A WHOLE
DIFFERENT LEAGUE

Outlaw leagues, forgotten teams and
other adventures in American sport

STEPHEN H. PROVOST

Cover photos

(clockwise from top)

<u>Front</u>
Molly Bolin, Iowa Cornets, Women's Basketball League
Jackie Robinson, Kansas City Monarchs, Negro American League
Red Grange, New York Yankees, American Football League I

<u>Back</u>
Dottie Schroeder, All-American Girls Professional Baseball League
Ed Lubanski, Detroit Thunderbirds, National Bowling League
Connie Hawkins, Pittsburgh Rens, American Basketball League

All material © 2019 Stephen H. Provost

Cover concept and design: Stephen H. Provost
All interior images are in the public domain, except as noted;
some images used with attribution under Creative Commons licenses.

Dragon Crown Books 2019
All rights reserved.

ISBN: 1-949971-00-7
ISBN-13: 978-1-949971-00-2

Dedication

To all the visionaries who dared to dream and, against all odds, sought to make those dreams come true. You brought us more joy than you'll ever know.

Praise for other works

"A well-written novel with modern prose and social concerns, the complex idea of mixing morality and mortality is a fresh twist on the human condition. … **Memortality** is one of those books that will incite more questions than it answers. And for fandom, that's a good thing."

— Ricky L. Brown, Amazing Stories

"Punchy and fast paced, **Memortality** reads like a graphic novel. … (Provost's) style makes the trippy landscapes and mind-bending plot points more believable and adds a thrilling edge to this vivid crossover fantasy."

— Foreword Reviews

"Profusely illustrated throughout, **Highway 99** is unreservedly recommended as an essential and core addition to every community and academic library's California History collections."

— California Bookwatch

"As informed and informative as it is entertaining and absorbing, **Fresno Growing Up** is very highly recommended for personal, community, and academic library 20th Century American History collections.

— John Burroughs, Reviewer's Bookwatch

"… an engaging narrative that pulls the reader into the story and onto the road. … I highly recommend **Highway 99: The History of California's Main Street**, whether you're a roadside archaeology nut or just someone who enjoys a ripping story peppered with vintage photographs."

— Barbara Gossett,
Society for Commercial Archaeology Journal

Contents

Acknowledgments

My thanks to Molly Kazmer and Cardte Hicks for providing personal insights during interviews for the WBL section of this work.

Introduction

My father would wonder why it's taken me this long to write a sports book. As a child, I spent countless hours in my room poring over old record books, making mental note of home runs, batting averages, championship game scores and the like.

The Baseball Encyclopedia. The Sports Encyclopedias of Basketball and Football. These were Bibles, not-so-graphic novels and best friends all rolled into one. When I wasn't leafing through these, I was cataloging my sports card collections, putting names to faces (and teams), and through it all memorizing reams of statistics — some of which seemed obscure, even to me.

It runs in the family, at least one generation back. My dad, a political science professor and sports buff, could rattle off the score of every Rose Bowl from the game's inception in 1903 until sometime in the '80s. His favorite was the first one he ever listened to (yes, listened — this was before the advent of television): USC's 7-3 upset of Duke on a late touchdown in 1939. Those seven points were the only points Duke allowed all year.

I inherited my father's enjoyment of statistics and trivia. Living next door to a Major League Baseball player (Bill Buckner, when he played left field for the Dodgers in the mid '70s), helped motivate me, too. I followed his progress daily in the paper, even after he was traded to the Cubs, and took special joy in the fact that he won a National League batting title in Chicago with a .324 average in 1980. We won't mention the '86 Series; I still think he got a bad rap.

It wasn't just Buckner whose stats I internalized. There were hundreds of players, living and dead, whose numbers fascinated me. I still remember Hack Wilson's 190 RBI and the fact that both Hank Greenberg and Jimmy Foxx came within a mere two home runs of tying Babe Ruth's legendary 60. More obscure: I also recalled that a pitcher named Charles "Old Hoss" Radbourn won an astonishing 60 games for the Providence Grays of the National League in 1884 (that figure has since been adjusted to 59). Speaking of Providence, I remember that the NFL team in that city was known as the Steam Roller, the single most awesome sports team nickname of all time.

I discovered that the 1932 NFL championship game was played on an indoor field that was shorter than regulation size, anticipating Arena Football by more than a half-century. And that one of the two leagues that merged to form the NBA once had two teams in Akron, both sponsored by tire companies: the Goodyear Wingfoots and the Firestone Non-Skids.

One Christmas, my father gave me a thick book with a white cover by George Gipe called *The Great American Sports Book*. It contained all sorts of stories, some obscure and all fascinating, that covered things like the cycling craze of the 1890s and boxing stories I'd never heard. I devoured it from cover to cover. That book is, in part, the inspiration for the present work.

"What might have been" has always fascinated me, and never more so than with sports leagues that, for one reason or another, didn't make it — which means almost all of them. Of all the startup leagues in the 20th century, only one achieved true parity, and it was the first to try: the Western League, which expanded from the Midwest to the East Coast and rebranded itself as the American League in 1900. Two other startups achieved success by forcing full-scale mergers with established leagues. The Basketball Association of American, founded in 1946, merged with the older National Basketball League three years later to form the NBA. Then, 20 years later, the NFL agreed to accept all the teams from the American Football League in a new, combined circuit.

There were also three leagues that forced partial mergers. The All-America Football Conference started play in 1946 and, after four years, the NFL accepted three of its teams as members: the four-time champion Cleveland Browns, the San Francisco 49ers and the original Baltimore Colts, which folded after a single season (a second franchise by the same name joined the league three years later). In 1976, the NBA absorbed four of the seven American Basketball Association teams. And in 1979, the National Hockey League absorbed four franchises from the World Hockey Association.

Other leagues were less fortunate, but no less interesting.

The National Bowling League came and went two years before I was born. But it included the only top-tier pro sports team my hometown has ever hosted: the Fresno Bombers. They built a huge bowling center on the outskirts of town that was torn down before I hit puberty. Of course, I had to know more, and what I discovered is contained in one of the chapters here.

I'm old enough to remember watching games in the World Football League and American Basketball Association, and I still mourn the premature demise of the USFL. Other leagues came and went before my time, but their stories are just as interesting. This text isn't meant to be exhaustive; it's a sampling of my favorite stories surrounding dreams and visions from American sports fans and entrepreneurs that ended in rude awakenings.

There are fewer such alternatives these days. The golden age of outlaw leagues lasted roughly 30 years and coincided with the postwar Baby Boom generation, when the sky seemed to be the limit and visionaries had more freedom to build their fields of dreams. From

1946 to 1974, new leagues cropped up with astonishing frequency. The year after World War II ended, the AAFC and BAA both started play, while the Pacific Coast League was trying to become baseball's third major league. The dawn of the '60s saw the creation of the AFL and American Basketball League, as well as never-realized plans for a Continental League in baseball. Then, the period from 1967 to '74 witnessed the advent of the ABA, WHL and WBA.

Since that time, however, few leagues have been able to muster the courage (or the money) needed to mount a serious challenge to the establishment. Only the USFL and the XFL in football posed credible challenges, and both played during the spring, avoiding direct competition with the NFL. Times were clearly changing. Organized Baseball's antitrust exemption has held would-be challengers at bay for more than a century. But even without such codified protection, the very nature of sports is different today than it once was. The sheer amount of capital available to our entrenched, iconic leagues makes it virtually impossible for upstarts to challenge them for player talent. The era of entrepreneurs entering the arena on a shoestring and a prayer has passed, probably for good.

But the memories remain … and they're worth revisiting. The existence of the outlaw leagues that sprang up in the 20th century is a reminder that not everything of interest in the sporting world takes place on national television, in New York or Los Angeles. Some dreams are born and die before half-empty high school gyms or on fields with rutted turf and rickety fences. There's a lot that has been forgotten — or would be if it weren't written down someplace like this.

What follows is a record of those things. Of what was, what almost was and what might have been had things turned out a little bit different.

Imagine for just a moment a different, happier ending for these dreams, and remember if you will the excitement and optimism that gave them birth.

Such dreams still exist. They're just in A Whole Different League.

This work is divided into four sections, each arranged chronologically. Standings for representative seasons are also included.

Part I
Baseball

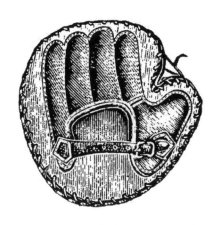

The Pittsburgh Crawfords in 1932, with pitcher Satchel Paige, third from left in the top row, and catcher Josh Gibson standing next to him at at top center.

Bright Stars in a Black Sky

Gus Greenlee and Branch Rickey came from two different worlds. Rickey, the general manager of the Brooklyn Gus Greenlee and Branch Rickey came from two different worlds. Rickey, the general manager of the Brooklyn Dodgers, had already spent four decades in organized baseball by the time they crossed paths in 1945. Greenlee had come to the game more recently and had organized his own brand of baseball using the proceeds from his numbers racket, popular nightclub and other illegal or barely legal activities.

If you were a black man living in Pittsburgh during the first half of the 20th century, that was how you got ahead. The numbers game was a form of private lottery in which players placed bets of as little as a penny on a three-digit number to be determined the following day, often the last three digits of racetrack betting totals or stock exchange volume. During the Depression, especially, such games were popular in working-class neighborhoods, in much the same way state lotteries are popular today.

Numbers games were so popular in Pittsburgh, where they were lightly regulated, that they produced more than $100,000 a week in profits. Earnings like that made Gus Greenlee a rich man and, when he became involved in baseball, helped put Pittsburgh at the center of the universe for Negro League baseball in the 1930s.

Pioneers

There wasn't just one Negro League, but several, dating back to the 19th century. Back then, organized baseball had been integrated, if only marginally so. Although teams were overwhelmingly white, a few black players did take the field. Foremost among them: Moses Fleetwood Walker and John "Bud" Fowler.

In 1872, Bud Fowler broke in at age 14 with an otherwise all-white professional team based in New Castle, Pennsylvania. He never made it to the majors, but he did play for several minor-league clubs over the years. In 1878, he pitched three games — including a two-hitter over eight innings — and managed a couple of hits for the Lynn (Mass.) Live Oaks in the International Association. He moved around after that, got married and eventually got a job as a barber in Stillwater, Minn., where he signed with a team in the Northwestern League.

Fowler was less effective as a pitcher, struggling with a sore arm and the switch that year from underhand to overhand pitching. But he made up for any decline on the mound by batting .302 and leading the league in hits. When he wasn't pitching, he moved around as needed, playing in the infield, outfield and behind the plate.

The Stillwater team went out of business after that season.

Walker, like Fowler, played in the Northwestern League (though a year earlier), where he was the Toledo Blue Stockings' regular catcher in 1883, hitting .251 and earning praise from The Toledo Blade: "Walker has played more games and has been of greater value behind the bat than any catcher in the league."

The Blue Stockings' success was such that they accepted an invitation the following year to join the American Association, which was then the second major league. Walker continued to play well, improving his batting average to .263, but he made 37 errors and suffered an injury that led to his release before the season ended. He never made it back to the big leagues, perhaps in part because of an incident that had taken place a year earlier.

When Toledo was still in the Northwestern League, the Blue Stockings hosted the National League's Chicago White Stockings in August of 1883. The team that would later become the Cubs (and should not be confused with the modern White Sox) was led by future

Hall of Famer Adrian "Cap" Anson, an unapologetic racist who saw no place for nonwhite players on the diamond.

Walker, who was suffering from a sore hand, wasn't expected to play in the game, but when Anson said his team wouldn't play "with no damned n-----," the Toledo club not only came to his defense but forced the issue. The Blue Stockings inserted Walker into the lineup, then threatened to withhold the visitors' share of the gate receipts if they pulled out. Having traveled from Chicago for the game, Anson was left with little choice but to back down. Still, he declared: "We'll play this here game but won't play never no more with the n----- in."

Moses Fleetwood Walker

The line in the sand had been drawn, and it would not be crossed by any big-league ballclub until Rickey did so by bringing Jackie Robinson to the Dodgers in 1947. Anson continued to play nearly up to the turn of the century, and his voice as one of the most influential players of his era carried a lot of weight. It also emboldened other racists to boycott interracial play. When Toledo traveled to Richmond, Virginia for a game in September of 1884, the Blue Sox were threatened with violence should Walker take the field:

A letter addressed to the manager of the Toledo Base Ball Club warned: "We the undersigned, do hereby warn you not to put up Walker, the Negro catcher, the evenings that you play in Richmond, as we could mention the name of 75 determined men who have sworn to mob Walker if he comes to ground in a suit. We hope you will listen to our words of warning, so that there will be no trouble: but if you do not, there certainly will be. We only write this to prevent much blood shed, as you alone can prevent."

The situation was defused when the Blue Sox released Walker. Toledo finished eighth in the 13-team league that season and did not return for the 1885 campaign.

Walker continued to play, earning a spot on the Newark Little Giants of the International League, where he teamed up with 21-year-old black ace George Stovey to form a potent battery. Stovey won 34 games during the 1887 season, while Walker hit a .264 and stole 36 bases. Two exhibition games, however, were pivotal to his future and the future of black baseball. In one, the New York Giants came to town and were beaten, thanks in large measure to Stovey and Walker. The pitcher held the Giants to two runs, and Walker threw out Giants player-manager John Montgomery Ward attempting to steal second base.

Ward was so impressed, he started asking around about the pair's availability, but word got back to Anson, who renewed his opposition, and Ward backed off. When Anson's White Stockings came to Newark for an exhibition, the Little Giants kept the two star players out of the lineup. Even more noteworthy, the International League adopted a resolution the same day refusing to approve any further signings of black player.

Things got tougher for black players from then on, as Bud Fowler could attest. After leaving Stillwater, he landed with the Keokuk Hawkeyes of the newly formed Western League in 1885. The circuit would later become the American League, but was still in its infancy then, playing its inaugural season with six teams from Cleveland west to Omaha. Keokuk replaced Omaha at midseason, and Fowler hit a respectable .278 with a couple of doubles in eight games.

But the rest of his career found him with one team one season and another the next, eventually bragging that he'd played in every state in the union. A team in Lafayette, Ind., signed him sight unseen in 1888 — then promptly released him when he arrived and they realized he was black. In 1892, he played with Lincoln in the Nebraska State League, a circuit described by Sporting Life as "the only league in the country which permits the employment of colored players."

Fowler, like other black players, was starting to run out of options. By this time, he was 34 years old and billing himself as the oldest active player in the country. (In an era long before online fact-checks, he sought to bolster his growing reputation by spreading the story that he was a decade older than he was.) That knack for self-promotion led him to his next venture: as a baseball executive running his own all-black team.

Fowler's last stop as a player was in the Michigan State League, where he played under manager — and future Hall of Fame shortstop — Honus Wagner in Adrian, a town about 70 miles southwest of Detroit. Before that, however, he met with J. Wallace Page, the owner of a local fence company and presented him with an intriguing idea. Page wanted a way to advertise his fences, and Fowler proposed barnstorming all-black baseball club as the perfect vehicle.

All-black baseball was still a relatively new concept at the time. The Cuban Giants had been formed in 1885 as the first all-black baseball team, and two years later, organizers formed the first league of all-black teams. The National Colored Baseball League was a loosely organized outfit with six teams that played anywhere between one and seven games. The league was barely a blip, lasting only a couple of weeks before canceling the rest of the season because of poor attendance.

Page liked Fowler's idea and agreed to sponsor the team that became known as the Page Fence Giants. The name "Giants" was a popular nickname for black baseball teams of the era, because it was used as a code word, Buck O'Neil explained in his book I Was Right On Time. After a brief stay in Memphis during his rookie season in 1937, O'Neil moved to the Kansas City Monarchs the following year and stayed there until 1955 — first as a player, then also as manager for his last eight seasons. He became the first black coach in the major leagues with the Chicago Cubs in 1962.

According to O'Neil, "Giants" was adopted as a code word to identify black teams because many newspapers refused to print pictures of African-Americans in their pages. This trend was especially prevalent during the barnstorming era. O'Neil wrote that someone seeing a newspaper or store-window ad announcing a game between a local semipro club and the River City Giants, it meant you could be sure the visitors were a black team.

Barnstorming could take teams to places they weren't particularly welcome. Sure, white fans enjoyed seeing them play (sometimes, more white spectators than black turned out), but they often didn't want them in white hotels. Foster solved this problem for the Page Fence Giants by procuring a railroad car made to his specifications that included sleeping quarters. The car, which was also staffed by a porter and a cook, was essentially a hotel on wheels. It gave players a place to sleep without having to worry about whether they'd be accepted at the local inn.

Fowler played and also served as manager for the team, which would take the field more than 150 times that season. Two of those games were against the Cincinnati Reds, which the Giants lost by scores of 11-7 and 16-2, but they were far more successful overall, winning 118 and losing 36. The Giants set the tone for later barnstorming clubs by incorporating plenty of showmanship on their tour. At each stop, players would don firefighter hats and ride bicycles around town, publicizing their games. (The bicycles, incidentally, were supplied by the team's secondary sponsor, Monarch Bicycle of Massachusetts.) The games themselves included extra entertainment value, too: shortstop Grant "Home Run" Johnson, who reputedly hit 60 home runs during his rookie season in semipro ball, once did a cartwheel while circling the bases.

The following year, with Fowler having left the team, the Page Fence Giants beat the Cuban X-Giants from Trenton, N.J., in 10 out of 15 games for a mythical "Colored Championship of the United States." It was one of several such series played during the tail end of the 19th century and featuring teams like the Original (or Genuine) Cuban Giants, who beat the offshoot X-Giants for the 1897 title, and the Chicago Unions, who wound up on the losing end of two such series in 1899.

Cuban connection

A number of teams incorporated "Cuban" into their names even though the players on their rosters weren't Cuban at all, but African-American. This made sense because, even as the color line was hardening against blacks, Latino players were still accepted in organized baseball. If blacks could pass as Latino, they still could gain at least a degree of acceptance by whites. The Cuban Giants, for instance, reportedly developed the habit of speaking in gibberish to one another during games, with the goal of convincing crowds they were Cuban.

But organized baseball was careful to be sure no one of African ancestry found a way into the big leagues via Latin America. When the Cincinnati Reds went on an exhibition tour of Cuba in 1908, they encountered a pair of strong prospects in Rafael Almeida and Armando Marsans. The Reds ownership wound up signing them both, but not before receiving assurances from a scout that he personally knew both players' parents and guaranteed "that none of them have other but pure Caucasian blood in their veins."

The same could not be said for a third Cuban prospect, Jose Mendez, who might have been the best player of the bunch. During the Reds' tour, Mendez pitched a one-hit shutout to defeat Cincinnati. It was the beginning of a remarkable stretch in which he strung together 45 consecutive scoreless innings. His earned-run average that season? An astounding 0.80. But while Marsans and Almeida were relatively light skinned, or "swarthy," there was no disguising Mendez's African ancestry. Even his nickname, "Black Diamond," was in reference to his dark complexion.

So, while Marsans played eight seasons in the majors (hitting .317 with 35 stolen bases in 1912), and Almeida three, Mendez never made the big leagues. Instead, when came to the U.S. in 1908, he played with the all-black Brooklyn Royal Giants. He continued to play in Cuba through 1915, then caught on with a series of black ballclubs: the Los Angeles White Sox, Chicago American Giants, Detroit Stars and, for the final seven seasons of his career, the Kansas City Monarchs.

Perhaps the highlight of Mendez's career was the deciding game of the inaugural Negro World Series in 1924. The best-of-nine series, pitting the Monarchs of the Negro National League against Eastern Colored League champion Hilldale, was knotted at four games apiece. Mendez, who was doing double-duty as the team's manager, was pushing 40, had recently undergone surgery and had been told by his doctor in no uncertain terms that he had not been cleared to pitch. Failure to heed that advice, the doctor warned, could result in permanent injury.

Mendez's response? "I don't care. I want to win today."

And win he did. Mendez not only beat Hilldale to wrap up the championship, but he shut out the ECL champs 5-0.

He would retire in 1926 at the age of 41, having played longer than either Almeida or Marsan. Unlike either of them, he was elected to the Baseball Hall of Fame. The network between Cuba and the Negro Leagues worked both ways, with players finding greater acceptance — and better pay — in Latin America than they did in their home country. In fact, teams from Cuba, Puerto Rico, Mexico and the Dominican Republic sought out African-Americans to strengthen their rosters. One such player was Home Run Johnson, Bud Fowler's former teammate with the Page Fence Giants, who had his best season ever for Havana at the age of 38 in 1911. His .410 average and 28 RBI were both career highs.

League play begins

Johnson was also part of the first successful all-black league, the National Association of Colored Baseball Clubs, which ran for three seasons from 1907 to 1909. It came on the heels of an innovative attempt to create an international, multiracial league the previous year. A Philadelphia bakery-chain owner formed the International League of Independent Base Ball Clubs and announced that it which would consist of two black teams, two Cuban ballclubs and a white squad.

Two teams quickly dropped out and were replaced, but the circuit did manage to make it to the end of its modest eight-game season, with the Philadelphia Giants claiming the title and a silver cup donated by the founder.

The following year, the champions of that league joined three other teams (the Cuban Giants, Brooklyn Royal Giants and Cuban Stars) in forming the National Association. The league's membership was remarkably stable, with the same four teams participating in each of its three campaigns. Johnson played for Philadelphia in the circuit's inaugural season, helping the Giants claim the title, but moved to Brooklyn during the league's second year, helping the Royal Giants to a first-place finish, four games ahead of his former team.

Brooklyn repeated as champion in 1909, and a 1910 season was supposedly planned, but the league appears to have vanished after that.

Today, new leagues are formed from scratch with rosters of completely new teams: None of the teams in the ABA, WFL, XFL, WHA, etc. existed before the league itself was formed. But that wasn't the case in the early 20th century. Then, club teams and barnstorming outfits came together to form associations with (often loosely) set schedules. This is how the first Negro National League came into being.

The catalyst was a man named Andrew "Rube" Foster, a pitcher of legendary status who joined the Chicago Union Giants in 1902 and reportedly compiled a 51-4 record on the mound in 1905. The right-hander was so good that New York Giants manager John McGraw is said to have enlisted his services as an informal pitching coach; Foster was credited with teaching Hall of Famer Christy Mathewson how to throw a screwball. Frank Chance of the Cubs hailed him as "the most finished product I've ever seen in the pitcher's box."

But Foster was more than a player; he was also an organizer. Like Bud Fowler before him, he put together his own team — the Chicago American Giants — building his roster from players from the Philadelphia Giants and the Chicago Union Giants (since renamed the Leland Giants after owner Frank Leland). That roster, which included Home Run Johnson and Rube Foster himself, racking up a record of 128-6 in its inaugural season, 1910. Foster called his team "the greatest baseball talent ever assembled," and McGraw reportedly said nine of his players could have made the New York Giants if they'd been white.

Foster struck a deal with Charles Comisky's son-in-law to use South Side Park, the 15,000-seat stadium that had been used by the White Sox as recently as 1910. The American Giants would play there until Christmas Day 1940, when it was destroyed by fire, and their use of the former big-league facility helped solidify their position as the nation's premier black team.

Through this period, team bookings were still controlled primarily by white promoters, who would take a significant cut by renting out ballparks and arranging games against white teams. Oddly, while blacks were prohibited from playing in organized baseball, there was no such ban on them playing against white players in exhibitions or winter leagues in places such as Cuba. Exhibitions didn't count for anything, so there was no danger of black teams "embarrassing" white players the way Jack Johnson had when he won the heavyweight title in 1908, in an event that sparked race riots. When white teams lost, as they often did, their fans could always claim the players weren't taking the games seriously and were just playing to stay in shape or put on a good show.

The players themselves knew differently.

Hall of Famer Heinie Manush, who played on a team of all-stars that lost three out of five games to the Chicago American Giants in 1929, recalled a game the following year in which outfielder James "Cool Papa" Bell robbed him of an extra-base hit by saying, "I sure am glad you colored players aren't in our league. I wouldn't ever hit .300." (For the record, Manush reached that mark 10 times in 17 big-league seasons and hit .330 for his career.)

Other Hall of Famers taking part in that '29 series included Harry Heilmann, who finished his career with a lifetime batting average of .341, and Charlie Gehringer (.320). But even with all that firepower, the white all-stars were largely baffled by the American Giants' pitching. After losing 12-11 in a slugfest to open the series, they managed to score just one run in two of the games and only two in a third. Only one of the games, a 10-1 Chicago blowout, was decided by more than two runs.

Willie "El Diablo" Wells and George "Mule" Suttles, who had hit more than 40 home runs. between them a couple of years earlier for the St. Louis Stars, led the offensive assault. Wells hit .500 for the series with two triples and stole home twice, once with the winning run in the opener. Suttles had two triples of his own in that game among three hits against all-star pitching.

"They say Suttles used the heaviest bat ever swung," Gehringer later recalled. "Looking back, I think it was true. He hit some boomers."

Bill Foster, younger brother of Rube Foster and the Negro Leagues' all-time winningest pitcher, pitched three games in the series, winning twice and losing a 2-0 decision.

Rube takes the reins

Foster's big brother had spent the 1910s building his reputation and wresting power from the white promoters who had dominated the game, economically speaking. As more blacks migrated north from the hostile, segregated South, many of them wound up in Chicago, the biggest city in the Midwest, and more of them wanted entertainment. Foster's American Giants provided it.

But the landscape was changing. The number of available white semipro teams was shrinking, with large numbers of young men joining the armed forces during World War I. Baseball was gradually becoming more organized, and within a few years, Branch Rickey would create the first farm system of minor-league teams, binding the major and minor leagues more closely together. Barnstorming was becoming more of a challenge, and white teams were no closer to accepting blacks.

In 1914, Foster had predicted that "before another season rolls around, colored ball players ... will be holding down jobs in organized baseball."

It didn't happen. If anything, the schism between white and black baseball was growing.

Instead, the migration of African-Americans northward heightened tensions in places like Chicago, where the black population had risen by at least 50 percent, to as many as 150,000, with the influx of 50,000 new residents from 1916 to 1919. Many found jobs in stockyard packing firms and settled in a so-called "black belt" on the city's South Side.

As the population in the Chicago area grew more diverse, tensions between the city's white and black residents rose. In the summer of 1919, a black teenager in a raft crossed an imaginary line separating "black" and "white" sections of a beach along Lake Michigan. He was stoned by a group of white youths, fell out of the raft and drowned. Eyewitnesses asked a police officer to arrest one of the youths, but when he refused, an irate crowd began to beat the youngster. The rioting spread from there and lasted a full week, ending with 23 blacks and 15 whites dead and more than 500 people injured. White rioters torched more than 1,000 black-owned homes.

Foster was on a barnstorming tour in Michigan with his American Giants when it happened, and stayed away until things settled, as a contingent of the state militia occupied the American Giants' home field. It was clear that baseball wasn't heading toward integration, as Foster had hoped. Instead, it was moving in the opposite direction. The only reasonable course, he concluded, was to start a formal league of all-black teams that would make its own rules and guarantee opponents would be available on a regular basis.

Foster called a meeting in Kansas City to form the Negro National League in 1920 — the same year the National Football League was formed. Charter members were located across the Midwest, in Cincinnati, Dayton, Detroit, Indianapolis, Kansas City and St. Louis, with two teams in Chicago. But like the NFL of the 1920s, the league was prone to seeing teams join and drop out, with the weak franchises more numerous than the strong ones.

Teams that failed to last often played in smaller cities without a separate black press; the Dayton Marcos, for instance, dropped out after the inaugural season (although they rejoined for a single campaign in 1926). Only two teams — the American Giants and Kansas City Monarchs — remained in the league for all 12 seasons of its existence. The Giants, Monarchs and St. Louis Stars were the only teams to win championships, with Foster's team claiming five pennants, the Monarchs four and the Stars three.

In 1923, the NLL gained a rival in the form of the Eastern Colored League, which was founded in 1923 and featured teams in a concentrated geographic area that extended from New York east to Harrisburg, Pa., and south to Washington, D.C. As with the NLL, a small number of teams dominated the circuit, with Hilldale winning three pennants and Atlantic City two in its five years of existence. For four of those seasons, the champion met the NLL winner in a Colored World Series, with the Midwest league winning three of those four meetings.

Don't look back

The NNL, which started out in the Midwest, eventually expanded into the South, with the Birmingham Black Barons and Memphis Red Sox joining in 1924. The circuit also featured a club in Nashville called the Elite Giants in 1930. The Black Barons' roster from 1927 to 1930 featured a young right-handed pitcher named Leroy Robert Paige, more well known as Satchel.

In his first two seasons with the Barons, Paige racked up records of 5-1 and 11-4, with a career-high 167 strikeouts in 1928. But, as good as Paige was, he was as well known for his wit and flair as he was for his pitching prowess ... which was considerable. By his own count, he claimed to have pitched 250 shutouts and 50 no-hitters in a career that spanned 2,500 games (winning 80 percent of them) for 250 teams. Once, he claimed, he pitched 62 consecutive scoreless innings: three more than Orel Hershiser's current major-league record.

How much of that was accurate? It was pretty much anybody's guess. Complete statistics from the Negro Leagues were spotty at best — thanks to the numerous exhibitions, barnstorming tours and a lack of consistent coverage in the press. So, it's hard to tell how many of Paige's claims were on the level and how many were poetic embellishment. How many no-hitters did he really throw? At one point, he merely said they were "so many" that "I disremember the number."

Even Paige's age was something of a mystery. Although records showed he was born on July 7, 1906, he teased members of the media by taking a page out of Bud Fowler's book and suggesting he was even older. When reporters assumed he'd been born before the turn of the century, Paige did nothing to dispel the notion, claiming that a goat "ate the Bible with the birth certificate in it."

Regardless of his age or the accuracy of the stats he kept, there was little doubt that Paige was, in fact, an ageless wonder. Like Muhammad Ali, he may have boasted beyond his abilities, but those abilities were so substantial that he could make even the most outrageous claims seem almost believable. He was, in fact, 42 years old when he made his major league debut as a "rookie" with the Cleveland Indians in 1948, and he did post a 6-1 record that year. He did pitch three scoreless innings for the Kansas City A's against the Red Sox at the age of 59 in 1965. (There was a bit of poetic justice to this particular happy ending: The Red Sox had been the last team to integrate their roster, in 1959, more than a decade after Paige joined the big leagues.)

Paige's most enduring quote has to do with his age, the last of six maxims he had printed on his business card: "Don't look back. Something might be gaining on you." The card also contained such counsel as to "avoid runnin' at all times" and "if your stomach disputes you, lay down and pacify it with cool thoughts."

Paige pacified batters with an array of pitches from his "Bat Dodger" to his "Midnight Creeper," from a "Wobbly Ball" to his "Hesitation Pitch," in which he paused during his delivery to make batters swing too soon. He was so confident in them that he would intentionally load the bases with nobody out, then tell his teammates to sit down in the field while he proceeded to strike out the side.

Paige had been pitching for more than two decades by the time Bill Veeck signed him to play for the Indians. Veeck, who would sign 3-foot, 7-inch midget for a single at-bat with the St. Louis Browns three years later, was known for his innovative marketing; hence The Sporting News accused him of signing Paige as a publicity stunt and thereby "demeaning" the sport. By season's end, however, the publication had changed its tune, naming Paige its rookie of the year after he built up a 1.42 earned-run average through six relief appearances — then promptly threw back-to-back shutouts. In doing so, he became the oldest pitcher ever to do so.

By that time, he was 22 years removed from his pro baseball debut in 1926 with the Chattanooga White Sox of the Southern Negro League, a minor league that fed the Negro National League.

1920 Negro National League			
	W	L	Pct.
Chicago American Giants	32	13	.711
Detroit Stars	35	23	.603
Kansas City Monarchs	41	29	.586
Indianapolis ABCs	39	35	.527
Cuban Stars	21	24	.467
St. Louis Giants	25	32	.439
Dayton Marcos	8	18	.308
Chicago Giants	4	24	.143

Collapse and resurgence

Ironically, that was the year that marked the beginning of the end for the NNL. It was reported in September that league founder Rube Foster had been confined to a psychiatric hospital for eight days, after which he was declared "mentally irresponsible" and committed to a facility in Kankakee, Illinois. There was no word on how all this had transpired, but the Associated Negro Press attributed it to "the effects of his strenuous labors" in behalf of the league and his refusal to stop when his friends expressed concern. He took a couple of weeks off in Michigan, but was called back to deal with unspecified but "urgent" league business. Within the month, he had experienced what the ANP called a "crash." The press service attributed it to stress, coupled with the lingering effects of exposure to gas the previous year while he was trying to stop a water heater leak.

Two years later, the only other all-black major league fell apart midseason when its founder, Ed Bolden, suffered a nervous breakdown. Bolden, who ran the Eastern Colored League's most successful team, the Hilldale club from the Philadelphia suburb of Darby, withdrew it from the circuit the following season. One important addition to the league that year, however, was the Homestead Grays, one of the dominant teams in Negro League history. Formed in 1910, they played independently for nearly two decades before joining the ECL, only to have it collapse.

The Grays and five other teams from that circuit — including Hilldale and the two-time ECL champion Bacharach Giants from Atlantic City — teamed up in 1929 to form the American Negro League, but it lasted only one season.

The Baltimore Black Sox won the title.

There was no East Coast league in 1930, as the Great Depression left half of urban blacks out of work and took a bite out of ticket sales that ultimately proved fatal for the NNL, as well. That league played its final season in 1931, but Homestead Grays owner Cumberland Posey took the initiative in trying to raise it from the ashes. His new East-West League, however, failed to attract the Chicago American Giants (who instead played in the Negro Southern League) and lasted just one season. The Grays and Black Sox each played 82 games, but none of the five other ballclubs managed more than 51.

Posey's Grays were led by batting champion Bill Perkins, who hit .408, but Homestead was in third place in June. That didn't bother Posey, who also owned the first-place Detroit Wolves. The Wolves' roster featured a number of players from the NNL's final champion, the St. Louis Stars. Among them: Cool Papa Bell, Willie Wells and Mule Suttles. But the Wolves failed to draw enough fans to justify their continued existence, so Posey simply merged them with the Grays.

Part of Posey's motivation in forming the EWL was to marginalize Gus Greenlee and his crosstown rival Pittsburgh Crawfords. Greenlee had purchased the team in 1931 and had immediately set out to challenge the Grays for supremacy, not only in Pittsburgh but nationally. Greenlee hired future Hall of Famer Oscar Charleston as a playing manager, and the team featured the most famous battery in black baseball history: Paige pitching to slugging catcher Josh Gibson, who was hailed as the Negro Leagues' answer to Babe Ruth.

Gibson, who reportedly hit a total of 800 home runs in league and barnstorming games during his career, averaged one for fewer than every 16 at-bats. He died of a brain tumor at the age of 35, just months before Jackie Robinson broke baseball's color barrier, but his legend endured. Monte Irvin, an all-star with the New York Giants who played eight seasons in the National League starting in 1948, had already spent nine years in the Negro Leagues at that point and had seen what Gibson could do.

"He was the best hitter I've ever seen," said Irvin. "He would come to the plate, and you would be in awe.

Worth noting: Irvin's teammates on the Giants included one Willie Howard Mays.

Walter Johnson, one of only two pitchers in major league history to win more than 400 games, described Gibson as a catcher who would have been worth $200,000 — if it weren't for baseball's color line. "He can do everything," Johnson said. "He hits the ball a mile, catches it so easily he might as well be in a rocking chair (and) throws like a bullet."

In 1932, Paige, Gibson and Charleston played for the Crawfords in a brand-new $100,000 ballpark built by Greenlee. It was the nation's first black-built and black-owned ballpark. When Posey's East-West League collapsed, Greenlee seized the initiative to form a new Negro National League built around his Crawfords. Six other teams joined them, including the American Giants (now known as Cole's American Giants), the Brooklyn Royal Giants and Baltimore Black Sox. Posey's Grays were also charter members, but they were thrown out of the league midseason for raiding the Detroit Stars' roster.

They would return the following year.

The Crawfords won or shared three of the first four league titles before the Grays broke through with consecutive titles in 1937 and '38. The team would move to Washington, D.C., and win six straight pennants from 1940 to 1945. The American Giants, the league's westernmost franchise, left the circuit in 1937 to become charter members of a new eight-team league based in the Midwest and South, the Negro American League.

The Kansas City Monarchs, Memphis Red Sox and Birmingham Black Barons were charter members and mainstays of the league. All four played in the circuit until 1952 (with the exception of one season for Birmingham), when Chicago called it quits. The league finally disbanded in 1962, having lasted 13 seasons longer than the second NNL. A short-lived member of the league played its games in Toledo during the 1939 season and in Indianapolis the following year: the Crawfords. Greenlee sold the team and the new ownership had moved it west, but it folded after just two seasons.

The NAL's marquee franchise was Kansas City, which won five of the first six pennants and prevailed in a newly revived Negro World Series with a sweep of the NNL's Grays in 1942. The Monarchs thus became the only team to win championships in both the first and second versions of the series, representing the first Negro National League in 1924 and the Negro American League 18 years later. The Grays, however, proved even more successful, winning the next two series and taking home three titles in eight years.

The final series was held in 1948, the last season of operation for the second NNL.

The reason for its demise? The integration of Major League Baseball, that elusive goal pursued in vain by Rube Foster that finally became a possibility during the early 1940s following the death of baseball's first commissioner, Kenesaw Mountain Landis.

1949 Negro American League	W	L	Pct.
Eastern Division			
Baltimore Elite Giants	59	30	.663
New York Cubans	26	20	.565
Indianapolis Clowns	37	44	.457
Philadelphia Stars	31	38	.449
Louisville Buckeyes	19	64	.229
Western Division			
Kansas City Monarchs	54	37	.593
Chicago American Giants	48	35	.578
Birmingham Black Barons	45	39	.536
Houston Eagles	34	35	.493
Memphis Red Sox	39	50	.438

Toward integration

If Cap Anson had drawn baseball's color line, Landis had helped ensure it remained all but etched it in stone — but not by making the ban on black players in organized baseball official. On the contrary: There never was any official rule banning black players from the big leagues, and Landis didn't create one. But he enforced the unwritten rule by refusing to end the not-so-gentlemanly agreement among owners to keep the color line in place.

Make no mistake: Landis had the power to end the policy, had he wished to do so. This was the same man who expelled star outfielder Joe Jackson of the Chicago White Sox for allegedly conspiring to throw the 1919 World Series, even though Jackson's performance in the Series told a different story. Indeed, it was the so-called "Black Sox" scandal that had led team owners to create the office of commissioner in order to clean up the sport's image, but Landis had refused to accept the position unless he were given broad leeway to act with near impunity.

Fearing a loss of credibility, the owners agreed to his conditions, giving him the power to investigate "upon his own initiative, any act ...suspected to be detrimental to the best interests of ... base ball." Upon conducting such an investigation, he was empowered to determine the appropriate response and "take such action either against major leagues, major league clubs, or individuals, as the case may be."

Long story short: Landis could have, by fiat, eradicated the color line with a stroke of his pen. But he chose not to.

Instead, he took the opposite tack.

When a reporter pressed him on the issue in 1942, Landis answered: "You fellows say I'm responsible."

The reporter followed up: "If you are not, why don't you defend yourself?

"There is no man living who wants the friendship of the Negro people more than I," Landis protested.

Then why didn't he erase the color line?

"No comment," Landis answered.

Landis let his actions do the talking for him. In 1942, the Chicago White Sox gave two black players — Jackie Robinson and Baltimore Elite Giants pitcher Nate Moreland — a tryout in Southern California. Jimmy Dykes, the White Sox manager, said they'd be welcome, but that they would have to "get after Landis" to make it happen.

A couple of months later, the Negro American League champion Kansas City Monarchs set up a barnstorming tour against a team of all-stars led by former Cy Young and MVP pitcher Dizzy Dean. Cleveland Indians ace Bob Feller was also scheduled to appear, but was in the Navy, which prohibited him from appearing. Other members of the team included three-time all-star Cecil Travis of the Senators — who was coming off a season in which he had led the American League in hits and posted a .359 batting average — along with journeymen like Johnny Grodzicki of the Cardinals, Claude Corbitt of the Dodgers, Emmett Mueller of the Phillies, Ken Silvestri of the Yankees, and George Archie of the Senators.

The commissioner canceled the tour after three games by charging that such exhibitions were "allegedly played for relief, but actually as commercial enterprises." As part of his decree, he forbade major and minor league teams from allowing their ballparks to be used, and prohibiting players from participating, in such exhibitions. Landis made no specific reference to the Dizzy Dean All-Stars or their opponents, but it was hard to ignore to important facts from the first three games:

The Monarchs had won all three by a combined score of 24-5.

The games had drawn crowds of 29,000 at Wrigley Field in Chicago, 22,000 at Griffith Stadium in Washington and 22,000 at Forbes Field in Pittsburgh. The last of these cities was home to the Homestead Grays, the Negro National League powerhouse that, at times, drew crowds bigger than those that attended Pirates home games. Indeed, the 22,000 figure was bigger than the crowd for any Pirates game so far that season.

Despite such setbacks, at least some baseball executives were ready to integrate. Bill Veeck wrote in his autobiography that he wanted to purchase the Philadelphia Phillies in 1942 and met with the team's owner, Gary Nugent, to arrange a deal — with Harlem Globetrotters owner Abe Saperstein as a facilitator. Saperstein, who had bought the Birmingham Black Barons in 1940, would recall Veeck's scheme in the Aug. 14, 1954 edition of the Philadelphia Independent:

"I'll tell you one thing about Veeck, something that few people know," he said. "The Phillies were for sale and Veeck attempted to buy them. But Bill Cox raised more money and got the club. Do you know what Veeck planned to do? He was going to take the Phils to spring training in Florida and then — on the day the season opened — dispose of the entire team. Meanwhile, with a team composed entirely of Negroes, who would have trained separately, he could have opened the National League season. I don't think there was a team in either league, back in 1943, that could have stopped the team he was going to assemble."

According to Veeck, he made the mistake of telling Landis about his plan, and the commissioner instructed National League President Ford Frick to block it. Whether the story is entirely true or not is difficult to determine, and some scholars have raised doubts about the truth of it. For one thing, Veeck seems to have merely assumed that Landis was the one who opposed him. For another, they say it's odd that no one in the press got wind of the story. But Veeck appears to have been careful to keep his idea under wraps until he spilled the beans himself to Landis, and Saperstein's corroboration suggests there was at least something to it.

The fact is, Veeck would pursue a similar (if less ambitious) course after he purchased the Cleveland Indians three years later. Veeck signed Larry Doby as the first black player in the American League and also procured the services of the Negro Leagues' best pitcher, Paige, to help the Indians to a World Series in 1948. When he signed Paige, he kept that a secret, just as he had kept his abortive attempt to buy the Phillies a secret three years earlier.

But Veeck wasn't the only big-league executive with his eye on the Negro Leagues and their considerable pool of talent. Over in the National League, Rickey was having similar ideas. Greenlee, he decided, could help him do it.

The former owner of the Pittsburgh Crawfords decided he wanted back into the game, so he applied for membership in both the Negro American and National Leagues. Both rejected him, so he decided to do what any ambitious sports entrepreneur would do: form his own league. He reconstituted the Crawfords to be the marquee franchise of what he dubbed the United States League. Other teams to play during the league's first season were the Atlanta Black Crackers, Brooklyn Brown Dodgers, Chicago Brown Bombers, Motor City Giants, Philadelphia Daisies and St. Louis Stars.

Kenesaw Mountain Landis

The Brooklyn franchise was significant because that's where Rickey's Brooklyn Dodgers played their games. The Dodgers had been making noise about trying to integrate the game since at least 1942. That summer, manager Leo Durocher was quoted in an interview: "I'd play the colored boys on my team if the big shots give the OK," but suggested he'd been hindered from doing so by a "grapevine understanding" that black players were off-limits.

When Landis got wind of the interview, he summoned Durocher to his office, and the manager emerged afterward, claiming he'd been misquoted. It's worth noting that Durocher was on thin ice with the commissioner at the time: The previous year, he'd given a friend of his, actor George Raft, four tickets to sit in his private box. But Landis heard about it and told Durocher's boss, Dodgers GM Larry MacPhail, who suggested that the club could avoid the appearance of impropriety by giving Raft four tickets to a different box.

Durocher, however, refused to budge.

It's impossible to know whether Landis brought up the Raft incident in his meeting with Durocher, but the fact that the manager claimed to have been misquoted when he emerged suggests that something was said that convinced him to recant. Perhaps he simply felt this particular battle, at this particular time, was not worth fighting. Or perhaps he had, indeed, been misquoted. Besides, MacPhail wasn't particularly keen on breaking the color barrier. In his view, Landis hadn't been clear enough, confirming what Durocher had said about the so-called grapevine understanding: "There has been an unwritten law tantamount to an agreement between major league clubs on the racial issue."

MacPhail insisted there was "no real demand" for black players, that few of them were good enough to play in the majors anyway, and that it would be unfair to "raid" the rosters of Negro League teams.

Some in the Negro Leagues agreed with him on this last point.

"If they take our best boys, we will be but a hollow shell of what we are today," Homestead Grays manager Vic Harris said in 1942. He preferred to maintain segregated teams, strengthen the Negro Leagues and then "challenge the best white team in the majors and play them."

Landis died in 1944, and the new commissioner, Happy Chandler, was far more amenable to the idea of integration than his predecessor had been. Whereas Landis had used his office to avoid the question, Chandler was unequivocal from the outset: "If they can fight and die on Okinawa, Guadalcanal, in the South Pacific, they can play baseball in America," he said. "And when I give my word, you can count on it."

But that didn't mean everyone was immediately on board with the idea. MacPhail moved across town in 1943 to become general manager of the Yankees, and two years later, New York Mayor Fiorello LaGuardia appointed a committee to study baseball's color line. MacPhail responded with a strongly worded letter warning that it should be preserved. That letter contained some of the same sentiments he had expressed in 1942 after Durocher's meeting with Landis. It asserted that that there were "few, if any, negro players who could qualify for play in the major leagues at this time. A major league player must have something besides natural ability." MacPhail concluded by writing: "I have no hesitancy in saying that the Yankees have no intention of signing negro players under contract or reservation to negro clubs."

But the man who replaced MacPhail as general manager of the Dodgers — Rickey — was much closer to Chandler on the subject. In fact, he was way ahead of him. In 1945, the same year MacPhail sent his letter to LaGuardia, Rickey came out publicly in support of Greenlee's United States League. And it wasn't just verbal support: Rickey called a press conference to declare that Greenlee's league was welcome to use Ebbets Field, as well as any other ballpark in the Dodgers farm system.

Rickey, in fact, had invented the very concept of the farm system when he was working for the St. Louis Cardinals, and had used it to develop young players and choose the best of them to stock teams that would win four World Series — in 1926, 1931, 1934 and 1942. It was the last of these that proved to be his swan song with the Cardinals before he left to join the Dodgers. The U.S. League, he figured, could serve the same function. In backing Greenlee's endeavor, he dismissed the Negro National and American Leagues as phony and irrelevant. There did not exist, he argued, "in a true sense such a thing as organized Negro baseball." Greenlee's new circuit would fill that void. If it sounded presumptuous, it was. Greenlee had, after all, been the founder of the Negro National League, and who was Rickey? A white man with a white man's agenda, and it was clear what it was: raid Negro League teams for talent to make his Brooklyn Dodgers a contender. But Rickey had put them in a pickle, and they knew it. They knew that, if the color line were broken, the raids that MacPhail had warned of would certainly occur, and that their teams would struggle to survive as a result. On the other hand, they couldn't very well oppose the idea of black players in the majors, for fear of incurring the wrath of black fans who had been hoping against hope for that very thing.

The U.S. League served its purpose and disappeared part way through a second season in 1946, in which it fielded just three teams in addition to the Crawfords: the Boston Blues, Cleveland Clippers and a Milwaukee club. The Brooklyn team was noticeably absent. Rickey didn't need it anymore, having signed Jackie Robinson to a contract on Oct. 23, 1945.

Postscript: During Jackie Robinson's 10 years with the Dodgers, from 1947 to 1956, the team won six National League pennants — the same number it had won in 57 years prior to that — and its very first World Series, in 1955. Don Newcombe, who had begun his career with the Newark Eagles of the Negro National League, and Roy Campanella, who had played nine seasons in the NNL, were on that 1955 team, as well.

Campanella would hit 242 big-league home runs and make eight consecutive all-star teams, beginning in 1949. Newcombe, the first black pitcher to win a World Series game in 1949, was also the first pitcher to be named Rookie of the Year, MVP and Cy Young recipient during his career — a feat not duplicated until 2011. The year after the Dodgers won the World Series, he became the first pitcher to win the Cy Young Award and MVP in the same season.

Rickey's plan had worked. Like a charm.

Homestead Grays, 1943

Colored World Series		
1924	Kansas City Monarchs (NNL) d. Hilldale (ECL)	5-4
1925	Hilldale (ECL) d. Kansas City Monarchs (NNL)	5-1
1926	Chicago American Giants (NNL) d. Bacharach Giants (ECL)	5-3
1927	Chicago American Giants (NNL) d. Bacharach Giants (ECL)	5-3
Negro World Series		
1942	Kansas City Monarchs (NAL) d. Homestead Grays (NNL)	4-0
1943	Homestead Grays (NNL) d. Birmingham Black Barons (NAL)	4-3
1944	Homestead Grays (NNL) d. Birmingham Black Barons (NAL)	4-1
1945	Cleveland Buckeyes (NAL) d. Homestead Grays (NNL)	4-0
1946	Newark Eagles (NNL) d. Kansas City Monarchs (NAL)	4-3
1947	New York Cubans (NNL) d. Cleveland Buckeyes (NAL)	4-1
1948	Homestead Grays (NNL) d. Birmingham Black Barons (NAL)	4-1

Please Release Me

In the summer of 1968, Curt Flood appeared on the cover of Sports Illustrated, the premier weekly chronicle of American athletics. The photographer captured Flood mid-flight, leaping for a long fly ball against the backdrop of the ivy-covered outfield wall at Chicago's Wrigley Field, home of the Cubs. Yellow lettering on the magazine's cover proclaims the St. Louis Cardinals star "baseball's best centerfielder."

Curt Flood

Indeed, Flood hit .301 that year and was in the midst of a run in which he would hit .300 or better in five of six seasons with the Cards. The seven-time Gold Glove winner had hit a career-high .335 a year earlier, leading St. Louis to a World Series championship.

Yet the infamous Sports Illustrated curse was in full effect. Although the Cards would return to the Fall Classic in '68, they blew a 3-1 lead and might have won if Flood hadn't misplayed a fly ball in the seventh inning of Game 7. He became the goat of the series.

Three years later, Flood found himself out of baseball for a challenge to baseball's reserve clause that effectively ended his career — even as it paved the way for players of the next generation to cash in with multimillion-dollar contracts in the years ahead.

This section isn't about Flood, per se, but about events a half century earlier that set the stage for his struggle to upend a system stacked against baseball's biggest stars. Those events involved two short-lived leagues of the early 20th century that, like Flood, challenged baseball's reserve clause.

It was the owner of a team in one of those leagues who built Wrigley Field, where Flood was captured by *Sports Illustrated*'s photographer more than five decades later. Except it wasn't called Wrigley Field back then. And it wasn't originally home to the Cubs at all:

It had been built for a team called the Chicago Whales that played in something called the Federal League back in 1914.

The reserve clause

The Federal League wasn't the first league to challenge the twin pillars of baseball's establishment, the National and American leagues, although it would be the last. The major leagues were able to maintain their dominance in part through the use of the reserve clause, which allowed teams to retain the rights to players even after their contacts expired.

Under this clause, players couldn't sign with any other team — even after the contracts expired. This gave teams immense bargaining power, as they effectively had players over a barrel. The choices were simple: "You can play for us, or not at all. We can trade you, release you, send you down to the minors, sell your contract or do whatever we want. You've just got to live with it."

It was the reserve clause that led Flood to take a stand in 1970, when the Cardinals offered him a contract for less than what he felt he was worth. "I'm a human being," he said. "I'm not a piece of property. I am not a consignment of goods."

But that's how he was being treated.

Flood wasn't the first player to chafe at the reserve clause. Eight decades earlier, it had been part of the impetus behind the formation of the Players' League, an attempt by players to form their own circuit in defiance of the established National League and American Association. The league was the brainchild of John Montgomery Ward, star shortstop for the New York Giants who also happened to be a graduate of Columbia Law School. Ward formed professional baseball's first union, the Brotherhood of Professional Base Ball Players, in 1885 and two years later wrote an essay in which he aired the same grievances Flood would later articulate.

Baseball players were being treated like "chattel," he wrote, and the reserve clause "has been used as a handle for the manipulation of a traffic in players, a sort of speculation in livestock, by which they are bought, sold, and transferred like so many sheep."

Ward, who was white, went so far as to draw on language that evoked memories of the antebellum South.

"Like a fugitive-slave law, the reserve-rule denies him a harbor or a livelihood, and carries him back, bound and shackled, to the club from which he attempted to escape," Ward wrote. Once a team had succeeded in procuring a player's services via signature, Ward added, "his professional liberty is gone forever."

Predictably, owners in the National League and American Association (a major league at the time) did not take kindly to Ward's critiques. The two leagues refused to recognize the Brotherhood, forcing Ward to take more drastic action: He would form a third major league, known as the Players' League, which would not recognize the reserve clause and which would invite players from the two established leagues to join.

John Montgomery Ward

The league formed in 1890 — the same year Congress passed the anti-monopoly Sherman Antitrust Act, which would come to play a key role in this saga. Two-thirds of National League players bolted for the upstart league, as did others from the Association; Ward himself played shortstop for the Brooklyn squad, which was named Ward's Wonders in his honor.

The National League sued the renegade players for breach of contract and also tried hauling Ward into court, but it lost those cases.

Despite those successes, the Players' League had one fatal flaw: In order to finance the enterprise, Ward had been forced to secure the backing of Wall Street financiers; when they failed to recoup their investments after the league's initial season, they pulled their money from the PL and threw their support to the National League. Without their backing, the upstart circuit collapsed after a single season.

Ward, who had been a pitcher earlier in his career, retired four years later as the only man to have collected more than 2,000 hits at the plate and more than 100 wins on the mound — a distinction he retains to this day. After retiring, he became a practicing attorney, but he never lost interest in baseball, and we haven't heard the last of him in this account.

The Players' League, meanwhile, wasn't the only casualty of baseball's first labor war. The American Association — likewise weakened by the three-way tussle — failed a year later. Before it did, however, one of its teams was involved in an incident that demonstrated the importance of the reserve clause ... at least from the owners' point of view.

Lou Bierbauer, star second baseman for the AA's Philadelphia team, had bolted for the

PL, where he played for Ward's Wonders. When the league folded, most of the players who'd defected returned to their original teams. But for some reason, Philadelphia failed to reserve their rights to Bierbauer.

This opened the door to the Pittsburgh Alleghenys of the National League, who had suffered at the turnstiles thanks to a dismal performance on the field and competition from the PL's Pittsburgh Burghers — who had absconded with most of their best players. Things had gotten so bad that, for one game, the Alleghenys drew a "crowd" of just 17 fans.

Coming off an abysmal 23-113 season, the Alleghenys were desperate. They noticed that Philadelphia had failed to reserve Bierbauer, who had hit .306 with a team-leading seven home runs for the Wonders. So, they leapt into action: Manager Ned Scanlon paid a midwinter visit to Bierbauer on Presque Isle in Lake Erie in order to sign him. According to author Alfred Spink, Scanlon was forced to cross the iced-over harbor in a winter storm in order to reach Bierbauer and get him to sign on the dotted line.

Philadelphia protested, but to no avail, having failed to reserve Bierbauer. An arbitrator agreed that the second baseman was a free agent, and Philadelphia was forced to accept a signing it considered "piratical."

That allegation meant the end of the Alleghenys name, with the team thenceforth being known as the Pittsburgh Pirates.

The Pirates' fortunes improved immediately: Even though they finished in last place again the next season, they improved their record to 55-80, and a year later managed to post a winning record. The team finally won the pennant in 1901 and took part in the first-ever World Series two years later.

Of course, the Pirates remain in business more than 125 years later. The Philadelphia team, by contrast, lasted just one more season before folding along with the rest of the American Association.

The AA's collapse left top players with even fewer options, especially considering the reserve clause remained intact.

It was strengthened even further when the Western League changed its name to the American League and agreed to abide by it after the turn of the century.

Two other leagues, however, did *not* agree — and were, in consequence, branded "outlaws" by the establishment.

1890 Players' League	W	L	Pct.
Boston Reds	81	48	.628
Brooklyn Ward's Wonders	76	56	.576
New York Giants	74	57	.565
Chicago Pirates	75	62	.547
Philadelphia Athletics	68	63	.519
Pittsburgh Burghers	60	68	.469
Cleveland Infants	55	75	.423
Buffalo Bisons	36	96	.273

Forgotten league

The first of these was the United States League, which never managed to play a full season, although it tried twice to do so. Plans for the league were announced in December of 2011, with teams set to play in New York, Brooklyn, Richmond and Washington, as well as the smaller Reading, Pa., whose franchise was owned by league president William Witman.

Soon, there was stalk that the league would also field teams in Pittsburgh, Chicago, Indianapolis, Baltimore and Kansas City. Sites for games were also being procured, with the Indianapolis team planning to play its games at the site of an old cemetery.

That idea turned out to be dead on arrival, however: Indianapolis didn't make the cut.

Charles White, a boxing referee who owned the New York franchise, had an even wilder idea: He wanted to build a playing field on the roof of the new Grand Central Station. Among the advantages: The roof was so large that home-run balls would no longer be lost, and the central location would be convenient for fans. One optimistic news report proclaimed, "It would be the most centrally located ballpark in the country, and all attendance figures would be knocked into smithereens."

Other promotions, such as vaudeville and motion picture shows, were planned for the nighttime hours at the ballparks.

By mid-January, Baltimore and Kansas City had been dropped from the list of franchises, and a lineup of eight teams had been all but finalized, with Pittsburgh, Cincinnati and Cleveland joining the five teams originally announced. (Chicago would ultimately replace Brooklyn on the list.) The Pittsburgh team, managed by former Pirates ace Deacon

Phillippe, was named the Filipinos in his honor.

Meanwhile, the league began courting players. Witman, who had previously run the Pennsylvania State League, predicted that the USL would have "no trouble getting ballplayers outside of the other leagues." adding that it wouldn't take "contract jumpers."

He declared: "There are enough good players lying around loose to make all the high-class teams we want."

One of the first names to surface was that of Dick Rudolph, a star pitcher with Toronto of the International League, who was reportedly offered a three-year contract to play in the USL. Ultimately, however, Rudolph wound up signing with the Boston Braves, for whom he won two games in the 1914 World Series.

Owners of the league's Richmond franchise said they were in talks with former Cubs third baseman Harry Steinfeldt, the fourth member of the famed Tinker-to-Evers-to-Chance infield, about a possible contract. (Steinfeldt did join the league, but instead as manager of the Cincinnati Pippins.) In Reading, meanwhile, rumor had it that Witman wanted to sign the legendary Adrian "Cap" Anson … even though Anson was just a couple of months shy of his 60th birthday. Anson, however, never played in the league.

The league vowed not to go after players under contract to existing teams, but the reserve clause was another matter.

"No contract jumpers will be played," Richmond co-owner Ernest Landgraf said. "We are going to protect the contracts of all ballclubs, but we are not going to recognize a reserve clause. We have none in our contracts. …"

Still, the league was unable to land any big names. Perhaps the most notable player who did sign was Jack Cronin, a pitcher who had spent all or part of seven seasons in the majors, but who had compiled a meager 43-58 record there and hadn't pitched a big-league game in eight years. He was nearly 38 years old when he joined the USL, having spent six years in the Eastern League before sitting out the 1911 season altogether. He did, however, win his first start for Reading, a 6-2 victory at New York in both teams' second game, striking out 12 batters in the process.

The season had opened a day earlier, on May 1, with the same two teams playing to a 10-10 tie before the game was called because of darkness.

Witman dubbed it an auspicious beginning, with 21,000 fans having turned out for the four season-opening games, including 8,500 who passed through the turnstiles in Richmond. Witman chided naysayers for predicting the league would never even get off the ground. "Now that we are actually started, you will see millionaires falling over themselves to get a piece of a good thing," he crowed, quickly adding, however, that "we have loads of money behind us and don't need any help."

Attendance in New York was less than one-third of the Richmond figure, but still encouraging: The Reading Times reported that the team's backers planned to build a new bleacher in anticipation of even larger crowds in the future as the club played its way through what was to be a 126-game season.

If you build it, they will come.

But they didn't.

Crowds quickly thinned out to the point that just 50 fans showed up for a May 27 game in New York. It didn't help attendance that the Knickerbockers had won just two of their first 17 games, and they didn't play another after that, ceasing operations with their Grand Central Station ballpark still an unrealized dream. Cleveland dropped out of the league after just three weeks, and a mere 11 fans showed up at one game in Cincinnati. A rumor circulated at the beginning of June that Witman's Reading team would move to Indianapolis, but the same news report said the team's players were already moving on to other teams and that nothing was left of the team except "one bat bag, a mask, the suits and Manager (Leo) Groom." The Indianapolis transfer never took place, and Witman filed for bankruptcy a couple of days later. The "loads of money" he had bragged about a month earlier were nowhere to be found; neither were millionaires falling over themselves to invest in the failing enterprise.

The league finally gave up the ghost after about five weeks of play, with Chicago beating Pittsburgh 7-5 in the final game June 8. The victorious Filipinos finished the truncated season with the league's best record at 19-8.

But amazingly, that wasn't the end of the USL. Not quite, anyway.

On Jan. 6, 2013, a group of investors led by Witman decided to try again, putting up $125,000 to incorporate the United States League of Professional Baseball Clubs. Once again, an eight-team lineup was planned, with Richmond, Reading, New York, Washington and Pittsburgh returning to join entries in Baltimore, Syracuse and Trenton, N.J.

By the time the league was formally organized March 6, however, the only two markets that had much success the previous season, Pittsburgh and Richmond, were no longer on the list. Pittsburgh's owners, notably, had abandoned the league for the new Federal League, a vote of no-confidence that should have raised a red flag for the U.S. League's future. Even more ominous, however, was the fact that the latter franchise had been replaced by the Lynchburg Shoemakers, a Class C team representing a city less than one-quarter the size of Richmond. The team had been so bad the previous year that it had been mired in last place when it was dropped from the Virginia State League in mid-June because it was unable to pay its players' salaries.

Despite this, a report surfaced that the club had offered Ty Cobb $15,000 to play for the Shoemakers. Whether there was anything to this or it was just a publicity stunt is hard to tell, but a few days later, Witman put the kibosh on the idea by saying Cobb wouldn't be able to play in the USL unless the Detroit Tigers released him from his contract. Since that wasn't about to happen, the idea died a quick death.

The extravagant "offer" to Cobb notwithstanding, the league showed a keen interest in curbing costs from the outset. The list of cities was one example: Newark replaced Trenton, Philadelphia took Pittsburgh's slot, and Brooklyn joined in place of Syracuse. As a result, travel distances were much reduced from 1912, with no Midwestern clubs and every team situated on or close to the Eastern Seaboard.

The league planned to play a season of about 120 games beginning May 10. But just three days into the season, Washington withdrew to play as an independent club, and New York refused to play a game at Newark because it hadn't been paid its guarantee. The league contracted to six teams, dropping New York, but a day later decided to give up the ghost altogether, citing poor attendance and depleted cash reserves (sound familiar?). But the USL wasn't the only league to emerge in 1913 as a potential challenge to the established leagues and the reserve clause. Another, more dangerous foe was waiting in the wings.

1912 United States Baseball League	W	L	Pct.
Pittsburgh Filipinos	19	7	.731
Richmond Rebels	15	11	.577
Reading	12	9	.571
Cincinnati Pippins	12	10	.545
Washington Senators	6	7	.462
Chicago Green Sox	10	12	.455
Cleveland Forest City	8	13	.381
New York Knickerbockers	2	15	.118

Bold challenge

The Federal League had something the USL never did: money. Its owners had a combined net worth of $50 million, the equivalent of $1.24 billion today. Their number included people like Harry F. Sinclair, the founder of Sinclair Oil, whose green dinosaur mascot still stands watch outside gas stations across the country today.

The Feds had money to burn, which is exactly what you need if you want to start a bidding war with the establishment. Perhaps more than any other upstart league before or since, the Federal League was in a position to pose a serious challenge to the big boys … because some of its owners were big boys in their own right. They could afford, monetarily speaking, to set their sights high, so they did.

Like the United States League, they made overtures to Ty Cobb, and like the USL, they came up empty, as they did in offers to Tris Speaker, Shoeless Joe Jackson, Christy Mathewson and Sam Crawford. But the Feds didn't let those setbacks stop them: They went out and signed a number of other players from the two established leagues in 1914, and by April 1 of that year, they had lured 39 players away from the National League and 20 more away from the AL.

Among them:

• Former Cubs shortstop Joe Tinker, the famed double-play sparkplug, most recently of Cincinnati.

• "Prince" Hal Chase, who had spent eight-plus seasons with the New York Yankees (earlier known as the Highlanders) before a recent trade to the White Sox. Chase would top the Federal League in homers with 17 in 2015, then win a National League batting title with Cincinnati the following year.

• Russ Ford, who'd spend five years as a pitcher with the Highlanders/Yankees, including a 26-6 season in 1910.

• Mordecai "Three-Finger" Brown, who'd strung together six consecutive 20-win seasons for the Cubs during a period when the team played in four World Series.

• Veteran Phillies infielders Otto Knabe and Mickey Doolan, two-thirds of that team's double-play combo.

• Cardinals outfielder Steve Evans and utility player Lee Magee.

The Feds' biggest coup, however, wasn't any of those established players, but an outfielder who'd played a mere five games with the New York Highlanders in 1912 before toiling for the entire 1913 season with the Hartford Senators of the Class B Eastern Association. There, he proceeded to win the league batting championship with a .345 average and led the team in every hitting category.

His name was Benjamin Michael Kauff, otherwise known as Benny.

Prior to the 1914 season, Sinclair's Indianapolis Hoosiers offered Kauff twice his previous salary to jump ship. It wasn't as though he'd been making that much in the first place, but $4,000 was still a good deal of money to a man who had spent the past season feeling forgotten in Hartford, Conn.

He would be even more successful in Indianapolis than he had been in Hartford — so impressive, in fact, that that people started calling him "The Ty Cobb of the Feds."

We'll hear more about Mr. Kauff later. But first, some background about the league itself. Kauff wasn't in the Federal League during its first year, and indeed, most history books don't even refer to that inaugural season. That's because the league didn't start out as particularly noteworthy. It debuted in 1913 as a regional operation with few illusions of being anything other than a minor league. In fact, J.J. Alcock of the *Chicago Tribune* wrote that "in everything but the size of its cities, the league deserved the ranking of about Class D as a minor circuit."

Like the USL it was considered an "outlaw" league — one that didn't recognize the reserve clause and which filled its roster with free agents. In fact, some news reports from early 1913 depicted the new league as rising from the ashes of the United States League's first failed season. it was true that the ownership of the U.S. League's successful pittsburgh Filipinos franchise had moved its team to the federal league, bringing manager Deacon Phillippe with them. But the FederalL wasn't really a "new USL." It was a more direct descendent of the Columbian League, which had been proposed by a man named John T. Powers the previous year. the league, however, had never gotten off the ground. Powers' St. Louis investor had withdrawn, forcing him to shelve the idea, but he returned in 1913 with a similar template for the Federal League, which like its predecessor would be based in major midwestern cities.

Ultimately, the Feds set up shop in four of the same cities that had been scheduled to be part of Powers' previous venture: Indianapolis, Cleveland, St. Louis and Chicago. Added to the mix this time were franchises in Pittsburgh and the Cincinnati suburb of Covington, Ky. (chosen because the ballpark they'd intended to use in Cincy was unavailable). The field in Covington held just 4,200 fans, and the site ultimately didn't work out, so the franchise relocated at midseason to Kansas City, another Columbian League market.

Overall, however, the Feds accomplished something the USL had never managed: They finished the season.

Indianapolis won the pennant in a runaway with a 75-45 record 10 games ahead of second-place Cleveland. And with that inaugural season in the books, the Feds began thinking bigger.

A lot bigger.

Chicago manufacturer Jim Gilmore replaced Powers as the head of the league and immediately began making plans to take the Feds into the big time. Expanding beyond its

Midwest base, the league added teams in the two biggest metropolitan areas not served by a major league team: Baltimore and Buffalo. A third new franchise, rumored to be headed for Peoria, never got off the ground, and an application from a Philadelphia-based group led by former Phillies owner Horace Fogel was rejected. Gilmore said point-blank that he wanted nothing to do with Fogel, who had been banned from organized baseball two years earlier for falsely accusing the National League of rigging the pennant race in favor of the New York Giants.

Newspaper headlines proclaimed that the FL had declared "war" on the baseball establishment, and that wasn't far wrong.

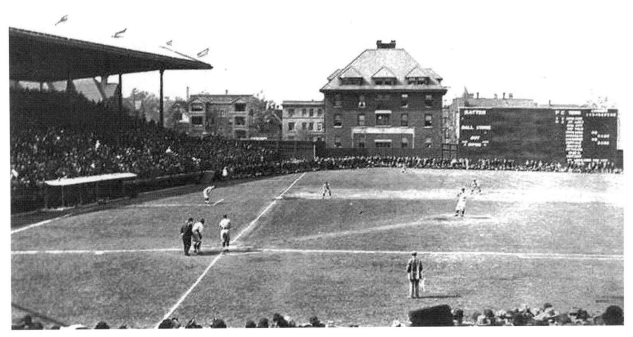

Weeghman Park, as it looked in its first season (1914); these days, it's Wrigley Field.

Wrigley before Wrigley

Gilmore knew he had to play hardball financially as well as on the baseball field. So, he brought in fellow Chicagoan, a flamboyant gentleman by the name of "Lucky" Charlie Weeghman, who owned of a dozen lunch counters in the Windy City. Weeghman became the co-owner and face of the Chicago franchise. In its first season, the team had been known as the Browns or Keeleys — for star pitcher/manager Burt "Speed" Keeley, who had spent a couple of years with Washington in the American League.

But Keeley didn't stay with the team the following season: Weeghman had someone else in mind for the managing job. So, the club became known simply as the Chicago Feds … to be rechristened the Whales the following season. Ever see a Whale in Lake Michigan? I didn't think so. But for that season, a whole team of them played a few hundred yards from its shores.

With his marquee franchise in place, Gilmore set out to promote the construction of modern, state-of-the-art ballparks for the Federal clubs. Soon, construction was begun on new facilities in Indianapolis, Buffalo and elsewhere, including Chicago's North Side. Weeghman Park would be the league's crown jewel and, through numerous upgrades and renovations, would stand the test of time to host its first World Series game more than a century later. Amazingly, it was built in just two short months.

The Chicago team had played its previous season at DePaul University, but a ballpark befitting a big-league team was needed for its sophomore campaign. With the Cubs playing on the city's West Side and the White Sox holding forth in the south, one piece of property stood out as the perfect site for a ballpark: a plot once owned by a Lutheran seminary, which had sold the land and relocated when urban Chicago had begun to encroach on its pastoral haven.

Weeghman wasn't the first to recognize its potential. A few years earlier, a man named Charles Havenor had formed a partnership that purchased the land from the seminary for $175,000. Havenor owned the Milwaukee franchise in the American Association, a high minor league with ambitions of attaining big-league status. His idea was to build a ballpark on the seminary site and install a team there in the upgraded American Association. Havenor's fellow owners, however, ultimately thought better of challenging the major leagues and remained a part of the baseball establishment — which blocked him from putting a minor-league team in Chicago.

His vision thwarted, Havenor sold his share of the property to investment partners, who in turn leased it to Weeghman as the site for his new ballpark.

Construction on the 14,000-seat stadium began on Feb. 23, 1914, just two months before Opening Day. It would have a single-deck, covered grandstand behind home plate and down the left-field line, with a large scoreboard in left field. Home runs could be hit down the lines, where the fence was 300 feet from home plate, but center field was cavernous: The left- and right-field walls converged at a near-right angle 450 feet away.

Eliza Hall, the student building from the old seminary, would become a target for batters aiming for an easy home run down the line in left field. They teed off during the season's first homestand, hitting one ball after another over the fence near the foul pole. It quickly became evident that the fence would need to be moved back, but there was a problem: Eliza Hall had been leased to a private party and was being used as a residence.

Weeghman, however, found a loophole: That lease didn't include the back porch, which he ordered demolished to make way for more room inside the ballpark.

Before work even got under way on the Chicago ballpark, the league was making headlines on the personnel front.

In December of 2013 the Feds league scored their first big signings when a pair of major-leaguers defected: shortstop Joe Tinker and pitcher Mordecai Brown. Brown inked a three-year deal with St. Louis, and Tinker accepted a three-year $36,000 contract to join the Chicago Feds, where he would replace Keeley as a playing manager. Before agreeing to join the Feds, Tinker had been included in a deal that would have sent him from Cincinnati to Brooklyn, but Tinker wanted no part of the Big Apple. "I want to play in Chicago, and organized baseball won't let me," he said. "I won't go to Brooklyn."

Brooklyn, however, would come to the Federal League.

It happened this way: The Cleveland Green Sox, who had been managed by pitching great Cy Young, announced in December that they were dropping out of the league because they couldn't find a place to play in 1914. Club President Charles Zimmerman put it bluntly: "We absolutely would not consider returning to Luna Park next season. Last year's experience there was enough. Other sites are in the hands of people with whom we are unable to do business."

The Cleveland franchise was transferred to Toronto, but that situation turned out to be temporary: About six weeks later, it was moved again, this time to Brooklyn. The team would be financed by Robert Ward, owner of a bakery that would lend the ballclub its name: the Tip-Tops. Ward entrusted the team's business operations to another Ward, who was no relation. This was none other than John Montgomery Ward, the same man who had spearheaded the formation of the Players' League nearly a quarter-century earlier.

John Ward hadn't lost his fervor for defending players against the reserve clause, and the Federal League gave him the perfect platform to continue that fight. It was, in a sense, heir to the mantle of the Players' League that Ward had formed in the waning years of the previous century. His dedication to the cause was captured in a message that appeared on the right-field wall on Opening Day of the 1914 season. It began with the declaration that "Ballplayers are all human" and touted the team's colorful uniforms as a contrast to those of the "drab monopoly era."

John Ward also served as attorney for the league, and it was in the courtroom that the Feds would pose perhaps their biggest challenge to the baseball establishment.

It was there that they ran into a mountain: a judge who also happened to be the future commissioner of baseball: Kenesaw Mountain Landis.

The Federal League's first season as a major league was greeted with the kind of enthusiasm that had eluded the U.S. League two years earlier. USL organizers had been pleased with a total turnout of 21,000 to their four season-openers, but estimates placed attendance at that same figure for the Feds' Chicago opener alone. The Chicago Tribune wrote that "every seat in the place was taken, a great many were standing up in the back of the grandstand, and more than 2,000 were on the field in the circus seats placed there for the occasion." Others watched the spectacle from roofs and buildings across the way.

There was a parade, a flagpole ceremony and a 21-gun salute.

Gilmore and Weeghman were described as being "so overjoyed with the spectacle that they almost wept," and the reporter enthused that "there is little doubt that it was an epochal day in the history of the national game."

Weeghman's team capped a near-perfect day by winning the game 9-1, but there was trouble brewing: Kansas City starter Chief Johnson, who had jumped to the Federal League from Cincinnati, was served with legal papers at the end of the second inning that admonished him against playing any more for the Packers until further notice (Despite the injunction, Johnson ended up appearing in 20 games that season). Legal issues were never far from the playing field for the "outlaw" Federal League.

Benny Kauff dominated the league at the plate, winning the batting title with a whopping .370 batting average — a mark that still stands more than a century later as the record for anyone in a rookie season. He led the league in half a dozen other offensive categories, as well, including hits, doubles, total bases and steals. Kauff's firepower was enough to catapult the Hoosiers to the head of the pack, and they won the FL pennant by a game and a half over Weeghman's Chicago nine.

Despite its success on the field, Indianapolis struggled financially as the smallest market in the league, running up a reported debt of $70,000. So, after the end of the season, Sinclair bought out his partners and moved the club to Newark, and Kauff wound up with the Brooklyn Tip-Tops as part of the deal. Sinclair didn't get the prize he really wanted: a seat at the table in New York City. He had hoped to move the Hoosiers to the Big Apple and hire Giants manager John McGraw to run the team. But the Yankees and Giants thwarted his efforts to play in Manhattan, and McGraw turned down a $100,000 contract.

Newark would have to do.

That setback wasn't the only one the Feds suffered during the offseason. More frustrating still was Walter Johnson's decision to renege on a contract he signed with the

Chicago Feds. Johnson, the best pitcher in baseball, agreed on Dec. 3 to leave the Washington Senators and join the ChiFeds for two years. The incentive: an annual salary of $17,500 and a $6,000 signing bonus. A little over two weeks later, however, Johnson had a change of heart after speaking with the Senators' manager and re-signed with Washington for three years. His new contract paid him $5,000 less a year than what Chicago had offered and was just $500 more than what he'd earned the year before.

But it wasn't about the money.

Someone had clearly gotten to Johnson and threatened him with legal action for violating the reserve clause.

"After a conference with Manager Griffith and legal authorities, I am convinced the option in my last year's contract with the Washington ballclub was binding," he said in a statement, "and I am going to return to the Washington ball club and fulfill my agreement at the terms offered me by that club."

One can only imagine how things might have ended up if Johnson had displayed the kind of courage Curt Flood showed a half-century later. As it was, however, Charlie Weeghman and the Feds were forced to swallow a bitter defeat at the hands of the establishment. But they'd only lost the battle, not the war ... at least not yet. And the Federal League owners were about to prove that they could to play hardball, too. Three weeks after Johnson caved and returned to the Senators, the upstart league sent its lawyers into a federal courtroom, where they filed an antitrust suit against organized baseball.

The National and American leagues, working in concert, were a monopoly, the FL charged, and should not be allowed to continue as such.

The trial was assigned to Kenesaw Mountain Landis, a federal judge who would, five years later, become the first commissioner of baseball (his name was a variant spelling of Kennesaw Mountain in Georgia, the place where his father was wounded in battle during the Civil War). From the Feds' point of view, Landis must have seemed like a great choice. Appointed by trust-busting president Teddy Roosevelt, he had once fined the quintessential monopoly, Standard Oil, a whopping $29 million. Surely, he would look favorably on a complaint that baseball, too, was a monopoly.

The trial was over a mere 17 days later, which must have seemed like a good sign, as well.

But Landis took his time rendering a decision, withholding judgment for nearly a year, and by that time, a lot had changed.

As the Federal League's second season as a major league progressed, things got progressively worse. Newark failed to make the splash Sinclair had hoped for, posting a winning record but finishing far back in the pack. Without Kauff in the lineup, the team batting average fell 45 points from the previous year, with just one member of the starting lineup hitting over .300. The pitching was just as problematic. Sinclair had parted ways with Kauff but had managed to retain the rights to the team's best pitcher from the previous year, Cy Falkenberg. But Falkenberg, who'd won 25 games with a league-leading nine shutouts for Indianapolis, was just 9-11 with no shutouts in Newark. By the time mid-August rolled around, the Peppers (as they were now known) had traded him to Brooklyn for Tom Seaton.

But Seaton was just as bad, going 2-6, and the Peppers — who had been in first place when Seaton came aboard — went into a tailspin, losing 23 of their last 39 games. They finished fifth, having failed to arouse the level of excitement needed to pry fans away from the Giants and Yankees across the state line.

Brooklyn finished even further back, managing seventh place in the eight-team league even though Kauff won his second straight batting crown and teammate Lee Magee ranked third among the league's hitters. With both teams in the New York metro area floundering, the Feds needed things to get better elsewhere.

They didn't.

Kansas City, which had barely held on to its franchise after 1914, was in trouble financially, and so was Buffalo. In August, Gilmore floated the idea of selling bleacher tickets for 10 cents apiece to drive up attendance. Youngsters, he said, "cannot afford to pay a quarter, and there are many men who do not feel that they can spend that amount for amusement."

It had the feel of a desperate move, and indeed, Gilmore told the press around the same time that the league hadn't made any money in its second season. He added, however, that it didn't expect to; the league's backers, he asserted, didn't care, as they were in the baseball business for the love of the game. That led the reporter writing the story to editorialize, "Mr. Gilmore, undoubtedly, is trying to kid himself."

The league president, however, was under no illusions concerning the gravity of the situation. "It was probably in May that some of us realized it was going to be a very poor season from a financial standpoint," he would say later. By July, he said, he had reached the conclusion that the league couldn't survive. "My opinion was we were fighting a hopeless task."

The pennant race was a thriller, with five teams in contention late in the season and the top three finishing within a half-game of one another (Chicago won the title by a less than a single percentage point over St. Louis by splitting a doubleheader with Pittsburgh on the season's final day, relegating the Rebels to third place).

Federal case

Despite the league's financial woes, owners and executives put on a brave face. The St. Louis Terriers proclaimed they couldn't wait for the 1916 season, and after the season ended, Gilmore came up with a plan to extract as much as he could from the established leagues in exchange for the Feds folding their tent. He shared his idea with Sinclair and Robert Ward, the Brooklyn owner, but kept the rest of the league in the dark.

Gilmore, Ward and Sinclair rented an office suite in New York, then secured an option to buy a plot of land at Lenox Boulevard and 143rd Street in Upper Manhattan. They enlisted the services of a New York architect (who also happened to be vice president of the Pittsburgh Rebels) to draft plans for a mammoth 55,000-seat stadium that would enable the Federal League to "invade" New York. All this was done in a very public manner, and on some level, it probably seemed credible. Before the Feds had played their first season as a major league, they had insisted that each of the eight teams build a new ballpark, and they'd been trying to get a foothold in New York for some time. It made sense.

It was, however, in Gilmore's words, "one big bluff."

He never intended to build that stadium, and he had no intention of playing a 1916 season, either. Gilmore knew it was best to negotiate from a position of strength, and the bogus stadium plans were merely a ploy to create some leverage and bring the established leagues to table. In order to make it work, however, he had to keep it a secret — even from the league's other owners. Soon, he had organized baseball's attention.

Gilmore opened the talks by angling for a merger, demanding that the American League absorb the Brooklyn Tip-Tops and Pittsburgh Rebels, while Newark and Baltimore would join the senior circuit. Kansas City and Buffalo would fold, while Weeghman would be allowed to buy the Cubs, and St. Louis Terriers owner Phil Ball would have the right to purchase one of the two established St. Louis ballclubs.

The merger, however, never happened. The NL vetoed the idea, having no interest in accepting competition for the Dodgers (then known as the Robins) in Brooklyn or the Pirates in Northwest Pennsylvania. Still, other aspects of the proposal survived: Weeghman was, in fact, given the opportunity to purchase the Cubs, which he did for $50,000, and Ball was allowed to buy the St. Louis Browns.

The Pittsburgh Rebels wouldn't survive, but their owners would receive a $50,000 buyout.

Robert Ward of Brooklyn got one of the sweetest deals. Ward had rebuilt Washington Park — the Dodgers' former home before they moved about a mile up the road to then-new

Ebbets Field in 1913 — to house his Tip-Tops, and the established leagues agreed to pay him $20,000 a year for 20 years for his trouble. (The Washington Senators considered moving there in the fall of 1916 but ultimately stayed put, and the ballpark was used for such things as ice skating and storage before it was finally torn down.)

Kansas City got nothing, as the Packers had gone belly-up at midseason and had been operated by the league the rest of the way. Buffalo was left out of the deal as well.

That left one franchise unaccounted for: the last-place Baltimore Terrapins. Gilmore had been stringing the Terrapins management along throughout the fall with a series of letters suggesting a player signing and professing his faith in the club "to draw wonderful crowds and easily pay expenses" in 1916. When Stuart Janney, an attorney for the Terrapins, confronted Gilmore, in November about rumors that a deal was in the works, he denied it flat-out.

The Terrapins owners were furious when, a month later, they found out the truth. When Gilmore asked if they would accept a $75,000 payment, they turned him down cold, demanding the same opportunity to purchase a big-league team that Ball and Weeghman had received. Their motivation was simple: They wanted to have a team in Baltimore and were willing to pay handsomely to get one. They offered to pay $250,000, five times as much as Weeghman was paying for the Cubs, only to be told by White Sox owner Charles Comiskey that Baltimore was "a minor-league city, and not a hell of a good one at that."

Charles Ebbets of the Brooklyn Robins stooped to racism in denigrating Baltimore: "You have too many colored (sic) population to start with," he said. "They are a cheap population when it gets down to paying their money at the gate." (In a dose of irony, this is the same Ebbets whose ballpark would, three decades later, be the home field for the man destined to shatter baseball's color barrier.)

The Terrapins wouldn't forget these slights.

A couple of months after the Gilmore deal ended the Federal League for good, Judge Landis finally got around to ruling on the Feds 1915 lawsuit. He dismissed the case, not based on its merits, but on what he feared would happen if the Federal League were to prevail: Simply put, he believed the established leagues would be too badly damaged by such a decision. Even though the plaintiffs had presented "a very full argument" based on "a very simply proposition," Landis couldn't bring himself to rule in their favor because he believed that doing so would be "if not destructive, vitally injurious" to the National and American leagues.

The story might have ended right there had it not been for the jilted Baltimore ownership group, which filed another antitrust lawsuit in September 1917. A jury ruled in their favor, awarding them $254,000 — more than what they'd offered to purchase a team in organized baseball. They never saw that money, though: The U.S. Supreme Court reversed that decision five years later, ruling that baseball was not a form of interstate commerce and was, therefore, not subject to the Sherman Act.

The ruling stood up to later challenges, even though courts ruled that other major sports leagues were, in fact, subject to the Sherman Act. Still, the Supreme Court refused to overturn baseball's exemption when Curt Flood challenged its legality years later, even though Justice Harry Blackmun admitted it was "an aberration" and "an anomaly." His reasoning was that the decision, while inconsistent and illogical, had been in force for so long that it was up to Congress to fix it. The court, in other words, punted.

Many players who suited up for Federal League teams ended their careers when the league gave up the ghost. A few, however, caught on with major league ballclubs and flourished. The established leagues had blackballed players who signed with FL teams in violation of the reserve clause; as part of the peace settlement with the Feds, they agreed to lift that ban.

Edd Roush, an outfielder for Indianapolis and Newark, signed with the New York Giants before moving quickly to Cincinnati and winning a pair of batting titles for the Reds in 1917 and 1919. Prince Hal Chase also won a batting title for the Reds, in 1916, a year after he led the Federal League in home runs for the Buffalo Blues. Chase, however, was implicated in a number of shady dealings involving bribery and gambling on ballgames. He was indicted (but never convicted) as an alleged middleman in the Black Sox scandal of 1919, effectively ending his career when baseball appointed its first commissioner: the same person who had heard the first antitrust case against the same owners who had now hired him. Kenesaw Mountain Landis.

Man vs. Mountain

It was Landis who ended the career of another former Federal Leaguer, too — none other than the famed Ty Cobb of the Feds.

Benny Kauff caught on with the New York Giants after the FL folded and, though he was never the player he'd been for the Feds, he earned a regular spot in the lineup, batting .308 in 1917 and .315 a year later. He helped the Giants make the World Series that year, and although they lost to the White Sox in six games, he was instrumental in one of New York's two victories, hitting a pair of home runs and driving in three of the Giants' five runs as they won Game 4 in a shutout.

Three years later, though, Kauff was out of baseball, thanks to Landis.

In December of 1919, Kauff was charged with selling a stolen car along with a pair of employees at the auto parts business he owned. A grand jury indicted him, but the trial was delayed several times at Kauff's request, and Landis eventually got tired of waiting. On April 7, 1922, he banned Kauff from baseball. When the case finally went to trial, Kauff, claimed he hadn't known the car was hot. He hadn't been there when his two employees stole it, and he hadn't been there when they divvied up the money they made from selling it. He also had what he thought was a valid bill of sale.

After just an hour of deliberations, the jury voted to acquit him.

Landis, however, was not eager to do the same. This was, after all, the same man who banned Shoeless Joe Jackson for life for his alleged role in the Black Sox series — a series in which Jackson hit .375 with a home run and six RBI. Unlike Jackson, Kauff wasn't even accused of throwing ballgames; his alleged crime, of which he had been acquitted, had occurred away from the diamond and had nothing to do with baseball.

That didn't seem to matter to Landis, though. Maybe the commissioner wanted to make Kauff wait the same way Kauff had made him wait for the case to go to trial.

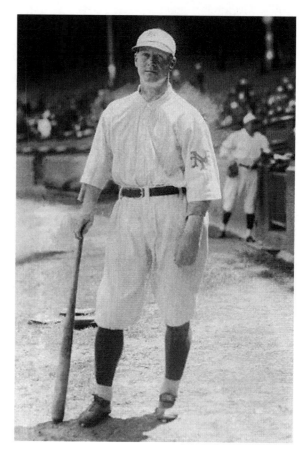

Benny Kauff with the New York Giants, after his Federal League days.

Regardless, whether by design or indifference, the commissioner spent months ignoring Kauff's petition for reinstatement, and with the season nearing an end in September, Kauff decided he'd had enough. He walked into the New York Supreme Court and obtained a temporary injunction requiring that he be reinstated, at least until the court could grant him a full hearing. Then he came out of the courtroom and called Landis an egotistical "czar," accusing him of dishing out arbitrary punishment on matters beyond his jurisdiction.

Even Landis' admirers probably agreed with some of Kauff's assessment. He had been hired to bring a greater degree of order to organized baseball, and one of his friends once called him "a great showman, theatrical in appearance. ... People always crowded into his courtroom, knowing there would be something going on. There were few dull moments."

Kauff's comments could not have endeared him to Landis, but he thought he had a good case. And he did. The judge even went so far as to declare that Kauff had been the victim of "an apparent injustice."

But it didn't matter.

As it turned out, the case hinged on Kauff's employment with the New York Giants, and since his contract had expired in October, he had no basis on which to seek an injunction. The upshot: He'd been too patient with Landis. He'd waited too long to act. And now that the ball was back in Landis' court, he proceeded to hit it — and Kauff — out of the park. Permanently. Landis even went so far as to say that he felt the jury had been wrong in acquitting Kauff, calling the verdict "one of the worst travesties of justice" he'd ever seen.

So ended the career of Benny Kauff, the Ty Cobb of the Feds, six years after the Federal League itself met its end.

Few people remember him today, perhaps because "Say it ain't so, Benny" just doesn't roll off the tongue.

1915 Federal League	W	L	Pct.
Chicago Whales	86	66	.566
St. Louis Terriers	87	67	.565
Pittsburgh Rebels	86	67	.562
Kansas City Packers	81	72	.529
Newark Peppers	80	72	.526
Buffalo Blues	74	78	.487
Brooklyn Tip-Tops	70	82	.471
Baltimore Terrapins	47	107	.593

Diamond Girls

The owner of the Chicago Cubs was worried. In the autumn of 1942, a staffer from the Office of War Information advised a gathering of baseball owners that 3 or 4 million men would be joining the armed forces, and that millions more would "transfer from their nonessential occupations to war jobs."

Pro sports had to rank pretty high on that list of nonessential occupations, and the war's impact was already being felt. The day after Japan attacked Pearl Harbor, Cleveland ace Bob Feller enlisted in the U.S. Army, becoming the first baseball player to do so. He would miss three full seasons and most of a fourth before returning to resume his Hall of Fame career. And that was just the beginning.

Ted Williams of the Red Sox, the last major leaguer to hit better than .400 in a season, joined the Army two years later, in May of 1942. His greatest rival, Joe DiMaggio, just two years removed from his record 56-game hitting streak, joined the Army in February of 1943. The Yankee Clipper was away from the game that summer and for two more seasons after that.

In the National Football League, the Philadelphia Eagles and Pittsburgh Steelers dealt with the manpower crunch by fielding a combined team called the Steagles in 1943; then, the Steelers combined with the Chicago Cardinals the following season on a team known as "Card-Pitt." There was no telling how long the war might continue or how many players might be lost.

Already, women were stepping up to fill many positions left vacant by men who had joined the armed forces. The percentage of women in the workforce rose 10 percentage points to 37 percent between 1940 and '45. Five million entered the workforce, going to work in factories as riveters, welders and crane operators. They built ships and worked with munitions. The aviation industry saw the biggest influx of women during wartime, but women went to work in other jobs traditionally held by men, driving fire engines, working as train conductors and serving as gas station attendants. In sports, they were golf caddies, pin-setters at bowling alleys (before they were automated), even coaches and baseball umpires. If they could call balls and strikes, they could play the game, too, couldn't they?

That was the question that occurred to Cubs owner Philip K. Wrigley as he considered the very real possibility that Major League Baseball might be forced to cancel one or more seasons because of World War II. Wrigley himself was a big supporter on the home front: Instead of spending money to advertise his company's chewing gum, he devoted his entire radio budget to promoting the war effort.

So, even when baseball staved off the possibility of a canceled season, Wrigley forged ahead with an idea he'd come up with to fill the void: a professional women's softball league. As originally conceived, the All-American Girls Softball League would have teams in a mix of major Midwestern cities such as Chicago, St. Louis and Cleveland, along with towns crucial to the war industry, like Gary, Indiana. He hoped the teams could play in big league ballparks while teams were on the road, but other owners didn't care for that idea, and Wrigley was forced to go it alone.

One way his new league would differ from the major is that its contracts wouldn't contain a reserve clause, binding players to a single team. Instead, players signed personal services contracts that could be renewed from year to year. Wrigley described himself as "probably the only one in professional baseball in the last 40 years who has never felt that the reserve clause ... was really essential."

He continued: "I have the old-fashioned idea that if a man likes his job, he will give it his best. If he does not like it, no contract on earth can cause him to put forth his best efforts." The new league, he suggested, would provide a good testing ground for a different way of doing things.

Wrigley was clearly thinking outside the box. And the one figure from the major leagues who supported him in this bold new endeavor, Brooklyn Dodgers executive Branch Rickey, would develop a reputation as even more of a maverick than Wrigley. Rickey accepted a position as trustee in Wrigley's new league and, although didn't play an active role in the project, lent credibility to it as a respected general manager for the Cardinals and, now, the Dodgers.

Wrigley's fellow owners weren't the only ones opposed to his idea. When Wrigley began holding tryouts, Chicago's softball establishment tried to sue him for "raiding" its players. The lawsuit went nowhere, because the Chicago group was an amateur organization that didn't pay its players. As a result, it reorganized the following year as a professional organization: the Chicago National Girls' Baseball League.

Like the All-American Girls League, it would last until 1954.

This fight seems to have made Wrigley think twice about placing a team in the Cubs' home ballpark Wrigley Field. When all was said and done, the Windy City would host a team in the league during just one season: The expansion Chicago Colleens, who didn't play at Wrigley Field but at the much smaller Shewbridge Field (which today is a small high school athletic field). The Colleens would wind up fielding a team during just one of the league's seasons, in 1948, and finished dead last.

The opposition of his fellow owners meant big league ballparks were no longer an option, so Wrigley opted to focus on smaller markets. Ultimately, four were chosen, each within a couple of hours' drive of Chicago.

Two of them, Kenosha and Racine, were just 10 miles apart in Wisconsin. South Bend, Ind., home to the University of Notre Dame, would host the third team, with the fourth based in Rockford, Ill., home to one of the earliest professional baseball teams way back in 1871 (the Rockford Forest Citys had played in the inaugural season of the National Association, forerunner of the National League). At least two other cities, Rock Island in Illinois and Oshkosh in Wisconsin, were reportedly under consideration but didn't make the final cut.

Wrigley set aside $100,000 for the venture, including $22,500 for each of the four markets, which would be matched in each city by local interests. But the league itself would own all the teams, and Wrigley announced it would be a nonprofit venture: "Proceeds will be used to expand," he said. "We eventually hope to build a structure of minor leagues. The league itself will control the players, rather than the clubs, to maintain a balance of talent insuring close competition."

Filling the rosters

Wrigley launched a search for those players via a series of tryouts in Chicago, Los Angeles, Nashville, New Orleans, St. Louis and elsewhere. The search even extended up into Canada, with 100 players invited to a spring training event at Wrigley Field set for May 17, 1943. Sixty of them would be chosen to participate, with 15 assigned to each of the four teams, although some were being signed to contracts before that. The minimum salary was set at $50 a week, with players responsible for their own expenses at home but the league picking up the tab on the road.

Ann Harnett was the first woman to sign a contract with the new league, going on to play four seasons with Kenosha and one with the Peoria Redwings. Gladys Davis and Helen Sandiford of Toronto signed in early April, followed by catcher Dorothy Maguire of Cleveland; pitcher Gloria Marks of San Diego; infielders Esther Ziske of Milwaukee and Helen Buchanan of Toledo; and outfielders Edythe Perlick of Chicago and Clara Schillace of Melrose Park, Ill.

Among them, Schillace would play four seasons, Perlick eight seasons and Marks a single season with the Racine Belles; Sandiford played one year, with the Rockford Peaches. Perlick, who played in the Chicago fast-pitch league before joining the new circuit, stole 481 bases in her career, including 88 in 1946, and she was chosen as an all-star in 1943, 1947 and 1948.

"I started out sliding into the bases, but after many strawberries and a sprained ankle, I decided I was fast enough to avoid sliding," she said later. "If you studied the pitchers, you'd know just when to get the jump on them. And most of the time I was fast enough to beat it out successfully."

Sliding could be problematic because the teams wore skirts, rather than pants like their male counterparts.

"The uniform was a dress, with a skirt that ended 3 to 4 inches above the knee and tights underneath that went only partway down the thigh," recalled Joyce Hill (Westerman), a catcher and utility player who spent eight years in the league with five different teams. "You were basically sliding on bare skin."

Mary "Bonnie" Baker, whose quintessential good looks helped her become the face of the league, later recalled that her manager with the South Bend Blue Sox, Bert Neihof, used to turn away when any of his players took off to steal second. It was just too painful to watch. Baker said someone designed sliding pads for the players to slip on before they went to bat, to protect their legs in case they got on base. The problem was, they didn't — get on base, that is. Pretty soon, they started to view the pads as a jinx and refused to wear them.

"So, we just contended with the strawberries," Baker said in a later interview. "Besides, they were ugly looking things — they hung out the bottom of your skirt."

Skirts weren't just mandatory on the field, but whenever the players went out in public.

"I remember traveling all night to Rockford, Illiniois, for one game, and we made a rest stop," said Dottie Schroeder, "but we had to take off our slacks and put on skirts before we got off the bus. It was the middle of the night. There was nothing out there but soybeans."

The uniforms, with their flared skirts, were part of a program to ensure that the players weren't viewed as too masculine. This was a priority for the league because, even during wartime, the presence of women in traditionally male-dominated fields created tension. The "Rosie the Riveter" campaign sought to strike a balance between toughness and femininity, and some factory operators gave the women who worked there lessons in how to apply makeup. Wrigley sought to strike the same balance with his new league. Team members were sent to charm school, and were fined if they were seen drinking or smoking in public.

No chewing tobacco, either.

"We understood why they wanted it," Vivian Anderson of the Milwaukee Chicks would say later. "They didn't want us to be classified as hoodlums for playing a man's game."

What they wanted was someone like Baker, a catcher and utility infielder for 10 seasons in the league. Baker's best season came in 1946 when she hit career highs in batting average (.286) and stolen bases (94); she also managed the Kalamazoo Lassies in 1950, before the league passed a rule requiring that managers be men. One of the Canadian players who caught on with the league, the Regina native was said to have been the inspiration for Geena Davis' character in the 1992 film, *A League of Their Own*.

Baker recalled earning her nickname during a barnstorming tour with a team from Moose Jaw, Saskatchewan, when a Scottish public address announcer in Chicago introduced her as she came up to bat in 1939.

"When it was my turn to bat, she announced me as Mary Baker, of course, but then he added, 'It's Mary, but it should be Bonnie with that wonderful disposition she has.' The name just stuck."

During the league's inaugural season, The *Kenosha Evening News* described her as having "a gorgeous smile, dark eyes fringed by long lashes" and "dark hair that off the field she wears in a smart up-sweep." The newspaper concluded: "Mary Baker has a truly regal bearing and knows how to wear clothes and set off her tall beauty."

Baker didn't think it was necessarily fair that she got so much attention: "I used to feel very badly sometimes because I really did get a lot of publicity, and there were other stars on the team," she said. "Matter of fact, there's this one girl in South Bend, I think she still hates me. She was an outfielder and she hit two home runs this one particular game and I got a game-winning single. Who do you think got the headlines?"

Baker appeared on an episode of the TV game show *What's My Line?* where she had the panel fooled about her occupation until Arlene Francis guessed it on the last question. She also had the lead position in a *Life* photo essay spotlighting the league in the magazine's June 4, 1945 issue. The magazine pointed out that she had set a grade-school record by throwing a ball 345 feet, and that she also "rides, swims and bowls."

That description was relatively on point compared to others, which often focused on things that had nothing to do with athletics. The *Kenosha Evening News* identified Dorothy Hunter's favorite hobby as knitting and Clara Schillace's fondness for cooking spaghetti. It also cited Shirley Jameson's "roguish eyes that refuse to behave; a saucy turned-up little Irish pug nose, and enough concentrated personality to lend oomph to a carload of Hollywood starlets."

The players were allowed to enjoy a few perks, though, baking them pies or even giving them nylon stockings. The latter, Dottie Schroeder would later point out, were "hard to come

Dottie Schroeder was the only player to take the field for each of the league's 12 seasons.

by during the war."

Like Baker, Schroeder caught and played infield, and also like Baker, she wound up featured in a magazine: Her photo adorned the cover of *Parade* magazine in August 1948. She was just 15 when she attended one of the league's regional tryouts.

"I read in the Chicago Tribune about the tryouts in St. Louis," she said in a 1990 interview with *The Indianapolis News*. "My father took me out. Only two out of 60 or 70 girls were picked to go on to spring training at Wrigley Field."

Schroeder wound up on the South Bend Blue Sox, where she stayed for two seasons, but she later also played for the Kenosha Comets and Fort Wayne Daisies (where she played six seasons) before concluding her career with the Kalamazoo Lassies.

By the time it was over, she had played all 12 seasons in the league, becoming the only player to do so. She finished her career holding league records for runs batted in and walks, ranking second in hits and third in home runs.

Rules of the game

All this fit perfectly with the league's emphasis on ensuring the players' femininity didn't become lost amid all their on-field heroics. To league founders, the two weren't incompatible; indeed, organizers believed they should go hand-in-glove. The charm school guide emphasized that "the girls in our League are becoming the heroines of youngsters as well as grownups all over the world. People want to be able to respect their heroines at all times."

The guide included a series of beauty routines for players to follow and prescribed a beauty kit containing cleansing cream, lipstick, rouge, cream deodorant, a mild astringent (to be applied "moderately but carefully"), face powder (for brunettes!), hand lotion and hair remover. Wardrobe suggestions were also included, along with advice on etiquette introduced with a quote from Emily post: "Charm cannot exist without good manners."

Players were advised to speak in a low tone, rather than a high-pitched voice, and were urged not to speak too loudly — especially when using other people's names or making personal remarks. Other no-nos: bragging about personal possessions or achievements, staring, arguing or bumping into others. Hair couldn't be too short, either.

"Femininity is the keynote of our league," president Ken Sells said. "No pants-wearing, tough-talking female softballer will play on our four teams."

The Chicago Tribune elaborated: "The muscular, boyish type is out, no matter if she's a potential Babe Ruth or Bob Feller."

To ensure these guidelines were followed, the league assigned each team a full-time uniformed chaperone, who was paid $250 to $300 a month to perform a variety of functions. Chaperones were part social secretary, part mother hen. They were responsible to ensure that players kept up appearances by adhering to league guidelines, and were expected to keep tabs on them at all times. Their job included approving players' living quarters, dining establishments and social engagements; handling meals, hotel rooms and transportation costs on road trips; enforce curfews; and administering first aid. That was just for starters.

Male ballplayers were never subjected to the kind of guidelines and oversight the women in Wrigley's league had to deal with. And the rules on the field were different, too, falling somewhere between softball and baseball.

In traditional softball, 10 players were stationed in the field. But the league eliminated the deep shortstop position, conforming to the baseball standard. The pitching mound, which had been 35 feet from home plate in softball, was moved back to 40 feet in an effort to boost run production (pitchers, however, still delivered the ball underhanded, at least at first). Bats were lengthened by 2 inches to 36 inches, and the batter's box was the same width as the one used in baseball, rather than the narrower one used in softball.

The game's resemblance to baseball soon led to uncertainty over what, exactly, the league should call itself. Less than three months after the first season began, it rebranded itself as the All-American Girls Base Ball League, then changed its mind at the end of the season and started calling itself the All-American Girls Professional Ball League. In 1946, organizers changed it to the All-American Girls Baseball League, which stuck until 1951, when it was shortened to American Girls Baseball League.

And it *did* become more like baseball as time went by. The league began allowing sidearm pitching in 1946, when the distance between the pitcher and hitter increased to 43 feet. Two years later, it allowed pitchers to throw overhand.

The overhand delivery hurt underhand pitchers who had honed their skills under the league's original rules, and teams moved some outfielders to the mound to take advantage of the change. Doris "Slammin' Sammye" Sams played, and excelled at, both positions — so much so that, in 1947, she became the only player in league history to be named an all-star as both a pitcher and outfielder. Sams, who joined the league in 1946, played nine seasons with the Lassies, first in Muskegon and then in Kalamazoo, winning the Player of the Year Award twice — one of only two players to do so.

As a pitcher, Sams tossed a perfect game in a 2-0 victory over Fort Wayne before 6,000 fans on Aug. 8, 1947. As a hitter, she hit better than .300 in each of her last four seasons. She was one of the most successful at adjusting to the league's continual changes in pitching distance, ball size and other metrics that kept players on their toes from one season to the next. The distance from pitcher to plate didn't remain static at 43 feet, where it stood when she threw her perfect game. It was lengthened again to 50 feet in 1948, and to 55 midway through the following season. It was moved to 56 feet in 1953 and to 60 the following year for the league's final campaign. The distance between bases gradually grew, too: from 65 feet to 68, 70, 72, 75 and, ultimately, 85.

The size of the ball, meanwhile, was reduced several times. It started out at 12 inches, the same size as the ball used today in slow-pitch softball. It was reduced to 11.5 inches in 1944 and, five years later, it was down to 10 inches. Midway through the league's last season, it switched to the same 9-inch ball used in the men's game.

The smaller ball and longer pitching distance that year helped hitters like Joanne Weaver of the Fort Wayne Daisies, who set league records for batting average at .429 and home runs with 29. She and Eleanor Callow of the Rockford Peaches became the only players to hit 20 or more home runs and steal 20 or more bases in a season, with Callow accomplishing the feat that same year. To illustrate how big a difference the rule changes made, Callow had never hit more than eight home runs and Weaver had never managed more than five before the 1954 campaign.

It was a far cry from the first season, when Eleanor Dapkus of Racine hit 10 home runs (a record that stood for nine years until Sams broke it by hitting 12 for the Kalamazoo Lassies in 1952).

Eddie Stumpf, left, managed the Rockford Peaches in 1943 and the Kenosha Comets in 1945. He also managed in the league's 1943 All-Star Game and served as a scout throughout the '40s.

On the field

That first season was split into two halves, with the Racine Belles winning the first half by .003 percentage points over the South Bend Blue Sox and the Kenosha Comets taking the second half. The Blue Sox, who finished second in both halves, posted the best overall record but failed to qualify for the championship series, won by Racine in three straight games.

Terrie Davis would win the batting title with a .332 average, while Helen Nichol dominated on the mound, finishing the season as the league leader in wins (31-8), earned-run average (1.81) and strikeouts (220). Nichol was the league's best pitcher in its sophomore season, as well, although her effectiveness declined as the league transitioned to an overhand delivery. Still, she finished her career in 1952 as the league's all-time leader in wins with 163, and strikeouts with 1,076.

The first season featured an event of particular note: a doubleheader scheduled for 6 p.m.

July 1 at Wrigley Field. The days were long in early summer, but even with daylight savings in effect, such a late starting time meant one thing: The first game of the twin bill might be completed during daylight, but the second game certainly wouldn't be. If you're familiar with baseball lore, you know that Wrigley Field was the last big-league ballpark in America to install lights — and that the professional night baseball game under the lights wasn't played there until 1988. Or was it?

It turns out that's not quite true. The first professional night baseball game played at Wrigley happened 45 years before that, three days before Independence Day in 1943, when two teams of All-American Girls all-stars took the field for the second game, sometime around 8 p.m. The first game featured the Fort Sheridan Comettes and Camp Grant Rockettes, two team representing the Women's Auxiliary Army Corps, and was followed by WAAC drills and a "fashion parade" of WAAC uniforms. The idea was to recruit members to the Corps, the women's branch of the U.S. Army. About 150 members of the Corps would be in the stands to provide information about the program.

The main event matched players from the two Wisconsin teams, Racine and Kenosha, against players from the South Bend Blue Sox and Rockford Peaches.

Banks of temporary lights were installed for the occasion, but they didn't always provide enough illumination as the lengthening shadows gave way to nightfall.

"The lights weren't all that great, but we were used to that — we had to play with whatever we had," said Shirley Jameson, an outfielder from Kenosha who was enjoying her best season. "Besides, just the fact that we were playing in Wrigley Field was enough. We'd have done it whether it was light or dark, because we were all on Cloud Nine."

According to *The Racine Journal Times*, fan balloting placed nine of the 15 Racine team members on the Wisconsin squad, including Perlick, Schillace and future player of the year (1945) Sophie Kurys. The pitching staff was led by Nichol, the league's top hurler.

That combination proved far too potent for the opposition, as the Wisconsin team routed the Illinois-Indiana squad 16-0 behind a combined two-hitter from Nichol and three other pitchers. Even the league's best hitter, Davis of Rockford, was ineffective against them, going hitless in two at-bats. Kurys led the way for Wisconsin, going 3-for-4, scoring three runs and driving in two.

It wasn't the last night game for the league at Wrigley: It would stage another doubleheader under the lights in its second year, this time to benefit the Red Cross.

The league expanded by two teams for that second season: the Milwaukee Chicks and its westernmost franchise, the Minneapolis Millerettes. Unlike the first four teams, both the new franchises were owned by Wrigley, who was pursuing his original vision of finding a foothold in larger cities. The experiment, however, didn't end up working too well.

Neither Minneapolis nor Milwaukee had a major league team at that point, but both had teams in the then-Double-A American Association that played in larger ballparks, where the Girls League also played. The Chicks — who were sometimes called the Schnitts, a German word for a smaller glass of bear with more foam — often had to play during the day because the Brewers had games scheduled in the ballpark at night.

Unfortunately, the press in these larger markets didn't give their teams the kind of coverage their small-market counterparts, and local businesses didn't support them at the same level, either. The Millerettes, named for the Minneapolis Millers men's team, drew such small crowds that visiting teams couldn't justify the expense of traveling so far from the league's Chicago-area base to play their games. After mid-July, the team's remaining home games were canceled, and the Millerettes became a traveling team.

The Chicks took the second-half championship and won the league title, with Kenosha again the runner-up, but the champions left Milwaukee for Grand Rapids in the offseason, while the Millerettes moved to Fort Wayne and were renamed the Daisies.

1943 All-American Girls Professional Baseball League	W	L	Pct.
First Half			
Racine Belles	34	20	.630
South Bend Blue Sox	28	26	.519
Kenosha Comets	23	31	.426
Rockford Peaches	23	31	.426
Second Half			
Kenosha Comets	33	21	.611
South Bend Blue Sox	30	24	.556
Racine Belles	29	25	.521
Rockford Peaches	20	34	.370
Championship: Racine d. Kenosha 3 games to 1.			

Peak and decline

The league's inability to find traction in larger markets might have helped sour Wrigley on the project. Another factor in his loss of interest may have been a realization that the war wasn't going to shut down the major leagues, after all. After the 1944 season, he sold the league to his top ad agent, Arthur Meyerhoff, for $10,000.

Under Meyerhoff's leadership, the league added the Muskegon Lassies and Peoria Redwings to its roster in 1946, and the circuit split into two divisions in 1948 when it reached 10 teams with the addition of the Chicago Colleens and Springfield (Ill.) Sallies. The 1947 season was the high-water mark for the league in terms of popularity, with its eight teams drawing an average of more than 98,000 fans for the season. The following year, the league's total attendance approached 1 million, although the average dipped a bit with the addition of the Colleens and Sallies.

Still, only one team (South Bend) made money, and the league's fortunes would continue to decline from there. The Colleens and Sallies were dropped after only one season and spent the next two years as traveling "rookie" teams dedicated to developing young talent and promoting the league beyond its base.

Despite its success at the gate, South Bend didn't win a league title until it went back-to-back in 1951 and '52 under new manager Karl Winsch, a former pitching prospect in the Phillies organization and husband to the team's star pitcher, Jean Faut. The two had married in 1947 and had a son the following year, making Faut one of the few players in the league with a family. She won Player of the Year honors in '51 and barely missed repeating after posting a remarkable 20-2 record on the mound the next year. Not to be denied, she went out and won the award again in 1953, which turned out to be her final season.

Faut had the circuit's lowest earned-run average in each of her last four seasons and finished her career with two no-hitters and two of the five perfect games in league history. She retired at the peak of her career in part because her husband's role as manager was creating friction between her and her teammates. Midway through the 1951 season, six starters on the 18-player team walked out because of friction with Winsch.

The Blue Sox won the championship anyway.

Faut's son Larry later recounted that the situation was difficult for her because the other players didn't trust her: They were afraid she would report to her husband behind their backs. Her own relationship with Winsch was, meanwhile, tempestuous.

"It was a very uncomfortable situation for me, and I decided to retire from baseball to get away from it," Faut said. "It got to the point where it was affecting our teamwork and we didn't have the team spirit we should have had. We could have done a whole lot more as a team that year if that situation hadn't been there, but I was stuck in the middle, so I just bowed out."

It was a move, however, that she wound up regretting: "I'm extremely unhappy about the fact that I didn't play in 1954. Some of the players said to me that if I had played, the team would have won the league in its last year. I never forgot that because I know I could have played another year."

Instead of quitting athletics, Faut turned to another sport, bowling, where she competed professionally, once bowled a 299 game and boasted a 195 average more than four decades after retiring from softball.

Even with Faut's exploits and strong performances by other players, fewer people were coming to the ballpark starting in 1948. With attendance continuing to decline, owners bought out Meyerhoff in 1950, putting an end to the league's centralized management structure. Now, it was every owner for himself. Before, the league office had overseen the scouting process and had allocated players to each team; now, there was a player draft. Each team was also responsible for its own publicity and promotion. But the change failed to halt declining attendance, as fans found other things to occupy their time in the postwar period, not the least of which was the new medium of television. And now, each team owner had to grapple with the financial consequences on his own.

By July of 1951, Kenosha announced it was folding and two others teams (Battle Creek and Peoria) were on "shaky" ground, according to a press report in *The Racine Journal Times*. In deciding to call it quits, the Kenosha Comets, charter members of the league, cited meager attendance of just 460 paid admissions per game. The culprits, they said, were bad weather and television.

Kenosha's demise came less a season after the nearby Racine Belles, another charter member, suspended operations. The Comets had hoped the Belles' fans, who lived just a few minutes up the road, might drive south to follow their former rival, but that hadn't happened. The Belles franchise, meanwhile, had been transferred to Battle Creek, Mich., but several players from Racine — including Edythe Perlick, one of the first players to sign — stayed in Chicago with the rival Chicago National Girls Softball League, rather than moving to Michigan. The depleted Battle Creek squad won just 10 of its first 50 games.

The Belles ended up surviving another season in Battle Creek, but Peoria called it quits at the end of the year, reducing the league to six teams. The league's geographic center had shifted by this time, having moved east from Chicago as half of the loop's six teams were now in Michigan. In Battle Creek, the Belles lasted one more year before moving to Muskegon in 1953 and finishing dead last. They played the last part of the season as a traveling team, and there was talk of a move to St. Joseph, Mich., but that never materialized and the franchise went out of business. Meanwhile, the Grand Rapids Chicks announced in September 1953 that they were folding, citing more than $15,000 in losses.

The Chicks' demise left the league with just four teams and dimmed prospects that it could continue in 1954, but the team owner reconsidered his decision when he realized that, if the league folded, he wouldn't be able to sell his players to another team. Besides, the Chicks were coming off a successful season in which they defeated Kalamazoo for the league title. Even with the Chicks on board, league owners voted in January to suspend operations for the '54 season. They later reconsidered, however, and went ahead with the season under a five-team format.

It turned out to be the final year for the league, with the South Bend Blue Sox defeating the Fort Wayne Daisies for the championship.

The Chicago National Girls Softball League went out of business the same year.

Memories of the All-American Girls League would be revived in 1992 with the release of *A League of Their Own*, a fictionalized version of events directed by Penny Marshall, and starring Geena Davis and Tom Hanks. In the film, the Rockford Peaches and Racine Belles are shown meeting for the championship in 1943. In real life, however, the Peaches finished in last place. (The Belles did win the title by beating Kenosha.)

Years later, most people had forgotten what really happened. But the film, which grossed $132.4 million, ensured that the league itself would be remembered. The movie was selected in 2012 for inclusion in the National Film Registry as "culturally, historically or aesthetically significant."

The same could have been said for the league itself.

1954 All-American Girls Professional Baseball League			
	W	L	Pct.
Fort Wayne Daisies	54	40	.574
South Bend Blue Sox	48	44	.522
Grand Rapids Chicks	46	45	.505
Kalamazoo Lassies	48	48	.500
Rockford Peaches	37	55	.402

Championship: Kalamazoo d. Fort Wayne, 3 games to 2.

Gateway to the West

If it hadn't been for Pearl Harbor, the Baltimore Orioles might be the Los Angeles Browns. Seriously.

Two days. That's how close the Browns were to moving west in 1941 when Japanese aircraft bombed an American naval base near Honolulu and pulled the United States into World War II.

Had they pulled it off, they would have brought Major League Baseball to the West Coast a full 17 years before it ultimately arrived.

As the fourth decade of the 20th century dawned, things were changing in St. Louis, both on and off the field. The Missouri city had been the fourth most populous city at the turn of the century, behind New York, Chicago and Philadelphia — each of which hosted two baseball teams. So did St. Louis. But the city had started falling down the list since then, and by 1940 had dropped to eighth place. The new No. 4 on the list was a city that didn't have two teams or even one: the burgeoning City of the Angels.

At the same time, things were even worse on the field for the Browns, who had long played second fiddle to the Cardinals in St. Louis. Heading into 1941, the Browns had suffered through 11 straight losing seasons, while the Cards had been to three World Series in the same span of time, winning two of them. (Adding insult to injury, when the Browns finally *did* qualify for their only Fall Classic, in 1944, they lost … to the Cardinals.)

The Browns' performance at the gate was just as pathetic as their showing on the field. In 1940, they finished dead last among big league ballclubs, averaging barely more than 3,000 fans a game. But that was an improvement over the previous year, when they averaged a fewer than 1,400 as the team struggled through a pathetic 43-111 season.

"I have been identified with the Browns in St. Louis for five years, and we have lost money every season," owner Don Barnes said.

Clearly, he was running out of patience. So were the people of Los Angeles, who were hungry for big league baseball and had been campaigning for several years to get a franchise.

"Certain interests of Los Angeles have approached me with reference to the possibility of moving the St. Louis Browns out there," Barnes said in December, before a meeting of American League owners. While he had "always been opposed to the removal of the Browns from St. Louis in the past," he continued, those interests had convinced him that Los Angeles "would be the most logical and desirable city, as modern methods of rapid transportation now place major league baseball within the realm of possibility on the West Coast."

L.A. fans had offered to guarantee Barnes attendance of 500,000 a year, nearly five times what the Browns had drawn in 1939. An offer like that was hard to ignore.

Meanwhile, improved air transportation and faster trains made it possible to play games in California while losing only two days a week. A team in Chicago, for instance, could leave the Windy City on Sunday evening in time to open a three-game series Tuesday afternoon, then depart Thursday evening and arrive back in Chicago for a Saturday afternoon game.

Barnes believed he had the support he needed from AL owners to make the move. They were scheduled to meet Dec. 9 in Chicago, and he'd made a powerful case.

What could go wrong?

But two days before that scheduled meeting, the Japanese bombed Pearl Harbor, and everything changed. Suddenly, the West Coast was seen as a huge potential target for enemy aggression. It was the wrong time to make such a move. Instead of enthusiastic support for the move, Barnes was met with the opposite: unanimous opposition. The owners, to a man, voted against it, and West Coast baseball would have to wait for nearly two decades.

1903 Pacific Coast League	W	L	Pct.
Los Angeles Angels	133	78	.630
Sacramento Sacts	105	105	.500
Seattle Indians	98	100	.495
San Francisco Seals	107	110	.493
Portland Browns	95	108	.468
Oakland Oaks	89	126	.414

Third major league?

Well, that's not entirely true. Baseball had been a big deal out West for some time; it's just that the Major Leagues hadn't been involved. The Pacific Coast League had been entertaining fans of the game since 1903, with teams playing in eight major markets — the same number as in the American and National Leagues. As of 1945, the population of cities in the majors (other than New York) averaged about 1.3 million, not too far ahead of the PCL figure of 900,000.

During some seasons, the league played as many as 200 games — with the San Francisco Seals posting the odd-looking record of 100-100 in 1950 — and its membership was stable: No franchises switched cities from 1938 to 1955. Nearly all the major cities in the West were represented, with six of the eight teams paired off to produce natural rivalries: Hollywood and Los Angeles, Seattle and Portland, Oakland and San Francisco. It was the perfect setup.

The league had plenty of talent, too. It had produced players like Tony Lazzeri, who hit 60 home runs for the Salt Lake City Bees in 1925, a year before joining the Yankees' famed "Murderers' Row." Lefty O'Doul hit .378 and captured the league's first MVP award in 1927 with the San Francisco Seals, two years before he won the first of two National League batting titles. Then, of course, there was Joe DiMaggio, who played three full seasons for the Seals — hitting .398 with 34 homers in 1935 — before joining the Yankees in '36.

Eventual Hall of Famers who spent time in the PCL included Lefty Gomez, Ernie Lombardi, Bobby Doerr and Mickey Cochrane.

Talk of making the PCL a third major league had appeared in the press as early as 1919, when the Oregon Daily Journal reported that Portland Beavers owner William McCredie was musing about the idea of taking

Spring training sites for PCL teams in 1915.

the league independent. McCredie's ideas carried some weight. After the earthquake of 1906, he had drawn upon his personal fortune to help keep other teams in the league afloat, and he'd served a term in Congress from 1909-11.

Nothing came of that talk, and McCredie sold the Beavers in 1921. But the idea didn't go away, and it came to the fore again as the league began to prosper.

The PCL reached new heights in the 1940s, with attendance skyrocketing. Before the end of World War II, it was outdrawing the National and American leagues. In 1945, average attendance for Sunday games was about 12,000, with some crowds as high as 20,000. Although it's not an exact comparison, 11 of 16 big league clubs drew an average of 9,000 fans or fewer for all their games that same year.

By then, the biggest advocate of transforming the PCL into a major league was its president, Clarence "Pants" Rowland, who had managed the Chicago White Sox and worked as an American League umpire for seven years. By 1944, he had joined the Pacific Coast League as president of the Los Angeles Angels. Rowland was already looking ahead to the end of the war — and was starting a campaign to take the PCL to the big leagues.

In 1945, the league took a step in that direction. It moved to protect its interests by making it more expensive for the majors to raid its rosters, proposing that draft prices be doubled from their current level to $15,000.

The big boys balked at that: No deal.

But Rowland wasn't about to give up, vowing to push his case anew once World War II was history.

"We'll keep after them, because we have a legitimate request," he said, acknowledging that perhaps "wartime conditions don't warrant an increase (in the draft price), but in a few years, we'll see to it that the big leagues don't pick up key players for a song." The West Coast would "simply have to get major league baseball when the war is over. This Pacific Coast area is the fastest growing in the nation."

The war ended in September of that year, and two months later, Rowland was back, petitioning owners to bestow major league status on the PCL. Most of the league's teams weren't tied to any big-league club (the exception being the Los Angeles Angels, who were affiliated with the Cubs and played at their own Wrigley Field) and were ready to step up to the plate.

Again, however, the answer was no.

Commissioner Ford Frick demurred that the league had neither the income nor the seating capacity at its ballparks to warrant such a designation. Still, Frick invited the league to resubmit its proposal the following year. He also expressed the belief that "eventually, the Pacific Coast League will advance and become the third major league," and that this might happen "sooner than most of us expected."

In an attempt to bolster its appeal, San Francisco owner Paul Fagan put forth the idea of expanding the league's footprint into cities like Denver, Dallas and Houston. Fagan, a wealthy banker, took over the Seals in 1946 and told the previous owner, "I only know two baseball names — Bob Feller and Joe DiMaggio. I don't know what they will cost. I want 'em."

Fagan didn't get either one, but he did spend $1 million to upgrade Seals Stadium and constructed a spring training facility in the remote village of Hana on Maui. (If you've ever driven the road to Hana, you know that, even today, it's not a quick jaunt to the other side of the island.) He also set player salaries at the major league minimum, paid manager Lefty O'Doul a premium and made his team the first in the minors to travel regularly by air.

The investments paid off, with the Seals setting a minor-league attendance record of 670,563 and winning the pennant in 1946 … but they still didn't qualify for the majors.

Other teams in the PCL didn't have the wherewithal to match Fagan's investments, and the league never did expand into Texas or Colorado. Still, the idea of promoting the PCL to big league status stayed alive. By 1952, attendance had cooled in the West, but talk of a third major league had heated up again. Frick declared on a trip to Los Angeles that "there is not a single doubt in my mind that the Pacific Coast League eventually will become a third major league."

Of course, he'd said that before. Was he sincere, or was he just biding his time, continuing to delay until the majors themselves expanded to the West Coast? In the summer of 1953, talk surfaced that Bill Veeck might move the St. Louis Browns to L.A. This prompted an immediate backlash from Cubs and Angels owner P.K. Wrigley, who said, "If you take Los Angeles out of the Pacific Coast League, you would wreck that circuit. I'm not going to turn against the men out there with whom I've been doing business for 30 years."

Still, Veeck had powerful backers for the move, including Union Oil and Yankees owner Del Webb, who was trying to set up a deal under which a group of investors would buy Veeck's stock and move the team to L.A., although other cities were also in the mix: Baltimore, Kansas City, Montreal and Minneapolis were mentioned.

One of those cities, Baltimore, ultimately got the Browns, with Webb blaming a lack of support in L.A. "I did everything I could, but nobody came up with any dough," he said. "If the people in Los Angeles had worked hard and presented something definite, I think it would have been a different story. Baltimore demonstrated what can be done."

1957 Pacific Coast League	W	L	Pct.
San Francisco Seals	101	67	.601
Vancouver Mounties	97	70	.581
Hollywood Stars	94	74	.560
San Diego Padres	89	79	.530
Seattle Rainiers	87	80	.521
Los Angeles Angels	80	88	.476
Sacramento Solons	63	105	.375
Portland Beavers	60	108	.357

Open status

The PCL had dodged a bullet, but that didn't mean Organized Baseball was ready to confer the coveted major league status on the circuit… at least, not right away. Two years earlier, Frick had proposed a new status, somewhere between Triple-A and the big leagues, which he called an "open classification." It was, in effect, a probationary status: If a league

Pants Rowland during his managing days with the Chicago White Sox.

could prove itself over a five-year period, it could apply to become a major league. Criteria included annual paid attendance, across the league, of at least 3.5 million over the five years; total population of 15 million; and a seating capacity of at least 25,000 in each ballpark. If these conditions were met, the league could seek to move up to the majors if three-quarters of its club owners approved.

Former Dodgers and Yankees executive Larry McPhail mused that the PCL could qualify by joining forces with the Texas League and incorporating cities from that region. Frank Shaughnessy, president of the International League, said his league could team up with the American Association to form a fourth major league, with teams in places like Montreal, Toronto, Buffalo, Kansas City and New Jersey.

A big concession was that the majors would finally meet Pants Rowland's demand of a $15,000 draft price, on top of which, players in open-classification leagues would be shielded from any major league draft for a period of five years. Despite these stipulations, however, the Seals' Fagan was unimpressed. To him, it was all or nothing: "Either we're a minor league or are under the commissioner of baseball with the same rights as the National and American leagues," he said. "There is no in-between."

Still, minor league owners voted unanimously in favor of the idea in December of 1951, with the big leagues approving it a few days later. The PCL applied for the designation almost immediately, and its application was approved as the new year dawned, elevating the league to a level that no other minor league ever had attained … or ever would. Now all the PCL had to do was prove itself over the next five years, and the majors would have no choice but to make it the third major league.

Or so it seemed.

The PCL produced some exciting baseball during the period. In 1954, San Diego beat Hollywood for the pennant in a one-game playoff. In Los Angeles, Angels slugger Steve Bilko won three consecutive home run crowns from 1955 to '57, clearing the fence an average of nearly 50 times a season during that stretch (Bilko never managed to duplicate that success in the majors, although he did hit 20 home runs with American League version of the Angels in 1961).

As 1957 approached, the league's five-year probationary period was drawing to a close. But that same year, the Brooklyn Dodgers and New York Giants both announced their intention to move west. In one fell swoop, not only was big league status off the table for the PCL, the league's very survival was threatened as it faced the loss of three teams (Los Angeles, Hollywood and San Francisco) in its two biggest markets. Could it even maintain its open classification, based on Frick's criteria, if it lost such a large population base? Moreover, news of the Giants' and Dodgers' plans was already hurting attendance, where Hollywood faced a loss of $500,000 at the gate.

PCL President Leslie O'Connor put it bluntly in a message to the majors: "You created our problem. Tell us what you can do to help us rather than destroy us." For one thing, he wanted help in finding new cities for the displaced teams; for another, he asked for a percentage of radio and TV money the majors would make from their West Coast operations. And, beyond this, the owners were adamant that they didn't want to lose their open status.

Despite their resolve, however, it soon became apparent that this wouldn't be possible. By September, O'Connor was scrambling to ensure the league's survival at even the Triple-A level. Ultimately, the PCL did manage to endure, with the Giants and Dodgers agreeing to pay $900,000 to the league and new homes being found for the three teams that had been uprooted. The Angels would move to Spokane, the Seals to Phoenix and the Stars to Salt Lake City.

Thus ended the era of big-league dreams for the Pacific Coast League, but as it turned out, another bid to create a third major league was just around the corner.

Shea Gets His Way

Many new leagues were created around the middle of the century to fill a growing demand for big-league sports west of the Mississippi.

The Continental League did the opposite

The proposed third baseball league was envisioned as a response to the westward expansion. Its original purpose was, in fact, to add a team in the east — specifically, in New York City, which the Giants and Dodgers had just forsaken for San Francisco and Los Angeles, respectively.

When the new circuit was announced in 1959, it had been a year since the National League abandoned the Big Apple. Attorney William Shea had tried to lure the Phillies, Reds and Pirates to take their place, but to no avail. Frustrated, he decided to try a different approach: He would create a whole new league, built around an entirely new franchise in New York.

Shea talked Branch Rickey out of retirement at age 78 to spearhead the project. Rickey had played baseball and football professionally shortly after the turn of the century, but he had far more impact as a front office executive. Known as an innovator, Rickey had helped design the familiar two-birds logo for the Cardinals in St. Louis, where he had also set up baseball's first farm system. The Cards owned 32 teams and had working agreements with eight others by 1940, but Rickey was ready for a new challenge.

Moving to Brooklyn in '42, he became general manager of the Dodgers, with whom he would establish the first full-time spring training site for the Brooklyn Dodgers (in Vero Beach, Florida). Most famously, of course, Rickey signed Jackie Robinson to a contract with the Dodgers, breaking baseball's color barrier in 1947. The Dodgers made it to the World Series six of the 10 years Robinson played with the team.

But not everything was coming up roses for Rickey.

By 1950, he owned a 25 percent interest in the Dodgers, as did Walter O'Malley and a third partner, Pfizer Chemicals President John L. Smith. The three had an agreement that, if one of them decided to sell his share, the other two would get first crack at it. When Smith died, though, O'Malley had the inside track. As the lawyer for Smith's widow, it was easy enough to obtain Smith's 25 percent … whereupon he set his sights on taking complete control. In an effort to squeeze Rickey out, he refused to renew his contract as general manager; Rickey agreed to sell, but demanded $1 million.

Dodgers announcer Red Barber would later recall how tensions between them boiled over during the final game of the 1950 season, with the Dodgers hosting the Philadelphia Phillies and the National League pennant on the line.

In the private box was right next to the announcers' booth, Barber recalled, the two men "yelled and screamed at each other, and as I broadcast the game, I had to turn the mike away from them in an effort not to pick up their verbal battle."

The Phillies won and earned a trip to the World Series that year, but the battle between Rickey and O'Malley was far from over.

O'Malley balked at Rickey's asking price, and there was so much bad blood between the two that there was no way Rickey could stay with the organization. Still, unwilling to let O'Malley get the best of him, he sought the advice of Pittsburgh Pirates owner John Galbreath, who introduced him to New York real estate deal-maker William Zeckendorf.

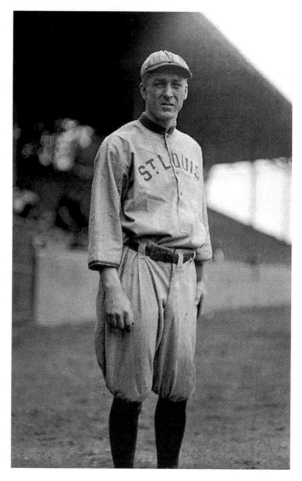

Branch Rickey played with the St. Louis Browns in 1906 and '07. He managed the Browns from 1913 to 1915 and the Cardinals from 1919 to 1925 before moving into the front office.

Zeckendorf agreed to offer Rickey the $1 million he was asking for, plus an extra $50,000. The idea was simple. With a second bidder at the table, O'Malley would have to meet the offer and pony up $1,050,000 if he wanted Rickey's share. Rickey would get his asking price, and Zeckendorf would be $50,000 richer for his trouble. The pair gambled that O'Malley wanted a controlling interest in the Dodgers so badly he would be willing to pay (if grudgingly) their price once he was backed into a corner.

They were right.

Rickey got his $1 million … and a new job to boot when Galbreath hired him to run the Pirates.

O'Malley was livid, and Rickey, though he had gotten the best of the deal, never forgave his former partner for forcing him out. So, when Shea approached Rickey nine years later with his idea for a new league, there was more at stake than baseball or even economics. O'Malley had pulled his Dodgers out of Brooklyn a year earlier in their move to Los Angeles, leaving the New York market ripe for the picking. If Rickey could play a role in putting a new team there — and that team wound up being successful — it would be the best sort of in-your-face vengeance against O'Malley.

Rickey jumped at the chance.

Terms and conditions

In the summer of 1959, Shea announced the league's formation, with franchises set for Denver, Minneapolis-St. Paul, Houston, Toronto and, of course, New York — all cities that would one day be admitted to the Major Leagues … some much sooner than others. Other cities under consideration included Atlanta, Buffalo, Dallas, Indianapolis, Miami, Montreal, New Orleans, Seattle and San Juan, Puerto Rico. (Atlanta, Buffalo and Dallas were ultimately selected.)

The plan was to play 154 games starting in 1961, with hopes that the league would one day participate in a round-robin World Series including the CL along with the two established leagues.

"We will want to be included in the World Series when our champion is able to give a good account of itself," said Jack Kent Cooke. Cooke, an Ontario native who owned the planned Toronto franchise, budgeted as much as $2.5 million of his own money to make the league a success. "The day will come when the Continental League will win the World Series, and we will really be made then." (That day never did come, and Cooke's Toronto team never even took the field, but he would end up owning a number of major pro sports franchises, including the Los Angeles Lakers and Los Angeles Kings.)

Shea expressed the same kind of confidence, predicting the league would have at least eight teams and possibly as many as 12. He wouldn't settle for anything less than big league status, rejecting the idea that the Continentals might accept the same "open" classification that had been bestowed upon the Pacific Coast League between 1952 and '58, placing it somewhere between Triple-A status and the majors.

Shea proclaimed that the new league was "proceeding on the basis of complete and unqualified cooperation of the two existing major leagues." The AL and NL, he said, "must accept us." The new venture wouldn't "cost them a thing. It creates vast new areas of interest and income with no risk on their part. How could they object to a deal like that?"

Well …

The new league was horning in on a several territories that the National and American leagues considered fertile ground for expansion — even if they had been dragging their feet. But that was just part of a bigger objection: The established leagues simply didn't want any competition. Commissioner Ford Frick realized he had the new league over a barrel: If it wanted recognition as a third major league, it would have to go through him. So, he set forth a litany of conditions the newcomers would have to meet in order qualify, involving everything from population thresholds for member cities to salary levels and player limits. One of those conditions was designed to hit the Continental League's wealthy owners where it hurt: in the pocketbook. They would have to pay indemnities to any Triple-A franchises their teams displaced.

The American Association worried that so many of its teams would be affected that it might have to go out of business, and owners in the International League expressed similar concerns.

The Continentals tried to negotiate in good faith, but the Triple-A leagues realized they had all the leverage. Under Frick's conditions, the CL couldn't move forward as a major league without their cooperation. So, while the Continentals tried to negotiate in good faith, there was little incentive for cooperation from the other end of the bargaining table.

When the St. Louis Browns had moved to Baltimore following the 1953 season, they had paid the International League team there a tad more than $48,000 and forked over an additional $350,000 to the league: a total of just under $400,000. True, that was seven years ago, but inflation had only added about $37,000 to that figure over that time. Just two years earlier, the Giants and Dodgers had paid the Pacific Coast League a total of $900,000 between them for the privilege of displacing the Seals and Angels, so it must have come as a shock to the Continentals when the International League demanded $850,000 for *each team*.

Shea called the figure "ridiculous," but word from the American Association was even more troubling. After initially asking for a cool $1 million for each of its teams, the league refused to even discuss the matter until after the 1960 season.

As if that wasn't bad enough, the Continentals faced an even bigger problem. By the spring of 1960, it was clear that the two established leagues had no intention of parting with any of their players. One idea had involved trimming big league rosters from 25 to 23, thus providing players for the new circuit. But the established teams had zero incentive to do that.

Rickey then went back to his old drawing board. Having invented baseball's farm system, he sought to reinvent it by striking a deal with the newly formed Western Carolina League. As a Class D league, it represented the bottom of the barrel, but you had to start somewhere, right? Rickey's pact with the new league was unique in several respects. Most notably, all the clubs would have working agreements with the Continental League as a whole, rather than individual teams. The players would be pooled and signed to individual teams, all of which would train together, and the CL would pay their salaries.

"This is a revival of the minor leagues at the grass roots level," Rickey said. "With this step, we have placed a very important rung on the ladder that will lead us to the top of baseball."

That rung, however, collapsed a week later when, predictably, Frick refused to support it. "I will not permit this operation the way Branch Rickey has outlined it," he said. "It would be a complete evasion of all the player limits. ... They cannot pool players or make agreements with clubs not yet in organized baseball. Of course, they can organize and operate in any way they please, but not within the structure of organized baseball."

The Continentals were back to Square One. By summer, they still hadn't signed any players and were faced with the prospect of operating with a collection of former amateurs and castoffs at best. It was hardly the kind of quality needed to run a major league. As it had been in the past, the reserve clause stood at the heart of the issue: Under the Supreme Court decision in the Federal League case, teams were still able to keep players from becoming free agents indefinitely. This meant the Continentals were severely limited in the number — and quality — of players they could sign.

Over before it starts

Fast running out of options, the Continentals pinned their hopes on a Senate bill by Estes Kefauver, a former Democratic candidate for president, that would have prevented any team from controlling more than 100 players at a time. The bill would allow ballclubs to have absolute control over 40 players at a time, plus 60 others in their first four years of organized ball, with everyone else being subject to an unrestricted draft. It also would identify any effort to obstruct a new league as an antitrust violation.

It effectively gutted the reserve clause.

Having hit roadblocks erected by Frick and company at every turn, Shea was blunt in assessing the importance of the bill to the new league's viability.

"The Kefauver bill is the only hope the Continental League has of getting players and going into business," he said in May. "It must be obvious to all now what always has been clear to me — that they (the majors) don't want us in organized baseball and are doing everything possible to hinder us. If the bill fails ... our only alternatives are war or quit. That is, unless the majors do an about face and agree to cooperate."

There was little chance of that. Frick testified to the Senate that the bill would decimate the minor leagues, leaving only enough players for about one-third of the 151 clubs operating that year to continue. George Trautman, president of the body that governed minor league baseball, concurred that the legislation "would be disastrous to the minor leagues, particularly in the lower classifications."

Such dire warnings must have resonated with the senators, because the bill went nowhere. Toward the end of June, the Senate voted overwhelmingly to kill it, 73-12.

Suddenly, the Continental League found itself out of ammunition, and the death knell came when the majors began talking in earnest about expansion. In August, Rickey's old nemesis, Walter O'Malley, announced that his National League expansion committee "immediately will recommend expansion, and that we would like to do it by 1961."

On the same day, the Continental League folded without ever having played a game or signed a ballplayer. But fact of the matter is that Shea and Rickey had gotten exactly what they'd wanted in the first place.

"We accomplished the job I started," Shea declared. "And I believe my city will be one of the first to get a team. It's been a lot of work, but I set out to get a team for New York, and this is it."

Rickey hugged Shea and told him, "I may never see you again, (but) you did a great job."

Within two years, the majors had expanded by four teams, fully half as many as the CL would have included. In 1962, National League executives added teams in two projected Continental League cities, Houston and New York, but the American League beat them to the punch: In 1961, the original Washington Senators moved into another Continental League site, becoming the Minnesota Twins, and the AL added a second new team, the Los Angeles Angels.

The Angels had to pay O'Malley an indemnity of their own to share his still-new Los Angeles territory. O'Malley had blocked a previous attempt by retired Detroit slugger Hank Greenberg and former St. Louis Browns owner Bill Veeck to secure an expansion team in L.A. He had no interest in sharing the West Coast's largest market — especially with Veeck, who was known as baseball's best promoter.

But with the Continental League having increased pressure for both leagues to expand, O'Malley acquiesced to a later bid at Southland expansion, by singing cowboy Gene Autry.

He received an indemnity, but the payment was just $350,000, far less than what Triple-A teams had been demanding from the CL and less, even, than what the Browns had paid to move to Baltimore.

So it was that Branch Rickey, once again, got the better of his old nemesis.

New York got a new team, O'Malley got a new rival and Rickey, I imagine, got a good deal of satisfaction from it all.

As for William Shea, not only did he live to see the New York Mets play baseball, he got to see them win one of the most dramatic World Series ever in 1969. Better still, they clinched the series in Game 5, playing at home in the stadium that had been built for them — a stadium named after the man who had made it all possible.

Shea Stadium in 1965, a year after it opened as Flushing Queens Stadium.

Part II
Basketball

NBA Orphans

You've probably never heard of Milt Schoon, who played a season in the National Professional Basketball League, which you've probably never heard of, either. Schoon played for the Denver Refiners. I can hear you asking under your breath, "The Denver who?"

The NPBL was formed in 1950 around four rejects: teams the National Basketball Association didn't want. The NBA was trying to find its footing, having been cobbled together the previous year in an unwieldy merger of two rival leagues. The older of the two was the National Basketball League, whose roots dated back to an era when industrial teams dominated the landscape. Companies in the nation's heartland sponsored teams to promote their products, their rosters often consisting of players who worked for them during the daytime and took to the hardwood on nights or weekends.

The NBL had been begun in 1935 as the Midwest Basketball Conference, with John Wooden playing for the Indianapolis Kautskys, a team named after a chain of grocery stores. Another team in Indianapolis was sponsored by the U.S. Tire Company, and Firestone Tires backed a team in Akron. The Chicago team, sponsored by the Duffy Floral Company, only played five games but qualified for the playoffs by winning three of them. The Florals, as they were known, went on to upset both division champions and claim the title.

Two years later, the league changed its name to the National Basketball League, but it was still a collection of mostly industrial teams representing small or middle-sized towns around the Great Lakes. Even though it became recognized as the premier league in America, in terms of talent, it remained a regional league.

That left a void the Basketball Association of America sought to fill. In 1946, the new league organized with high hopes and plenty of ambition. Unlike the NBL, it placed teams in major cities and secured large arenas to showcase them. The BAA's approach was the way of the future, but the NBL still had the best players and the new league struggled, with more than one-third of its members folding after the first season.

After another season of barely keeping its head above water, the younger circuit made a bold move by raiding the NBL — not just for players but entire teams. Four of them accepted invitations to join the upstart league, including the powerful Rochester Royals and the Minneapolis Lakers, who featured the game's first superstar, center George Mikan. Both the

Lakers and Royals were initially loyal to the NBL but reconsidered when Fort Wayne and Indianapolis made the jump. (The Indiana teams had been admitted on condition that they shed their corporate team names: The Fort Wayne Zollner Pistons became simply the Pistons, dropping the name of the piston company owner who also owned the team. The Indianapolis Kautskys became, instead, the Jets.)

With the NBL badly weakened but the BAA still hemorrhaging cash, the stage was set for a full-scale merger the following season. Anderson, Waterloo, Sheboygan, Denver, and Syracuse from the NBL joined what was now a 17-team Frankenstein's monster of a league. So did an NBL club called Tri-Cities, which represented three towns that straddled the Illinois-Iowa state line: Moline, Rock Island and Davenport. Syracuse was in the Eastern Division but played most of its games against its historical rivals from the NBL in the West.

Before long, there were indications that this arrangement wouldn't last. At the conclusion of the season, the Anderson Packers issued a demand for the coming season: The league, they said, should ensure that each team played the same number of games against all the other members. League officials, however, said it was impossible to meet such a demand under the current format, so they booted the team from the league in April.

The format itself came under fire at a meeting later that month in New York, where President Maurice Podoloff declared it "unwieldy" and "impractical."

"It posed all sorts of schedule and traveling problems," he said. "An ideal setup would be 10 teams, 12 at most, operating in two divisions."

Scheduling wasn't the only problem. There was concern that small Midwestern markets such as Anderson, Waterloo and Sheboygan simply couldn't support big-time basketball. Anderson, for instance, was a community of fewer than 50,000, and the Packers played their games in the 4,500-seat Wigwam Arena. Seating capacity at Municipal Auditorium in Sheboygan (population 42,000) was even smaller at 3,500. Waterloo was slightly larger and played in a more spacious arena, but the three towns were by far the smallest in the NBA.

"They haven't got the big city arenas we have," Podoloff would say.

Sheboygan and Waterloo, however, had no desire to quit the merged league. In search of a compromise, Podoloff floated the possibility of a "companion league" comprising Waterloo, Sheboygan, Anderson and teams in other Midwest cities such as Racine, Grand Rapids and Des Moines. The alternative, however, came with an implicit threat: "Instead of throwing out smaller members bodily, we are trying to arrange an alternative in the form of an affiliated league."

Team owners in Waterloo and Sheboygan, however, said they wanted no part of what seemed like a minor league. Threat or no threat, their answer was no.

Knowing that Podoloff was on the verge of expelling them from the league, they beat him to the punch, withdrawing from the NBA and announcing plans to form a rival organization. Denver joined them. Although it was a larger market, the city had posed a different problem for the NBA: As the only team west of the Mississippi prior to 1960, it was so far away from all the others that travel costs proved prohibitive. It also had proven to be the league's biggest money loser.

The new organization, as proposed, looked very much like a reconstituted NBL: a regional Midwestern league composed of small and mid-sized markets, some of which had been suggested by Podoloff in his "affiliate" plan. Ten new cities in five heartland states and Colorado were listed as possibilities when plans for the league were announced. But in the end, only four new clubs joined the four NBA refugees in the new circuit, which was christened the NPBL: Grand Rapids, St. Paul, Louisville and Kansas City.

Commissioner Doxie Moore, who had coached in both Anderson and Sheboygan, played up the contrast with the NBA. The new league, he said, would feature basketball towns in the heartland rather than remote big cities that had shown little appetite for the game. "This eight-team league is more compact than any major pro basketball league ever has been," Moore said on the eve of the season openers. "It is a basketball-loving league made up of cities that want basketball for the love of the game."

The Sheboygan Armory in Wisconsin was home to the Sheboygan Redskins, who played in three different basketball leagues during the 1940s and early '50s: The National Basketball League, the NBA and the National Professional Basketball League. *Royalbroil.*

Game of a lifetime

Even though two large-market NBA teams — Chicago and St. Louis — had also folded, the new league bypassed those sites. Its largest city would be Kansas City, followed closely by Denver, which changed its name from the Nuggets to the Frontier Refiners under new ownership. (If that name sounds a little goofy, keep in mind that the franchise was founded in 1932 as the Denver Safeway Pigs.) But being in a new league didn't solve the old problem of being 600 miles away from the closest team they played. The Refiners, who also played some games in Cheyenne, Wyoming, were sponsored by a refining company in a throwback to the old industrial sponsorships, made a go of it but eventually folded and were replaced by a team in Evansville. Before that happened, however, their center had the game of a lifetime.

Milt Schoon is listed at anywhere from 6-foot-7 to 6-foot-10 in various accounts, but there's no doubt he was tall. In fact, he was best known, before that night in 1951, as a member of what had been affectionately known as "The World's Tallest Team." That was the nickname bestowed on the basketball team at Valparaiso, a Lutheran college in northwestern Indiana.

Coach Loren Ellis arrived in 1941 and built a program that had went 4-13 that his first season into a national power. The squad's best player was 6-foot-3 forward Bob Dille, Valparaiso's first basketball All-American, but it was built around a group of big men that included Schoon as well as the Warnke brothers, Don and Wally, both of whom checked in at 6-foot-10. It was Schoon who was assigned to guard George Mikan when then-undefeated and top-ranked DePaul of Chicago rolled into town for a midseason game. Schoon held Mikan to nine points as the Crusaders shocked the Blue Demons 65-57.

Once Schoon graduated, he signed with the Detroit Falcons of the newly formed BAA in 1946, where he averaged fewer than 3 points a game and found himself out of a job when the team folded at the end of its only season. The most noteworthy fact about that first pro season may have been Schoon's number: 68. According to one source, as of 2016, he was the only player to ever wear that number in the BAA or NBA.

Schoon caught on the following year with the Flint Dow A.C.'s, and industrial team that played in the NBL. He averaged 6.3 points a game as Flint's starting center and got to tangle again with Mikan, whose Minneapolis Lakers were playing in the league that season. But Flint was atrocious, winning only eight of its 60 games and finishing dead last in the Eastern Division. It folded at the end of the season, and Schoon moved to the Sheboygan Redskins, his third team in as many years, shifting to a backup role but playing on a winning team for the only time during his five years in four pro leagues.

He stayed with the Redskins the following season when they joined the NBA, averaging 8 points a game. But Sheboygan lost nearly twice as many games as it won and left the league at year's end to become a charter member of the new NPBL. Schoon didn't go with them, but he did join the new league when the Denver Refiners bought his contract from the Redskins.

Schoon was known as a banger who liked to mix it up under the basket, not a big offensive theat. Over his first four pro seasons, he'd averaged just 6 points a game and offered no indication that he would ever set the world on fire with his scoring. He'd suited up in 215 games and the most he'd ever scored in a single game was 24 points. Although his scoring improved in the NBPL (rising to 11.7 points a game), his best output that season was 21.

But on January 21, 1951, something happened that transformed him from ordinary to almost superhuman, if only for a single game. In what would prove to be the Refiners' final home game of the season — and ever — a 99-72 romp over the Kansas City Hi-Spots before fewer than 1,000 fans. The victory was all the more satisfying to those few in attendance because they got to see Schoon set a record for the most points ever scored by a single player in a professional basketball game.

He made 29 shots from the field and six free throws for a total of 64 points, one more than the previous record set by future Hall of Famer Joe Fulks with the Philadelphia Warriors two years earlier. The record would stand for nearly a decade, until Elgin Baylor broke it with a 71-point onslaught for the Lakers in 1960 — a game in which he also grabbed 25 rebounds. (Baylor, another future Hall of Famer, had tied the record by scoring 64 points of his own the previous year, and Wilt Chamberlain would shatter it two years down the line with his still-unmatched 100-point outing.)

Lost in the shuffle was Hal Hutchinson, who set a team record for the Hi-Spots with 30 points.

The win over Kansas City moved the Refiners into a tie with Waterloo for the lead in the NBPL's Western Division. Unfortunately, it came on the same day as an announcement from coach Jimmy Darden that the Refiners were calling it quits because of poor attendance. They'd meet their obligations to play three more games on the road, but after that, the franchise would fold.

Did Schoon know about the team's impending doom and decide to give the few fans who showed up at least one great memory of the Refiners? Or did he just have one of those once-in-a-lifetime games?

Either way, his epic performance marked the beginning of the end, not just for the Refiners but for the league as a whole. It turned out to be Schoon's last game in a pro basketball league: He didn't bother to accompany the team on its final road trip, and neither did two other key players. The result was predictable: The Refiners lost their final game, at Sheboygan 157-72. Sheboygan's point total was the most by any pro team in a single game until that time, and its 85-point margin of victory set a record that still stands.

Meanwhile, the team Denver beat thanks to Schoon's historic performance, Kansas City, wound up dropping out of the league, too, leaving the NPBL without its two largest markets. The league had already lost St. Paul and Grand Rapids in December, while Louisville would close up shop in mid-February, leaving only three of the four NBA refugees to carry on.

The league hastily added the Evansville Agogans, an independent team that had beaten the Refiners in an exhibition, but it was hardly enough to stop the bleeding. Evansville played six league games and lost them all before the NPBL vanished without even bothering to play a championship series between the two division winners. Sheboygan and Waterloo both declared themselves to be the true champions of a now-nonexistent league.

Sheboygan continued for one more season as an independent team, playing teams like the Toledo Mercuries and the Prairie Ramblers, a team of Bradley University graduates. They even played the Lakers in an exhibition game, dropping a 105-84 decision in February of 1952. That same month they welcomed a familiar face back to their lineup: Milt Schoon, who rejoined the Redskins for a date against the Prairie Ramblers.

The Ramblers had beaten Sheboygan the previous month, handing the Redskins their first loss of the season. But in the rematch, Schoon showed he could still make an impact on the court: He led all scorers with 19 points as Sheboygan ran away with an 80-58 victory. The Sheboygan Press reported: "Big Milt Schoon's presence around the slot probably made the difference in this one. … Not up to his peak, he still played good ball in socking away a half dozen baskets."

He turned up over the next couple of years for playing for teams like the Busch Jewelers of Rockford, Chick Doster's Zephyr Oilers of Chicago Heights and the Aurora Jungle Florists.

Schoon apparently had an opportunity to continue his pro career back east, but he turned the offer down and went to work instead for International Harvester. Asked why he chose to retire from the game, Schoon said the reason was simple: He hated the East Coast in general, he didn't like Boston and he couldn't stand New York.

But for one game with the Denver Refiners in 1951, he was bigger than all of them put together.

1950–51 National Professional Basketball League

	W	L	Pct.
Eastern Division			
Sheboygan Redskins	29	16	.644
Anderson Packers	22	22	.500
Louisville Alumnites	18	17	.514
Grand Rapids Hornets	6	13	.315
Evansville Agogans	0	6	.000
Western Division			
Waterloo Hawks	32	24	.571
Denver Refiners	18	16	.529
St. Paul Lights	12	8	.600
Kansas City Hi-Spots	4	19	.174

Louisville, Grand Rapids, St. Paul and Kansas City and Denver folded.
Evansville replaced Denver.

A Globetrotter's Revenge

When Stephen Curry revolutionized basketball by taking — and making — ridiculously long shots, he made the NBA look like a Harlem Globetrotters highlight reel.

And, in addition to his own undeniable talent, he had the Globetrotters' owner to thank for it.

Curry hit more than 400 3-point shots in the 2016 season, an astonishing figure considering no one else had ever hit as many as 300. In doing so, he set the tone for a shift in the game from the low post to beyond the 3-point arc. In short order, even 7-foot big men were adding the long ball to their repertoire.

He could never have done so without Abe Saperstein, the promoter and entrepreneur who helped turn the Globetrotters into an institution.

The NBA added the 3-point shot based on its popularity in the American Basketball Association, which challenged the established league for nine years before finally calling it quits in 1976.

Like any upstart venture, the ABA had sought to distinguish itself through innovations. For one thing, it played with a red-white-and-blue basketball. For another, it awarded three points instead of two for any shot made from beyond a certain distance.

After the ABA folded in 1976, the NBA absorbed four of its teams. Three years later, it also adopted the 3-point shot.

Most people probably think the ABA invented the concept, or at least was the first league to use it.

Wrong and wrong again.

The 3-point shot had been tested in a college game between Fordham and Columbia back in 1945, but it was Saperstein who took it mainstream, adopting it as a feature of a league he founded in 1961: the American Basketball League.

Despite the similarity in their names, the Saperstein's ABL was an entirely different beast from the later ABA. It wasn't as successful, lasting just a year and a half, and it's largely forgotten today. But without it, we might never have gotten to enjoy Curry's 3-point prowess, and pro basketball might still be the rough-and-tumble low-post game it was when Wilt Chamberlain and Bill Russell waged their epic battles in the 1960s.

Chamberlain, interestingly, played a year for Saperstein's Globetrotters because he'd left college early, and at the time, the NBA didn't accept players whose class had yet to graduate. That was in 1958, a few short years before Saperstein launched the ABL, which many viewed as an act of revenge toward the NBA for denying him a franchise in Los Angeles. This is the story of that league.

First, however, some background.

Conquering the globe

Abraham Michael Saperstein was born in London on the Fourth of July in 1902, but he was really a Chicago kid, having moved to the City of Big Shoulders at the age of 5.

The original Globetrotters were Chicago kids, too. None of them came from Harlem, and the team didn't play a single game there until the 1960s. The name was a promotional tool Saperstein came up with to establish it as an African-American institution.

The Globetrotters started life in 1927 as the Savoy Big Five, with Saperstein as their coach. The name stemmed from Chicago's Savoy Ballroom, which sponsored them and hosted their games. Saperstein, just 24 at the time, changed their name to the New York Harlem Globe Trotters two years later. The team followed in the footsteps of the New York Renaissance, or Rens, an all-black team that had debuted four years earlier, representing the Renaissance Ballroom — which *was*, in fact, in Harlem.

The Rens were one of the premier teams of their era, compiling a record of 112-8 in the winter of 1932-33, including a winning streak of 88 games. Six of their eight losses came against the Original Celtics (who represented New York, not Boston), the premier all-white team at the time. The Rens, to their credit, gave as good as they got: They beat the Celtics eight times that season. Celtics center Joe Lapchick called Rens Hall of Famer Charles "Tarzan" Cooper the best center who had ever played the game. John Wooden, who would coach the UCLA Bruins to an 88-game winning streak of their own, played against the Rens as a member of the Indianapolis Kautskys. Of the Rens, he said: "To this day, I have never seen a team play better basketball."

The Globetrotters were playing good basketball, too. Most people today know them as an exhibition team, "Clown Princes of Basketball" almost as famous for their comedy as for their prowess on the hardwood. But it wasn't always that way. Once upon a time, the Trotters were a real competitive force to be reckoned with, fast catching up with the rival Rens.

In 1939, the Rens won the inaugural World Professional Basketball Tournament in Chicago, beating the Globetrotters in the third round en route to the title. But the Trotters got revenge the following year, beating the Rens by a single point in the quarterfinals and going on to win the tournament with a 31-29 victory over the Chicago Bruins. The Bruins, owned by Chicago Bears founder George Halas, played in the National Basketball League, one of two forerunners of the NBA.

The winner of the tournament, held in Chicago from 1939 to 1948, was generally considered the world champion. The Globetrotters, who also placed third in the event four years later, gradually supplanted the Rens as the nation's premier all-black team. The Rens would play their final games representing Dayton, Ohio, in 1949 as part of the NBL's final season. The league was integrated at the time, allowing for an all-black team at a time when the rival Basketball Association of America was open only to white players. The Rens disbanded when the two leagues merged in 1950, although three black players (one of whom was Globetrotter Nat "Sweetwater" Clifton) promptly broke the color barrier that same year. Meanwhile, Saperstein bought the rights to the Renaissance name, which he would resurrect upon forming the ABL.

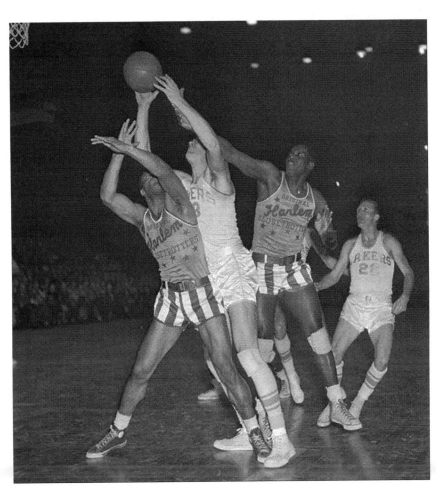

George Mikan of the Minneapolis Lakers, center, struggles to get off a shot against the Harlem Globetrotters in their 1948 game. *Melanie Warner.*

While the Rens were fading into history, the Globetrotters were thriving. They scored their biggest victory in 1948, when 18,000 fans — the largest crowd ever to watch a pro basketball game in Chicago at that time — packed Chicago Stadium to watch the all-black Trotters take on the all-white Minneapolis Lakers.

Saperstein's team came in riding a 102-game winning streak, while the Lakers boasted the sport's first true superstar in center George Mikan.

Long before 7-foot centers were the norm, the 6-foot-10 Mikan towered over the Globetrotters' 6-3 pivot man, Goose Tatum. Mikan outscored Tatum 18-0 in the first half as the Lakers took a 32-23 lead, but the Globetrotters rallied to win it 61-59 on a 30-foot shot by Elmer Robinson in the closing seconds.

The Trotters also won a rematch, 49-45, a year later, but the Lakers would wind up being Saperstein's foil, and the impetus for him to form the ABL, a decade down the road.

California schemin'

In early 1959, Saperstein announced plans to seek an expansion NBA franchise in Los Angeles. But he probably didn't make any friends in the league by the way he went about it.

"If the NBA doesn't come to the coast by 1960, it's crazy," he said. "Those who run the NBA are a bunch of mossbacks. They're not malleable. They don't adjust to conditions. They're putting their money on a dead horse in Cincinnati and Detroit, and leaving potentially great cities like San Francisco, Los Angeles and Seattle go to waste."

Saperstein's comments would prove prescient: within less than a decade, each of those three cities would host an NBA team. Saperstein, however, wouldn't be a part of any of them.

In seeking a franchise in Los Angeles, Saperstein apparently felt the NBA owed him one for bringing fans into its arenas on nights when the Globetrotters served as the opening act before the league's regular games. On most nights, the Globetrotters were a bigger attraction than the NBA contest. Despite this, the NBA was wary of Saperstein. He owned a minority's interest in the Philadelphia Warriors, but he had also purchased an NBA team in the past ... only to back out and let the team go under.

The team in question was the Chicago Stags, a charter member of the BAA that Saperstein purchased in 1950 after it ran into financial problems. Saperstein renamed it the Bruins (the same name as the team his Globetrotters had defeated for the 1940 world championship), but had trouble re-signing the Stags' players, some of whom bolted for a short-lived rival league.

Rather than pursue the matter further, he simply folded up shop and let the team fail. Not a good omen, to say the least, especially with the league looking at Chicago as a possible expansion site.

Saperstein's blunt criticism of the NBA — for continuing to operate in smaller

Midwestern markets when California beckoned — probably didn't help, either.

Ironically, it was one of those shaky franchises that moved to L.A. with league approval, preempting Saperstein and scotching his plans. That team was, of course, the Lakers, the team he'd helped put on the map with the 1948 game against his Globetrotters.

Saperstein, naturally, was livid at this turn of events. Not only was he frozen out of Los Angeles, but the NBA soon added a new team to his hometown of Chicago, the Packers, who would begin play in 1961.

Saperstein's solution was simple: He would form a league of his own. Actually, he'd been toying with the idea even before the NBA made it clear he wasn't at the top of its L.A. list. That was fine with Saperstein, who had bemoaned the NBA's trend toward high-scoring games that offered little in the way of defense. In the 1953-54 season, its teams had averaged fewer than 80 points a game, but that figure increased every year over the course of the next eight seasons, topping out at 118.8 (which was still a record more than a half-century later) in 1961-62, the year the ABL would start play.

Abe Saperstein

"The men who run the game can't see that offense is strangling defense — and may ruin the game," Saperstein bemoaned in 1958, the year when average scores first topped 100 points. "People want to see a game, not just a point-scoring exhibition."

It was an ironic statement coming from a man who owned the most famous exhibition basketball team ever assembled.

Further irony: Saperstein blamed increasingly dominant play by big men under the basket for the out-of-control scoring. In announcing the formation of the ABL in April of 1960, Saperstein crowed: "Our rules will be a lot different than the National Basketball Association's, where it is a game of towering giants and towering scores. We will devise rules to return defense to basketball and make it a game for the little guy as well as the big guy."

The irony lay in the fact that, in 1958, Saperstein had signed the era's most dominant big man, Wilt Chamberlain, to play with his Globetrotters for $50,000.

But at least he was consistent in this much: When asked whether Chamberlain was a candidate to play in his new league, Saperstein didn't hesitate in saying "no."

Saperstein had two ideas for limiting the dominance of big men and pulling the game out from under the basket. One involved the shape of the key, which had originally been shaped like (naturally), a key and was just 6 feet wide under the basket. Ever since 1937, offensive players had been prohibited from spending longer than 3 seconds in the key at any one time; if they were caught doing so, their team would lose possession of the ball.

The NBA doubled the width of its key in 1951 in response to the dominance of big men (particularly George Mikan of the Lakers), who had taken advantage of the narrow lane to "camp out" under the basket, awaiting lob passes from teammates that led to easy layups. In a column he penned for the Minneapolis Star that year, Mikan himself explained (and defended) the reasoning behind the rule change.

"The old-fashioned pivot man, who stood in the corner of the keyhole all game long, is extinct from the pro game. Now he has to run like a forward." This, he wrote made for a more lively and interesting game: "Nobody's loitering in the lane and because the pivot man is moving, the whole attack is faster. It's a wider attack. It uses more of the floor. There's more going on 'outside' than there ever was."

The change had checked the dominance of big men, but they only got bigger and more adept at dealing with the new landscape. Chamberlain, who stood 7 feet, 1 inch tall, would score 100 points all by himself in the Philadelphia Warriors' 169-147 victory over the New York Knicks in 1962, the year NBA scoring reached its zenith. It was precisely this sort of offensive shootout that Saperstein wanted to avoid, so he widened the key further, borrowing the trapezoidal shape that had been adopted for international play in 1956. The international key was 20 feet wide at the end line, making it even harder for big men to bide their time underneath the basket without violating the 3-second rule.

The second innovation was the 3-point shot, which Saperstein felt would tilt the balance of power away from the key and toward hot-shooting guards: "the little guy."

Bill Sharman, who would coach two teams in the ABL, recalled that Saperstein ran the idea by him first. He wanted to call it "the 25-foot home run," but Sharman didn't think that term worked for basketball. He also suggested that 25 feet from the rim might be a little too far out. The distance was adjusted to 25 feet from the backboard, or 23 feet, 9 inches from the center of the hoop.

A league takes shape

When word first leaked out that Saperstein was considering a new league, inquiries began to come in from across the country. Interested parties from places as diverse as Wichita, Toledo, San Diego and Baltimore contacted Saperstein, but none of them would make the cut. Host cities were chosen strategically to avoid direct competition with the NBA (except in Chicago and Los Angeles, where the NBA had only recently arrived) and give the league a true national footprint. This stood in contrast to the National Basketball Association, which, despite its name, remained a regional outfit confined to the Northeast and Midwest in 1961, with the sole exception of the recently transplanted Los Angeles Lakers. Not only did the ABL place franchises in L.A. and San Francisco, it considered including teams from several other Western cities.

Saperstein originally intended to begin play in 1960 with six teams. In addition to Los Angeles and San Francisco, the list included Washington, Cleveland, Chicago and Kansas City. But he later announced he was postponing the inaugural season a year and would be adding teams in two other cities. Applicants from Portland, Salt Lake City, Honolulu, Pittsburgh and Vancouver were considered, with Portland and Pittsburgh winning approval. By October of 1960, however, Portland was out and Hawaii was in.

The Hawaii Chiefs would be owned by Art Kim, who had Saperstein knew from way back. Kim had gotten involved with the Globetrotters in 1946. He'd worked to organize games for the team and had supervised some of its "foils" — the Washington Generals, New York Nationals and Hawaii Surfriders.

Kim himself was from Maui, so having a team in Hawaii was personal for him, and Saperstein liked the idea of a team in the islands enough to overlook the obvious drawbacks of travel costs and jet lag. Those costs would be mitigated by extended trips to the islands, with teams playing several consecutive games there and the Chiefs likewise stringing together a number of games on the mainland.

Even though Saperstein had felt slighted by the NBA when it declined to award him a Los Angeles franchise, he didn't own the L.A. Jets. Instead, the team was run by Vito Guarino and Len Corbosiero, who had themselves petitioned the older league for a franchise in the Southland, only to be rejected when the Lakers moved. Saperstein did, however, own the ABL's Chicago Majors, and he also owned the name of the Pittsburgh franchise, which was called the Rens in honor of the Globetrotters' biggest all-black rivals during the 1930s and '40s.

The ABL definitely had a big-league feel — at least on the surface. But peel back that thin veneer, and the reality was less impressive. In Los Angeles, the Jets were unable to book any dates at the Sports Arena because the Lakers had locked up nearly exclusive rights to play there. The ABL club was allowed to play six home dates in the 15,000-seat arena; for the remaining 33 dates on the Jets' home schedule, they would be exiled to the Olympic Auditorium, a structure that dated to 1925 and was better known, over the course of its history, for blue-collar events like wrestling and roller derby.

Two other teams played in big-league cities but had more modest origins, having transferred from the semipro National Industrial Basketball League. Teams in the NIBL harkened back to an earlier era, when manufacturers fielded teams of employees to promote their products by playing basketball. Teams had names that reflected their sponsors, like the Fort Wayne General Electrics, Los Angeles Kirby's Shoes and the perennial champion Bartlesville Phillips 66ers.

By the time the ABL came along, the NIBL was in decline, with its best players moving to the NBA as salaries there began to eclipse what the manufacturers were willing to pay. The league's final champion, the Cleveland Sweeny Pipers (named for Ed Sweeny's plumbing company) was invited to join the ABL, and the owner of the New York Tuck Tapers (named for a company that made construction tape), was granted the new league's Washington franchise and retained the familiar Tapers name.

When it came to finding a place to play, the Pipers had it even worse than the L.A. Jets: Over the course of their first season, they played on no fewer than eight different "home" courts, ranging from the 9,900-seat Cleveland Arena all the way down to high school gyms as far afield as Sandusky and Columbus. Even the arena was no palace. Built in 1937, it would later serve as the first home for the Cleveland Cavaliers, who only played their four years before it was closed and later demolished in the mid-'70s.

Playing in multiple arenas was a common practice in the ABL, which sometimes scheduled doubleheaders involving four different teams and relied heavily on the Globetrotters to fill the stands as an opening act for league games.

The Pipers might not have known where "home" really was, but they did have a few things going for them. For one, they had a top-flight coach in John McClendon, who became the first African-American head coach in professional sports when he agreed to lead the Cleveland franchise.

McClendon's resume was impressive: He had led Tennessee State to three consecutive NAIA (small school) national championships from 1957 to 1959 before leaving to coach the Sweeny Pipers during their debut Industrial League season. He brought his Tennessee State backcourt with him: Ron Hamilton and John "Rabbit" Barnhill (Barnhill would stay with the Pipers when they joined the ABL and play 10 pro seasons after that).

Under McClendon, the Pipers not only dethroned Bartlesville as NIBL champion, they won the AAU national tournament, as well.

The Boss and The Hawk

By this time, Sweeny had turned management of the Pipers over to a brash 30-year-old Ohio native who was the heir to a shipping fortune: George Michael Steinbrenner III.

Yes, *that* George Steinbrenner.

The man who would become famous as owner of baseball's marquee franchise, the New York Yankees, took the reins of the Pipers against his father's wishes and, significantly, without his financial backing. Almost immediately, he began making his mark with the kind of aggressive management style that would mark his tenure with the Yankees: a hands-on (some would say meddlesome) approach to his team, a knack for signing big-name players and a flair for the dramatic. But it was McClendon, not Steinbrenner, who was the architect of the Pipers early success. Not only did McClendon bring Barnhill with him to the ABL, he got an even bigger Tennessee State star to join the Pipers. Dick Barnett had been the Syracuse Nationals' top pick in the NBA draft two years earlier and was coming off a season in which he averaged 17 points a game for the Nats.

Steinbrenner offered Barnett a one-year deal worth $13,000 to play for the Pipers, $1,500 more than what Syracuse was offering.

The money, along with the prospect of reuniting with McClendon, convinced Barnett to take the offer. The Nats protested, saying they had an option to retain Barnett, and obtained a restraining order that prohibited him from playing for the Pipers. He missed 30 games before Steinbrenner struck a deal with the Syracuse general manager to obtain his services. The late start, however, didn't affect him: Barnett would go on to average 26.2 points for the Pipers, the second-highest figure in the league.

The Pipers weren't the only team to land NBA-level talent, but the league's biggest star was a player the NBA didn't even want.

Connie Hawkins, along with the Lakers' Elgin Baylor, set the stage for the kind of gravity-defying heroics that would become the hallmark of Julius Erving, Magic Johnson and Michael Jordan. Hawkins had signed to play college ball at the University of Iowa, but was kicked off the team when it was learned that he had taken a $250 loan from an acquaintance named Jack Molinas, referred to in one internet headline as "basketball's one-man corruption machine."

Molinas, an All-American at Columbia University, who had played well enough as a rookie for the Fort Wayne Pistons in 1954 to qualify for the All-Star Game. But he was suspended before the game was played and banned from the NBA for betting on games. Molinas' questionable activity dated back to his time at Columbia, where was alleged to have shaved points and even thrown games for bookies while playing for the Lions.

After he left the NBA, he waded even deeper into the underworld. He was accused of rigging a boxing match by drugging a fighter and fixing a horse race by shocking the entries with a remote-control buzzer. In 1961 was charged as the head in a gambling ring that led to the arrests of 37 players from 22 colleges, including Columbia. Found guilty of bribing players to fix games from 1957 to 1961, he was sent to prison in 1963, where he served a five-year term before his release … whereupon he turned to trafficking pornography and furs from Taiwan.

Molinas was dead by the age of 43, having taken an assassin's bullet to the head beside the swimming pool at his Hollywood Hills home.

Hawkins' story has a much happier ending, but his dealings with Molinas cost him the best years of a spectacular career in pro basketball. He was never implicated in any gambling activities, but Molina's point-shaving conspiracies were the equivalent of baseball's Black Sox scandal: Anyone even remotely connected was viewed as tainted. Hawkins, like Molinas, was banned from the NBA, but the ABL had no reservations about signing the 19-year-old kid who had never even played college ball, especially after authorities declined to charge him with any wrongdoing.

"Hawkins is ready for any pro club in the country right now," Rens coach Neil Johnston said after signing him to a contract in the fall of 1961.

Hawkins lost no time in becoming a phenomenon. He scored 22 points in Pittsburgh's first game, a win over Cleveland, and followed that up with 27 as a crowd of 13,817 fans turned out to watch the Rens defeat Chicago. With Hawkins on a hot streak, some other teams began to grumble that he shouldn't be allowed to play because he hadn't gone to college. This complaint was ultimately dismissed — the ABL as a whole doubtless knew they had a star in the making — and Hawkins continued to impress. Against Hawaii, he scored 11 of his 20 points in the fourth quarter, including the go-ahead basket, as Pittsburgh erased a nine-point deficit to beat the Chiefs.

Hawkins just kept getting better as the year progressed, scoring 49 points in a December loss to Cleveland and pouring in a league-record 54 in another loss to the Pipers the following month.

He would finish the season as the league's scoring champion, averaging 27.5 points per game, and would be voted the MVP.

Other stars

Another victim of college scandal, 7-footer Bill Spivey, would average 22.7 points a game for Hawaii. Spivey had been caught up in the point-shaving controversy of 1951 while playing for the University of Kentucky. He faced a criminal complaint, but a jury voted 9-3 in favor of acquitting him on bribery and perjury charges, which were ultimately dropped when prosecutors declined to pursue a second trial. Despite the lack of a conviction, the NBA banned Spivey anyway, unwilling to take a chance that he might have been guilty. He went

on to join the Trotters' traveling circus for three years as a member of their nightly set-up opponents, and was past 30 when he joined the ABL's Chiefs. He stuck with the league as it began its second season and averaged 22.5 points that year before it folded, but he never played top-level pro ball after that.

George Yardley with the Syracuse Nationals in 1959.

The ABL's best 3-point shooter never played in the NBA, either. Tony Jackson was banned for failing to report a point-shaving bribe he didn't take. He didn't even take it seriously. It didn't matter. The NBA wanted nothing to do with him, and he wound up playing with the Chicago Majors, leading the league in 3-pointers with 141 in league's first season and topping the list before the league went under the next year. He scored 53 points in one game near the end of that first season, but he never played a minute in the NBA. His main claim to fame after leaving the

ABL was a record he set in its successor, the ABA … but not for making the most difficult of shots, the 3-pointer. Instead, it was for making the easiest: the free throw. He once sank 24 of them in a single game.

One star who hadn't been touched by scandal was Bill Bridges of Kansas City, who signed out of the University of Kansas and would wind up playing 13 seasons in the NBA. With the Steers, Bridges averaged 21.4 points in his first season and was leading the league by a wide margin at 29.2 in his sophomore campaign when the ABL folded. Bridges broke Hawkins' single-game scoring record with 55 points against Oakland in the second week of December and added 49 the next night against Chicago. When the ABL folded less than three weeks later, Bridges wound up as the league's all-time leading rebounder and second-best scorer, behind Hawkins.

In Los Angeles, the Jets signed 6-5 forward George Yardley, who had averaged 19 points a game over a seven-year NBA career. Yardley, like Barnett, had played most recently with the Syracuse Nats, averaging 20 points and eight rebounds a game in the 1959-60 season. His best season had come in 1957-58, when he averaged a league-leading 27.8 points a game and became the first player in NBA history to score more than 2,000 points in a season. Yardley had retired the previous year, having told his wife the family would move to California once their oldest child started school. The Jets offered him the chance to keep that promise while, at the same time, returning to the court. Even though he only played when the Jets were at home, he would lead the team in scoring with an average of 19.2 points in 25 games. After that, he never played pro basketball again.

The Jets also attracted Sharman, the Celtics legend, to L.A. as a player-coach, a significant coup for the league. Sharman had three times averaged more than 20 points a game in Boston and had led the NBA in free-throw percentage seven times, but he was, at heart, a California boy: Born in the San Joaquin Valley farming town of Porterville, he had starred in college at USC, where he'd played baseball in addition to basketball. Sharman would become the only coach to win titles in three pro basketball leagues, and the only man to coach three pro teams in Los Angeles: the Jets, the ABA's Stars and the NBA Lakers.

1961–62 American Basketball League	W	L	Pct.
Eastern Division			
Cleveland Pipers	45	36	.556
Pittsburgh Rens	41	40	.506
Chicago Majors	39	44	.470
Washington / New York Tapers	31	50	.448
Western Division			
Kansas City Steers	54	25	.684
Los Angeles Jets	24	15	.600
San Francisco Saints	38	38	.500
Hawaii Chiefs	29	53	.354

Kansas City d. Cleveland 2-1 in first-half playoffs.
Cleveland d. Kansas City 3-2 for championship.
Los Angeles disbanded during the season.

A champion without a league

As the ABL began its first season, the Jets were expected to be one of the top teams, and through the first half of the season, they challenged the Kansas City Steers for supremacy in the Western Division. Despite a winning record, however, they had problems at the turnstiles. They drew a crowd of more than 8,300 to their home opener at the Sports Arena, a 119-116 win over Chicago, but they played the rest of their home games at the Olympic Auditorium and never again approached that figure. Their next game, at the Olympic, drew just 1,364 fans for a loss to San Francisco, and things got even worse in December, when back-to-back wins over the Saints attracted anemic attendance figures of 522 and 256, respectively.

A thrilling one-point win over Hawaii in San Francisco on Jan. 10 gave them a 24-15 record, good for second place in the Western Division behind the Steers. But the team folded its tent after that, talking vaguely about the possibility of reorganizing the following year and playing down the freeway in Long Beach, but that didn't happen. Long Beach did get an ABL team in 1962, but it was the Hawaii Chiefs, who relocated to the mainland after a year playing in Honolulu and Hilo.

The loss of the Jets was the second major blow to the ABL during the first half of Season 1. The Washington Tapers, having lost twice as much money as they'd expected ($105,000) through the end of 1961, abruptly pulled up stakes and announced they were moving to Long Island on New Year's Day, where they would rebrand themselves as the New York Tapers.

The first half of the season ended with a three-game playoff between Kansas City and Cleveland, the leaders in the Western and Eastern divisions, respectively. Kansas City won the best-of-three series Under the ABL's innovative, if chaotic playoff system, the Steers earned the right to meet the winner of a postseason tourney involving the league's other six teams following the second half.

That winner turned out to be Cleveland, which had sacked McClendon as its head coach but had brought in an equally notable replacement: Sharman, who signed on after the Jets folded. The Pipers turned the tables on the Steers by beating them 3-2 in a best-of-5 championship series during the second week of April, but that wasn't the biggest victory Cleveland would enjoy in the spring of '62.

Five weeks later, Steinbrenner announced that Ohio State All-American Jerry Lucas, the nation's most sought-after college player, had agreed to a two-year contract with the Pipers. The Cincinnati Royals of the NBA had offered far more money, $105,000 for three years (and a new car!), while his base salary with Cleveland would be just $10,000 each year. But he was also given $40,000 in investments and Steinbrenner had promised to push for a shorter, later-starting season, which would allow Lucas to finish his degree before he started playing.

Steinbrenner then used his newfound leverage in an attempt to get the Pipers into the NBA … much to the chagrin of both the jilted Royals and the remaining ABL teams. But Steinbrenner couldn't come up with the money needed to seal the deal, and the ABL was threatening to sue. Thus, the NBA reversed course and denied the Pipers' application, which meant the team — and Lucas — had no place to play.

Actually, Lucas did. Just not with the Pipers. He wound up joining the Royals, after all, leading the NBA in field goal percentage and scoring 17.7 points a game en route to being named the league's rookie of the year.

The Pipers? They folded, leaving Cleveland without pro basketball until the Cavaliers came along in 1970 and Steinbrenner without a team until he acquired the Yankees three years after that. In fact, the city of Cleveland didn't win another pro basketball title until 2016, when the Cavs finally broke one of the longest droughts in the nation.

Take 2 and a legacy

With the Pipers out of business, the ABL itself announced it was folding, then backtracked and soldiered on into a second season with six teams, minus Cleveland and the disbanded L.A. Jets. The league abandoned the San Francisco market, which the NBA had claimed by moving the Philadelphia Warriors westward during the offseason, but remained in the Bay Area with a team called the Oakland Oaks.

Since the NBA had vacated the City of Brotherly Love, the ABL swooped in and claimed it by moving the New York Tapers to their third city in less than two years. Hawaii moved to Long Beach, leaving Chicago, Kansas City and Pittsburgh as the only holdovers from the first season. (In fact, it turned out that the Tapers owner was also keeping the Rens afloat.) Denver was supposed to get a new team for the second season but didn't, leaving the loop with six teams in a single division. Even Saperstein was saying the chances of success were a 100-to-1 shot.

He couldn't buck those odds. The ABL folded at the end of 1962.

Connie Hawkins went on to play the next four years with the Globetrotters before finally catching on with the ABA's Pittsburgh Pipers (no connection to the Cleveland Pipers). He hadn't lost a step, leading the new league in scoring and being named its most valuable player, just as he had in the ABL. He finally made it to the NBA in 1970, averaging 20 points or better during each of his first three seasons with the Phoenix Suns before he began to slow down, ultimately retiring in '76. One can only imagine what his career might have looked like had the NBA not blackballed him for eight seasons.

The ABL may have lost its brief battle with the NBA, but it can be argued that it won the war. Today's NBA is stocked with a dozen teams west of the Mississippi — including two in Los Angeles. NBA teams still averaged more than 100 points a game, but for the most part they remained far below the 118-point average posted the year Wilt scored 100 (although they were on the rise again in 2019). And the game itself looks a whole lot like the game Saperstein envisioned, one that makes the little guy just as important as the big man, if not more so. His 3-point shot, adopted by the NBA in 1979, has gradually supplanted the low-post game as the dominant feature of the pro offense. Players like Stephen Curry, James Harden and Klay Thompson have taken the baton from once-dominant pivot men like Shaquille O'Neal and Tim Duncan. Even the tall guys are shooting 3s (Kevin Durant, anyone? Kristaps Porzingis?).

Saperstein could never have imagined how much his innovation would affect the game. Tony Jackson of Chicago led the ABL, making more than 141 shots from beyond the arc in the league's only full season.

That wouldn't even make the top 250 in NBA history.

Saperstein was a visionary. No one bought his vision at the time, but today, it's bringing in millions upon millions of dollars for people with names like Curry, Durant and Harden. And things have come full circle: Today's NBA has brought pro basketball back to where it was when the Trotters were playing the Lakers and the Rens. It's competition. It's entertainment. And that's not a contradiction.

1962 American Basketball League	W	L	Pct.
Kansas City Steers	22	9	.710
Long Beach Chiefs	16	8	.667
Pittsburgh Rens	12	10	.545
Oakland Oaks	11	14	.440
Philadelphia Tapers	10	18	.375
Chicago Majors	8	20	.357

League disbanded Dec. 31.
Kansas City declared champion.

Beyond the Arc

If George Mikan hadn't been so tall and so good at basketball, he might have been mistaken for your average nerd. Part of it was the fact that he was damned smart: He earned a law degree after his playing days were over. But part of it was the stereotypical set of glasses he wore on the court, which made him look like a professor or a librarian or an oversized Leonard Hofstadter from *The Big Bang Theory*.

One day when he was 12, Mikan's father was whittling, and a sliver of wood flew out into George's eye. Two years later, Mikan was already 6-foot-5 and went out for basketball at Joliet Catholic High School. But his eyesight suffered as a result of that splinter, and he was forced to wear thick glasses. That didn't sit well with his high school coach, who kicked him off the team.

It was the coach who turned out to be truly shortsighted, because Mikan went on to become the best player of his era and the first true basketball superstar. In listing players who changed the face of the game, historians often rank him behind a number of more recent phenoms, people like Michael Jordan and Magic Johnson, Kobe Bryant and LeBron James, Shaquille O'Neal, Kareem Abdul-Jabbar and Wilt Chamberlain.

But as O'Neal said, "Without No. 99, there is no me."

Mikan, No. 99, won a national championship at DePaul University, then led the short-lived Chicago American Gears pro team to the World Basketball Tournament title as a rookie. The next year, he joined the Minneapolis Lakers of the National Basketball League and won a championship there, too, initiating a dynasty for the team long before Wilt, Kareem, Magic or Shaq wore purple and gold. When the franchise moved to the rival Basketball Association of America the next year, Mikan won another title, and another the following year. Then, from 1952 to '54, he led the franchise to its first threepeat.

Overall, Minneapolis won five NBA titles in a span of six years. No other Laker since has been part of such a run. The only reason the Lakers failed to win six consecutive titles? Mikan broke his leg before the divisional finals, which the Lakers lost to the Rochester Royals. He did all this wearing a pair of round, Coke-bottle glasses that made the look fashionable long before John Lennon or Harry Potter. They also might have had something to do with an innovation that became perhaps the most distinctive piece of sports equipment in the second half of the 20th century. Interviewed by Terry Pluto for his book *Loose Balls*, Mikan said he didn't care for the traditional brown ball. As a spectator after he retired, he had trouble seeing it from the balcony in some of the NBA's dimly arenas.

When organizers were forming a new basketball league to compete with the NBA in the mid-1960s, they asked Mikan to be the league's commissioner. He was the perfect choice: a basketball icon who also happened to be a lawyer. After Mikan agreed to take the job, it didn't take him long to bring up his problem with the NBA's dull, brown basketball. Taking note of the new league's name — the American Basketball Association — he decided the colors of the ball should reflect the brand. What could be more American than red, white and blue? Those became the colors of the ball used by the ABA and popularized over the next decade.

1967–68 American Basketball Assocation	W	L	Pct.
Eastern Division			
Pittsburgh Pipers	54	24	.692
Minnesota Muskies	50	28	.641
Indiana Pacers	38	40	.487
Kentucky Colonels	36	42	.462
New Jersey Americans	36	42	.462
Western Division			
New Orleans Buccaneers	48	30	.615
Dallas Chaparrals	46	32	.590
Denver Rockets	45	33	.577
Houston Mavericks	29	49	.372
Anaheim Amigos	25	53	.321
Oakland Oaks	22	56	.282

Pittsburgh d. New Orleans 4 games to 3 for the championship.

Heir to the ABL

The new league also decided to borrow an innovation from the old American Basketball League: the 3-point shot. The new league not only adopted a name that was similar to its predecessor, it was, in many ways, its natural descendent. One of the founding owners, Art Kim, had owned the Hawaii Chiefs of the ABL and had moved the club to Long Beach for its abbreviated second season. In the ensuing years, he hadn't lost his appetite for basketball or his conviction that a team south of Los Angeles could be successful. He'd spent that time working for the Globetrotters, but he was ready for something different, so when ABA founder Dennis Murphy contacted him, he was intrigued by the idea of joining the nascent league.

When it came to choosing a location for the franchise, Kim kept his eyes on Southern California. But this time, instead of Long Beach, he chose Anaheim: His Amigos would be a charter member of the new league, playing most of their games at the Anaheim Convention Center (although three were played in Hawaii). Kim's biggest signing — figuratively and literally — was Larry Bunce, a 7-foot center who had averaged 15 points a game at Utah State. Bunce was the first and, at the time, only 7-footer in the league when he stepped onto the court in 1967.

According to ABA founder Murphy, another owner in the new league had been involved in the Pittsburgh ABL franchise: theater owner Gabe Rubin, who signed on as owner of new the Pittsburgh Pipers. A more important link in Pittsburgh, however, was on the playing floor. Connie Hawkins.

A league MVP with the Rens in his only full pro season, Hawkins found himself still on the NBA blacklist and therefore without a team when the ABL folded. He played four years with the Harlem Globetrotters but wanted to get back to competitive basketball. The ABA gave him the perfect opportunity.

Hawkins made the most of it, averaging a league-best 26.8 points a game in his first season with Pittsburgh and leading the Pipers to the ABA title. He was the league's MVP that year, just as he had been in the ABL. The next season he was even better, averaging better than 30 points a game for the Pipers, who had moved to Minnesota during the offseason. But injuries kept him out of nearly half his games that year, and he wound up having surgery on his knee.

After that season, he finally joined the NBA. Hawkins sued the league for blacklisting him and received a $1.3 million cash settlement; more important, he got a contract with the Phoenix Suns. Hawkins was an all-star during his first four seasons in the league, averaging 20 points or better for three consecutive years before recurring knee problems slowed him down. In all, he played seven NBA seasons with three teams before retiring in 1976.

One can only imagine how high The Hawk might have flown had he not been blacklisted at what would have been the height of his career.

Apart from Hawkins, the most important connection to the old ABL was Bill Sharman, who had coached the L.A. Jets and Cleveland Pipers in that league. Murphy told Pluto in

Loose Balls that he'd known Sharman through connections at USC (Sharman's alma mater), and that it was Sharman who helped him come up with the name American Basketball Association. Murphy thought about asking Sharman to be commissioner of the new league, but he was coaching the San Francisco Warriors in the NBA at the time, so he couldn't take the job.

Sharman would eventually leave the Warriors to coach the Los Angeles Stars in 1968, leading them to the league championship series despite a fourth-place finish in his second season. The following year, the team moved to Salt Lake City and won it all as the Utah Stars, but Sharman missed Southern California, so when an opportunity arose to coach the Los Angeles Lakers, he took it. He lost no time in coaching the Lakers to their first title in Los Angeles, during a season when they compiled a still-record winning streak of 33 games and won 69 games, at the time the most ever in a single season.

Sharman was named ABA coach of the year in 1970 and added the same honor in the NBA two years later, but perhaps the biggest impact he had on the upstart league was his suggestion to Murphy that the league adopt the 3-point shot the old ABL had used.

Murphy took that suggestion, and it changed the face of basketball.

The first time the 3-pointer made headlines in a big way, it was thanks to a point guard named Jerry Harkness, who had played a handful of games for the New York Knicks in 1963 but was released and got a sales job with Quaker Oats in Chicago, playing semipro ball in his spare time. When he read about plans to start a new league three years later, he wrote a letter to the Indianapolis Star, asking how to get a tryout with the fledgling Pacers: "I'll never be satisfied until I prove to myself once and for all that I can't play pro basketball," the letter read. "I don't ask for a contract or anything else. All I want is a chance to try out. I'm willing to quit my job if you'll give me that chance."

He got the chance, and the contract, to boot, averaging 7 points a game in 71 games with the Pacers during their first season. None of those games, and none of the points he scored, was bigger than the 3-point shot he sank in the team's 15th game, against the Chaparrals in Dallas. Trailing 118-116 with one second left, the Pacers' Oliver Darden inbounded the ball to Harkness under his own basket. With no other options, Harkness heaved the ball the length of the court toward the basket.

It went in.

"I didn't aim it or anything," he said in the locker room after the game. "I knew I could get one shot off, though, so I let it fly."

At the time, they measured the shot at 92 feet, and although it was later adjusted to 88, it remained the longest successful shot in pro basketball history until 2001. When the shot went in, his ecstatic teammates mobbed him … and immediately huddled up to prepare for overtime. They thought he'd hit a regular 2-point shot. One of the officials had to come over and remind them that, in the ABA, a shot from that far out was worth three points, so the Pacers had actually won.

It proved to be the highlight of Harkness' career. He played a few games into the following season before being sidelined with back problems that forced his retirement.

A colorful cast

The ABA had more than its share of memorable moments and talented players.

ABA rosters included a plethora of stars who shone just as brightly in the NBA. In addition to Hawkins and the incomparable three-time MVP Julius "Dr. J" Erving, it had Moses Malone, Spencer Haywood, Rick Barry, Artis Gilmore, George Gervin, David Thompson, George McGinnis, Zelmo Beaty and Billy Cunningham. Others such as Mel Daniels, Ron Boone, Roger Brown, Dan Issel, Billy Paultz and Louie Dampier spent their best years (or all of them) in the upstart league, but their work on the hardwood was no less impressive.

But there was also a cast of colorful and sometimes eccentric supporting characters: players who weren't quite all-stars but who helped give the league a flavor all its own.

Take Charlie "Helicopter" Hentz, for instance. Many people still remember Darryl Dawkins' monster dunks for the Philadelphia 76ers, which shattered a pair of glass backboards in late 1979, exploits that led the NBA to install breakaway rims. But Hentz, a 6-foot-6 forward for the ABA's Pittsburgh Condors, had shattered two backboards of his own a decade earlier, and had done it in a single game.

One minute into the second quarter of a game against the Carolina Cougars in Raleigh, N.C., Hentz executed a two-handed dunk that brought the entire basket down, shattering the glass backboard into a thousand pieces. It took an hour for a maintenance crew to locate and install a wooden replacement, but the original glass backboard remained in place at the other end of the court.

For the time being.

With a little more than a minute left in the game, Hentz repeated the feat on the second backboard. With so little time left on the clock and Carolina ahead by 15 points, officials agreed to call the game at that point.

Hentz had made his mark on the ABA, but he wouldn't be around long. He appeared in

Connie Hawkins led the Pittsburgh Pipers to the first ABA championship in 1968.

57 games for the Condors that season, averaging 6.0 points and 6.8 rebounds a game, but it turned out to be his only year in the ABA.

Another player who made his mark in a single game was Larry Miller, a 6-foot-4 guard who was the ACC men's player of the year for the University of North Carolina in 1966 and '67. Miller had averaged a little over 13 points a game during his college career, but he had once scored 46 in a high school game, accounting for more than two-thirds of his team's total points. So, there was some indication he had it in him to really break out. That's what he did for the Carolina Cougars on March 18, 1972, when he erupted for a league-record point total against the Memphis Pros.

Miller was closing in on the end of his best pro season when it happened. His 67 points set an all-time league record in a 139-125 win over the Pros, and he did it without hitting a single 3-point shot. At the time, it was the most points ever scored by a guard in a professional basketball game, though it was eclipsed five years later by Pete Maravich's 68 against the New York Knicks, with Kobe Bryant setting the current standard thanks to his 81-point effort against Toronto in 2006.

Miller's fortunes took a turn for the worse after that. Two days after his monster game, lightning struck his house and it burned to the ground and he suffered a cut to his shooting hand that required 11 stitches.

Even though he averaged a career-high 18.4 points a game, the Cougars let Miller go after the season, refusing his demand for a better contract and trading him to San Diego. The next season was the last in which his scoring average reached double figures, and three seasons after his record performance, he was out of basketball at the age of 28. But his 67 points still stood as the most ever scored by one player in an ABA game when the league folded in 1976. It's a record that can never be broken.

Another prolific scorer who didn't last long in the league was Les Selvage, the ABA's first mad bomber. When the league debuted, most players used the 3-point shot as basketball's version of a Hail Mary, a gambit to be employed late in a lopsided contest on the slim chance of getting back into the game. Not Selvage. His team, the Anaheim Amigos, was often playing from behind, but that had little bearing on Selvage's shot selection. He shot 3s like they were going out of style, behaving in 1967 like a proto-Stephen Curry.

That year, *Sports Illustrated* even described him, like Curry as having "a build that is not prepossessing and a little-boy face."

The magazine focused on Selvage in a piece about the 3-point shot during the league's first season, contrasting him with NBA great Oscar Robertson, who had tried to shoot a few 3s for the heck of it, only to give up after a few minutes, declaring the distance to be out of his range. At the time the article went to press, Selvage had already launched 107 treys and hit 47 of them, or 44 percent, far better than his shooting percentage from inside the 3-point line: a mere 32 percent. His coach speculated that his wrists were so strong that he might make more shots in close if he banked the ball off the backboard.

In one game, Selvage shot 26 3-pointers and made 10 of them.

He had cooled down a bit by season's end, with his 3-point percentage falling to 32 percent. Still, he hit 147 bombs in 461 attempts, averaging 14 points a game. He made more 3-pointers by himself than nine of the other 10 *teams* in the league. Despite his exploits, however, the Amigos finished with the second-worst record in the league while playing in front of the ABA's smallest crowds (just 1,283 on average for their home games). Owner Art Kim had no appetite for further the financial bleeding and sold the team to a construction company owner named James Kirst, who jettisoned virtually the entire roster when he moved the Amigos up the freeway to become the L.A. Stars.

Selvage didn't play in the league the following season and played a grand total of four games with the Stars in the 1969-70 season, his last as a pro. During those four games, he tried four 3-pointers and didn't hit any of them before disappearing for good. Still, the 147 he made in 1967-68 ranked him 18th in the number of *career* 3-pointers made during the ABA's entire nine seasons of existence.

He died in 1991.

Temper, temper

Another early star in the league was Levern Tart, who picked up the nickname "Jelly" while playing for the Oakland Oaks. Tart set a short-lived ABA record early on with 49 points in a loss to Anaheim on Halloween, 1967. Tart scored almost 27 points a game for the Oaks through the first half of the season, only to be dealt to the New Jersey Americans. Tart made the all-star team that season, but his scoring dropped off significantly the next year before he returned to form with another all-star season in his third year. But he only played one more season after that, going through six teams during his time in the league.

Part of the problem for Tart may have been that Rick Barry kept following him around. Barry, had already spent two seasons with the NBA's San Francisco Warriors — leading the league in scoring with a career-high 35.6 average in his second year — when he became the first big-name player to sign with the ABA. Part of the allure was the fact that the Oakland Oaks, owned in part by singer Pat Boone, signed Barry's father-in-law Bruce Hale to coach the team. Barry was barred from playing for the Oaks during their first season because of his contract with the Warriors, but they knew he'd be free to play in their second year, so Tart was expendable. He became even more expendable when he clashed with Hale one night during a game against Minnesota.

In the space of a week, Tart lit up the Muskies for 70 points over two games; still, the Oaks lost them both and were mired in a six-game losing streak despite Tart's exploits. Unfortunately, Tart wasn't just good, he was cocky. After an explosive first half against the Muskies, he went cold and Hale tried to send in a substitute. Tart, however, refused to come out of the game three times. Hale had clearly had enough, and the Oaks traded Tart immediately after his 34-point effort against the Muskies on Jan. 18 for guard Barry Leibowitz.

"Naturally, we hate to lose a player of Tart's ability, but we feel this deal will benefit the Oaks in many ways, and it fits with our building program for the future," Hale said. "I've been very high on Barry. He is a fine all-around performer and a team leader."

If Hale was counting using Leibowitz to build for the future, he counted wrong. Leibowitz played 35 games for the Oaks, averaging less than half what Tart had, and was out of pro basketball after that season. Of course, it didn't matter, since the Oaks had Barry coming in the following season, when he would take them from last place to first and an ABA championship.

After a disappointing season with three teams in 1969-70, Tart regained his touch the following year with the New York Americans, where he led the team with 24.2 points a game. But the Americans acquired Barry the following season and didn't need two high-scoring stars competing to take shots, so Tart was traded in February of '71. He played out the season with the Texas Chaparrals before retiring at the end of the year.

If Tart's quick temper and attitude made him a liability, he had nothing on John Brisker of Pittsburgh, who was even more talented … and even more volatile. Tart might have threatened to punch people out, but Brisker followed through. He burst on the scene in 1969 as Pittsburgh's replacement for Hawkins, who had jumped to the NBA's Phoenix Suns, and while Brisker couldn't quite fill Hawkins' shoes, he came close. He was an all-star in 1970-71 and again the following season, averaging 29.3 and 28.9 points a game respectively.

But Brisker was even more well known for his violent temper than his scoring prowess. He appeared on the cover of Pittsburgh's 1970 media guide attired in a sombrero and poised to draw a pair of six-shooters. That wasn't just for show. He actually came to games with a gun in his bag, and one of his teammates, Charlie Williams, said he worried that Brisker might actually pull it out and shoot someone.

He didn't care who he fought. In 1971, Brisker was headed home from a World Series game in Pittsburgh when he got in an argument with another man over a cab. Brisker had hailed the taxi, but another man said he'd reserved it ahead of time; Brisker, already seated inside, refused to leave, and a fistfight ensued. Police arrived, but Brisker fought with them, too, sending two of the three officers to the hospital with chest pains and an injured hand, respectively.

It was no different on the court, where Brisker earned a similar reputation with his fists. After being ejected from a game against Denver for throwing an elbow at the Rockets' Art Becker, he stormed back out onto the court and tried to clobber Becker three times before police escorted him to the locker room. More than one ABA player reportedly needed facial surgery after bloody confrontations with Brisker, and opponents started taking drastic measures.

Players steered clear of him, fearing retaliation if they fouled him. Dallas coach Tom Nissalke, however, countered by offering his players an incentive to stand up to Brisker: Nissalke put a $500 bounty on Brisker's head, payable to the first Chaparrals player who socked him. One of his players responded by sending Brisker to the floor with one punch at the opening tipoff. (The bounty remained in effect whenever the Chaps played Pittsburgh, in case Brisker ever got out of line.) The Utah Stars went even further, cooking up a promotion called "John Brisker Intimidation Night." Heavyweight contender Ron Lyle appeared on the cover of that program that night in a fighting stance, and four other boxers showed up at the arena, too.

"Not that anyone on the Utah Stars team fears John Brisker," the program said. "But just in case the husky, sometimes ill-tempered, Pittsburgh Condor forward gets out of line tonight the Stars' management has taken steps to keep all in control. Surrounding the court tonight will be five of the top boxers the Intermountain Area has ever produced. For tonight is 'John Brisker Intimidation Night' and it is the intention of the Stars to turn the tables on the high scoring Condor. Tonight it is Brisker who is on foreign soil and with the likes of Ron Lyle … Don and Gene Fullmer, Rex Layne and Tony Doyle standing in the wings, best he doesn't get far out of line."

Fullmer was a former world middleweight champion. Lyle would go on to challenge Muhammad Ali for the heavyweight title and knock down George Foreman twice in a nontitle bout. Layne had beaten heavyweight champs Ezzard Charles and Jersey Joe Walcott. If Brisker wanted to start a fight, they weren't the sort of people he'd want to mess with.

Brisker didn't cause any trouble that night with his fists, but he didn't seem fazed by the stunt, scoring 37 points as the Condors topped the Stars 135-129.

In fact, nothing seemed to faze Brisker, who was ready to take the next step in his career. After three seasons in Pittsburgh, he followed in the footsteps of Connie Hawkins and Spencer Haywood (who he'd known in Detroit before they turned pro) by jumping to the NBA. He joined Haywood in Seattle, signing a six-year, $1 million deal with the SuperSonics, but he was never able to replicate his ABA successes on the big stage.

During his first season with the Sonics, he played under Nissalke, the same coach who had put a price on his head in the ABA. But it wasn't Nissalke who turned out to be a problem. Brisker had and uneasy but workable relationship with him, but the Sonics management didn't: With the Sonics far below .500, they fired Nissalke at midseason and named assistant Bucky Buckwalter as interim coach. In the offseason, they in turn replaced Buckwalter with Celtics legend Bill Russell, an old-school disciplinarian who had little patience for the temperamental Brisker. The fiery swing man made the wrong kind of impression on his new coach when, just four days into training camp, he decked teammate Joby Wright during a scrimmage. Four teeth flew out of Wright's mouth and landed on the court, and he wound up with a broken jaw. (Afterward, a Seattle newspaper columnist responded by inducting him into a Seattle Boxing Hall of Fame.)

Brisker could still score in bunches, racking up 47 points against Kansas City-Omaha on Nov. 25, but nothing he did seemed to impress Russell, who didn't think he played enough defense. Midway through the year, he sent him down to the feeder Eastern Basketball Association, where Brisker lost no time setting out to prove him wrong, scoring 51 and 58 points in the only two games he played for the Cherry Hill Rookies.

Russell remained unmoved.

Although Brisker returned to the Sonics the following season, he mostly rode the bench and averaged a mere 7.7 points a game. His last hurrah came in a Jan. 31 game against Portland, when he came off the bench to score 16 of his game-high 28 points in a furious fourth-quarter rally as the Sonics overcame a 21-point deficit to pull out the victory. Teammate Slick Watts would recall that, after the game, Brisker fixed Russell with the kind of menacing, in-your-face glare that put everyone in the Sonics locker room on edge.

He only played eight more games after that, and owner Sam Schulman ultimately let him go — with three years left on his six-year, $1 million contract — for creating "dissention" on the team. Brisker negotiated a $325,000 buyout and never played in the NBA again, but things only got worse from there. After the season, a restaurant and nightclub he'd purchased went belly-up, leaving him with $40,000 in debts. "The IRS padlocked the front door," his brother Ralph recalled.

Then his wife of five years filed for divorce in 1977, claiming he had beaten her up so badly he'd left her deaf in one ear. Brisker found a new girlfriend, Khalilah Rashad, who gave birth to his second child. He wanted a new start, and Haywood remembered him talking about going back to his roots in Africa. He'd long been interested in his cultural heritage, having decorated his suburban Seattle homes with African artifacts, and he'd been to Nigeria in 1975, where he'd thought about buying a soccer team.

In 1978, three years after he played his last game, Brisker boarded a plane bound for Africa where he reportedly planned to start an "import-export business." The last time anyone heard from him was April 11, when Rashad got a phone call from Kampala, Uganda. Brisker told her he would send for her and their daughter, but she never heard from him again. Nobody did.

It wasn't long before rumors started swirling about what had happened to him. Haywood later said Brisker had shown him a picture, before he left, of someone who looked like Ugandan dictator Idi Amin ... but he couldn't be sure. One story maintained that he became a mercenary and was executed after Amin's overthrow in 1979; another maintained that he had insulted an African ruler at a banquet and had been shot dead on the spot. Given Brisker's temper, either seems at least plausible. But it also seems possible that, amid mounting debts and facing the prospect of paying a divorce settlement, he just wanted to disappear.

There's no real evidence for any of it. Brisker was ruled legally dead in 1985, and no one knows what really happened to him. All that's certain is that nobody's heard from him since that last phone call in 1978, and with the passage of time, many have forgotten that John Brisker was once one of the best players in the ABA.

Stability? What stability?

The league had its share of gimmicks: A wrestling bear was brought in as a halftime attraction during one game, and there was a cow-milking contest at another. Teams move from one city to another more often than carpetbagging politicians, changing names at the drop of a hat, with only Indiana, Denver and Kentucky staying put for the league's entire nine-year run.

The Houston Mavericks (who drew just 89 fans to one game) became the Carolina Cougars after two seasons, then the Spirits of St. Louis. The Nuggets had been pegged to play in Kansas City but couldn't find an arena and moved to Denver before the start of the league's first season. Originally called the Larks (after the Colorado state bird), they changed their name to Rockets when the owner of Ringsby Rockets Trucking bought the company, before eventually becoming the Nuggets.

The Dallas Chaparrals changed their name to Texas, then back to Dallas before moving to San Antonio as the Spurs.

The Minnesota Muskies morphed into the Miami Floridians, then just the plain Floridians.

The Pittsburgh Pipers moved to Minnesota, then back again the following season and later became the Condors … but only after jettisoning a plan to call themselves the Pioneers.

The Oakland Oaks became the Washington Caps, then the Virginia Squires.

The New Jersey Americans turned into the New York Nets (and are now the Brooklyn Nets of the NBA).

The ABA's only expansion team, the San Diego Conquistadors, became the San Diego Sails briefly before folding. The Conquistadors, who doubtless had one of the longest one-word nicknames in sports history, were known affectionately as the Q's and pulled off what appeared to be, at the time, the biggest signing in league history: Wilt Chamberlain. The NBA great was near the tail end of his career and no longer scoring the way he had in his younger days, but he still had led the league in rebounding for the Lakers for the seventh time in eight years the previous season, 1972-73.

The Q's signed Chamberlain to be their player-coach, but he never played a single game for them after a court sided with the Lakers, who said he was still under contract to them. The court did allow Wilt to coach in San Diego, but he was far less effective on the bench than on the court, and even missed one game to sign copies of a new book. He left the team after one season, having coached the Q's to a 37-47 record, declining to re-sign because the team just couldn't afford him.

The New Orleans Buccaneers, league runners-up in their first season, became the Memphis Pros two years later, then changed their name to the Tams and then the Sounds.

"Tams" was actually an acronym for Tennessee, Arkansas and Mississippi, because the team owner sought to draw fans from all three states (though, in reality, few fans from any state attended their games). That owner was Charles O. Finley, who also owned baseball's Oakland A's and used that team's green-and-gold color scheme for the Tams. Two years later, however, the Tams were moved to Baltimore, where they became the Hustlers. The league didn't like the not-too-family-friendly nature of that name, so they changed it to Claws, but the league revoked the franchise and folded the team after just three exhibition games when the new owners failed to supply cash guarantees.

Despite that instability, the ABA was every bit as competitive on the court as the NBA was during the 1970s. If you want proof, all you have to do is look at the box scores. During the younger league's existence, its teams played more than 150 exhibition games against NBA squads, winning 79 and losing 76. The best players in the two leagues also met for a pair of interleague all-star games in 1971 and '72, with the NBA winning both games but only by a combined score of seven points.

Julius Erving of New York, left, and Willie Wise of Utah battle for the ball during the 1973-74 ABA season.

The ABA's own final all-star game in 1976 was an extravaganza that featured entertainment by Glen Campbell and Charlie Rich, along with another innovation: pro basketball's first slam dunk contest (won by Erving). Nearly 18,000 fans attended the game between a team of ABA stars and the first-place Nuggets at Denver's McNichols Arena, but despite that success, the writing was on the wall for the troubled league.

The ABA had long been divided between the haves and have-nots. Teams in cities without much big-league history or competition, in any sport, drew well: the Indiana Pacers and Kentucky Colonels were consistently at or near the top of the league's attendance chart. Utah and Carolina usually did well, too, but places like St. Louis, Miami, Dallas, Los Angeles, San Diego and Houston — larger cities where there was more competition for the entertainment dollar — struggled to attract fans and media coverage. The New York Nets were the big exception, with the presence of Dr. J selling thousands of tickets.

When 1976 rolled around, the league was in dire straits. Baltimore folded before the season began and was quickly followed by the San Diego Sails and the once-stable Stars in Utah. Virginia and St. Louis managed to make it through the season, but only barely, and by the end, the Squires had folded, leaving the league with just six franchises. Of those, four joined the NBA: Denver, New York, Indiana and San Antonio.

Kentucky, in some ways the league's most stable franchise, was left out of the deal — accepting a $3 million buyout from the NBA in exchange for closing up shop.

The ghost of the Spirits

St. Louis was a different case. The Spirits' move to St. Louis had been a colossal failure; the team had drawn well in Carolina, despite losing money, but found few followers in Missouri. At season's end, brothers Ozzie and Daniel Silna, who owned the team, announced it would be moving to Salt Lake City and would be rechristened the Utah Rockies.

The Silnas, who had made their fortune in the polyester business hoped their team and the Kentucky Colonels would both be welcomed in the NBA. It made sense, to their way of thinking: Absorbing all six remaining ABA squads would have given the league 24 teams, a balanced membership that would have made scheduling easier. But when the dust cleared, the older league agreed to take just four.

St. Louis and Kentucky were on the outs.

The Silnas were none too happy about that development. This wasn't the first time their NBA dreams had been dashed: They'd tried to purchase the Detroit Pistons a few years earlier, and when that deal didn't pan out, they'd bought the ABA's Carolina Cougars and moved them to St. Louis. Now they found themselves once more on the outside looking in.

"We expected and hoped to be part of the NBA for quite a long time," Ozzie Silna said in an interview for the ESPN documentary *Free Spirits*. "We shouldn't have been treated as badly as we were. There was no reason to leave us out."

The Silnas were determined to be fairly compensated, not just for their team but for their disappointment. So instead of accepting the same $3 million payment the Kentucky Colonels had received, they took a slightly smaller sum ($2.2 million), and negotiated a novel bonus: They would receive one-seventh of the television revenues earned by the four ABA teams that would be joining the NBA "for as long as the NBA or its successors continues in existence."

This might have seemed like a good deal for the NBA at the time. This was before the advent of huge TV contracts and before the era when Magic Johnson, Larry Bird and Michael Jordan made pro basketball into a hand-over-fist moneymaker.

The Silnas reaped $522,000 from the deal in its first year, a tidy sum but nothing like what they'd end up making as the years went by. Over the next 38 seasons, they would rake in 100 times what the Colonels got: a whopping $300 million. The NBA was losing so much money on the settlement that, in 2014, it struck a deal to terminate the agreement for an additional upfront payment of $500 million.

That's $800 million total, which would have been enough in 2014 to do what the Silnas had wanted to do in the first place: Buy an NBA team. In fact, all but the four most valuable franchises in the league were worth less than $800 million in 2014. So, I suppose you could say that's what the Spirits of St. Louis were ultimately worth. Not bad for a team that lost 60 percent of its games during two seasons in Missouri and drew a paltry 2,700 fans per game in the final year of its existence

That's not quite the last word on the Spirits of St. Louis, however. Their continuing legacy lives on in an announcer who got his start with the team. The 22-year-old Syracuse University dropout who called the Spirits' games for KMOX would go on to cover the Olympics, Major League Baseball and pretty much any other sporting event you can think of. In time, he become the face of NBC Sports. His name: Bob Costas.

ABA championship series		
1968	Pittsburgh Pipers d. New Orleans Buccaneers	4-3
1969	Oakland Oaks d. Indiana Pacers	4-1
1970	Indiana Pacers d. Los Angeles Stars	4-2
1971	Utah Stars d. Kentucky Colonels	4-3
1972	Indiana Pacers d. New York Nets	4-2
1973	Indiana Pacers d. Kentucky Colonels	4-3
1974	New York Nets d. Utah Stars	4-1
1975	Kentucky Colonels d. Indiana Pacers	4-1
1976	New York Nets d. Denver Nuggets	4-2

Ahead of its Time

Billie Jean King struck a major blow for women in athletics with her straight-sets victory in her 1973 *Battle of the Sexes* tennis match with Bobby Riggs. And, in the ensuing decades, stars like Chris Evert, Martina Navratilova, Steffi Graf and Serena Williams vaulted women's tennis onto something close to equal footing with the men's game: From 2010 to 2014, television viewership was higher for the women's U.S. Open final was higher than it was for the men's championship.

There was even something close to paycheck parity. Although 71 of the top 100 men made more than their counterparts in the women's rankings, both singles champions at Wimbledon got the same prize money in 2018. It wasn't perfect, but it was a lot better than most other sports. In fact, outside of women's golf and the Olympics every four years, women in most sports didn't even have a national stage on which to compete.

Among the five major U.S. team sports, there's been no truly big-time league for women in either hockey or football, and it took World War II to spur the creation of the All-American Girls Professional Baseball League, which lasted scarcely a decade before folding, never to be replaced. King had founded World Team Tennis — which showcased men and women equally — the same year she defeated Riggs, but equality was still a long way away.

"Until team sports are accepted the same way they are for men, we haven't even arrived," she said. "Everyone talks about our success; all I can think about is, we haven't even started."

Which team sport was the best prospect?

King, speaking in the summer of 1981, cited the Women's Basketball League, which had been around for three seasons. "They really are the pioneers now for women in team sports," she said, advising the league to "grow slowly. Don't be overanxious. Don't expand too quickly."

Unfortunately, the league failed to take that sort of advice and never made it to a fourth season. By November, just four months after King praised the WBL, it was out of business. But that doesn't mean it was a bad idea; on the contrary, it was simply about 20 years ahead of its time.

One man's vision

Bill Byrne, the man behind the WBL, had hoped the 1980 Olympics would build excitement for his newest venture. Women's basketball had made its debut as an Olympic sport in 1976, with the U.S. winning a silver medal (behind Russia, which hadn't lost a game for 17 years).

Byrne believed the future of the sport was bright. He had started out as an organizer of local slow-pitch softball and basketball leagues before founding the National Scouting Organization, which gave him access to a number of professional athletes. From there, he founded the Columbus Bucks of the Midwest Football League, where he wound up as commissioner before leaving for the new World Football League. He served there as director of player personnel for the Chicago Fire, then worked for the Shreveport Steamer before that team folded along with the rest of the WFL in the middle of the league's second season.

After that, Byrne returned to his original passions: softball and basketball. In 1977, he founded the American Professional Slo-Pitch League, which began with a dozen teams and featured a few former big-league baseball stars, such as Joe Pepitone and Norm Cash. The league might have been mistaken for a drinking game, considering some of its team nicknames: the Milwaukee Schlitz, Cincinnati Suds and Kentucky Bourbons. It lasted four years before merging with a rival circuit, and the combined league soldiered on for two more seasons before petering out. Perhaps its biggest claim to fame was its 1979 championship game, a 5-3 victory for the Schlitz over the Bourbons that was the first event ever televised on ESPN.

Such ventures, however, only served as appetizers for the main course: the first-ever pro basketball league for women.

Byrne had been involved, peripherally, in an earlier effort to start such a league, which had used his scouting service to contact coaches about potential talent. That league was to be built around the Indianapolis Pink Panthers, recently formed by Karen Logan and Jolene Ammons. The pair had been star players for the All-American Red Heads, a sort of women's version of the Harlem Globetrotters that had been barnstorming around the country, playing against men's teams, since 1936 (and would continue to do so until 1986). The Red Heads' gimmick was that every player on the team either had naturally or dyed red hair. Ammons had spent 11 years with the Red Heads and Logan had been with them for three, but the pair decided to go their own way and form the Pink Panthers, who would be charter members of the new six-team Women's Professional Basketball Association.

The Pink Panthers were scheduled to open the WPBA season against the Arkansas

Lassies, another traveling team that had accepted membership in the new league. The barnstorming Lassies played 180 games a year, mostly against teams of high school coaches and athletic directors, and had been around for at least a decade. They never actually played in Arkansas — the team was actually based in Michigan, where it expected to play its home games once the league got started. Other franchises in the new circuit were supposedly lined up for Atlanta, Winston-Salem, Allentown, Chicago, Fort Wayne and Iowa in what was envisioned as a 12-team league.

None of those teams ever played a game. In fact, the only game ever played in the WPBA was the opener on Jan. 5, 1975: The Lassies defeated the Pink Panthers 65-63 on a steal and last-second basket. A report in *The Indianapolis News* declared, "the WPBA has become a reality." But the report also indicated both teams were surprised at the low turnout for the game, played just outside Indianapolis, in the heart of basketball country.

"I am very disappointed at the lack of response for the Panthers," league founder Conrad Stephens said. "The local paper didn't even cover the game. If the town paper can't back its local team in such an eventful game, perhaps the team needs to relocate. I am considering doing just that."

The Pink Panthers did, in fact, relocate to Phoenix, but they didn't last long there, either. Before the month was done, Logan took time out to compete in the *Women Superstars* made-for-TV competition on ABC. There, she placed second to volleyball star Mary Jo Peppler, missing out on the title only because she was assessed a 5-second penalty in the obstacle course. The last reference to the Pink Panthers in the press came Feb. 9, when a columnist reported that the team was in limbo and Logan had departed for California.

She kept herself in the limelight by beating Lakers superstar Jerry West in a televised game of H-O-R-S-E inspired by the King-Riggs *Battle of the Sexes* tennis match.

WBL takes shape

When Byrne decided to start his own league, it was natural that he should contact Logan, who not only signed to play for the Chicago Hustle but also designed the league's smaller ball, 1.5 inches less in circumference and 3 ounces lighter than a regulation NBA ball. The ball, designed to boost scoring and fit more comfortably in women's smaller hands, became the standard for women's basketball.

Teams in the league would play 34 games of four 10-minute quarters, using a 30-second shot clock. To fill their rosters, they could call upon an increasingly large pool of players created in the aftermath of Title IX, the 1972 law that forbade discrimination in education (and, by extension, school-based athletic activities) based on a person's sex.

Byrne touted the new venture by pointing out that women's basketball was, indeed, growing by leaps and bounds at the college level. In 1973, he said, 483 schools had women's programs — a figure that had grown to 882 by the time the league announced its formation five years later. "We conducted a marketing study on this 2½ years ago and it showed us the time was right" for a women's league, he said.

A businessman in Iowa was the first to make a firm commitment, which included a $50,000 franchise fee. The Hawkeye State, while not a major market, had proven a popular venue for a six-player version of girls high school basketball: Capacity crowds of 14,000 had attended a five-day tournament at the Des Moines Veterans Memorial Auditorium earlier in the year.

The Iowa Cornets hoped to develop a regional fan base by playing games in various cities across the state, including Des Moines and Cedar Rapids. Team owner George Nissen, who owned a gymnastics equipment company, likened the venture to farming: "If you put enough fertilizer on, it will grow." He admitted the league was a "calculated risk" but added that "the soccer league started this way, and it has become successful" — a reference to the North American Soccer League, which would soon encounter problems of its own and would end up calling it quits six years later.

In retrospect, it was not the most auspicious comparison.

Also not auspicious: Two of the league's most notable draft choices — Ann Meyers of UCLA and Carol Blazejowski of Montclair State — both passed on the league in order to maintain their eligibility for the 1980 Olympics. The WBL would have to wait, but that wasn't an issue, because it figured to get a major boost from the Games, after which the stars who had played on the U.S. National Team would be eager to join its ranks.

When the Olympics went on without the U.S., that plan went up in smoke, but both Meyers and Blazejowski did end up playing in the WBL. More on that later.

Another standout, Lusia Harris, also wound up playing in the WBL after initially declining. The Houston Angels weren't the only team she rebuffed: Harris, a 6-foot-3 center who averaged a shade under 26 points a game during her college career at Delta State, was chosen with the 137th pick of the NBA draft — ahead of 36 men. Alvin Scott, the player drafted right behind her, wound up playing eight seasons in the NBA, but Harris never worked out with the Jazz: It turned out she was pregnant at the time. (Team officials later joked they owned the future draft rights to her unborn child.)

In an interesting twist, volleyball superstar Mary Jo Peppler, who had beaten Logan for the Women Superstars title, signed with the Chicago Hustle.

Molly Bolin, second from right, shared the league's MVP award during her second season with the Iowa Cornets. Also pictured standing, from left: Tanya Crevier, Mary Schrad (mostly obscured), Joan Uhl, DK Thomas and Suzanne Alt. Rod Lein, general manager/acting coach, is facing the camera during a first-season game at Minnesota. *Molly Kazmer collection.*

A star is born

But the first player to sign a contract with the league was "Machine Gun" Molly Bolin, who inked a $6,000 deal with the Cornets.

Bolin had been a high school phenom in Moravia, Iowa, but the version of the game she played there would be barely recognizable today. Under Iowa's rules for six-on-six high school girls basketball, three forwards were stationed in — and confined to — the front court with three guards playing the entire game in the backcourt. Players could only dribble twice before they had to pass the ball, and the ball was taken back to halfcourt after each possession, so the guards never got to play offense and the forwards never had to play defense.

Because only three players were eligible to score, a team's top shooter often racked up big numbers, and that's what Bolin did. Then known as Molly Van Benthuysen, she averaged just under 55 points a game during her senior season, once setting a record for points in a single game at 83. On the flipside, though, the format didn't allow her to learn the art of the dribble drive, and she never became known as a strong defender.

Bolin's lack of dribbling ability hindered her during tryouts for the 1975 Pan American Games, but in some ways, it may have helped her in the long run. The Iowa game's emphasis on quick passing and shooting foreshadowed the kind of play that would set the Golden State Warriors apart during their NBA dynasty in late 2010s. One writer even described Warriors sharpshooter Stephen Curry as the "male Machine Gun Molly." (Bolin, coincidentally, wore the same number, 30, with the Cornets as Curry would later don for the Warriors.)

The Cornets signed Bolin as a local draw, but she quickly proved herself to be a lot more. Though she was no longer playing the old six-on-six game, it wasn't long before she started using her patented pull-up jumper to roll up big numbers.

"That high-scoring mentality was ingrained from those early days," Bolin, now Molly Kazmer, recalled. "In my mind, once a goal was achieved, my personal bar of expectations also rose, so I not only believed I could score a lot of points in a game — but I expected to if given the chance."

Against just one team, the Minnesota Fillies, she scored at least 50 points no fewer than four times. She set a league record with 53 points in a single game near the end of the league's first season. During the second season, she broke that record with 54 points and then again with 55, both times against the Fillies, adding a 50-point performance in a playoff game against Minnesota.

Kazmer, remembered rising to the occasion against the Fillies.

"They were a good team and a big rival always in our way of making the playoffs," she recalled. "Whenever we played them, it always seemed to be a crucial game for positioning and we got had big crowds or the game was televised. So, I was always really pumped up in those games and the freedom I had to shoot the ball in season two just sort of took over in a flashback to my high school days. ..."

The record-breaking 55-point performance was even more impressive because she went down with a dislocated shoulder during the game — a press photo shows a trainer attending to Bolin as she lay stretched out on the court. Amazingly, she hit 18 of 19 shots she took during the game. The injury, she said, dated back to childhood.

"I had a torn rotator cuff starting with a playground game in high school when a boy I beat twisted my arm behind my back and threw my ball down the street!" she said. "But it was never treated and about once a year, if I hit my shoulder wrong, (it) would go out of socket. It was painful but I had to relax and get it back in place, which wasn't fun, either. ... It went out a time or two after my career was over, and the pain was so bad I threw up — so I was just conditioned to ignore pain when I played!"

Bolin paced the Cornets in scoring with 16.7 points a game during her first season and set a league record by averaging 32.8 points in her sophomore campaign, leading the Cornets to the finals both years.

1979–80 Women's Basketball League	W	L	Pct.
Eastern Division			
New York Stars	28	7	.800
New Orleans Pride	21	13	.618
New Jersey Gems	19	17	.528
St. Louis Streak	15	21	.417
Washington Metros	3	7	.300
Philadelphia Fox	2	8	.200
Midwestern Division			
Iowa Cornets	24	12	.667
Minnesota Fillies	22	12	.647
Chicago Hustle	17	19	.472
Milwaukee Does	10	24	.294
Western Division			
Houston Angels	19	14	.576
San Francisco Pioneers	18	18	.500
California Dreams	11	18	.393
Dallas Diamonds	7	28	.200

New York d. Iowa 4 games to 1 for the championship.
Philadelphia and Washington disbanded after 10 games.
California disbanded after 29 games.

Teams come, teams go

Unfortunately, the Iowa team disbanded after those two seasons despite being the league's top draw. The team pulled in crowds ranging from 1,500 to 3,500, compared with fewer than 1,000 for some teams. But there were other problems. Nissen, the owner, had a lot of assets tied up in Iran, which were forfeit when the Shah was overthrown in the 1979 Islamic Revolution. That same year, he spent $1 million to make a movie about a fictional women's basketball team that featured a number of Cornets players alongside "Pistol" Pete Maravich ... and tanked at the box office. Before long, Nissen could no longer afford the team and tried to sell it to a former deejay. The check bounced, and Nissen was left holding the bag. Having lost $700,000 on the team, he decided to fold the franchise.

Molly Bolin in the 1980 WBL All-Star Game.
Molly Kazmer collection.

The league was chaotic like that from the outset. Byrne originally hoped for a 12-team league, saying he had "firm" commitments for franchises in Philadelphia, Baltimore, St. Louis, Los Angeles, Seattle, Denver and Winston-Salem. None of those cities was represented when the league tipped off. Byrne also mentioned possible franchises out west in Las Vegas, Phoenix, San Francisco and Portland. But none of those came to pass, either, and he ultimately settled for an eight-team circuit, with each of the franchises east of the Continental Divide: the Chicago Hustle, Dayton Rockets, Houston Angels, Iowa Cornets, Milwaukee Does (as in female deer, counterparts to the NBA's Bucks), Minnesota Fillies, New Jersey Gems and New York Stars.

The Stars were formed just nine days before the season started.

Houston won the championship, defeating Iowa in the deciding game in a best-of-five series, and Rita Easterling of Chicago (the league's No. 2 overall pick after Meyers) won MVP honors for a season that included a then-record 44-point outing. Chicago turned out to be the league's marquee franchise, averaging several thousand fans a game and winding up as one of only three teams to play all three seasons (Minnesota and New Jersey were the others).

The Dayton franchise folded after the first season, but Byrne, undeterred, approved seven expansion teams for Year 2 and adopting a three-division format. St. Louis and Dallas got new teams, as did Washington, Philadelphia and New Orleans, where the Pride was led by former Lakers coach Butch van Breda Kolff. Two new West Coast teams — the San Francisco Pioneers and Long Beach-based California Dream — gave the league a national footprint for the first time, but the Dream ended prematurely when financial problems forced that franchise to fold late in the season.

Things were even worse for the Philadelphia Fox and Washington Metros, both of which disbanded after just 10 games. The Fox team was founded, basically, on a lick and a promise ... that wasn't kept. Eric Kraus, a New York businessman, came up with 20 percent of the $100,000 franchise fee, with the remainder due after the league came up with another $250,000 in start-up funding. It never did, and Kraus didn't pay the other $80,000, either. The Fox folded after drawing fewer than 1,000 fans to each of its first three home games, and Fox players responded by filing a lawsuit against Byrne alleging breach of contract and unfair labor practices. Even the general manager, Dave Wohl, wasn't aware of the money problems.

"There was a misrepresentation that there was money behind the club," he said. "I felt it would be solvent for a year. As it turned out, there were no investors."

The league did have a new marquee attraction in Meyers, the No. 1 pick in the league's inaugural draft who had sat out its first season. Before joining the WBL, however, she tried landing a job in the NBA: The Indiana Pacers signed her to a $50,000 contract and gave her a shot at making the roster. She didn't make the cut, but signed with the New Jersey Gems shortly afterward for even more money: $130,000 over three years. She played one year and was the league's co-MVP with Bolin (who averaged 32.8 points a game), but the Gems missed the playoffs and Meyers left, later saying she stopped getting paychecks in the summer of 1980.

The New York Stars, who signed former New York Knick Dean Meminger as head coach for their second season, were the class of the league. The team's most visible players were 6-foot-3 center Althea Gwyn (the team's top scorer and rebounder), and identical 5-foot-11 twins Faye and Kaye Young, who were featured in an ad campaign for Dannon Yogurt.

Posters and promotions

The Youngs were good players, but they were also attractive, and the league wasn't above using that to market its product. Bolin, who got an endorsement deal with Sport Shake, and Janie Fincher of the Chicago Hustle both had posters made that highlighted their good looks in an era when an iconic Farrah Fawcett poster was ubiquitous in teenage boys' rooms across the country. The Houston Angels even shared a nickname with the popular TV show that made Fawcett famous, *Charlie's Angels*. In a league with nicknames that included Fox, Dream, Diamonds and Gems, the Angels were hardly alone.

The posters provided Bolin with a way to make up for a salary gap between her and many of the other players that had left her on the short end. While players like Meyers and Blazejowski were signing for six figures, Bolin was stuck at four. She made $3,000 for the ill-fated movie with Maravich, whom she became friends with while driving him to the set. But her salary of $900 a month meant she was only making about half as much as teammate Robin Tucker. They offered her a modest raise to $1,200 a month, but that wasn't enough, especially considering she and her husband had a toddler to support. At the time, Bolin was playing under a new coach who had her coming off the bench, so she didn't have a lot of bargaining power.

"So, I got the idea that I wanted to make and sell posters at our basketball games so I could make extra money. The team did agree to pay for the photographer and prints and I could keep all of the profits — so I agreed and signed my new contract — *still* far less than member of my team made and most of the players across the league."

Soon, Bolin was not only starting again but was one of the league's top stars, and the posters were in demand. She went through the whole first run of the posters and had to print a couple of more runs to keep up with the demand, selling them for $3 each and adding a photo print to T-shirts, which she sold for $10 each at games. The posters foreshadowed an era when athletes would make more money through merchandising and corporate tie-ins than they would for playing their games.

Unfortunately, Bolin's idea turned out to be ahead of its time, and it may have come at a cost to her legacy: "I'm thinking it was (because of) the posters that people wouldn't take me seriously."

Bolin wasn't the only one increasing her visibility. In New York, the Stars were trying to get noticed in the nation's No. 1 sports market by moving from a small campus arena in New Rochelle to Madison Square Garden for their second season. Not only did they have a new home, but a great product, as well: They tore through the league, posting a 28-7 record and losing just one game in the playoffs. They defeated Iowa for the championship, three games to one, despite a stellar performance by Bolin, who scored 49 points in Game 4 to keep the series alive. But neither team was around for the league's third season, with the Stars having lost a ton of money, some of it thanks to the $300,000 cost of renting the Garden.

Tragedy in Omaha

With the Cornets on the verge of folding, Bolin took her shooting talents to a newly formed rival league called the Ladies Pro Basketball Association, where she signed a guaranteed $30,000 deal with the Southern California Breeze as a player and assistant couch. The Breeze program touted her as its No. 1 draft choice and "the top female basketball player in the United States."

Even though she was only 22, Breeze executive Tony Mercurio was confident Bolin could fill an important role as liaison between the players and head coach Ken Cole, who had enjoyed considerable success in Australia. Mercurio said she would be in charge of the team's tryout camp and would be able to step in and assume coaching duties should Cole be suspended or miss a game for some other reason.

Bolin wasn't he first member of the Cornets to jump to the new league. Doris Draving, who had averaged 14.9 rebounds a game to lead the league in that category, signed with the Tucson Storms, while guard Robin Tucker joined the New Mexico Energee.

"I went to California to a new league and tried to take as many teammates as I could with me," Bolin recalled.

But one of the players who didn't join her was Connie Kunzmann, a 24-year-old forward who had been on the Cornets during both of the league's first two seasons. Like Bolin, Kunzmann had grown up playing six-on-six basketball in Iowa. A native of Everly, a town of a few hundred people in the northwest corner of the state, she was was one of four Iowa natives on the Cornets original roster, joining Bolin, Mary Schrad and Ronda Penquite. At 6-foot-1, she was as tall as anyone on the roster, forming a "twin towers" duo with center Draving, the team's No. 2 draft choice.

Bolin, Draving and Kunzmann formed the core of one of the league's best teams during their two seasons in Iowa. In their final game together, Bolin scored 36 points and Kunzmann added 20 as the Cornets fell the to the Stars in Game 4 of the 1980 finals.

But instead of jumping to the LPBA with her teammates, Kunzmann signed on with the WBL's new Nebraska Wranglers, a team based in Omaha. Just across the state line from Iowa, it was as close as she could get to her home state now that the Cornets were no longer in the league. It was also right next door to Wayne State College, where she graduated as the career leader in rebounding and the No. 2 all-time scorer.

"Connie wanted to stay closer to home and her family, and she went to play at Nebraska, who won the championship that year," Bolin said.

Signing with Nebraska carried another perk for Kunzmann: She got to play under former

Cornets coach Steve Kirk, who had taken the Wranglers job.

Karen Logan also signed with the new league as coach of the Tucson Storms. But the six-team circuit lasted barely a month, with only three of its teams even seeing action. Logan's Tucson team had its opener canceled when financial backing "disappeared," according to one news report. (Logan's next stop was Utah State University, her alma mater, where she was named women's basketball coach in June of 1982. She coached the Aggies for two seasons.)

Bolin, meanwhile returned to the WBL for the remainder of its third and final season, where she caught on with the San Francisco Pioneers, now led by former Stars head coach Meminger.

"Playing for Dean Meminger as my coach was quite an experience," Kazmer (Bolin) recalled. "He really pushed me, though he could be brutal sometimes!"

Also on that team was Cardte Hicks, a Long Beach State product who had been an alternate on the 1976 Olympic team and was lauded by Pioneers coach Frank LaPorte as "better than Blaze(jowski) and Meyers." In 1977, Hicks had gone to Holland, where she became the first woman to play on a men's pro team. A year later, still playing in Europe, she did something that no woman had ever done in a game before: She dunked the ball.

During her two seasons with the Pioneers, she averaged in double figures — including a 41-point effort in a 115-106 loss to the New Jersey Gems late in the '81 season — and pulled down plenty of rebounds because of her leaping ability.

"One of the girls passed me the ball so high that I got up with two hands and slammed it and hung on the rim," she said in a television interview. "And it was just, it was quiet. It was like, 'What just happened?' "

Her nicknames were "Spring Wonder" and "Magic." When she got up high enough to hang on the rim, she said, she would memorize the way the crowd and her teammates looked from those rarified heights. "Yes, I did enjoy being up there until I had to look down," she remembered. "High anxiety."

Hicks and Bolin, along with teammate Cindy Haugejorde, were named to the West squad for the All-Star Game, set for Feb. 9 in Albuquerque.

Kunzmann, meanwhile, was hitting her stride with the Nebraska Wranglers: She didn't make the all-star team, but she'd been named captain on a team that was turning out to be the class of the league. On Feb. 5, the Wranglers played Nancy Lieberman and Diamonds in Dallas, a game that featured the two division leaders. Dallas led the Coastal Division at 11-6, while Nebraska sat atop the Central Division at 16-4. The Diamonds won, handing the Wranglers just their fourth loss of the season, but Kunzmann showed why the team was a force to be reckoned with. She hit 7 of 8 shots for 19 points and pulled down 10 rebounds as she played what Lieberman called "the game of her life."

The next night, after the team returned to Omaha, she put on her Iowa Cornets jacket and headed out to a bar called Tiger Tom's. Her team had played seven games in nine days, and she was ready to relax during the all-star break. Kirk, meanwhile, headed to Albuquerque, where he'd been chosen to coach the East squad in the All-Star Game.

Kunzmann stayed at Tiger Tom's until closing, then accepted a ride from Lance Tibke, a security guard at a nuclear plant whom she'd met once before.

He drove her to a cemetery, and she was never seen again.

When Tibke resurfaced, however, he had a black eye. On Feb. 10, he confessed to stabbing Kunzmann and beating her over the head with a tire iron during a fight at the cemetery. There he buried her jacket, now soaked with blood and it was found a week after her death. With the search hampered by blizzard conditions and temperatures of nearly 50 below zero, it would take seven weeks before Kunzmann's body was recovered. Tibke had dumped her body in the Missouri River, and it was finally recovered in late March after two boys found it tangled in the limbs of a tree that had fallen into the river.

Kirk and Bolin were in New Mexico for the league's All-Star Game when the news of Kunzmann's disappearance surfaced. (Bolin would lead all scorers with 29 points for a West team that also included Blazejowski and Lieberman in a lopsided 125-92 victory over Kirk's East squad).

"While we were at the All-Star Game, the third season, the next morning I received a call that she was missing," Bolin said. "Apparently the guy confessed, since his truck got stuck on the boat ramp in the ice and snow. It was extremely sad and tragic as she loved basketball as much as I did and did not get to experience winning the championship that year."

Demise and aftermath

Bolin continued her hot shooting after the all-star break, averaging 30 points a game from then until the end of the season and finishing second to Blazejowski in the race for the scoring title. The Pioneers, however, had won just one of their first six games by the time she arrived and finished the season out of the playoffs at 14-22. Still, the team could play with (and beat) the league's best teams. With the season winding down, Bolin and Hicks combined for 50 points in a 104-98 upset of eventual champion Nebraska.

In New Jersey, the Gems survived for a third season despite losing Meyers. The Gems replaced her by signing Blazejowski to an even bigger deal, for $150,000 over three years.

League owners fired Byrne as commissioner as the WBL contracted to nine teams, with inaugural champion Houston also folding. The California Dream's former owner tried again with a new team, the Nebraska Wranglers and another expansion team was added: the New England Gulls. But the Gulls echoed a familiar refrain by missing paychecks and folding up their tent after just 12 games, having lost 10 of them.

The Gems, with Blazejowski, had one of the league's biggest names, but again failed to even make the championship round, losing to a Dallas Diamonds team led by another of the league's stars, Nancy Lieberman, who averaged 26.3 points a game and won Rookie of the Year honors in her first WBL season. The Diamonds, in turn, fell to Nebraska in the championship round, after which the league called it quits.

Hicks attributed its failure to "not enough coverage" and "not enough fans to fill the gymnasium to keep us paid. I remember getting paid and told not to cash the checks until enough money was in the accounts for us to cash." What coverage there was, she said, "was always centered on a few players that stood out because of political reasons; however, players like myself knew and understood the love of the game and took a back seat."

Despite those drawbacks, the league left Hicks with plenty of fond memories:

"Playing with the best women in the world, who laid the ground for others to follow our dreams. Having to travel to different cities and staying in hotels and just bonding with some of the many players I had the pleasure of meeting. The crowds were not as big as we all would have liked; however, we were all so happy to be playing: We enjoyed the game, knowing we were pros. Feeling like a celebrity and working in communities when called upon to do positive things. I enjoyed being coached by the best and putting on shows with my ability to dunk, not knowing how special it was."

After the WBL folded, founder Byrne would try again. In 1984, again hoping to capitalize on the Olympics — where the U.S. team actually played this time, winning the gold medal — he put together another league: the Women's American Basketball Association.

Lieberman signed with the Dallas team, again called the Diamonds, that would have paid her $250,000 over three years if the league had survived. Bolin was offered just $6,000, about what she'd earned during her first WBL season, to join the Columbus Minks, representing Byrne's hometown, where the league offices were located.

She turned it down, but agreed to play after the team lost its first few games. Byrne sweetened the deal by putting her up at his own house so she wouldn't have any expenses.

The WABA started out with four other teams in addition to Dallas and Columbus: the

Atlanta Comets, Chicago Spirit, Houston Shamrocks and Virginia Waves. The Comets practiced at the zoo, and team member Kara Haun recalled 100 being a large home crowd. The team didn't have any uniforms, so one of the assistant coaches went to a store, bought 10 T-shirts and had red numbers screened onto them.

The Minks played their home games at the Fairgrounds Coliseum in Columbus, while the team stayed "for almost a month on an old Army base," Bolin said. "They didn't turn on the heat until a certain date, so we were all freezing and getting sick."

The highlight of the Minks' season was a 92-90 victory over Dallas, which had won its first 10 games. Bolin scored 19 points for the Minks in the game, which featured a marquee matchup with Lieberman and should have been a preview of the finals. The Minks held a firm grip in second place behind Dallas for most of the season, but the team drew anemic crowds of a few hundred spectators, and Byrne was forced out as commissioner. Bolin left the team after nine games, having suffered a dislocated shoulder for the third time in four months and a broken nose when she was hit during a game. The league ultimately disbanded the team with five games left on its schedule. In fact, only two of the six franchises managed to make it to season's end, leaving first-place Dallas to face sixth-place Chicago (which had finished 6-14) for the "championship." Unsurprisingly, Dallas won.

Two years later, Bolin signed to be assistant commissioner of another new league called the National Women's Basketball Association, which planned franchises in Des Moines, Knoxville, Monroe (Louisiana), Virginia Beach, Charlotte and Southern California. Olympic gold medalist Cheryl Miller was the top draft pick and was "placed on the California Stars by the league's office" a press report said, because coaches for the league hadn't been hired. Miller and the Stars, however, never played a game, nor did any other team in the league. It quickly amassed $150,000 in debt and folded.

Hicks went back to Europe, where she played in Sweden, Italy and France, which she described as "a very fast-paced game," until 1994. "I enjoyed it and wished I never had to retire." She switched to volleyball in 1996, playing on the U.S. national team and received a master's in psychology from the University of Phoenix. She founded a nonprofit organization called The Legends, which (according to its website) "works to empower children, foster families and individuals by building healthy bodies, strong minds and productive lives."

Bolin, who became embroiled in a nasty divorce and custody case, retired from the sport after the NWBA folded.

"It was a tough road wanting to be a player then," she said. "I played a lot of pickup games around Orange County — mostly against men — and hoping to get another shot as the years passed me by. The custody case and, later, raising my young son, prevented me from taking any offers to play basketball overseas and I never felt it was in his best interest for me to leave the country."

Lieberman became the first woman to compete for a men's pro team as a member of the Springfield Flame of Massachusetts in the United States Basketball League during the summer of 1986 and was also a member of the Harlem Globetrotters' foil, the Washington Generals. She hit the court again during the WNBA's first season, when she played for the Phoenix Mercury and was the league's oldest player at age 39. After she retired, she served as head coach of the NBA Development League's Texas Legends and an assistant for the NBA's Sacramento Kings, as well as serving as a broadcaster.

Other former WBL stars also remained in the public eye. Kaye Young stepped away from the sport to marry her college sweetheart, future Pittsburgh Steelers head coach Bill Cowher. She died of skin cancer in 2010 at the age of 54.

Meyers, the sister of Milwaukee Bucks player Dave Meyers, also married a legend from another sport: former Los Angeles Dodgers pitcher Don Drysdale. She became involved in broadcasting, serving as an analyst for WNBA games and, later, for the NBA's Indiana Pacers and Phoenix Suns, retiring from the latter post in 2018. Blazejowski served as an executive in the NBA and, from 1997 to 2010 with the New York Liberty of the WNBA.

Donna Geils, one of only 20 women to play all three seasons in the WBL, started her own production company and worked as an executive with the PGA Tour for 17 years. She also spent nearly six years as president of the WNBA.

1984 Women's American Basketball Association	W	L	Pct.
Dallas Diamonds	19	2	.905
Columbus Minks	12	5	.706
Atlanta Comets	7	6	.538
Virginia Wave	5	9	.357
Chicago Spirit	6	14	.300
Houston Shamrocks	3	14	.176

Dallas defeated Chicago for the championship.
Atlanta, Columbus, Virginia and Houston disbanded.

David vs. Goliath

Maybe, this time, women's basketball would find some staying power. In the mid-1990s, not one but two leagues emerged with the kind of potential not seen since the WBL. One would sign more top players, while the other would have the money and the marketing muscle of the men's National Basketball Association behind it.

The sport had already been through plenty of fits and starts.

After the collapse of two short-lived circuits in the 1980s, something called the Liberty Basketball Association emerged in 1991 to stage an exhibition before an announced crowd of 10,753 in Auburn Hills, Mich. It featured some odd innovations: a court 4 feet shorter than the one used in the NBA, a foul line closer to the rim and a shorter basket: 9 feet, 2 inches. The players also wore skin-tight, one-piece uniforms more like something you might see in a superhero movie than on the basketball court. The Detroit Dazzlers defeated a team of league all-stars 104-87.

In addition to the Dazzlers, first-year franchises were announced as the Chicago Slammers, Los Angeles Lancers, New York Blasters and Philadelphia Freedoms (the same name once used by a World Team Tennis outfit), with a sixth team to be named later. The Slammers' name was meant to be taken literally: With a 9-foot-2 basket, organizers expected to see players dunking the ball.

"Play above the rim excites fans," league founder Jim Drucker said. "The lower baskets create the style, speed and power that has made men's pro basketball so popular."

Drucker wasn't a newcomer to basketball. He'd served from 1978 to 1986 as commissioner of the Continental Basketball Association, which for a time became the premier second-tier men's league below the NBA. During Drucker's tenure, he expanded the league's membership from eight to 14 teams, secured its first television contract, and saw franchise values rise from $5,000 to $500,000. He also instituted a "7-Point System" for keeping track of the league's standings, with three points awarded for each game won and an additional point for each *quarter* won.

ESPN was to televise at least five regular-season games during the LBA's first season, with each team playing between 10 and 40 games.

The league, however, never got beyond that single exhibition. Organizers cited the flagging economy in announcing it would be put on hold for at least a year, and two years later, Drucker said he was in no rush to jump-start the dormant concept.

Nancy Lieberman said, "I think this would be a great time" to start a women's pro league. "It's just going to take more than a Jim Drucker. It's going to take the NBA."

Her assessment turned out to be prescient, but it would be a few more years.

In the meantime, a league called the Women's Basketball Association got further than Drucker did, playing three seasons starting in 1993, but the schedules consisted of just 15 games, mostly in small venues, and the league's footprint was limited to the Midwest (the Kansas Crusaders, Nebraska Express and Chicago Twisters each won a championship). The league struggled, even in Iowa, where a couple of games in 1994 drew "crowds" of 44 and 125. It started out with six teams in its first season, then expanded to eight and had plans to become a national 12-team league in 1997.

Molly Bolin, the WBL's all-time leading scorer, was involved in trying to make that happen.

"I had been meeting with the president of Liberty Sports (no connection to the Liberty Basketball Association), who wanted a women's league as they expanded cable sports programming back in 1996," she said. "We were in talks to get a new league together when the NBA made announcement that the WNBA was being formed. Then Liberty was bought out by Fox Sports and all my 'free' time and efforts to help a new league get off the ground were for nothing."

Fox didn't share Liberty's vision for the league and, rather than competing with WNBA, pulled the plug.

Olympic springboard

Another group, however, didn't have the same reservations: organizers of a new circuit called the American Basketball League. Like the WBL before it, the ABL was formed to capitalize on a surge in popularity for the sport tied to the Olympic Games, where the U.S. team went undefeated to capture the 1996 gold medal in Atlanta. The league signed a number of stars from the Olympic team and placed a franchise in Atlanta with a nickname ("Glory") pegged to Olympic success. The team would play its home games in a 5,700-seat arena at Morehouse College that had been built for the Games, and the Glory's marquee player was Teresa Edwards, a Georgia native who had played in four Olympics herself.

The ABL hoped that, by getting a one-year head start on the WNBA, it could gain a clear advantage. Unlike the WNBA, which would play its games during the summer, it announced a more traditional fall-winter schedule, with eight teams in two divisions: the Glory, Columbus Quest, New England Blizzard and Richmond Rage in the East, with the Colorado Xplosion, Portland Power, San Jose Lasers and Seattle Reign in the West.

Nikki McCray, a member of the gold-medal Olympic team, scored 24 points for Columbus in the ABL's first game, as the Quest beat Colorado 87-76 before 5,300 fans in Springfield, Mo. The Quest would build on that success to win titles in each of the ABL's two years, with McCray winning MVP honors in its inaugural season.

The ABL as a whole seemed to be building momentum by its second season, with attendance up 23 percent. It added an expansion franchise, the Long Beach StingRays, and was signing some of the sport's top names. Among them: Olympian Katrina McClain in Atlanta and Kara Wolters, center for the unbeaten University of Connecticut team, who stayed close to home by signing with the New England Blizzard.

The Blizzard, which also signed UConn star Jennifer Rizzotti, capitalized on the hometown heroes' presence by building a strong local following. Although they played some of their games before just a few thousand spectators in Springfield, Mass., they drew big crowds when they played in Connecticut, averaging nearly 7,500 fans during their first season and pulling in a league-record 11,878 for a game in Hartford against San Jose. (The team would hire former Boston Celtics head coach K.C. Jones as its head coach the following season.)

League co-founder Gary Cavalli was pleased with the league's ability to sign so many top stars after its inaugural draft, especially with the WNBA tipping off before the ABL's second season. When it came to the signing war, the ABL was the clear winner.

"I wouldn't go so far as to characterize it as a landslide," Cavalli said, but "we identified 13 players out of college we felt we should have. ... Of the 13 we identified, we signed eight. The WNBA signed three."

The Glory signed 1995 college player of the year Saudia Roundtree from the University of Georgia, and 1996 award winner Kate Starbird from Stanford, joined the Seattle Reign. Two-time winner Dawn Staley (1991 and 1992), an Olympian from the University of Virginia, signed with the Richmond Rage.

Still, once the WNBA tipped off, it was clear who had the advantage with the fans. Nancy Lieberman, who signed to play in the WNBA, characterized it as "David and Goliath," with the ABL in the underdog role. And Cavalli himself admitted: "It's been very stressful. For every top player signed, it's been a battle going up against the most successful, prestigious basketball machine in the world."

Part of that stress came from player salaries. You get what you pay for, and in order to attract the nation's top talent, the ABL had to offer big bucks: Specifically, the league's minimum salary of $40,000 wasn't too far below the WNBA's *maximum* of $50,000. The average ABL salary during its third season was $90,000, three times what the average WNBA player made.

Despite its head start, the ABL was also at a disadvantage when it came to exposure. Notably, the league was absent from nine of the nation's 10 largest metro areas (San Jose being the exception), and lacked the kind of television contract the WNBA was able to land. The WNBA had games televised on NBC, ESPN and Lifetime, while the ABL had a game of the week on Black Entertainment Television and a deal with Prime Sports. The WNBA's first game featured teams in the nation's two biggest television markets: the New York Liberty and Los Angeles Sparks.

"The WNBA has been more of a marketing success and the ABL more of a competitive success," Marc Ganis of the Chicago sports consulting firm Sportscap told *The Baltimore Sun* in August of 1997, by which time each league had one season under its belt. Despite the ABL's advantage in terms of talent, the WNBA's television exposure and larger markets gave it a big advantage at the gate: It drew an average of more than 9,500 fans a game, nearly three times the average for the ABL.

One measure of the contrast: When the ABL expanded into Southern California with the StingRays in its second season, it put itself in direct competition with the Los Angeles Sparks of the WNBA. The Sparks, run by Lakers owner Jerry Buss, played at the NBA team's home arena, the 17,500-seat Great Western Forum in Inglewood. The StingRays toiled in the Pyramid, capacity 4,200, on the Cal State Long Beach campus.

L.A. Times columnist Bill Plaschke covered the StingRays' opening 98-91 victory over the rival San Jose Lasers, noting that Long Beach was "clearly superior to the Los Angeles Sparks," who hadn't scored that many points in any of their games the previous season. But the crowd of 3,108 on hand for the StingRays' opener was barely half the size of the smallest crowd the Sparks had drawn (5,987) the year before.

A fan named Anita Fitzgerald who attended the StingRays' opener concurred: "The play was incredible. They had much better players than the Sparks." She added, however, that "compared to the Sparks, it felt like a high school game."

"The best women's pro basketball team in the Southland," Plaschke concluded, "is big, fast and wondrously skilled. It also may be doomed."

Plaschke was right on both counts. The StingRays, led by ABL Defensive Player of the Year Yolanda Griffith, were so good, they finished second in the Western Conference at 26-

18 before defeating Colorado and Portland to reach the finals. There, they won their first two games at home before dropping three straight to the defending champions in Columbus and losing the best-of-five series.

The StingRays, however, folded after the season, victims of meager marketing and lackluster fan support. The Atlanta Glory also went out of business.

StingRays General Manager Bill McGillis later called his team's failure inevitable: "With no significant TV income, the math just doesn't work," he said. "If we had sold out every game in Long Beach, we still wouldn't have broken even."

Yolanda Griffith moved to another new team, the Chicago Condors, one of two expansion teams the ABL added (along with the Nashville Noise) to replace the Glory and StingRays for its third season. The Condors were one of the league's few forays into a major market — and turned out to be its last. They almost didn't get off the ground at all. On the day she was poised to announce the new team's name, General Manager Allison Hodges said, she received an ominous phone call from Cavalli telling her not to bother.

The league, he said, was "going under."

Cavalli called back a few minutes later and told her not to worry, after all: "I think we're OK."

Hodges did a good job selling the team to the Windy City, which also had supported the Chicago Hustle in the WBL. At nearly 5,000 fans a game, the Condors ranked second in attendance among the league's nine teams despite losing eight of their first 12 games. Hodges struck a deal for local radio coverage, but the league nixed the idea because it was trying to get a national radio contract — a contract that never materialized.

Hodges' team was $13,000 in the hole, but was expecting to cover that with $21,000 in merchandise sales. It never received that money, though, because the league declared bankruptcy just before Christmas of 1998 and liquidated its assets, grounding the Condors and the other eight teams for good. The all-star game, scheduled for January, was canceled, too.

Survivors

The WNBA, meanwhile, was still standing. It continues to operate 22 years after its founding. A number of players wound up with the WNBA, including former StingRay Yolanda Griffith, who made an immediate splash by winning the MVP and Defensive Player of the Year awards in her first season with Sacramento. She went on to earn all-star honors seven times.

StingRays head coach Maura McHugh also wound up in Sacramento, where she served as an assistant for the Monarchs beginning in 1999, then as head coach from 2001 to 2003. The Seattle Reign's Kate Starbird, who was shooting 43 percent from 3-point range when the ABL folded, landed with the Monarchs, as well, and played in the WNBA for four seasons.

"A lot of us realized that the ABL was a risky venture, but I believed in what the ABL was about," Starbird said when she learned the league had folded. "This summer, I was a little scared, but I really believed we'd play out the season. It was a shock today to get the phone call that we wouldn't be playing anymore."

Dawn Staley, the two-time college player of the year, was a first-team all-ABL choice in 1997 and a second-team selection in 1998. She went on to even more success in the WNBA, where she led the Charlotte Sting to the championship round in 2001 and to the conference finals each of the next two seasons. She was voted one of the top 15 players in league history in 2011.

Nikki McCray caught on with the Washington Mystics and played for five WNBA teams through 2006, earning all-star honors in her first three seasons. Andrea Nagy, who finished third on the ABL's assist chart with the StingRays, played a couple of seasons in Washington, as well, and four seasons in all. In her final year, she was reunited with her former coach, McHugh, on the Monarchs roster.

Jennifer Rizzotti played five seasons in the WNBA, with Houston and Cleveland. Her Blizzard teammate, Kara Wolters (the tallest player in UConn women's basketball history at 6-foot-7) went to Houston, as well, and played four seasons in all with the Comets, Indiana and Sacramento.

Among others making the leap: Jennifer Azzi of the San Jose Lasers, who played one year with the Detroit Shock before ending her career with three seasons on the Utah Starzz/San Antonio Silver Stars. Sheri Sam, also of the Lasers, played with seven different teams before retiring in 2008.

Edna Campbell of the Colorado Xplosion, who played six seasons with Seattle, Sacramento and San Antonio, continued her career despite being diagnosed with breast cancer; she later authored *The Breast Cancer Recovery Manual*. Debbie Black, Campbell's teammate in Colorado, played in the WNBA until 2005, as did Adrienne Goodson of the Chicago Condors and Natalie Williams of the Portland Power

Atlanta Glory star Teresa Edwards didn't play in the WNBA until 2003, when the Minnesota Lynx drafted her even though she was 38 years old; she played there for the next two seasons and later served as an assistant coach for three different teams (including a stint as interim head coach in Tulsa).

The success of the ABL's New England Blizzard at the gate seems to have caught the eye of the WNBA, which chose Connecticut as the new home for its Orlando franchise in 2003. It was the first time the league located a franchise in a non-NBA market.

1997–98 American Basketball League	W	L	Pct.
Eastern Conference			
Columbus Quest	36	8	.818
New England Blizzard	24	20	.545
Atlanta Glory	15	29	.340
Philadelphia Rage	13	31	.295
Western Conference			
Portland Power	27	17	.613
Long Beach StingRays	26	18	.591
San Jose Lasers	21	23	.477
Colorado Xplosion	21	23	.340
Seattle Reign	15	29	.340

Columbus d. Long Beach 3 games to 2 for the championship.

Part III
Football

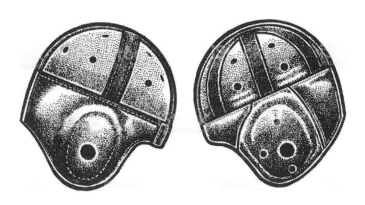

Red, Maroon and Honolulu Blue

Sports leagues in the prewar era bore little resemblance to their modern counterparts. Even one of the most audacious promoters of that day — a man named C.C. "Cash and Carry" Pyle — would have found himself in a state of shock had he been transported to Glendale, Ariz., for the 2015 Super Bowl.

This was an era before routine transcontinental flights, before billion-dollar stadiums, collective bargaining, steroids and cable television … or any television, for that matter. Baseball was king, and it provided the only semblance of stability in terms of league structure. Football and basketball, the other two legs of the "big three" in the American sporting triumvirate, remained largely regional affairs. Teams played in modest facilities and, often, small towns; many of them were sponsored by local businesses in much the same way the town barbershop or dry cleaner might sponsor a Little League team today.

The Green Bay Packers were first sponsored by a packing company, and basketball's Detroit Pistons don't owe their name to the Motor City's auto industry. They started out playing in Fort Wayne, Indiana, where team owner Fred Zollner employed more than 1,000 people making (naturally) pistons at his foundry. The team was, for many years, known as the Zollner Pistons.

Company teams and industrial leagues were common in the prewar period, when barnstorming was still in vogue and teams banded together to form loosely organized "associations." Schedules were cobbled together, with some teams playing only a few games and others booking a full slate. Some would disappear at midseason, unable to keep their commitments to the league or their players. Others might play exhibitions against traveling teams or interleague games that didn't count in the standings, in addition to their league commitments.

Leagues came and went with almost alarming regularity, appearing to great pomp and promise, then dissolving as teams dropped out, fortunes changed or fans lost interest. The National Football League had been born as a regional league, centered in the Northeast and Midwest. The charter member Decatur Staleys were sponsored by the Staley Starch

Company before they moved to Chicago and became the Bears, and the Duluth Kelleys (later the Eskimos) had the backing of the Kelley-Duluth Hardware Store when they joined the league in 1923.

1926 American Football League	W	L	T	PF	PA	Pct.
Philadelphia Quakers	8	2	0	93	52	.800
New York Yankees	10	5	0	212	82	.667
Cleveland Panthers	3	2	0	62	46	.600
Los Angeles Wildcats	6	6	2	105	83	.500
Chicago Bulls	5	6	3	88	69	.455
Boston Bulldogs	2	4	0	20	81	.333
Rock Island Independents	2	6	1	21	126	.250
Brooklyn Horsemen	1	3	0	25	68	.250
Newark Bears	0	3	2	7	26	.000

The NFL's first challenger

The league had played just six seasons when the aforementioned C.C. Pyle decided to offer an alternative, the first in a handful of leagues to go by the name American Football League in the prewar era. They had little or no relationship to one another and none to the most successful circuit under that name, which kicked off much later in 1960. But baseball's National League could exist alongside its American League counterpart, so who was to say the same arrangement wasn't possible in football? Pyle thought the country was ready, and he was just the guy to pull it off — or so he thought.

Pyle was a Chicago theater owner, sports agent and promoter extraordinaire. Among other things, he organized the first professional tennis tour, booking major arenas to showcase the likes of Suzanne Lenglen — winner of six Wimbledon singles titles — and three-time U.S. singles champion Mary K. Browne alongside four male tennis players. That was in 1926, and Pyle had developed the idea to promote the career of Lenglen, one of his clients.

That same year, he launched an even more ambitious project featuring an even more famous client: Harold "Red" Grange.

Grange had been a high school track and field star, also lettering in basketball, baseball and football. In his college career at the University of Illinois, the three-time All-American was so dominant that he averaged 168 yards per game rushing, not to mention his exploits passing, returning kicks and catching the ball. Known as "The Galloping Ghost" for the lightning quick running style that enabled him to elude tacklers with stunning frequency on the football field, Grange was a star of the highest order, even making the cover of *Time* magazine in 1925 ... and Pyle felt he deserved a contract of the highest order as a reward.

"This man Red Grange of Illinois is three or four men rolled into one for football purposes," sportswriter Damon Runyon gushed. "He is Jack Dempsey, Babe Ruth, Al Jolson, Paavo Nurmi and Man o' War. Put together, they spell Grange."

The Chicago Bears, who signed him to his first pro contract, took Grange on a 19-game barnstorming tour across the country that drew huge crowds and earned the Ghost $100,000. But that stupendous sum only whetted Pyle's appetite. He tried to get Grange part ownership of the team, but when Bears owner/coach George Halas balked at the idea of relinquishing that level of control, Pyle hatched another plan: He would apply to the NFL for a new team in the Big Apple. When league president Tim Mara nixed that idea, Pyle went one step further and decided to create an entirely new league built around his larger-than-life client.

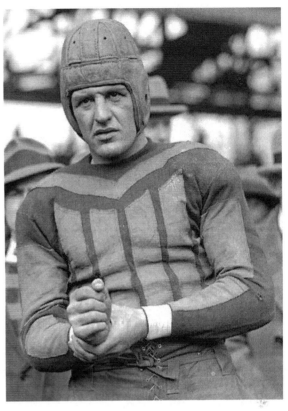

Red Grange in 1925, a year before he joined the first AFL as a member of the New York Yankees football team.

A year before the New York Yankees turned in arguably the most storied season in baseball history, Pyle rented their home field to showcase the Babe Ruth of football and created a team (called the Yankees, of course) to surround him. Then he organized a league of teams in major markets such as Cleveland, Philadelphia, Chicago and Boston. There was even a team representing Los Angeles, but the Wildcats — named for another Pyle client, University of Washington halfback George "Wildcat" Wilson — didn't play any games on the West Coast; they were a traveling team that used the Hollywood image to further burnish the league's big-time credentials.

The Wildcats were actually based in Rock Island, Illinois, home of another league team, the Independents, who had jumped from the NFL into the arms of the new league.

It was a move they quickly regretted.

Although Grange drew big crowds wherever he played, attendance for games not involving the Ghost was meager. The Brooklyn Horsemen, who took their name from two members of Notre Dame's famed "Four Horsemen," Harry Stuldreher and Elmer Layden, lasted just four games — three of them losses — before folding. The Newark Demons, winless in five starts, and Cleveland Panthers threw in the towel a week later, and the Boston Bulldogs dropped out a week after that. By season's end, only four of the original nine teams were still playing football, among them the homeless Wildcats. And, adding insult to injury, Grange's Yankees weren't even the best of those that remained. The Philadelphia Quakers closed their season with back-to-back victories over the Yankees to claim the title, then went down in ignominious fashion to the NFL's seventh-place team, the New York Giants, in a 31-0 postseason clash.

It was the last game a team from the AFL's first incarnation would ever play.

Grange went back to the Bears, where he played six more seasons, never again the dominant force he had once been.

An uncrowned champion

But the failure of the AFL didn't mark the end of challenges to the rival league, which despite its decisive victory over Pyle's upstarts was a far cry from the singular behemoth it is today. The league's 1926 roster of teams was bloated at 22 teams, which played schedules that ranged from four to 17 games. By the next season, membership had plummeted to a dozen, with one team playing five games and another 18.

Other games during the era were played against teams outside the league, some of which were every bit as good as their NFL counterparts even though they played in less formal associations such as the Ohio Valley League and the Anthracite League. The latter circuit consisted of five teams within roughly 10 miles of one another in Pennsylvania's coal country (hence the league name). The most successful of the bunch were the Maroons of Pottsville, a town of fewer than 25,000 not to be confused with the similarly sized Pottstown down the road, site of a different but also very successful football team a half-century later.

The Maroons, owned by a local surgeon named Doc Striegel, signed three players from the 1923 NFL champion Canton Bulldogs, then proceeded to go undefeated — allowing just a single touchdown all season — and clinch the 1924 Anthracite League title in their second season. The league promptly collapsed, and the Maroons stepped up to join the NFL ... and promptly won the league championship there, as well. Or so it appeared at the time.

The Maroons capped a hugely successful season by defeating their nearest competitor, the Chicago Cardinals, earning the right to play a lucrative game against the recently graduated Notre Dame All-Stars, the cream of the crop in collegiate football. The Frankford Yellowjackets, another strong franchise, based in Philadelphia, had been salivating over the opportunity to play against an Irish team featuring the "Four Horsemen." The Jackets, playing more games that season than any other NFL team, racked up 13 wins, but also suffered seven losses — including a 49-0 drubbing at the hands of the Maroons, whom they had defeated earlier in the season.

As owners of the league's best record, the "Anthracite Terrors" were the logical choice to face the Notre Dame stars. But when they proceeded to schedule the game against Notre Dame, not in Pottsville but in Philadelphia, the already embittered Yellowjackets flew into a rage. Philadelphia, they argued, was their home turf, and Pottsville had no right to play there.

The Maroons, on the other hand, had every motivation to do just that. Their own home field, at Minersville High School, seated only 5,000 fans, while Philly's major league baseball stadium, Shibe Park, was more than six times its size. A bigger venue meant the chance to sell more tickets and, consequently, make more money, so the Maroons were determined to play the game. NFL President Joe Carr, however, took the Yellowjackets' side in the dispute and warned Doc Striegel that his team would be kicked out of the league if it followed through with its plans.

Striegel didn't take kindly to being bullied, saying the league had granted permission for the game to go forward, only to change its tune after the contract was signed.

"I could not abrogate the contract honorably after it was made," Striegel said. And so, he defied Carr and played the game anyway.

It was a rousing success: 10,000 people showed up to watch a thrilling contest, as the Notre Dame stars thoroughly outplayed the Maroons in the first half, building a 7-0 lead. At halftime, according to one account, a telegram arrived from Carr at the NFL office with the news that he was fining the Maroons $500 and suspending their franchise, rendering them ineligible for the league title they had won on the field but had yet to be formally awarded.

The team responded with a vengeance, taking the field in the second half with "the gentle demeanor of Hyrcanian tigers during Lent," as one account put it.

The Maroons scored on a 17-yard touchdown pass but missed a chance to tie the score when Charles Berry's conversion attempt struck the crossbar and ricocheted back. In the end, however, Berry transformed himself from the goat into the hero. Pottsville drove into Notre

Dame territory with less than a minute to play and, unable to advance any further, gave Berry a chance to redeem himself. Once again, the kicker trotted out onto the field, and this time, he made good, atoning for his earlier miss with a 30-yard field goal that split the uprights and won the game.

If there had been any doubt who owned the best team in the NFL during the 1925 season, the win over Notre Dame erased it. The victory was a defining moment, not just for Pottsville, but for pro football as a whole, which gained a shot of credibility by proving it could compete with the much more popular college athletes of the day. But the NFL's top brass made good on its threat to suspend the Pottsville franchise and ordered the second-place Chicago Cardinals to play two more games and pad their record so their winning percentage would surpass that of the Maroons.

Those games were against the hapless Milwaukee Badgers and Hammond Pros, who between them had won just one of the 11 league games they'd played. To make matters worse, both teams had already disbanded for the season, and the Badgers even brought in four high school players from Englewood High School in Chicago to play under assumed names against the Cardinals. The result was predictable: The Cards scored 32 points in the fourth quarter alone and demolished the "Badgers" 58-0, adding another shutout two days later against Hammond to climb above Pottsville in the standings.

Pottsville's franchise was reinstated into the NFL the following season, when the Maroons finished a strong third behind the Yellowjackets (whom they played to a 0-0 tie) and the Bears. The franchise went into decline after that, eventually moving to Boston for one year before folding after the 1929 season. The bitterness over the city's "stolen" championship, however, lived on long after the team's demise.

No less a figure than Red Grange stated bluntly, "They won the championship in 1925 but were robbed of the honour by some misguided judgement."

Johnny McNally, another early standout and Hall of Famer who played for the Green Bay Packers, concurred: "Championships are won and lost on the field, and Pottsville won it there in 1925. The Cardinals were defeated in an honest contest by Pottsville and should not claim a championship they didn't win. I support the Maroons as the true champs of 1925."

In 1963, a committee representing members of the '25 Maroons informed the NFL that its collection of memorabilia would be withheld from the Hall of Fame unless the team was awarded the championship retroactively.

"We will donate our collection to the Hall of Fame Under one condition only," Pottsville businessman Joseph C. Zacko said. "And that is that the Pottsville Maroons must be recognized as the 1925 professional football world champions. The record books must be changed to correct the injustice perpetrated by the National Football League."

But the NFL didn't like being bullied any more than Doc Striegel had, and its owners voted 12-2 to retain the status quo. When the issue was reopened again in 2003, owners voted again (this time 30-2) against recognizing the Maroons as champions. This was despite the fact that the Cardinals' owner at the time refused to accept the championship, labeling it "bogus." It was, one report states, only after the team's ownership changed hands in 1933 that it began to claim the championship as its own.

According to some, the club's "theft" of the 1925 title from Pottsville activated a curse against the Cardinals franchise, which managed to win just one more title, in 1947. As of this writing, it has since gone 67 years without a championship, the longest streak in the NFL and the second-longest current drought in American professional sports, trailing only the Chicago Cubs.

1929 Ohio Valley League	W	L	T	PF	PA	Pct.
Portsmouth Spartans	12	2	1	352	22	.857
Ashland Amoco Yellowjackets	8	2	1	243	46	.800
Cincinnati National Guards	7	2	1	129	57	.778
Akron Awnings	8	3	1	109	62	.727
Ironton Tanks	5	6	0	138	85	.455
Middletown Armco Blues	3	5	1	47	119	.375
Chillicothe Eagles	3	7	0	91	84	.300

The Ohio Valley League

After the demise of the Anthracite League, another regional alliance of football clubs formed to provide top-level competition on the gridiron, this time in the Ohio Valley. The league, which lasted five seasons in the latter half of the 1920s, fielded a lineup that fluctuated between five and seven teams, playing in such industrial towns as Middletown, headquarters of the Armco steel company, which sponsored a team there and another in Ashland. Cincinnati, the largest city in the league, fielded a team called the Potters which was sponsored by Potter's Shoes and, later, by the local National Guard.

Two teams that played within about 25 miles of each other along the banks of the Ohio River would wind up having a lasting impact on the history of the sport. One was the three-time champion Ironton Tanks, who scored several victories over NFL teams during their history. The other was a team that began its existence under the guidance of legendary Olympian Jim Thorpe, the Portsmouth Shoe-Steels, whose name paid homage to its joint sponsorship by a shoe company and a steel mill.

Portsmouth, which won the league's final championship in 1929, developed a rivalry with Ironton that would have a profound impact on the history of the football games watched each year on Turkey Day in living rooms across the country.

Earlier, Thorpe had led the Canton Bulldogs to three Ohio state pro championships in four years and had taken the team from there into the newly formed American Professional Football Association in 1920. He had served nominally as president of the new league, where the Bulldogs won consecutive titles in 1922 and '23 (without Thorpe on the roster) — by which time it had changed its name to the National Football League. The team's successes in the league's formative years spurred the league to establish its Hall of Fame in the city of Canton even though it no longer fielded an NFL team.

By the time Thorpe signed on with Portsmouth in 1927, his career was winding down. At 39, he served as player-coach of the Shoe-Steels, but even though he was playing sick, he still managed to rush for 20 yards in a November showdown with Ironton, the defending champion — one more than the Shoe-Steels allowed the entire opposing side — in grinding out a 7-0 upset over the Tanks. The victory vaulted the Shoe-Steels into title contention, and they set up a Dec. 4 showdown with the league-leading Ashland Armcos with the title on the line.

Unfortunately for the Shoe-Steels, Thorpe's contract called for him to stay with the team for 10 games, and the contest with the Armcos would be No. 11. Thorpe promised to play the game anyway if he were able to reach an agreement with the Portsmouth owners, but he apparently never came to terms with them. Instead, he left at the end of November to check on a dog kennel he owned in Marion, Ohio, and never returned. He only played one pro football once more after that, a single game for the Chicago Cardinals the following season, and Portsmouth nearly beat Ashland without him. The Shoe-Steels held a 6-0 lead after three quarters before the Armcos returned a punt 54 yards to the 1-yard-line midway through the final period, then punched it in for a touchdown and nailed the decisive extra point.

The following year, the Portsmouth squad was back for more, without Thorpe and with a new, less awkward-sounding name: the Spartans. This time, they finished ahead of Ashland in the standings but couldn't match the Tanks, who beat them 14-0 in the season's final game. The Spartans finally broke through in 1929, as Ironton went through a down year and Portsmouth finished the season with 10 straight wins to claim the championship. It turned out to be the league's last hurrah, as it dissolved following the season, while the Spartans parlayed their success into an application for membership in the NFL.

It was accepted.

The Tanks, meanwhile, soldiered on as an independent club, scheduling games against opponents whenever and wherever they could find them. Even though they weren't members of the NFL, half of their 10 games came against members of the elite circuit, and they won three of those — a winning percentage that would have been good enough to tie them for fifth place in the 11-team league that year. The Tanks were coached by Greasy Neale, a future Hall of Famer who would later coach the Philadelphia Eagles to a pair of NFL championships. Under his guidance, they edged the NFL's second-best team, the New York Giants, 13-12, behind a pair of touchdown passes from star halfback Glenn Presnell — including one that tied the score with just 3 seconds left. Presnell then capped the comeback by kicking the game-winning extra point.

A few weeks later, the Tanks beat the third-place Chicago Bears decisively, 26-13.

But the Tanks' first two games against NFL clubs actually came against their old adversaries, the Spartans, with each team winning one of them by a single point.

To say that the Tanks-Spartans rivalry was fiercely contested would be an understatement. *Portsmouth Times* writer H. Coleman Grimes declared in 1929 that "the rivalry in the old days was as bitter as a feud between two of the fightingest clans in history." And his colleague at the *Times*, Dick Young, called the midseason game between the two squads in 1929 "the roughest football game ever played," contending the Tanks "devised every means known to football to injure Portsmouth and remove the stars from the game. Leg-twisting, slugging and kneeing were the main Tank objective."

The officials, Young wrote, turned a blind eye to the carnage.

That set up the rubber match on the final game of the season, set for Thanksgiving, Nov. 27. The Thanksgiving Day game had become a tradition for the Tanks, who had first played on the holiday in 1920 and had done so every year starting in 1922.

Spartans to Lions

Presnell, who still lived in Ironton when he died in 2004, less than 11 months shy of his 100th birthday, ended up going over to "the enemy" and playing for the Spartans after the Tanks gave up the ghost. He led the league in total yardage with 1,296 yards in 1933 and the following year kicked a 54-yard field goal that endured as a league record for nearly two decades. He was even responsible for choosing the team's new colors after the team left

Portsmouth for the big city lights that same year. Indianapolis and Columbus had both courted the team, but it would end up moving farther north instead — to Detroit.

The team had worn purple in Portsmouth, but new owner George Richards wanted a different look.

"Mr. Richards, the owner, the day I was up there and signed my contract, he said, 'There's a table out there in that next office covered with uniforms. Why don't you pick out the colors you like?'" Presnell recalled in a 2002 interview. "I went out — my wife was with me — we saw this Honolulu blue and silver, and we fell in love with it."

The Detroit Lions' colors remain the same to this day. And, just like their long-ago rivals from Ironton, they play a game every Thanksgiving Day.

Portsmouth Stadium, home of the Spartans, who played in the Ohio Valley League and the NFL before moving to Detroit and becoming the Lions.

NFL Wannabes

Most of the chapters in this book focus on failed leagues, but this one's a little different: It concerns a failed team that played in no fewer than three such leagues but was, in spite of that, anything but a failure.

The Los Angeles Bulldogs were born of a dream that would have brought NFL football to the West Coast before World War II. They were so successful that, in just their second season, they became the first major pro football team to compile a perfect record, going 8-0 in league play to win the championship of the second American Football League (the first being the one built around Red Grange).

In their first five years of existence, the Bulldogs went 39-7-4, and in 13 seasons, and posted a losing record just twice.

Yet somehow their success failed to land them the prize they most coveted: a spot in the NFL. They had the Cleveland Rams to thank for that … but more on that later.

Not only did the Bulldogs have a big-league vision, that had a brand-new playing field. Gilmore Stadium, was just two years old when the team began playing its games there in 1936. It seated 18,000 people, which may not seem like much when considering the L.A. Coliseum could accommodate crowds of more than 100,000, but pro football was nothing like the drawing card it is today. On the gridiron, college was king, and while USC and UCLA might come close to packing the Coliseum, pro teams were lucky to get a fraction of that support. In fact, Gilmore could have accommodated all the fans who attended NFL championship games in 1935, 1937 and 1941 in its single-deck horseshoe-shaped bleachers.

The man behind the stadium was E.B. Gilmore, whose father had been a real-life Jed Clampett. Arthur F. Gilmore had purchased a small plot of land west of downtown Los Angeles for his dairy. One day, he was out digging for water for his herd when the struck something else instead.

Oil.

Gilmore soon shifted his focus away from the dairy and started building derricks on the land instead. Before long, Gilmore owned one of the most successful oil companies in California, which ultimately grew to include a network of 3,500 independent service stations that sold "Blu-Green" gas under the red lion logo.

Gilmore's son took over the company in 1918 and took it to new heights. Earl Gilmore knew how to generate publicity. Inviting customers to "roar with Gilmore," he hired aviator Roscoe Turner to barnstorm up and down California with a real lion cub as his copilot. He sponsored a radio show, a song contest and Indy 500 drivers, among other things, putting the Gilmore name on all of it. In 1934, he built an outdoor stadium at Third and Fairfax, and slapped his name on that, too. It would become part of a major complex that also included Gilmore's Farmers Market (which opened later that year) and Gilmore Field for baseball (1939). The Farmers Market is still open today.

At Gilmore Stadium, auto racing was the big attraction — which made sense considering the business Gilmore was in. Football games, however, had also been part of the plans from the beginning. Plans called for the stadium to host games involving Cumnock School of Expression, where several USC players had attended before moving on to college, and the first mention of the project in the *Los Angeles Times* stated that Cumnock planned to lease the property from Gilmore for just this purpose.

Not long afterward, pro football was added to the schedule.

Pacific dreams

Two months before the stadium opened to motorcycle racing in May of 1934, an insurance broker named Thomas F. Bailey had announced the formation of the Pacific Football League. He'd been encouraged by a series of exhibitions in January featuring the world champion Chicago Bears at Los Angeles' Wrigley Field. A crowd of 20,000 had turned out in mid-January to watch the Bears defeat a team of West Coast all-stars 26-7. The visitors' star attraction, none other than Red Grange, scored one touchdown on a 67-yard run and another on a long catch-and-run play for the Bears.

Another game was scheduled for two weeks later, and the ticket office at Wrigley reported the heaviest demand for reserved tickets in the history of the ballpark. The crowd, in fact, turned out to be even bigger than it had been for the first game, with estimates ranging from 25,000 to 30,000. The result, however, the same, with the Bears winning this time by a score of 23-0. Southern California clearly had an appetite for professional football.

One headline from the first game described the Bears as doing "missionary work" on the Pacific Coast, and if that was the case, Bailey was converted: "The enthusiastic reception given the professional football games here in January by fans encouraged the establishment of a league on the West Coast," he declared.

Bailey's idea was simple: Give college graduates a chance to continue playing together after their college eligibility ran out. (And make some money in the process.)

"By pitting outstanding stars of each university against one another, we believe school rivalry will be maintained in the professional games," he said.

Eight teams were announced: four each in Southern California and the Bay Area. Teams in the south would be made up of players from USC, UCLA, Loyola and Santa Clara, while those in the north would fill their rosters from Stanford, Cal, USF and St. Mary's grads. Organizers said 28 college stars had already been signed, including star Southern Cal back Homer Griffith, who had accounted for the first two touchdowns of the Trojans' 1933 Rose Bowl triumph. Players from the winning team would get $75 after each game, with $50 going to each member of the losing team, and according to one source, there was even talk of a postseason title game against the NFL champion.

That proto-Super Bowl never came off. Griffith wound up playing for the Chicago Cardinals instead that year, and ultimately only six teams competed in the Pacific League (the USF and St. Mary's franchises having dropped out). Plans for a 10-game season never came to fruition, with teams playing anywhere from two to five games. The Berkeley Giants won the title with a 3-0 record, while the Southern California Maroons took second at 3-1-1, followed by the Westwood Cubs at 2-1-1.

Despite the success of the January exhibitions, the league games didn't draw nearly as well as Bailey had hoped, and ticket sales couldn't support the league's guaranteed player payments. These were eventually dropped, and players were instead paid a percentage of the gate. All three Southern California teams played games at Gilmore Stadium; in one case, a game between the Cubs and Del Ray Shamrocks served as the opening act for a Cumnock Academy high school game.

The season petered out then came to a less-than-glorious end when the NFL's Chicago Cardinals defeated four league teams on a West Coast swing, trouncing the Maroons 41-7 at Gilmore and shutting out the Berkeley Giants 21-0 — after the Giants refused to take the field unless they were paid in advance.

Despite such ominous sings, the league returned the following season with just four teams, all in the Southern California area (the Stanford Braves having moved to Hollywood). The American Legion stepped in to sponsor it, and the formal name was changed to the American Legion Football League ... although it was normally referred to as simply the Los Angeles pro league. The 1935 season lasted a little longer, with teams playing four to seven league contests and the Cubs beating the Maroons by a half-game to claim the title.

The American Legion disbanded the league at season's end, turning its attention to a new endeavor: It wanted a franchise in the National Football League. To this end, it hired a general manager named Harry Myers and gave him a $10,000 budget to field a new team, the Los Angeles Bulldogs, who were given a "probationary franchise" in the NFL. Myers hired former USC coach "Gloomy Gus" Henderson, more recently of the University of Iowa, to run the team, which scheduled a series of games as an independent team in 1936.

1937 American Football League	W	L	T	PF	PA	Pct.
Los Angeles Bulldogs	8	0	0	219	69	1.000
Rochester Tigers	3	3	1	94	115	.500
New York Yankees	2	3	1	57	115	.400
Cincinnati Bengals	2	3	2	102	89	.400
Boston Shamrocks	2	5	0	76	98	.286
Pittsburgh Americans	0	3	0	7	69	.000

The second AFL

But Myers' group wasn't the only one with big plans that year. A former New York Giants executive had already announced plans for a new league to rival the NFL. The name he chose came to be almost a cliché over the years, because it was used by so many rival leagues: the American Football League. This wasn't Red Grange's AFL of the 1920s, and it wasn't the AFL that would ultimately force a merger with the NFL in the 1960s. It was the brainchild of Harry March, a medical doctor who'd attended high school in the cradle of professional football (and site of its future Hall of Fame), Canton, Ohio.

March later coached his alma mater in 1904, but he was first and foremost a medical doctor, so two years later, he signed on as team physician for the Canton Bulldogs. The Bulldogs' roster would later include legendary Olympian Jim Thorpe and who would become charter members of the NFL, winning back-to-back titles without losing a single game in 1922 and '23. But it was with the Giants that March would make his biggest mark.

March had been the man behind Tim Mara's throne for the Giants; he'd been present at the meeting where Mara bought into the NFL in 1925, subsequently serving as team secretary and, later, president for the next eight years. Mara had been a New York bookie before he bought the team, but he didn't know much about football; March (who later wrote a book on the game's early history) provided that knowledge.

March owned a small piece of the Giants himself, but he sold it to Mara in 1932 and eventually wound up on the losing end of a dispute with Boston owner George Preston

Marshall and Brooklyn owner Dan Topping. Chagrined at this turn of events, March decided to seek retribution by challenging the NFL directly with a new league of his own.

Initial plans listed teams in a number of potential East Coast sites, including Hartford, Albany, Baltimore and three potential franchises in New Jersey … none of which ever played a game.

After an organizational meeting in April of 1935, the league announced a "firm" lineup of Boston, New York, Cleveland, Syracuse, Jersey City, Philadelphia and Providence — a lineup that didn't wind up being so firm, after all. None of the last three cities ended up fielding teams, and the list ultimately included just six franchises: the Boston Shamrocks, New York Yankees, Pittsburgh Americans, Cleveland Rams, Syracuse Braves and Rochester Tigers (who had originally been scheduled to play in Brooklyn).

The Shamrocks would win the league's first title in 1936 and would prove so successful at the gate that they forced Marshall to move his NFL team from Boston to Washington — where it has been ever since — the following season. But the Shamrocks' second season would be far less successful. They managed to sign the previous year's Heisman Trophy winner, Larry Kelley of Yale, to a one-game contract with an option to play more, but despite an Oct. 20 headline promising that Kelley would be in the lineup the following Sunday against Pittsburgh, Kelley was a no-show and never took the field in Boston. (In fact, he never played pro football anywhere and focused on his career as a teacher.) It was that kind of season for the Shamrocks, with the team winning just two games and closing the season in fifth place.

The league disbanded after that, and the Shamrocks played one more season as an independent team before folding.

Another AFL team, however, lasted a good deal longer. The Cleveland Rams had placed second to the Shamrocks that first season, losing just two games and tying two others while fielding a powerful defense that shut out three of their nine opponents. They managed a split with the league champion Shamrocks, losing their first meeting but winning the rematch, and were scheduled to host Boston in a game for the championship, but the Shamrocks owed their players back pay, and they refused to play until they received it. When it wasn't forthcoming, the game was canceled, and Boston claimed the title based on its superior record.

After the season, Cleveland bolted the league and applied for membership in the NFL — the same "probationary" slot the Bulldogs had been promised the year before. Los Angeles had been all but an adjunct member of the league in 1936, playing six of its 10 games against NFL teams (all at Gilmore Stadium) and emerging with a credible 3-2-1 record. The team drew good-sized crowds, too, including 17,000 for a 13-10 win over the Chicago Cardinals. Despite this strong showing, however, the Bulldogs suddenly found themselves with competition for the NFL opening they'd thought was in the bank: The league announced it was considering not only Cleveland, but also Houston as alternative sites for the new franchise.

When all was said and done, the league accepted the Rams, who fit best into its existing Northeast-Midwest geography.

It would not be the last time the Rams would undermine the 'Dogs.

Still, Los Angeles got a consolation prize: With the Rams having left the AFL, there was an opening there, and the Bulldogs accepted an invitation to replace them. They immediately dominated the league, led by Gordon Gore and Ed "Crazy Legs" Stark, who tied for second on the league's scoring list with 42 points apiece. Behind their efforts (Gore was not only an offensive threat, but a placekicker to boot), the Bulldogs won each of their eight scheduled AFL games by at least 10 points and became the first of just four major pro football teams ever to complete a perfect season. They didn't play any NFL teams that year, having been blacklisted as a member of the rival AFL.

1938 California Football League						
	W	L	T	PF	PA	Pct.
Stockton Shippers	4	0	0	53	16	1.000
Hollywood Stars	4	1	0	103	39	.800
Salinas Packers	2	3	0	89	78	.400
Fresno Crushers	2	5	0	51	90	.286
Oakland Cardinals	0	3	0	12	85	.000

Salinas and a third AFL

Their closest competition, it turned out, came from an independent team, the Salinas Iceberg Packers ("Iceberg" referred to the kind of lettuce grown in the Salinas Valley). The Packers had actually beaten the Bulldogs 21-17 the year before, and on that basis claimed the mythical title of Pacific Coast champions, setting up an intersectional contest with the "other" Packers — the NFL champs from Green Bay — who promptly dispatched them by a score of 42-7.

In 1937, the Bulldogs prevailed in each of their three meetings with Salinas, but it wasn't easy. Their first meeting of the year was also the Bulldogs' first home game, as they were returning from a six-game East Coast road swing to open the year. They'd won all six of those contests — five AFL games and an exhibition — while the Packers had won all four of their starts. A crowd of 15,000 turned out to see the Bulldogs shut out the Packers 13-0 with a pair of touchdowns in the second half.

Salinas bounced back two weeks later to blank the Rochester Tigers, a team the Bulldogs had beaten twice, by a score of 25-0, setting up a return match with the L.A. club in early December. The Packers, playing at Salinas High School this time before a capacity crowd of 3,000 (more than one-quarter of the farming town's population at the time), struck first with a touchdown on their opening drive. But the Bulldogs responded with 10 points in the second quarter and led 17-7 until a late score by Salinas made it 17-14 just before the final gun. A 40-yard field goal by Gerald Gore in the second quarter turned out to be the difference.

The two teams would meet one last time in 1937, with the Bulldogs prevailing 21-3 before 15,000 fans at Gilmore Stadium. Salinas once again opened the scoring, the *Los Angeles Times* reported, when Arleigh Williams, "the baldheaded California field goal artist," connected from 17 yards out in the second quarter. But the Bulldogs responded with a pair of second-quarter touchdowns and capped the scoring with another in the final period. Turnovers set up two of the Bulldogs' scores, and the *Times* confidently reported that the team had "earned a crack at the Washington Redskins or Chicago Bears, who will be in this vicinity right after the New Year dawns."

The Redskins had beaten the Bears for the NFL title two weeks earlier, but neither wound up playing the Bulldogs. The Redskins declined an offer of such a game, and the Bulldogs instead concluded their season with a 13-10 victory over a team of all-stars to finish with 16 wins in as many games overall (eight AFL starts and eight nonleague games). The closest thing to an AFL-NFL championship game was an all-star game played Jan. 30 at Los Angeles' Wrigley Field, in which a team composed primarily of NFL stars defeated an AFL side stocked with several Bulldogs 17-12. The charity game lacked the drama of an official contest, with only 2,500 fans showing up for what the *L.A. Times* dubbed a "drab" affair.

The AFL folded after that second season, leaving the Bulldogs once again a team without a league.

One possible landing spot was a newly formed California Football League, which featured Salinas Packers and four other teams: the Hollywood Stars, Stockton Shippers, Fresno Crushers and Oakland Cardinals. Paul Schissler, who had coached in the NFL for four years with two different teams, organized the league and ran the Hollywood team, which he hoped to build into a rival for the Bulldogs. The AFL champions, however, didn't end up joining the league, and the Iceberg Packers were a shadow of the team they'd been the previous two seasons. They opened their season with an exhibition rematch against the Bulldogs at Gilmore Stadium, but this time were no match for Los Angeles. The Bulldogs "literally toyed with the shorthanded Salinas Packers," the *Los Angeles Times* reported, coming away with a 34-0 victory "that might just as well have been 134 to 0."

Salinas didn't do much better in the new league, winning just one of its four games and finishing next-to-last. The Stockton Shippers finished a game ahead of the Stars to claim the championship with a perfect 4-0 record, then promptly disappeared from history along with the rest of the CFL when it folded after a single season.

The Bulldogs, meanwhile, compiled a record of 11-2-1 as an independent team, led by Gore, who was becoming a dominant force for the team. He scored routinely on runs long and short, kicked a 44-yard field goal in a win over the NFL's Pittsburgh Pirates and even had a pick-six on defense against Cincinnati, a fellow AFL refugee also operating as an independent that year.

After the team's second meeting with Pittsburgh in three days ended in a tie, Detroit Lions owner Dick Richards invaded the team's locker room and offered Gore $100 a game to jump ship. Gore declined the offer, and the Bulldogs went on to win their last five games of the season. They wound up with a 2-1-2 record against NFL teams (who were willing to play them once again now that they were out of the AFL), with their only loss in the series a 14-12 nail-biter against the Chicago Bears.

Of the victories, 28-7 victory over the Cleveland Rams in November had to be particularly satisfying. The Rams scored immediately when the Bulldogs fumbled on the first play after the opening kickoff, and Cleveland took the loose ball in for a touchdown. But they couldn't find the end zone the rest of the game, and the Bulldogs won going away.

The Bulldogs also beat Salinas twice more, and dispatched the Hollywood Stars 34-0, leaving little doubt that they would have dominated the CFL had they chosen to become members. Not only was the league gone after one uneventful season, so were the once-powerful Iceberg Packers, who packed it in for good after losing their final four games (including twice to the Bulldogs and in their season finale against the Hollywood Stars).

Stars owner Schissler wasn't done with West Coast football, however. He helped organize what would be the NFL's first annual postseason all-star game — an extravaganza touted in the press as "the first 'professional bowl football game'," or Pro Bowl. The format was different back then, with a team of all-stars facing the league champion New York Giants in a game that drew 15,000 fans to Wrigley Field in Los Angeles. The Giants won by a score of 13-10 in a contest notable for the fact that it featured three non-NFL players on the all-star team: Gore, Los Angeles teammate Bill Moore at right end, and the Hollywood Stars'

Owen Hanson at left guard. It was the only time players from outside the NFL competed in the game.

Games following the same format were played after each the next two seasons, both in L.A., both at Gilmore Stadium, using NFL players exclusively. The game moved back east after that and was discontinued in 1943, only to be revived after the 1950 season — again in Los Angeles, but this time at the Coliseum and featuring two competing teams of NFL stars.

Gore's appearance in that first game turned out to be his last representing the Bulldogs, as the Lions renewed their offer of an NFL contract and, this time, he accepted. Gore's NFL career would be brief: In a single season with the Lions, he played in seven games but only gained 7 yards from scrimmage in eight rushing attempts, caught a single pass for 20 yards and failed to complete his only pass.

Without Gore, the Bulldogs nonetheless forged ahead with more ambitious plans, joining another new league (called, predictably, the American Football League) and once again winning the championship in 1939. They failed to duplicate their unbeaten record from two years earlier, but only barely, losing just once and avenging that defeat in Columbus with three victories over the Bullies late in the season.

The last of these, before a crowd of 7,000 at Gilmore, was a classic. L.A. led 21-7 going into the fourth quarter, but Columbus tied the score with a pair of touchdowns. Los Angeles then drove to the Bullies' 25-yard line before Bob Davis intercepted a pass intended for Elvin Hutchison at the 1-yard line. As Hutchison moved in to make the tackle, Davis tried to elude him but, in doing so, stepped back over the goal line before being knocked out of bounds in the end zone. The play was ruled a safety, giving the Bulldogs their two-point margin of victory and the league title with a 7-1 record.

The Bullies apparently dropped to third place at 9-4, but the league ruled that two of their losses to the Bulldogs had been in nonleague games and also nullified their season-ending demolition of St. Louis. This gave Columbus a winning percentage of .818 to the Bulldogs' .800 and allowed the Bullies to claim a tainted championship. Regardless of the final standings, the two teams were clearly the class of the league, and when the Bulldogs dropped out the following season, it paved the way for the Bullies to claim the championship in 1940 and '41, the league's final two seasons.

Whether the Bulldogs left the AFL because it denied them the championship or whether the AFL punished the team by expelling them is unclear. What is clear is that, even without a league to call home, the Bulldogs were intent on continuing. A month after the season, they Bulldogs returned to the field for an exhibition against a team of California collegians that featured UCLA's Kenny Washington — who would eventually break the NFL's color barrier. Perhaps to the surprise of the 8,500 fans in attendance at Gilmore Stadium, the collegians built a 14-12 lead with two minutes left on the strength of Washington's two touchdown runs. Only a late field goal by the Bulldogs' Tillie Manton saved the day.

Washington would play a key role in what was to follow.

1939 American Football League	W	L	T	PF	PA	Pct.
Los Angeles Bulldogs	7	1	0	223	35	.875
Cincinnati Bengals	6	2	0	117	85	.750
Columbus Bullies	9	4	0	235	81	.692
Chicago Indians	4	3	0	55	51	.571
St. Louis Gunners	5	6	0	141	164	.455
Dayton Bombers	2	5	0	45	167	.286
Kenosha Cardinals	2	7	0	97	105	.222
Louisville Tanks	2	9	0	51	226	.182

Columbus champion with revised 9-2 mark.
L.A. beat Columbus in 3 of 4 head-to-head games.

Kenny and Jackie

About the same time the Bulldogs were edging Washington's all-stars, our old friend Harry Myers approached the board of directors for baseball's Pacific Coast League and suggested they back a similar league for football. The league would include six to eight teams playing a schedule of 16 or 20 games from Oct. 1 through the end of the year.

Myers quoted George Halas of the Bears as saying, "The idea of organizing a Pacific Coast league, backed by the league of baseball teams, is about the most sensible I have heard relative to coast football. It should be very successful."

That proposal died a month later, but as it turned out, the idea itself was far from dead.

Enter another familiar face, Paul Schissler. Before his coaching days in the NFL, Schissler had spent nearly a decade coaching at Oregon State, and although his California Football League had failed, he hadn't lost his love for the game or wavered in his belief that it could prosper on the West Coast — and not just in Los Angeles. One piece of evidence: A healthy crowd of 6,500 had turned out to see one of the Bullies-Bulldogs games, which had been played in Oregon. On its heels, Schissler set out to organize a game between the

Bulldogs and a team of all-stars in Portland two weeks into the new year.

There's no record in the press of whether such a game was played, but what is notable is the fact that Schissler soon resurfaced as part of a plan for a new league. The pitch to baseball's PCL owners had gone nowhere, but in August, an announcement came that a new league was about to happen anyway: a six-team circuit with Schissler serving on the league's board of directors and running a team in Hollywood called the Bears. The Bulldogs were to be members as well, and former star back Ed Stark had a team in Phoenix. Other entries were set for Bakersfield, Oakland and San Diego.

Myers was involved, as well, serving as temporary chairman, and a 10-game schedule was announced. A week later, the idea was up in the air again, with Myers declaring that too many potential players were eligible for military conscription, but organizers ultimately forged ahead, even as Bakersfield dropped out less than a month before opening weekend. The owner cited "business pressure" and reported he'd been unsuccessful in getting former Salinas Packers owner Ed Storm to take over the team.

When league play started, it was apparent that it would be a two-team race between the Bulldogs and Bears, who shared Gilmore Stadium as their home field. Each team beat the other twice but suffered no other losses, with the Bulldogs finishing 7-2-1 and the Bears at 6-2-0. The Oakland Giants were the only other team to win even one game, while the Phoenix Panthers and San Diego Bombers were both winless in just four starts.

One star of the new league was none other than Kenny Washington, who scored a pair of touchdowns and passed for four more to lead the Bears.

Washington had excelled for UCLA in baseball, where he was actually considered a better prospect than his teammate, Jackie Robinson. But he was even more accomplished on the football field, where he became the first consensus football All-American ever in 1939 after leading the nation in total offense. He played in the 1940 College All-Star Game against the Green Bay Packers, where he scored a touchdown and impressed Bears owner George Halas so much that he asked Washington to stick around for a couple of weeks. Halas wanted to draft Washington, but first he had to persuade his fellow owners to tear down pro football's color barrier.

They all agreed, with the exception of Washington owner George Preston Marshall, whose influence was enough to keep the UCLA phenom out of the NFL.

Back in California, Washington needed a place to play, and he found one with the newly formed Hollywood Bears.

He missed two games with an injury that first season, when the Bulldogs edged the Bears for the inaugural PCFL title, but he returned at full strength in 1941, and his presence made all the difference in the world. The league was down to four teams now, with Phoenix having folded and the new San Francisco Packers replacing the defunct Oakland Giants. But no matter how many teams there were in the league, Washington would have dominated. His seven rushing touchdowns tied him for most in the league, and his seven TD passes were more than twice as many as anyone else managed that year. Washington's efforts led the Bears to a perfect 8-0 season, including a three-game sweep of the Bulldogs (whose only other loss was by a single point in their season opener).

Not that the Bulldogs didn't try to level the playing field. Seeking someone to counter the athleticism of Washington, they settled on his college teammate Jackie Robinson. Robinson joined the Bulldogs for a Dec. 14 game against the San Francisco Packers, and he delivered a 41-yard scoring run to cap a 36-0 victory.

Jackie Robinson with the Kansas City Monarchs of the Negro American League in 1945.

The next week brought the season finale against the Washington and the Bears, and Robinson didn't disappoint. With the score tied 3-3 in the third quarter, he connected on a 23-yard pass to the Hollywood 19 and found another receiver just short of the goal line. Then, after the Bears stopped Los Angeles cold on three straight running plays, he completed a short pass for a touchdown to put the Bulldogs ahead.

Then it was Washington's turn. On the next drive, he ran for one first down, picked up six more yards on the ground and completed a pass to the L.A. 13-yard-line. That set up a pass to Glen Gavlin, who caught it at the 5 and ran in for the tying score. After the Bears held the Bulldogs on downs, Washington returned a punt to the Los Angeles 46, then followed that up with a 35-yard pass to Woody Strode for what turned out to be the winning touchdown.

Robinson tried to rally the Bulldogs, but the issue was decided when the Bears intercepted his pass at the Hollywood 30.

Kenny Washington had won this clash of the titans, and there wouldn't be another. With the Bears' win coming just two weeks after Pearl Harbor, Robinson found himself drafted into the military, ending his brief pro football career.

Washington avoided conscription for a painful reason: Knee problems kept him out of the service and also out of football in 1942. Without him, the high-flying Bears plunged back to earth, scoring a total of just 15 points in four league starts — all losses — during the 1942 season. The next year, they were out of business (at least temporarily), with Washington working as a Los Angeles police officer and Schissler busy coaching the March Field team in Southern California as a major in the Army Air Corps.

Washington returned to the PCFL in 1944 with the San Francisco Clippers, who finished second after losing three games to a different Hollywood team, the Rangers, and going 8-0 against everyone else. Hollywood finished the year at a perfect 11-0 and had four of the league's six top scorers, but Washington ranked third in touchdowns and points scored to earn all-league honors at halfback.

In 1945, with Schissler out of the military, he reformed his Hollywood Bears, and Washington was back on the roster. He had perhaps his finest season, scoring 92 points — more than twice as many as anyone else in the league — while leading the league in touchdowns (9), extra points (26) and field goals (4). He ranked second in rushing and third in passing for the Bears, who won the title by a half-game over the Oakland Giants. It wasn't really that close, though: Hollywood beat the Giants both times they met, the second time by a score of 48-0.

Hollywood drew an average of close to 13,500 for its nine games in Los Angeles, and the league appeared to be on solid footing, showcasing perhaps the nation's best player in Washington and offering the West Coast's version of major professional football. It might not have been the NFL, but it was the next-best thing.

The PCFL was poised to expand to nine teams under a new two-division format, with teams as far east as Salt Lake City, as far north as Tacoma and as far south as San Diego, just north of the Mexican border. The league even welcomed a team in Hawaii, before it was even a state and long before the World Football League expanded that far. The Warriors would find success with a second-place finish in 1946 and would win league titles the following two years.

Unfortunately, by then, the bottom had fallen out.

1946 Pacific Coast Football League

	W	L	T	PF	PA	Pct.
Northern Division						
Tacoma Indians	7	4	0	202	141	.640
San Francisco Clippers	6	4	0	206	130	.600
Salt Lake Gulls	2	5	1	81	137	.286
Sacramento Nuggets	2	5	1	67	201	.286
Oakland Giants	1	5	0	60	89	.167
Southern Division						
Los Angeles Bulldogs	9	2	1	318	185	.812
Hawaiian Warriors	8	4	0	97	105	.667
Hollywood Bears	5	5	1	187	196	.500
San Diego Bombers	1	7	0	65	164	.142

Championship game: Los Angeles 38, Tacoma 7

Bulldogs pre-empted

World War II drawing to a close, a major sports boom was at hand, and the NFL was ready to consider expanding to the West Coast. Groups in San Francisco and Los Angeles had applied for franchises in 1944, with the Los Angeles group including Bing Crosby and a member of the Wrigley family. Buffalo also applied, but none of the three cities was accepted. Instead, all three cities would be represented in the new All-America Football Conference that began play in 1946.

The arrival of the AAFC's Los Angeles Dons was a gut punch to the L.A. Bulldogs and Hollywood Bears, but the real knockout blow came soon afterward. The same Cleveland Rams who had kept the Bulldogs out of the NFL a decade earlier announced in January of 1946 that they were moving to Los Angeles.

The Rams weren't just an NFL team, but the league champion, having edged the Redskins for the title less than a month earlier. To make matters worse, the Rams then signed Kenny Washington away from the Bears, depriving the PCFL of its marquee player. By that time, Washington had undergone five operations on his knees, but he was still a big draw at the gate and a threat to break things open on the field.

(Woody Strode, who had played with Washington at UCLA and caught that game-winning pass from him against Jackie Robinson and the L.A. Bulldogs five years earlier, also signed with the Rams, playing one season in the NFL and later turning to acting. In 1960, he was nominated for a Golden Globe as Best Supporting Actor in *Spartacus*.)

When Washington signed with the Rams, he broke the color barrier in the NFL, just as Robinson would do a year later in Major League Baseball. But his departure spelled the beginning of the end for the PCFL, which limped along for three more seasons before closing up shop in 1948. That turned out to be Washington's final pro season, as well, with his bad knees forcing him out of the game at the age of 30. In his three NFL seasons, he showed flashes of brilliance, including a team-record 92-yard run from scrimmage, and averaged an impressive 6.1 yards per carry, but he never again attained the heights he'd reached with the Hollywood Bears.

Cleveland's departure for Los Angeles, meanwhile, paved the way for the AAFC's Cleveland Browns, who won all four league titles before joining the NFL and winning another one. The team they beat — and which beat them for the championship the following year?

You guessed it: the Los Angeles Rams.

PCFL championship games and interleague playoffs	
1940	Columbus Bullies (AFL) 31, Hollywood Bears (PCFL) 7
1941	Hollywood Bears (PCFL) 21, Columbus Bullies (AFL) 9
1942	No game
1943	No game
1944	Hollywood Rangers (AFL) 42, San Diego Bombers (PCFL) 7
	Hollywood Rangers (AFL) 21, San Diego Bombers (PCFL) 10
1945	No game
1946	Los Angeles 38, Tacoma 7

The Browns Had It Down

The Cleveland Browns were once the Boston Celtics of professional football.

No, really, they were.

The team that's never even *been* to a Super Bowl and hasn't won an NFL championship since 1964 was once so good it practically destroyed an entire league — and not just on the football field.

That league was the All-America Football Conference, which made debuted in 1946 during the postwar boom and appeared to be everything the National Football League wasn't. The NFL, it should be noted, wasn't the two-ton gorilla it is now. Quite to the contrary, it was mainly a Steel Belt league, with all its teams confined to a relatively narrow corridor stretching from Chicago eastward and up to Boston.

The league had struggled through the war years, enduring poor attendance in some markets and struggling to find enough players to make games *worth* attending. Many athletes had answered the call to duty, spending all or part of the previous four seasons fighting overseas, and rosters were so badly depleted that some teams were forced to join forces.

The Steelers couldn't even field a full team two years running. In 1943, they merged with the Philadelphia Eagles to form a two-headed monster known as the Steagles, with the teams' coaches sharing sideline duties. The following year, they teamed up with the Chicago Cardinals to form a team that sounded like it belonged in a Las Vegas poker tournament: Card-Pitt. (I guess the names Steeginals and Cardlers just didn't work for them.) Then, in 1945, the Boston and Brooklyn teams merged into a single entity that played in both cities but called itself simply the Yanks.

There was still a demand for football, especially on the West Coast, but the NFL was in no shape to expand. In April of 1944, applications from Los Angeles, San Francisco and Buffalo were considered, then rejected.

Into this void stepped a man named Arch Ward, who was sports editor of the *Chicago Tribune* but also a first-rate promoter. He'd been the brains behind two events that have become national institutions: the All-Star Game in Major League Baseball and the Golden Gloves amateur boxing tournament. Now, he set his sights on perhaps his most ambitious proposal to date: a football league that wouldn't be limited to the Steel Belt, but would span the nation — a truly All-America Football Conference.

A few short months after the NFL decided against expanding, Ward announced the formation of a new league that would have teams in (surprise) Buffalo, L.A. and San Francisco, as well as five to seven other cities. The owners included oil tycoons, celebrities and other familiar names. Former heavyweight champ Gene Tunney was on board in Baltimore; movie star Don Ameche led the Los Angeles group, which also included the likes of Louis B. Mayer, Bob Hope and Bing Crosby; and Lou Gehrig's widow — the league's secretary/treasurer — was involved in the New York franchise. The press referred to them collectively as the "millionaires' coffee klatch."

Chicago and Cleveland were also on the list, with the latter franchise awarded to a taxi company mogul named Arthur "Mickey" McBride. McBride had cut his teeth in the newspaper business as circulation manager for the *Cleveland News*. He'd gotten to know Ward at the time, and he'd developed an interest in football when he attended games with his son, a student at Notre Dame. He'd tried — unsuccessfully — to buy the Cleveland Rams in 1942, so the new league presented him with just the kind of opportunity he'd been looking for.

Although he hadn't been a football fan for long, McBride knew right out of the gate that he'd need a first-rate coach for his as-yet-unnamed team. True to his Notre Dame ties, he first set his sights on Irish coach Frank Leahy, who accepted a handshake deal with McBride to become coach and general manager. But Notre Dame got wind of the deal and persuaded Leahy to back out, leaving McBride back where he'd started.

The Massillon Miracle Man

Turns out, an even better coach was still available. Paul Brown was just 36 years old, but he'd already been successful at both the high school and college levels. The "Massillon Miracle Man," as he was known, had won six state titles in eight years at Massillon High School. There, he'd developed the sport's first playbook, insisted on strict discipline and opened his roster to African-American players at a time when many coaches refused to do so. His system produced a 35-game winning streak and four national championships before he took a job at Ohio State in 1941.

The following year, his Buckeyes won the Big Ten title and the national championship.

McBride paid handsomely for Brown's services, offering him what the owner said was "the biggest salary I ever heard of being paid for such a job" — $17,500 a year, or the equivalent of roughly $250,000 in 2018. Brown, who was serving in the military, also received a stipend until he was discharged and ownership of the team that ultimately would bear his name.

The origin of that name is more interesting than you might think. The team held a naming contest, and a Navy specialist named John Hartnett won $1,000 in June of 1945 for one of 36 people to choose the winning name: "Panthers." It wasn't exactly original. A team by that name had represented the city from 1919 until 1933, playing independent ball most of that time but also playing five games in Red Grange's first American Football League.

But that name didn't last long. A little more than two months later, it had been changed, with assistant coach Johnny Brickels announcing that a majority of entries had actually preferred that the team name have some association with its coach. Brown had initially objected to the idea, but ultimately agreed that the contest could be reopened and the judges could select another name. They did so, and a second $1,000 prize was duly awarded, this time to one William Thompson.

Brown, however, seems to have still been a bit embarrassed that the team would carry his name, so he encouraged a rumor that the team had actually been renamed in honor of Joe Louis — the "Brown Bomber." (The story didn't really make much sense, as it would have been natural to shorten such a name to "Bombers," rather than Browns. Besides, Louis had been born in Alabama and was living in Detroit — not Cleveland — at the time.)

The fans who voted to name the team in Brown's honor were clearly confident he wouldn't let them down.

And he didn't.

In his four seasons as coach of the team in the AAFC, the Browns won four championships, even posting a perfect 14-0 regular-season mark in 1948 (the league played a 14-game schedule a decade and a half before the NFL adopted it). The Browns were not only good, they were popular, outdrawing any single NFL team by a wide margin during that period. Football fans in the city had doubtless felt jilted by the Rams' departure for Los Angeles just a few months after the AAFC announced it was forming.

The Browns would have Cleveland all to themselves, but the league's new L.A. franchise, the Dons, would have unexpected competition in Southern California from the defending NFL champions. Still, they held their own, outdrawing the Rams two of the four seasons the teams went head to head and attracting a pro football record 82,576 fans to the Coliseum for a game against the New York Yankees in 1947. That record would be eclipsed a year later by another AAFC game, with 82,679 turning out to see the Browns edge the visiting 49ers 14-7, snapping San Francisco's 10-game winning streak.

1946 All-America Football Conference	W	L	T	PF	PA	Pct.
Eastern Division						
New York Yankees	10	3	1	270	192	.769
Brooklyn Dodgers	3	10	1	226	339	.231
Buffalo Bisons	3	10	1	249	370	.231
Miami Seahawks	3	11	0	167	378	.214
Western Division						
Cleveland Browns	12	2	0	423	137	.857
San Francisco 49ers	9	5	0	307	189	.643
Los Angeles Dons	7	5	2	305	290	.583
Chicago Rockets	5	6	3	263	315	.455

Championship game: Cleveland 14, New York 9

Loaded with talent

In fact, after a shaky start in its first year, the AAFC outdrew the NFL over the final three years of its existence.

Part of the reason was the league's talent.

Its stars included the likes of offensive back Glenn Dobbs from the University of Tulsa, who started out with the league's Brooklyn Dodgers before moving to the Dons. Dobbs led the league two divergent categories — total offense (2,094 yards) and punting (47.8-yard average) — during the league's first season, earning MVP honors despite playing for a Dodgers team that finished a dismal 3-10-1 record.

The Dons also had Angelo Bertelli, the 1943 Heisman Trophy winner from Notre Dame who signed with the team in its inaugural season and played two more seasons for the Chicago Rockets before knee problems ended his career. Neither he nor Dobbs ever played in the NFL, but there were other AAFC players who did.

Few people remember that Hall of Fame receiver Elroy "Crazylegs" Hirsch got his start with the AAFC's Chicago Rockets, where he played three seasons before joining the NFL Rams. Then, of course, there was Cleveland's dynamic duo: quarterback Otto Graham and tackle Lou Groza, who was better known for his prowess as a placekicker.

Cleveland Browns quarterback Otto Graham went out on top.

Graham played 10 seasons with the Browns (four in the AAFC and six in the NFL), leading the league in passing yards five times and never once failing to reach the championship game — winning seven of them. When he retired after a 38-14 win over the Rams in 1955, it came after a season in which he led the league in completion percentage, yards per attempt and quarterback rating. "Automatic Otto," as he was known, never missed a game in his career.

Groza, meanwhile, led the AAFC in field goals during two of his four seasons in the league, then did the same thing in the NFL for four consecutive years starting in 1950. He connected from 16 yards out with 28 seconds left in the championship game that year to give Cleveland a stunning victory over the Rams in the Browns' first NFL season. "The Toe," as he was known, played with the Browns through 1967, leading the league in field goal percentage as late as 1963 at the age of 39.

Meanwhile, Brown maintained his practice of welcoming African-American players to his roster, a policy that paid dividends with the signing of defensive lineman Bill Willis and fullback Marion Motley. Brown had faced Motley's high school team from Canton when the coach was still at Massillon High — the only team ever to beat Motley's crew over a three-year span in the late 1930s. He went on to attend the University of Nevada and was working at a steel mill in Canton when he learned about the AAFC and wrote Brown asking for a tryout.

Brown initially said no.

He considered Willis the real prize, but in an era of segregation, he needed another black player to room with him on the road. That led him to reconsider Motley, and both joined the team for its first season.

Motley led the AAFC in rushing during Cleveland's undefeated season in 1948, then duplicated the feat two years later when the Browns joined the NFL. Willis went right along with him and earned all-pro honors each of his four seasons in the established league. Both of them wound up in the Hall of Fame.

179

But the AAFC's talent wasn't just a thin layer of superstars at the top. Forty of the 66 players on the team of all-stars that defeated the Rams in the 1946 College All-Star Game signed with AAFC teams, including eight of the 11 starters. The upstart league had talent, it had big money backing it, and all but one of its teams played in football stadiums at a time when most NFL games were still played in ballparks built for baseball.

The league played in major metropolitan areas across the country, and its commissioner, James Crowley, had plenty of cachet as a former member of Knute Rockne's fabled Four Horsemen of Notre Dame. (Another former "horseman," Elmer Layden, was commissioner of the NFL at the same time.

Perhaps the league's biggest coup came after its original New York franchise pulled out before the start of the inaugural season. No problem. The AAFC simply persuaded an entire NFL *team* to jump ship and join the new kids on the block: Dan Topping, owner of the Brooklyn Tigers, ditched the established league for the AAFC, bringing most of the players from that team with him and reconstituting it as the New York (football) Yankees.

With so much going for the league, what could have possibly gone wrong?

For one thing, the Cleveland Browns were so thoroughly dominant that it became almost a foregone conclusion that they would win the title. During their four seasons in the league, they lost just four times: twice each to the L.A. Dons and San Francisco 49ers. When the 49ers snapped the Browns' 30-game unbeaten streak with a 56-28 drubbing at Kezar Stadium in October of 1949, there was, perhaps, hope that a changing of the guard might take place. But the Browns won the rematch 30-28 a few weeks later, then shut down the high-powered San Francisco offense 21-7 for the championship in the last AAFC game ever played.

Throughout its history, the new league was clearly divided into the haves and have-nots, with Cleveland epitomizing the former category, along with the two West Coast teams, Buffalo and, to some extent, the New York Yankees. Teams in Chicago, Baltimore, Brooklyn and Miami didn't fare nearly as well.

Lost at sea

The poor Miami Seahawks joined the league relatively late. After Gene Tunney couldn't find a place for his Baltimore team to play, that franchise was put on hold and the league's eighth franchise was awarded to a Miami group led by Atlanta restaurateur Harvey Hester, a former football coach at Wofford College who owned a place called Aunt Fannie's Cabin (and, later, another joint called the Hillbilly Rest-Runt).

The decision to place a franchise in Miami must have seemed like a good idea at the time. It marked the first time a major football league had ever ventured into the South. It would also give cold-weather teams another place to play (in addition to L.A. and San Francisco) late in the season, when winter descended on the Midwest and Northeast.

Despite these obvious advantages, though, there were red flags, as well. Hester was anything but a member of the "millionaires' coffee klatch." A man of relatively modest means, he wasn't in a position to put together a strong contender, and to make matters worse, he was getting a late start compared with the other owners. He was also introducing football to a relatively small city that had never seen it before. Miami in 1945 was growing fast, but it was still primarily a "snowbird" community for winter visitors from New York and New Jersey. With roughly 200,000 residents, it was less than half the size of any of the league's other cities.

The Cleveland Browns hosted the Miami Seahawks in both teams' first game ever, on Sept. 6, 1946. The Browns demolished the hapless Seahawks 44-0.

Hester rented Roddy Burdine Stadium (later to be renamed the Orange Bowl), which in 1946 had just 35,000 seats. He tried and failed to hire Bears quarterback Sid Luckman away from the Chicago Bears. All of this combined to create a perfect storm that would seal the Seahawks' fate after a single season. Miami's civic leaders didn't like the idea of Sunday football, so Hester was forced to schedule games on Monday nights long before Frank Gifford, Dandy Don and Howard Cosell held forth on ABC. There was no TV in those days, and no reason to think about going to see a football game on a Monday night.

The idea of playing late-season games in balmy Miami might have been good for cold-weather teams, but it was terrible for the Seahawks. Playing their first three — and seven of their first eight — games on the road, with a bye week thrown in for good measure, didn't give Hester a chance to introduce the team to its fan base. That might not have mattered much if the team had gotten off to a good start. Unfortunately for Hester, the opposite happened. By the time the Seahawks played their home opener, they had lost their first three games by a combined score of 95-28.

Their Monday night home debut in October was postponed until Tuesday when the remnants of a hurricane made the game unplayable. Not surprisingly, fewer than 8,000 fans showed up to watch the Seahawks drop to 0-4 with a 34-7 loss to San Francisco.

Miami Daily News reporter Matty Matthews began his account of the San Francisco game like this: "Unless a tidal wave of gridiron talent sweeps over the Miami franchise … within the next few weeks, professional football in the Magic City will need the country's foremost magicians to revive it."

Hester promised "drastic changes" and declared, "Our organization will field a winner here if it's the last thing I do."

Hester wasn't the only one who was frustrated. The Miami coach, Jack Meagher, wasn't used to losing. The Seahawks, like the Browns, were named in honor of their coach: Meagher had coached the Iowa Pre-Flight Seahawks during the war. Few people remember it now, but Iowa Pre-Flight was a major power at the time, a military team (Navy, to be exact) that played only three seasons from 1942 to 1944.

The team beat traditional powers Nebraska 46-0 and Michigan 26-14, and rose near the top of the national rankings. Pre-Flight even split a pair of games with Brown's Ohio State teams — losing in 1942 but avenging that setback the following year en route to a stellar season in which it wound up ranked second in the nation. They might have been national champions had it not been for a missed extra point in a 14-13 loss to unbeaten Notre Dame. Pre-Flight entered the game favored, but four of its starters and three reserves were transferred to other military bases the week before the game.

The next season, Meagher coached Pre-Flight to a No. 6 ranking as the team won its final 10 games by a cumulative score of 306-77 after an opening loss at Michigan.

When the Seahawks hired Meagher, who had previously found success at Rice and Auburn, it seemed like a real coup. But unlike Paul Brown, Meagher wasn't around long. He quit in frustration before Miami even played its second home game, a 20-7 loss Nov. 11 to the Chicago Rockets that dropped their record to 1-8.

He never coached another game after that.

Needless to say, not too many fans were interested in following a team whose playoff prospects had dwindled to zero after just a single game at home, and it didn't help that the AAFC's idea of playing late-fall games in Miami turned out to be a dud with the weatherman: Rain fell on the next five Monday night home games after the Seahawks lost their opener.

The team averaged barely 7,000 fans for their seven home games that season, including just 2,300 for their season finale against Brooklyn. At least those few fans who bothered to show up on yet another rainy night for that Dec. 13 game got their money's worth, as the

Seahawks rallied with two late touchdowns to beat Brooklyn 31-20 for only their third win of the season (the other two were against the equally pathetic Buffalo Bisons). After the season, Hester had no more money to spend on the team, and a "save the Seahawks" drive by other boosters failed to keep them in Miami. Instead, the Baltimore team that was originally supposed to be part of the league replaced the Seahawks for the 1947 season.

Despite losing most of his money, Hester continued to operate his restaurant until his death at age 70 in 1967. He even had bit parts in a pair of movies: *I'd Climb the Highest Mountain* in 1951 and *The Great Locomotive Chase* five years later.

The Seahawks, however, were history.

Haves and have-nots

But unfortunately for the AAFC, they weren't the league's only problem. All but one of the circuit's best teams were concentrated in the Western Division, where the worst entry (Chicago) finished only a game under .500. The New York Yankees had the East virtually all to themselves, finishing with a 10-3-1 record while Buffalo, Brooklyn and Miami could manage no more than three wins apiece. Despite Dobbs' presence in the Dodgers' backfield, the team failed to draw, averaging fewer than 14,000 fans a game as the only AAFC team playing in a baseball stadium — aging Ebbets Field.

The team and its fans suffered through two identical 3-10-1 seasons before the owner threw in the towel and the team was purchased by the owners of its baseball namesake. Branch Rickey, who had signed Jackie Robinson to play for the baseball Dodgers a year earlier, took charge of the team and began looking for innovative ways to improve its fortunes. He suggested the AAFC play a 28-game season instead of just 14 … and idea that went nowhere. And he hired Pepper Martin, the former St. Louis Cardinals all-star outfielder/third baseman, as a placekicker.

Martin, a scout for the baseball Dodgers who'd retired as a player a few years earlier, was 44 years old at the time, and his football experience consisted of some games with a semipro team in Oklahoma called the Hominy Indians back in the 1920s. But Carl Voyles, who coached the AAFC Dodgers, saw him placekicking in a touch football game during the baseball Dodgers' spring training stint in Vero Beach, Fla., and was impressed enough to sign him. In an exhibition against the Montreal Alouettes, he connected on all four extra points and even returned a punt 10 yards.

But Martin got off on the wrong foot, suffering a leg injury (described in one account as a "Charley horse") and never made a kick during the regular season. The Dodgers waived him a month into the campaign, and Rickey found a more suitable position for him as manager of the Miami Tourists minor-league club. As in baseball.

Rickey's foray into football turned out to be a bust, as the Dodgers were even worse in 1948 than they had been the two previous years, finishing 2-12-0. Not that it much mattered that year, as the Cleveland Browns were still beating everyone in sight. Their 14-0 record would stand as the best ever for the regular season until it was matched in 1972 by the Miami Dolphins, a team that, ironically, represented the same city as the hapless Seahawks had during their only AAFC season.

The imbalance between the league's two divisions was worse than ever in 1948, with the Yankees in decline and no other team rising to take their place in the East. While Cleveland was going undefeated, Buffalo (renamed the Bills after 1946 but bearing no relation to the current team) and Baltimore tied for the top spot in the East at 7-7. Buffalo won a playoff and the right to get slaughtered by the Browns 49-7 in the title game. Everyone would have preferred to see the Browns face the 49ers, who finished 12-2 that year behind star quarterback Frankie Albert's league-leading 29 touchdown passes, but the fact that San Francisco finished behind Cleveland in the Western Division standings meant the 'Niners had to stay home for the championship game.

Before the 1949 season, the AAFC and NFL discussed a possible merger, but George Preston Marshall of Washington didn't like the idea, and Cleveland owner McBride said he wanted no part of the older league. Since the Browns were the AAFC's marquee franchise, that put the kybosh on the idea … at least for the time being.

"If pro football returned to only the National League, it would just be going backward, like in the old days of poor scheduling with a couple of hardheads running the show," McBride said.

And that was that.

The AAFC soldiered on through a 1949 season that saw the Chicago Rockets rebrand themselves as the Hornets … and remain virtually ignored by fans in a city that preferred the NFL Bears and Cardinals. The Brooklyn Dodgers, meanwhile, finally gave up the ghost and merged with the Yankees, leaving the circuit with just seven teams. On the positive side, this meant the AAFC had to scrap its chronically unbalanced two-division format, all but ensuring that, for once, the two best teams would meet in the finals. The AAFC, however, was on its last legs.

Attendance in its final year was still higher, on average, than that for the NFL, but was down in every market.

	AAFC championship games	
1946	Cleveland Browns 14, New York Yankees 9 – at Cleveland	
1947	Cleveland Browns 14, New York Yankees 3 – at New York	
1948	Cleveland Browns 49, Buffalo Bills 7 – at Cleveland	
1949	Cleveland Browns 21, San Francisco 49ers 7 – at Cleveland	

Merger

The NFL had problems of its own. The New York Bulldogs were averaging barely 8,000 fans a game, while the Pittsburgh Steelers and even the venerable Green Bay Packers were reportedly close to bankruptcy. The Packers averaged fewer than 17,500 fans a game, and there was talk that they might be left out of any merger. When the deal was finally struck in December 1949 to bring the rival leagues together, the Packers survived, although they sold 9,500 additional shares of stock in the spring of 1950 to stay afloat.

Despite the NFL's struggles, it was clear that the older league got the better of the merger. Every NFL team survived, including the lowly Bulldogs, who got most of the AAFC Yankees' roster and a new name (Yanks) as part of the deal. Meanwhile, only three AAFC teams survived intact. McBride agreed to let his Browns take part in the merger, after all, while Cleveland's chief rival, San Francisco, also made the cut.

Teams that shared cities with NFL clubs went by the wayside: The Dons in L.A. and the Hornets in Chicago were history. That left just two other teams as merger candidates: Baltimore and Buffalo. Of the two, the Bills seemed the logical choice. Attendance was slightly better in Buffalo, and the team hadn't had a losing record for three consecutive seasons. Baltimore, by contrast, had finished dead last at 1-11 in 1949.

Despite this, it was Baltimore that ultimately took part in the merger, thanks in part to a $50,000 payment to Washington's Marshall for infringing on his team's territorial rights. Buffalo went by the wayside, although its owner received a stake in the Cleveland Browns as a consolation prize.

Buffalo had one last shot at joining the new merged league, but owners voted in January 1950 not to add a 14th team. Buffalo, Houston and Oakland all applied to join the league, with Buffalo the clear favorite despite Houston's pledge to build a 110,000-seat covered stadium for less than $6.5 million. Oakland's bid was shelved almost immediately as infringing on the 49ers' territorial rights. But there was a lot of sentiment in favor of Buffalo, which had raised $250,000 in guarantees to cover season tickets and operating costs.

Despite that, however, owners wound up split nearly down the middle on the city's bid and — since a unanimous vote was needed to admit any new team — the motion died. All three cities would get teams a decade later in the next (and most successful) league to challenge the big boys, the fourth AFL.

With the NFL-AAFC merger complete, the new league rebranded itself as the National-American Football League and exchanged its east-west divisional format for two "conferences," dubbed "National" and "American." It wasn't long, however, before the combined league began to eliminate most vestiges of the old AAFC, one by one. First to go was the NAFL name, which lasted just three months before the league started calling itself the NFL again.

The conference format was scrapped after three seasons.

The decision to admit lowly Baltimore turned out to have been a bad one. The team repeated its 1-11 record and became the only team in league history to allow more than 50 points in four different games (including a 70-27 loss at Los Angeles). The Colts drew just 6,800 fans to their final home game before owner Abraham Watner threw in the towel. The cemetery owner had lost $106,000 during the woeful 1950 season, and more red ink seemed a certainty if he tried to stick it out. The other owners refused his request to bolster the team's roster by contributing one veteran player each, and fewer than 2,500 fans had expressed interest in buying season tickets for the coming year.

On Jan. 18, 1951, the Baltimore Colts went out of business.

Marshall did return the $50,000 Watner had paid him for territorial rights.

The combined Bulldogs-Yankees team managed to survive a little longer than Watner's Colts, but ultimately suffered the same fate. The infusion of new talent rejuvenated the Bulldogs (now the Yanks), who rebounded from 1-10-1 season to post a 7-5 record in 1950. But attendance fluctuated wildly, and the improvement on the field turned out to be temporary. The Yanks dropped to 1-9-2 the following season and drew fewer than 9,500 fans on average to their four home games.

The Yanks fled the Big Apple under new ownership in 1952, relocating to Dallas as the Texans, but they didn't have any better luck there. After losing their first nine games, the new owners gave up on the team, and the league took over operations, moving the Texans to Hershey, Pennsylvania, of all places, and scheduling their final "home" game of the season at the Rubber Bowl in Akron, Ohio. Only 3,000 fans showed up to watch the team notch its only win of the season, 27-23 over the Bears.

The league now had a team without either a home or an owner, but as luck would have it, a businessman named Carroll Rosenbloom was interested in bringing pro football back to Baltimore. The NFL awarded the Texans franchise to Rosenbloom, who had made a fortune producing overalls, along with most of its roster. The team was promptly renamed the Colts.

Just like the old AAFC team.

Continental Drift

Happy Chandler was an innovator. The second commissioner of Major League Baseball had put pen to paper in 1947 to approve one of the most significant changes in the history of the game — its integration, with the Brooklyn Dodgers' signing of Jackie Robinson, the first black player in the majors. He established the first pension fund for players and became known as "the players' commissioner."

Perhaps for that reason, the owners weren't too happy with his leadership and refused to extend his contract when it came up for renewal in 1951.

No matter. Albert Benjamin Chandler simply returned to his home state of Kentucky and won election as governor of the state in 1955. It was the second time he'd held that post, having served previously from 1935-39, when he repealed the state sales tax and replaced it with Kentucky's first income tax — another innovation.

Now, he was being an innovator once again, but this time on the gridiron. He had lost a bid for an unprecedented third term as governor in 1962 and, in casting about for a new challenge, he found it in a newly formed third major football league.

Few people remember the Continental Football League today, sandwiched as it was between the high-flying AFL and the ill-fated World Football League of the early '70s. That's partly because it never decided quite what it wanted to be: a top-tier farm league for the established leagues or one of the big boys itself. In the end, it settled into a position somewhere between the two, aspiring at times to greatness but never quite achieving parity with the NFL and AFL.

It took its name from an ill-fated baseball endeavor also known as the Continental League, which announced its formation as a "third major league" the same year the American Football League was formed (1959) but ultimately never played a single game.

"Our level is the third league," Newark Bears owner Sol Rosen proclaimed in announcing the new endeavor in February 1965. "That's why we picked a name for our league that was synonymous with what the Continental League implied in baseball."

Rosen's Bears bad been extremely successful in the Atlantic Coast Football League, compiling a record of 23-2-1 over two seasons and making the finals both years — with a title to their credit in 1963. Emboldened by his team's on-field success, Rosen filled out an application for the Bears to join the AFL. When it was rejected, Rosen began pursuing the idea of starting a new league. The result of those efforts was the Continental League.

The league boasted that it was "dealing with men able to finance big budgets, such as those in the National and American Leagues. We'll bid for top player talent. We'll go for big crowds and national television."

This was just the sort of challenge that appealed to Chandler, who found himself out of politics but, as a former baseball commissioner, uncommonly qualified to lead the new endeavor. ("I've always been bitten by two bugs — the politics bug and the sports bug," he said at the time.) Chandler's leadership, announced a month after the league's formation, gave the circuit instant credibility, while his annual salary of roughly $40,000 and five-year contract hammered home the fact that the league meant business.

Unlike the AFL, which had kicked off five years earlier, the Continental Football League wasn't starting from scratch. It was formed with teams from two minor leagues: the 4-year-old United Football League, based in the upper Midwest, and the aforementioned ACFL, which would continue to operate independently despite losing four clubs to the new venture.

The upside: Much of the framework was already in place for the inaugural season, which was set to begin in just a few short months. Host cities had been identified, players were already under contract (no draft was needed) and stadium leases had been signed. The downside: The league's teams operated largely in smaller markets and came with a certain amount of baggage as minor-league and semipro outfits.

From the UFL came the Wheeling Ironmen and Charleston Rockets, natural rivals based in West Virginia, along with the champion Canton Bulldogs, Indianapolis Warriors and Montreal-based Quebec Rifles. Teams joining from the ACFL were the Hartford Charter Oaks, Newark Bears, Richmond Rebels and Springfield (Mass.) Acorns — none of them operating in what were considered "big league" cities at the time.

There was precedent for starting out small. Baseball's American League had begun as a regional minor league — the Western League — before rebranding itself and becoming a rival of the established National League back in 1901. In its early years, the NFL had operating in markets such as Canton, Akron, Dayton, Green Bay and Duluth. But that was a long time ago, and the Continental League was starting out with the equivalent of half a dozen Green Bays and a couple of medium-market towns.

Nevertheless, hopes were high that the new circuit could hold its own.

The opening date of Aug. 14 gave it a jump on the established leagues, and it announced a couple of new rules designed to make the game more exciting. One of them was adopted much later by the NFL: a sudden-death overtime period. The first team scoring in the extra period would be awarded the victory, and ties would be recorded only if neither team could manage any points for a full 15 minutes. The league also outlawed fair catches, and booting the ball out of the end zone on a kickoff would result in a 5-yard penalty and rekick.

"We want to be competitive with the other two leagues," said Chandler, who envisioned becoming a "threat" to the established leagues "in the next few years."

"We'll respect the contracts of their players, and we hope they will do the same with the ones we sign."

The new league, however, was far from stable. It extended an invitation to the Providence Steamroller to join from the ACFL, but the team declined, forcing the league to create a franchise from scratch for the city, a team dubbed the Rhode Island Indians.

Other teams were quickly shifted to new locations before the season could get under way. Indianapolis relocated to nearby Fort Wayne. The Springfield Acorns were sold to a group in Norfolk, Va., where the team was rechristened the Neptunes. Canton's ownership, unable to secure a lease for the 20,000-seat Fawcett Stadium and unwilling to continue play in a 6,000-seat high school stadium for another year, moved the team to Philadelphia in direct competition with the NFL's Eagles.

The Quebec Rifles from the UFL also found a new home. The Rifles had earned their nickname from head coach, Sam "The Rifle" Etcheverry, who had played quarterback with the Montreal Alouettes in the Canadian Football League, and they kept that moniker even though their namesake declined to make the move to a Toronto for the team's debut in the Continental League. Their new home, however, was far from paradise: They played their first season in a Triple-A baseball park.

Meanwhile, however, the league started thinking about expansion before it had even played a down. Groups in Rochester, Miami, Birmingham, Phoenix and Anaheim were said to be interested, and investors in Tulsa seemed even more serious. In May, Chandler granted them an expansion franchise for the 1966 season, and the owners of the team, to be called the Wildcatters, promptly signed legendary NFL quarterback Sammy Baugh to a five-year coaching deal worth a staggering $50,000 a year. Ownership agreed to pay a $250,000 franchise fee and planned to play games in Skelly Stadium at the University of Tulsa, which was being expanded to 40,000 seats.

There was just one problem: The stadium operators rejected the lease agreement because "they did not meet our financial requirements."

The Tulsa Wildcatters never played a game in the Continental League.

Those teams that did take the field during the league's first season found themselves up against an immovable object in the form of the Charleston Rockets. With a front four led by future Los Angeles Rams Pro Bowl selection Coy Bacon — one-quarter of the famed "Fearsome Foursome" — the Rockets allowed their opponents just 9.2 points a game in reeling off 14 consecutive wins. Just two teams managed to score more than 20 points against them (one of them, Philadelphia, losing in a 58-21 rout), and the Rockets held eight consecutive foes to single digits in one stretch that included three shutouts.

Charleston ran away with the Western Division title at 14-0, earning the right to face Eastern champ Toronto in for the championship. The Rifles finished the season at 11-3, but two of their losses were to the Rockets.

Happy Chandler

As the Rockets capped their perfect season with a 24-7 victory over Toronto in the championship game, owners voted to require that all teams in the league occupy or commit to building stadiums with at least 20,000 seats. The resolution came despite the fact that Charleston had drawn barely enough fans to fill half the 12,000 seats in Laidley Stadium for its championship triumph.

The owners also voted 8-1 to consider using optioned players sent down by the two established leagues. The rationale was simple: It would bring a few better-known players into the league, at least temporarily, and it would save money since the NFL or AFL would still be paying a portion of the player's salary. But it would also create the impression that the Continental League, rather than competing with the two established circuits, was settling for hand-me-downs or scraps dropped under the table.

For that reason, the vote didn't sit well with Chandler, who proclaimed that it "would make the CFL a minor league." Complaining that the decision went against the terms of his employment, he tore up his contract and waived his rights to be paid for the remaining four years, giving up roughly $160,000.

"When I took this job, the owners indicated they wanted to be a major league," Chandler said in January 1966. "They can't be a major league this way. ... I asked them to relieve me of my contract. I don't want any money. I'm all right financially."

The same could not be said for the league itself, which struggled throughout the season. The novelty wore off early — if it ever caught on at all — with the first 30 games producing an average attendance hovering at fewer than 10,000 fans. Only Richmond, Toronto and

Philadelphia surpassed that figure (and not by much), while league-leading Charleston barely managed 7,500 a game. Chandler tried to play the optimist, claiming that attendance was actually better than expected and noting that the AFL's New York and Oakland franchises had played to some home crowds of fewer than 5,000 people just two years earlier.

TV or not TV

Despite Chandler's attempts to spin the numbers, they didn't add up to a profit for the Continental League's owners. Indeed, by season's end, not a single team in the circuit had managed to make money, with the Rhode Island Indians deciding to cease operations after their final game, leaving the league with just nine teams. The Wheeling Ironmen, doormats of the Eastern Division with a woeful 2-12 record, ran out of money as well as one point, and Pittsburgh Steelers owner Art Rooney loaned the team some extra uniforms to use.

Part of the problem was the lack of a major television contract. With the CBS televising NFL games and NBC broadcasting the AFL, the Continental League had hopes of signing a deal with the third major network, ABC. Chandler had said before the inaugural season that he was in negotiations to sign a television contract, but apparently, nothing ever came of it. The closest the league ever got was a $500 deal to televise the 1966 championship game on "ABC's Wide World of Sports." It was the last professional football game televised on the network until 1970, with the debut of "Monday Night Football."

Another opportunity appeared to present itself when self-made millionaire Daniel Overmyer announced his intention to start a fourth broadcast television network to rival the Big Three. The United Network planned its debut in the fall of 1967, broadcasting eight hours a day on as many as 125 affiliated stations nationwide. It started out airing a two-hour late-night talk show called "The Las Vegas Show" live from that city's Hacienda Hotel. Hopes were high, and the Continental League secured a breakthrough three-year contract with the network to televise Saturday night games starting in the fall of 1967. The network planned to feed five games each night into regional areas.

Unfortunately for the league, it never happened. The United Network failed to attract enough viewers with "The Las Vegas Show" to make a profit and pulled the plug after just a month on the air. Nearly $700,000 in debt, it declared bankruptcy three months before the start of the Continental Football League season.

The United Network debacle was still in the future when the Continental League headed into its second season in 1966, with the Bears' Rosen replacing Chandler at the helm.

More changes were in the offing for Season 2. The Fort Wayne Warriors moved to

Montreal — the city the Rifles had abandoned a year earlier — where they became the Beavers. The Newark Bears, meanwhile, pulled up stakes and moved to Orlando, where they became the Panthers, the city's first professional sports team. Walt Disney World was still five years in the future, and Orlando was still a sleepy town of fewer than 100,000 residents at the time; a former area resident recently described it to me as little more than a gas stop between Tampa and Jacksonville. A slight exaggeration, perhaps, but Orlando in the mid-1960s hardly represented a step toward the big-time image the Continental League had initially hoped to cultivate.

To replace the failed Rhode Island franchise and fill the void left by the Bears in the New York region, the league awarded a franchise to a team called the Brooklyn Dodgers. And who better to serve as general manager of the new team than Jackie Robinson, who had made history for the baseball team of the same name?

"I know we won't be equal to the New York Giants and possibly at the start to the New York Jets, but we are going to play interesting football," Robinson predicted.

The Dodgers hired seven-time Pro Bowl defensive end Andy Robustelli, a future Hall of Famer who'd retired from the New York Giants two years earlier, as their head coach and began looking for a place to play. This proved to be a problem. The Jets had exclusive rights to Shea Stadium, and the Yankees rebuffed the Dodgers' request to play in the House That Ruth Built. As a result, they were exiled to Downing Stadium, a rundown 22,000-seat facility that was on Randall's Island in Manhattan, not Brooklyn. Built in 1936 as a WPA project, it would later serve as home field for the New York Stars of the World Football League, a team that lasted less than a year.

The Brooklyn Dodgers didn't fare much better. They drew a paltry 12,000 fans to their home opener — their best home crowd of the season — lost their first six games and wound up last in the Eastern Division. Their final home game was played at tiny, ancient Mt. Vernon Memorial Stadium in Westchester, where they treated the 4,100 fans who bothered to show up by upsetting division-leading Toronto 19-17.

It was the last game the Brooklyn franchise would play.

The league added some drama by expanding the playoff field to four teams, allowing the runners-up from each division to qualify. Philadelphia defeated Toronto 31-14 in the Eastern semifinal, then faced Orlando, which had knocked off defending champion Charleston 31-24 in the Western semi. The championship game was a far more interesting affair than the previous year's blowout had been, with Orlando running out to a 17-3 lead before the Bulldogs stormed back to tie it on a pair of touchdown passes by Bob Brodhead. The Bulldogs then won it in overtime when Jamie Caleb capped a 57-yard drive with a chip-shot field goal from 10 yards out, his second successful kick of the game.

But despite the excitement on the field and the presence of a national television audience on ABC, the game was a failure at the turnstiles, with just 5,226 fans filing into the stadium in Philadelphia to watch the home team prevail. The Bulldogs never got to defend their championship, folding after the season, and winning quarterback Bob Brodhead retired at age 28, taking a job as business manager of the Cleveland Browns. He later served a five-year stint as athletic director at Louisiana State University.

The losing quarterback in that title game, Don Jonas, went on to build a distinguished career on the field. He won league MVP honors that year, then repeated the feat in 1967 and '68, when his Panthers won back-to-back championships. In 1967, he threw for 3,446 yards and 41 touchdowns, (although he also served up 21 interceptions). Four years later, having moved to the Canadian Football League, he won that circuit's Most Outstanding Player Award after throwing for more than 4,000 yards and 27 touchdowns. After retiring from as a player, he became the first-ever head coach at the University of Central Florida.

One final footnote on the 1966 season: The Wheeling Ironmen featured a two-way player who would later make a name for himself as a coach in the NFL. Sam Wyche, who would lead the Cincinnati Bengals to a Super Bowl in 1988, completed 9 of 18 passes for the Ironmen and came up with three interceptions as a defensive back, but it didn't help the Ironmen much. After a 2-12 showing the year before, they finished this the '66 season winless in 14 games and allowed nearly twice as many points as they scored. Still, they somehow managed to survive to play a third season in the league and in fact persevered throughout its five-year history.

Take the money and run

Despite the absence of their defending champion, the Continental League soldiered on into the 1967 season, seeking to overcome its persistent woes by finally living up to its name. Expanding beyond the East and Midwest for the first time, the league announced plans to admit seven new teams in a new Pacific Division.

Many of the teams, however, weren't really new: Most were transplants from various semipro leagues out west. Three of them — Seattle, Eugene and Victoria — came from the Pacific Football League, where Seattle and Eugene had finished 1-2 in the standings. The addition of Eugene typified the league's problem with its "minor league" image. The city (which never had another pro football team) had a population that hovered around 60,000 at the time, and Bethel Park had just 10,000 seats — making a mockery of league owners' previous commitment to adopt a low-end threshold of twice that many. Still, the league wanted to expand, and despite its small stature, Eugene had led the PFL in attendance the year before. So, the Bombers were in.

Seattle was coming off a 10-0 season capped by a 48-13 rout of the San Jose Apaches in an interleague game dubbed the West Coast Championship. (The Apaches, notably, were also admitted to the Continental League's new Pacific Division.) The Seattle squad, which had been known as the Ramblers in the PFL, rebranded themselves as the Golden Jets … only to be threatened with a lawsuit by the New York Jets. They then promptly changed their name to the Rangers.

In addition to the three PFL clubs and San Jose, the league welcomed teams in Sacramento, Orange County and Sacramento into the fold. The Orange County entry, which would play its games in Anaheim, would (confusingly) be named the Ramblers.

The league must have seemed full of confidence in launching such an ambitious undertaking, but that ambition failed to mask the league's continued instability.

Franchises awarded to Milwaukee and Chicago in January never materialized. Richmond folded before the season started. Meanwhile, the defunct Brooklyn franchise, transferred to Akron in the offseason, ran into almost immediate trouble. Owner Frank Hurn lined up a staff with some impressive credentials, hiring former NFL quarterback Tobin Rote as general manager and 1948 Heisman Trophy winner Doak Walker as head coach. Rote signed a three-year contract, but he only lasted three exhibition games before getting the ax — along with Walker.

Hurn told the press, "I did not feel I was getting a professional job out of Rote and Walker, although I was paying them pro salaries."

But Hurn actually never paid them anything, and in fact took $30,000 from the pair to finance a team he couldn't afford before they got wise to him. So, he cut them loose. A con man with Chicago mob connections Hurn managed to run the Vulcans franchise into the ground in a few short weeks. He claimed to own 65 pieces of heavy equipment, all of which turned out to be figments of his fertile imagination. Moreover, he didn't live in the Chicago office building he listed as his address. Hurn even looked the part of the sleazy con artist he was: Vulcans lineman Bob Meeker recalled him wearing shark-skinned suits, white shirts, black ties and a perpetual 5 o'clock shadow.

Yet the city was so eager to have its own big-time football team that it overlooked the obvious. The league, similarly hungry for success, did the same.

Hurn had promised to pay Rote and Walker an estimated $40,000 between them, yet he had invested very little of his own money in the team. His mob connections had put up the

Doak Walker had a lot more fun playing football than coaching the Akron Vulcans.

$50,000 the league demanded to transfer the Brooklyn franchise to Ohio. As for Hurn himself, he simply didn't have any money. It was all talk.

"Hurn has spent only $2,000 of his own money on the operation," Rote declared after being handed his walking papers. "I personally have loaned him more than $10,700 and have a note to prove it."

Paydays brought not paychecks, but excuses. Those checks that were written bounced.

Rosen summoned Hurn to the league offices to demand an accounting of $50,000 the league said it was owed. But Hurn passed the buck, blaming the city of Akron for failing to support the team, with a team spokesman protesting that only 1,000 tickets had been sold to the season opener against the Toronto Rifles — another team soon to meet a strange and bitter end.

Rosen and the other owners apparently bought this explanation, because the commissioner issued a statement declaring that "Frank Hurn, owner of the Akron Vulcans, has satisfied the Continental Football League owners that he has obtained adequate financial support for the 1967 Eastern Division season." Exactly how Hurn had satisfied the owners, Rosen didn't say, but all the turmoil didn't help the Vulcans on the field, where they lost their opener to the Rifles 22-7.

A week later, one of those teams was out of business … but it wasn't the Vulcans. The Rifles, who had lost $400,000 the previous season on top of $300,000 the year before, simply ran out of money and were unable to compete with the Canadian Football League's Toronto Argonauts, who had signed away the Rifles' head coach, Leo Cahill, before the season. The Argos also snagged Rifles quarterback Tom Wilkinson, the Continental League's Rookie of the Year in '66, and running back Joe Williams, who had rushed for 2,338 yards in two seasons with the Rifles.

What amounted to a raid on the Continental squad left it decimated and with little heart to continue in light of the owners' immense debt. After those owners bowed out two games into the season, the league decided to keep operating the club as a traveling team, with hopes of keeping it going until the end of the season.

But those hopes were soon dashed, courtesy of the Akron Vulcans. Not surprisingly, Frank Hurn's assurances that he would get the team's finances under control amounted to nothing more than hot air. The league had delivered $3,000 to the Vulcans' dressing room before a Sept. 17 loss in Wheeling, which the players had vowed to skip if they weren't compensated. They hadn't been paid in two weeks. Meanwhile, an investigation showed that Hurn owed more than $70,000 in local debts, and the league was trying to collect on a $100,000 performance bond the owner had posted. Hurn was, however, nowhere to be found. He'd left town five days earlier, and no one seemed to know where he'd gone.

The league scrambled to find someone to take over the team, but two potential owners backed out. Leo Rymkus, the coach and general manager who had replaced Rote and Walker, fumed that it was "the biggest mess I've been associated with in my lifetime in football; I can't coach this way."

Perhaps the final nail in the coffin came when the team delivered its uniforms to the cleaners after the Wheeling game, and the cleaning establishment refused to return them, citing bills that hadn't been paid.

That same week, Rosen pulled the plug on both the Akron and Toronto franchises.

Sadly, it wasn't the last time Akron had its pro football hopes dashed. More than four decades later, a promoter Jamie Cuadra announced plans to form a pro football league called the New USFL. Several cities were mentioned as sites for potential franchises, but none was as highly touted as Akron, where an ownership group stepped forward and purchased the aging Rubber Bowl — the Vulcans old home field. Plans were made to refurbish the stadium, and a team name was even chosen that evoked memories of the Vulcans: the Akron Fire.

Those plans went up in smoke when Cuadra pleaded guilty to embezzling more than $1 million from two San Diego companies and using it to attract investors for the league. Cuadra turned out to be just another con artist, much like Frank Hurn.

What happened to Hurn? Having skipped town with the Vulcans on their last legs, he fled to Florida, triggering a nationwide manhunt. Sent back to Akron, he was sentenced to three years in prison — of which he served 10 months — and five years on probation. Free again, he returned to Florida, where he wrote bad checks in Tampa, and became involved in transporting stolen coal across state lines: 2,400 tons of it. Another scam involved an attempt to sell a coal mine he didn't own. Hurn was sentenced to prison again, this time for five years, before being paroled in 1983. His last known address was Sedona, Ariz.

1965 Continental Football League	W	L	T	PF	PA	Pct.
Eastern Division						
Toronto Rifles	11	3	0	412	258	.786
Philadelphia Bulldogs	10	4	0	414	341	.717
Norfolk Neptunes	9	5	0	326	280	.643
Newark Bears	5	9	0	307	310	.357
Wheeling Ironmen	2	12	0	175	290	.143
Western Division						
Charleston Rockets	14	0	0	462	129	1.000
Fort Wayne Warriors	8	6	0	351	256	.538
Richmond Rebels	6	8	0	283	385	.429
Rhode Island Indians	3	11	0	182	411	.214
Hartford Charter Oaks	2	12	0	203	455	.143

Championship game: Charleston 24, Toronto 7

Rhinos ramble on

The Continental League, meanwhile, was getting new addresses all the time. Even the new Pacific Division had its problems. The Long Beach Admirals (a franchise originally intended for Phoenix) lasted just one game — a lopsided home loss to Seattle — before asking seeking the league's permission for a transfer to Portland. Instead, the league revoked the franchise altogether.

There were a few bright spots out west, where the Orange County Ramblers and San Jose Apaches vied for the division title. The Ramblers were successors to the Orange County Rhinos of the old Western Football League, which had the distinction of being the first Los Angeles-area football team to appear regularly on local television back in 1957.

The following year, on-air announcer Sam Bacon started challenging the NFL Rams to a scrimmage. The Rams — who were no slouches that season at 8-4 — took up the gantlet and promptly destroyed the Rhinos 38-0 in one half of football at the Rose Bowl. Against regional semipro teams such as the Bakersfield Spoilers and the San Pedro Longshoremen, the Rhinos were much more effective. In 1966, they won the Western Football League title with a sterling 10-0 record and applied to join the Continental League.

They continued their success there under the new name and immediately kindled a rivalry with the new San Jose squad. The Apaches in some ways typified the Continental League's continued struggles to shed its image as a minor league. They wore used silver-and-black Raiders uniforms for their home games which they exchanged for white-and-red 49ers uniforms when they went on the road. The team van was a loaner from a local car dealership. Rather than competing with the NFL and AFL for top players, the Apaches were strictly a local bunch copying the big boys — about 20 of them castoffs from the Raiders and 49ers.

"We've boiled it down to a solid 35 (players), all from the Bay Area," their coach said, commenting on the roster before the season. "The vast majority of this group of young men is comprised of recent college graduates. We'll be running basically 49er offenses and defenses."

A little more than a decade later, the coach in question would not only run offenses for the 49ers themselves, he would redefine them, leading the NFL club to three Super Bowl championships and revolutionizing the way the entire league approached the game with his West Coast Offense. The Apaches, however, gave Bill Walsh his first head coaching gig, following seven years as an assistant at San Jose State, Cal and Stanford. His first taste of pro football had come just a year earlier, when he worked as Raiders' running backs coach.

Under Walsh, the Apaches got off to a strong start on the field, outscoring their first four opponents by an average score of 31-7 in an unbeaten string that set up a game against the second-place Ramblers. The Orange County team was 4-1 at that point and "in a state of shock" (according to one press account) coming off an upset loss to the Bombers in Eugene, Ore.

The Ramblers managed a 24-17 victory over the Apaches to retake first place, which is where they would finish the season, closing the year with five straight wins — including a key 14-3 decision at San Jose — while the increasingly injury-plagued Apaches lost three times in the space of four games to fall out of contention. San Jose's season finale, an anticlimactic 48-23 rout of the Sacramento Buccaneers, turned out to be the last game for both the Apaches and their up-and-coming coach. Competing in the same market as the Raiders and 49ers, the team managed to draw more than 4,000 fans to San Jose City College Stadium just once (a crowd of 4,391 against Orange County), a meager level of support that couldn't sustain the team beyond its inaugural season.

Walsh left the Continental League at year's end, too, accepting an offer from the legendary Paul Brown to become an assistant with the AFL's expansion Cincinnati Bengals. He would coach there for the next eight seasons and eventually begin his 10-year stint as head coach of the 49ers in 1979.

The Orange County Ramblers, meanwhile, earned the right to host the league championship game at Anaheim Stadium against the Orlando Panthers, champions of the East for the second straight year. Even with the home-field advantage, though, the Ramblers were overmatched, as Don Jonas threw five touchdown passes — four of them to Samuel Weir — in a 38-14 rout against a defense that had given up just four all season.

The two teams would meet again for the championship at the close of the next season, which brought yet more change to the Continental League. Rosen, the commissioner, bowed out following a season in which five of the league's 15 teams failed to complete their full schedules. Charter member Hartford folded, as did Montreal, Akron, Toronto and Long Beach.

Increasingly, the league sought to replenish its ranks by absorbing teams from other leagues — or entire leagues themselves. The problem with this approach was twofold. First, many of those teams were already on shaky ground when they applied for membership, and second, the leagues that produced them were invariably semipro outfits that played at a level below the Continental League.

Before the 1968 season, the league absorbed the Professional Football League of America, which had been formed as a direct outgrowth of the Continental League's birth: When the strongest five teams left the old UFL to form what they had hoped would be a third major league, the other three stuck together as the nucleus of the PFLA. Not only had those teams preferred to continue in a minor-league context, they hadn't been very good even at that level: Their combined record in the UFL's final season was paltry 11-31.

A few other teams had signed on to fill out the PFLA's membership, but despite its grandiose name, it always remained strictly a regional outfit, with only one team — Huntsville, Ala. — outside the Midwest.

Still, the Continental League needed new blood, so it pursued a merger.

The PFLA was supposed to contribute eight teams to a new, combined 20-team league, but only five (Chicago, league champion Alabama, Oklahoma City, Omaha and Quad Cities) ultimately made the transition, with the other three either deciding against the move or failing to meet the league's financial requirements. Joliet, a UFL member that had declined to join the Continental League in the first place, opted out again despite having made it to the PFLA title game a year earlier. The Continentals took up some of the slack by granting expansion teams to Indianapolis, Detroit and Little Rock, Ark.

Once the season started, it became clear that the PFLA teams would bring little to the table. The Chicago Owls did manage to lure Joe Williams back from the Canadian Football League, and he resumed a career in which he would become the all-time Continental League rushing leader. But even the PFLA champion Alabama Hawks failed to crack the .500 mark, as did almost other franchise brought in via the merger; only Omaha managed a winning record at 7-5. The biggest disaster was the Quad Cities franchise, which opened the season with a 63-6 loss to previously inept Wheeling (now renamed Ohio Valley) and drew a mere 3,000 fans to their home opener against the Owls before the league revoked the franchise and awarded a team to Las Vegas instead.

The expansion Michigan Arrows, based in Detroit, were just as bad, posting a dismal 1-11 record, but their roster was noteworthy for including a placekicker named Garo Yepremian. The Cypriot-born Yepremian had played for the NFL's Detroit Lions in 1966 and '67 before enlisting in the Army. When the Lions refused to sign him upon his return to Michigan in 1968, the Arrows offered him a contract. He responded by making 6 of 10 field goal attempts and averaging 36 yards punting for the team. His 60 percent showing was a league record for kickers with 10 or more attempts.

Yepremian would become far better known, however, for a botched play in the 1973 Super Bowl, when he came off the bench to attempt a field goal with his Miami Dolphins leading 14-0 in the waning moments. When the kick was blocked, and Yepremian picked up the ball and tried to throw it, only to have it slip out of his hands. Instead of catching it, he batted it up into the air … and into the hands of Washington defender Mike Bass, who returned it for a touchdown.

Miami held on to win 14-7, and Yepremian quipped afterward, "This is the first time the goat of the game is in the winner's locker room."

Another placekicker starred in the 1968 Continental League championship game, which ended as the previous one had, with Orlando defeating Orange County. Panthers quarterback Don Jonas, who had beaten the Ramblers with his arm the previous year, did the trick with his leg this time, kicking three field goals — including a 52-yarder that set a league record — to more than account for the difference in a 30-23 decision.

Revolving door

Their second straight loss in the title game turned out to be the Orange County Ramblers' swan song: They moved to San Bernardino after the season but never played a game there: The San Bernardino Sun reported May 20, 1969, that club chief executive Vic Saman's phone had been disconnected and that he could not be located. The league revoked the franchise and transferred the players' contracts to a newly formed Honolulu team.

The Hawaiian Monarchs, as they were to be called, made headlines by reportedly offering O.J. Simpson a $2 million contract that one news story said "reportedly involves pineapples." The former Heisman Trophy winner (and future murder suspect) was at an impasse in contract talks with the Buffalo Bills and was exploring his options. Two other Continental teams — the Indianapolis Capitols and San Antonio Toros — also reportedly made overtures, but Simpson ultimately remained with the Bills.

It was probably a good thing for him that he did, as the Monarchs never played a game in Hawaii. As was becoming almost predictable at this point, the league stepped in and announced that the team was failing to meet its obligations, canceled the franchise and awarded the player rights to a new franchise in Portland called the Loggers.

Meanwhile, Charleston, where the Rockets had won the league's inaugural title after a perfect season, left the league and was replaced by the Jersey Jays out of Jersey City.

The biggest change in membership for 1969 involved another merger. A year earlier, the semipro Texas Football League had rejected overtures to join forces with the Continental League, suggesting instead a postseason interleague title game between the two champions. A year later, TFL commissioner George Schwepps was singing a different tune, accepting a new proposal to join the Continental League as a full division of teams based in Texas and the surrounding area. Six teams ended up joining: the Dallas Rockets, Fort Worth Braves, Oklahoma (Tulsa) Thunderbirds, San Antonio Toros, Texarkana Titans and West Texas Rufneks (based in Midland-Odessa).

The Fort Worth team signed All-American running back Chris Gilbert from the University of Texas, the first player in college football history to rush for more than 1,000 yards in three consecutive seasons. The New York Jets, fresh off their stunning Super Bowl upset of Baltimore, drafted him in the fifth round, but Gilbert reportedly asked the Jets for more money than the team was paying its top choice.

"I made up my mind about a month ago what would be worth my while," he said during talks with the Jets. I don't know if they think I'm serious about it. They said I was asking more than their first-round draft choice. If they want me bad enough, they'll got ahead and pay it. Of course, if they don't, that's that."

Gilbert had made up his mind he wouldn't play for the Jets for less than $40,000. After all, they'd paid Joe Namath 10 times that much in 1965.

Talks with the Jets soon broke down.

That's when Tommy Mercer, a beer executive and owner of the Braves, stepped in with an offer that was said to be in five figures (the Jets themselves had reportedly been offering something in the low $20,000s). Mercer was no lightweight. He had been a partner with oilman Lamar Hunt — founder of the AFL and owner of the Kansas City Chiefs — in a minor league baseball team, and the pair had unsuccessfully sought to obtain a Dallas franchise in both the National and American Leagues.

Gilbert later recalled Mercer telling him that the league had a television contract and made him an offer he couldn't turn down: He would only have to play half the time on offense and only had to work out twice a week; the team would pay for his apartment and transportation, and Mercer guaranteed his salary. It also offered him a chance to stay close to Austin, where he was finishing up his degree. Ultimately, of course, there was no TV deal, but Gilbert signed the contract and suited up for the Braves.

In hindsight, however, Gilbert might have made the wrong decision. His teammates resented his big salary and never got to know him because he didn't practice or play with them often enough. His limited involvement also hurt his production: He wound up playing second fiddle to fellow Braves running back James Walker — a UC Santa Barbara product who led the league in rushing with more than 1,000 yards that season — and never wound up playing in the NFL. Still, Gilbert had no regrets. Mercer paid him the money he had promised, and Gilbert invested it in a new bank, turning a tidy profit from the venture.

(Mercer, it should be noted, wasn't always that generous. When sagging attendance hurt his bottom line in 1970, he demanded that his players sign contract amendments under which they would forfeit their salaries for the final two games in exchange for a cut of the gate receipts. Those who refused would be cut — and only four of them did.)

Unlike the Fort Worth Braves, the El Paso Jets never even wound up playing in the Continental League. The TFL team on the southwestern border was supposed to come along for the ride when the two leagues merged, but wound up suspending operations instead. The league, however, had bigger plans: It wanted to expand all the way into Mexico itself. In an ambitious move, it granted an expansion franchise to a 42-year-old used car dealer from San Antonio named Red McCombs, who hoped to have his Mexico Golden Aztecs play their games in Mexico City's mammoth Olympic Stadium, where the capacity had just been increased to 83,700 for the 1968 Summer Games. It was a far cry from the 10,000- or 20,000-seat facilities some of the league's franchises had called home.

Unfortunately, city officials in the capital demanded to set admission prices at a meager 38 cents apiece. Even with 83,000-plus seats available, McCombs knew he could never make any money that way, so he moved his team out of the capital and over to Monterrey, where 52,000-seat University Stadium was available to rent. The immediate results were sensational: The Aztecs drew a whopping 25,000 fans for their opening exhibition game against the Chicago Owls, followed by 19,000 a week later for a preseason win over the Las Vegas Cowboys. From there, however, attendance began to spiral downward, with just 3,000 fans turning out for the regular-season opener against the Oklahoma Thunderbirds.

Convinced he could do better in Mexico City, McCombs tried again to negotiate a lease there, but again came up empty, leaving the team effectively without a home. The team played four more games, all on the road, before finally calling it quits after a 17-3 victory at Dallas on Sept. 18.

Perhaps surprisingly, it wasn't the last the sports world would hear of Red McCombs, who three years later would get involved in another pro sports venture in a renegade league, helping to lease the Dallas Chaparrals of the American Basketball Association and move them to San Antonio. The deal allowed a consortium of McCombs and 35 other businessmen to move the team on the condition they would return it to Dallas if no deal to purchase the Chaps had been finalized within three years.

A year later, McCombs and his group agreed to purchase the Chaps (now renamed the Spurs), and eventually helped bring them into the established NBA along with three other ABA teams in 1976. A couple of years later, McCombs sold the Spurs and bought another NBA team, the Denver Nuggets. He sold them after six years later and purchased a controlling interest in the Spurs, which he held until 1993. His biggest sports purchase, however, brought him back into football when he acquired the NFL's Minnesota Vikings.

Minnesota was a long way from Mexico, and the Vikings were a far cry from the Aztecs.

A bang and a whimper

But whatever one might say about the problems the Continental League experienced in 1969, it was hard to top the league's championship game that season — which turned out to be the final game it ever played. The matchup pitted San Antonio from the TFL against the Indianapolis, which had shocked two-time defending champ Orlando in the semis 27-7 behind the arm of a 22-year-old quarterback named John Walton, who had played college ball at small Elizabeth City State in North Carolina.

Out of college in 1969, Walton had signed a free-agent contract with the Los Angeles Rams for $200, but found himself No. 3 on the depth chart behind Roman Gabriel — the NFL's Most Valuable Player that year. The chances of seeing playing time with the Rams were slim to none, so the team sent him to Indianapolis for seasoning, and he made the most of the opportunity, throwing 17 touchdown passes and earning all-league honors.

Walton's opposite number for that game was Toros quarterback Sal Olivas, a 23-year-old out of New Mexico State who had led the nation in total offense with the Aggies two years earlier.

The Capitols, playing at home on Dec. 13 before more than 10,000 fans, opened the scoring on a blocked punt and took a 14-0 lead on Walton's first scoring pass of the game, a 15-yarder to Al Moore. But San Antonio kept battling back, pulling even at 21 on Olivas' first touchdown pass before Walton struck back with a 51-yard strike to Joe Wynns in the waning seconds of the first half. The Toros knotted the score again at 28 on Olivas' 1-yard run in the third quarter, but Indy scored the next 10 points and was poised to hoist the trophy when the unthinkable happened: the Toros scored 10 points of their own in the final 24 seconds. Olivas (who finished the game with 314 yards passing) lofted a 29-yard scoring pass to R.A. Johnson, then the Toros recovered an onside kick to set up a 38-yard field goal by Jerry Moritz with 2 ticks left on the clock.

Moritz had a chance to give San Antonio the title in overtime with a relative chip shot: a 25-yard attempt. But the kick sailed wide to the right, and Walton responded by leading Indy on the game-winning drive, connecting on passes of 11, 21 and 15 yards to set up a 13-yard scoring run by John Nice with just 9 seconds left that sealed the victory. Final score: Indianapolis 44, San Antonio 38.

Coming off the spectacular championship class, the Continental League seemed on the verge of coming into its own. The TFL had provided a strong infusion of new talent, and the league had a pair of young, marketable stars in Olivas and Walton — who had just become the first black quarterback ever to win a pro football championship. Attendance was even up, with teams across the league averaging nearly 8,000 fans a game, compared to just 6,600 a year earlier. The Norfolk Neptunes averaged nearly 15,000 fans a game, while Fort Worth, Orlando and Sacramento were at or above 10,000.

But there were problems under the surface. A mere two days after the title game, the league revoked three key franchises: the Chicago Owls, Omaha Mustangs and Wheeling-based Ohio Valley Ironmen, one of just two remaining charter members. The reason given by Commissioner Jim Dunn was familiar. He announced it was "for failure to meet full 1969 commitments to the league," most of them financial. The same day, a group of promoters in Tennessee bought the Las Vegas Cowboys, intending to move them to Memphis.

Franchise shifts and failures were nothing new to the league, but this time, it turned out to be the beginning of the end. Omaha got a new franchise, but Arkansas and Alabama dropped out, as did the Jersey Jays. The most devastating blows, however, came with the withdrawal of perennial attendance leader Norfolk and two-time champion Orlando. Soon, only a single franchise was left east of the Mississippi River: the champion Indianapolis Capitols. Team president Art Savill realized his team would be faced with prohibitive travel costs if it decided to remain in the league. In mid-February, the Caps pulled out, too.

"In the event there is a change in the alignment, which will give us a reasonable chance for existence, we will be pleased to withdraw our withdrawal," Savill said at the time, "but I do not think the situation will be changed."

The league scrambled to shore up its eastern membership by adding a team in Hershey, Pa., to be called the Pennsylvania Bruins, but the Capitols weren't coming back. Savill instead began pushing for construction of a domed stadium that would make Indianapolis an NFL-worthy site. Meanwhile, his Caps joined Orlando, Jersey and Norfolk in bolting for the ACFL, one of the two leagues that had given birth to the Continental League six years earlier.

The promise of a new start quickly gave way to oblivion, however, as only Norfolk remained in the league past the 1970 season and the circuit suspended operations a year later. The league had relied on working agreements with NFL and AFL clubs, which treated the Atlantic Coast League like a farm system. Each of the league's eight teams was affiliated with a major club (Hartford had a deal with the Buffalo Bills, Pottstown with the Philadelphia Eagles and Bridgeport's owners even named their team after the parent club, the New York Jets). The arrangement allowed minor-league teams to bolster their rosters with young prospects in need of seasoning and veterans hoping to earn their way back to the big time.

But after the 1969 season, with the NFL and AFL poised to finally consummate their merger, Commissioner Pete Rozelle canceled all the combined league's minor-league affiliations. The NFL now had 26 teams, and the eight-team ACFL couldn't supply farm clubs for every one of them; the teams left out of this equation felt as though they would be at a disadvantage, so Rozelle nixed the entire program. This left the ACFL without a key source of talent, and it proved to be a crippling blow.

Ill fortune struck again when one of the league's marquee teams, the Orlando Panthers, had to compete without their best player: MVP quarterback Don Jonas fled north after the '69 season to conclude his stellar career in the Canadian Football League. Orlando's top draw in 1970? A 27-year-old newcomer named Pat who weighed in at a slim 122 pounds and whose sole responsibility was to hold the ball for the kicker on extra points. "Pat," in this case, as short for Patricia, and Palinkas was married to the Panthers' placekicker, Steve Palinkas. When she entered an August game against the Bridgeport Jets in August of 1970, she became the first woman to play in a professional football game. She promptly flubbed the snap, tried to run with the football and took a vicious hit from linebacker Wally Florence, who weighed nearly twice as much as she did.

"I tried to break her neck," Florence said at halftime. "I don't know what she's trying to prove. I'm out here trying to make a living, and she's out here prancing around, making folly with a man's game."

Palinkas shrugged it off, coming back in the second half to handle the snap perfectly on two occasions, each time allowing her husband to split the uprights. As to Florence's hit, she said: "I didn't feel a thing. When I went to the locker room at the half, I had a little headache. I took some aspirin and felt fine."

Palinkas didn't last long in the league, however, as the Panthers cut her husband after a leg injury reduced his range on field goals. Pat Palinkas quit the league along with him, and she wasn't the only casualty. The Orlando franchise itself folded at season's end, while former Continental League rival Indianapolis took a step down to the regional Midwest Football League.

1968 Continental Football League

	W	L	PF	PA	Pct.
Atlantic Division					
Orlando Panthers	10	2	378	160	.833
Ohio Valley Ironmen	9	3	388	257	.750
Charleston Rockets	8	3	287	180	.727
Norfolk Neptunes	7	5	361	222	.583
Alabama Hawks	5	7	175	290	.416
Michigan Arrows	1	11	130	418	.083
Central Division					
Indianapolis Capitols	8	4	300	169	.667
Omaha Mustangs	7	5	242	261	.583
Chicago Owls	6	6	284	241	.500
Oklahoma City Plainsmen	5	6	199	265	.454
Arkansas Diamonds	2	10	177	425	.167
Las Vegas Cowboys	1	9	105	325	.100
Quad Cities Raiders	0	2	15	84	.000
Pacific Division					
Orange County Ramblers	11	1	331	146	.917
Seattle Rangers	7	5	302	206	.583
Sacramento Capitols	5	7	218	248	.416
Spokane Shockers	3	9	161	302	.250

Championship game: Orlando 30, Orange County 23

Leftovers

In early 1970, the Continental League attempted to soldier on, only to be met with another obstacle: the announced formation in early March of another league, to be called the Trans-American Football League. Hershey withdrew its application and cast its lot in with the new league, as did Mercer's Fort Worth team and the San Antonio Toros — who promptly made an offer of $250,000 to Heisman Trophy winner Steve Owens of Oklahoma. The league announced its intention to field eight teams in the fall of 1970, with the others being in Los Angeles, Chicago, Memphis, Tampa and Birmingham.

A little more than a week after it announced its formation, however, the league pushed its projected starting date back a year to 1971, with San Antonio and Fort Worth apparently deciding to stay put in the TFL portion of the Continental League, after all. At this point, there weren't many teams left outside of Texas. Sacramento, Seattle, Spokane and the resurrected Omaha franchise were still in the picture, but every other team had either folded or bolted for the ACFL.

In the midst of all this turmoil, Dunn resigned as commissioner March 10 and was replaced by Sacramento Capitols owner Lee Baldarelli.

On March 10, Dunn resigned as commissioner and was succeeded by Sacramento Capitols owner Lee Baldarelli, who promptly announced a series of rule changes designed to make the Continental League (or what was left of it) more compelling. For one thing, the league had decided to adopt the equivalent of basketball's three-point shot for field goals: Kicks longer than 35 yards would be worth four points, and kicks of more than 45 yards would be worth five. Even more radically, the league had voted to implement the so-called "eight-point rule" previously used in the Pacific Football League. Under this rule, teams that had fallen behind by eight points or more would be allowed to receive a kickoff after scoring instead of kicking the ball away.

"In a real sense, CFL football will not be over until the final second of play," Baldarelli announced. "Our purpose is to bring good professional football to our communities. We further wish to be known as the innovators of the new rules of football."

Neither of these innovations ever caught on, and no one ever got a chance to see how they might work in a Continental Football League game. The end came when Baldarelli's Sacramento team itself went out of business in early July, after the commissioner reported he had only been able to sell 1,250 season tickets of the 3,000 needed to keep the team viable.

The remaining Texas teams played in a six-team standalone TFL in the fall, with Olivas leading the Toros to a 21-17 victory over the Braves for the title in November. The Toros and the rest of the league then turned right around and returned to the gridiron April 1 under the auspices of the delayed Trans-American Football League, which had decided to try playing football in the spring. At the time, it was a novel concept, later copied by the USFL, XFL, Alliance of American Football and several other leagues that never made it off the drawing board.

"We're very enthusiastic about this new idea," Toros co-owner Henry Hight gushed. "We've received a lot of favorable comment on the idea, and even television has expressed a keen interest in it."

The Toros and Braves made up two teams in the four-team TAFL Southwest Division — the only division that actually played any games in the spring of 1971. The idea was for three other divisions to go online the following spring — something that never occurred. Low attendance and (inevitably) the lack of a television contract for what was then a strictly regional league doomed the concept before it could go any further. The Texarkana Titans topped the regular-season standings with a 5-0 record and faced San Antonio for the league championship in June, with the Toros prevailing 20-19.

The San Antonio squad moved into yet another new league the following year, setting up shop in the Southwestern Football League along with franchises in Phoenix, Las Vegas, Los Angeles and Dallas-Fort Worth. There, the Toros went undefeated and won yet another league title.

After the season, San Antonio owner Hight pitched American expansion to Canadian Football League, touting a southern division that could include teams in Las Vegas, Los Angeles, Phoenix, San Antonio and Seattle. The Canadian circuit didn't take him up on the idea, although it did expand south of the border for two seasons, in 1994 and '95, before retreating to the Great White North when the NFL moved into its most successful market, Baltimore. Instead, the Southwestern League expanded the following year, adding teams in Albuquerque, Reno and Oklahoma City. The Las Vegas Casinos made news by offering Rams quarterback Roman Gabriel a $100,000 contract to play eight games. Gabriel never did play for the Casinos, but the New Mexico Thunderbirds got a strong arm of their own in the form of Toros quarterback Sal Olivas.

"I am convinced that Sal can play football for an NFL team," New Mexico general manager John Radasovich said in the summer of 1973. "In fact, the way he's performed over the past in the Southwestern League, I'm amazed that no NFL team has picked him up. We are doing everything we can to see that Sal has a fair shot at the pros."

Olivas never made it to the NFL, and the Southwestern League called it quits after just two years.

A World of Trouble

Bigger was better. That was the idea behind the World Football League, which burst onto the scene in 1974 with big plans and a big name. How could you get any bigger than a "world" league, right?

Actually, you could. The very same week the WFL announced its plans, an outfit called the Universal Football League declared its intention to begin play in '74 with teams in eight North American cities — including Toronto and Mexico City. Proposed innovations included 12 players instead of 11, a three-down format ala the Canadian Football League, and kickoffs from the 20-yard-line instead of the 40 to encourage runbacks.

"We're asking for $3 million in cash for each of the franchises," said Tony Razzano, a sports agent who planned to organize the league with attorney and fellow Dayton resident Louis S. Goldman. "We've received verbal commitments from a number of cities, but there's nothing in writing yet."

Razzano spoke of plans to sign players such as Sonny Sixkiller and Joe Theismann but admitted no one was under contract, and the league never got past the theoretical stage. It's one thing to ask for $3 million; it's quite another to get someone to cough it up, especially when a similar blueprint had been placed on the drawing board by Gary Davidson, who had plenty of experience in this sort of thing.

Davidson had already played a role in launching upstart basketball and hockey leagues, both of which — the ABA and WHA — were still in business at the time. Now he had his sights set on the big enchilada, pro football, which was rising fast to challenge baseball's identity as the national pastime. And Davidson wasn't just thinking nationally; as the new league's name boldly stated, he was thinking globally.

"As it stands now, I don't know the exact number of interested parties involved, but we've been talking to 20 or 30 groups from Osaka, Japan, all the way to Rome," he said in announcing the league's formation at the start of October 1973. "There's a little bit of travel problems, though, so we'll probably limit ourselves to Europe or Asia the first year."

The league never got nearly that far and, in fact — despite designs on Mexico City and Tokyo — no member ever played outside the United States. But the initial roster of teams did include a franchise in Honolulu and another in Toronto, the latter belonging to John F.

Bassett, owner of the World Hockey Association's Toronto Toros. Bassett had deep pockets, to some degree lined by his media magnate father, which gave the league an instant shot of credibility. (The elder Bassett owned both Toronto newspapers along with the Canadian Broadcasting Corp., and he'd ventured into the football arena himself as an owner of the CFL's Toronto Argonauts.)

Those pockets were deep enough to put together a $3 million-plus package that lured three star players away from the Miami Dolphins, where they'd been at the core of a team that completed an unbeaten run through the NFL in 1972, culminating in a Super Bowl victory. Fullback Larry Csonka had led that team in rushing, Paul Warfield had been the Dolphins' top receiver, and Jim Kiick had rushed for more than 500 yards that season. With

Larry Csonka in 1972

a year left on their NFL contracts, the three pledged to join the Northmen in 1975.

It wasn't a hard decision: Csonka had only been making $60,000 a year with the Dolphins.

"Money isn't always the only consideration," he said. "In this case, it is one of the considerations, of course, but there are others which I do not wish to discuss. We had a figure in the back of our heads. The Toronto club offered us more than we anticipated — even more than we had asked for in the exploratory package."

Other considerations were also behind the decision by Oakland Raiders quarterback Ken Stabler to jump leagues, signing a contract with the Birmingham Americans, though he admitted the money was pre-eminent.

"The most important factor was money," the Alabama native said in announcing a three-year, $350,000 deal to play in his home state starting in 1976. "Getting back to the South was also pretty important. I was born in the South and played football in the South. Oakland could have offered me as much money as Birmingham, but they couldn't have let me play in the South."

Indeed, the new league couldn't have come along at a better time for NFL players, who were unhappy with their salary levels and, in the spring of '74, murmuring about the possibility of a walkout. The players were unhappy about the so-called Rozelle Rule, which permitted NFL Commissioner Pete Rozelle to compensate any team losing a free agent if the team couldn't reach an agreement with the player's new squad. As a result of the rule, few teams were willing to sign free agents, fearing Rozelle might deprive them of key players as compensation.

"It makes you wonder why the owners don't start talking seriously about a contract," mused O.J. Simpson, who knew the value of leverage: A few years earlier, he had reportedly been offered contracts with three different Continental League teams before signing a four-year deal with the Buffalo Bills worth $215,000. "For the players, the new league is the best thing since the AFL. I think it ought to mean an average yearly increase of $10,000 to $15,000 for the players."

NFL players did, in fact, go on strike over the Rozelle Rule and other issues, but they returned to the field without a collective bargaining agreement before the season could start. It was a short-term victory for the commissioner and league owners, but the players took their case to court and won a ruling that the Rozelle Rule violated the Sherman Antitrust Act.

Even before the abortive strike, however, some NFL players decided it was worth it to test the waters with the upstart league. The first was Virgil Carter, who had led the NFL in passing percentage with the Cincinnati Bengals in 1971 but had recently been traded to the San Diego Chargers. He chose the newly minted Chicago Fire instead, signing a two-year deal worth a reported $100,000.

The Hawaiians, meanwhile, signed several players away from the established league, led by Cowboys running back Calvin Hill and 49ers All-Pro tight end Ted Kwalick. Hill signed a three-year deal, and Kwalick inked a multiyear deal worth an estimated $500,000 that reportedly included a condominium and (yes) a pineapple plantation.

The competition between the two leagues wasn't just good for veterans, but for players coming out of college, too. Among them was Danny White, an All-American quarterback from Arizona State who had selected by the Dallas Cowboys but faced the prospect of playing behind Roger Staubach and Craig Morton. The Cowboys still wanted White as their quarterback of the future, though, and — apparently nervous about the new league — doubled their offer to him. That's when Bassett called him from Toronto and asked him very simply what it would take for him to suit up as a Northman.

White responded by quoting Bassett a figure that was twice what the Cowboys had offered and, without missing a beat, the Toronto owner said he had a deal.

"It's a very opportune time for me to graduate," White noted.

(It was an opportune time for Morton, too, as he signed with a contract with the WFL's Houston Texans, leaving the Cowboys without two of the three quarterbacks they'd counted on having in 1974.)

Shifting sands

While the owners were opening their wallets to raid the NFL, not everything was rosy in the house that Gary Davidson was building. Many of the contracts being signed didn't take effect until 1975 or later, because the stars jumping to the new league wouldn't be free of their existing contracts until then. That meant the new league would have to make it through its first season using a motley assemblage of NFL castoffs, greenhorn college graduates and refugees from the minor leagues.

One of those leagues, the Southwestern Football League, even sued the WFL for $5 million in early 1974. The upshot of the case: San Antonio Toros owner Henry Hight claimed the new league was violating his circuit's territorial rights by setting up shop in areas where the SFL had established teams — even though teams from both organizations would be competing in only one of those markets (Los Angeles).

"The WFL has stated that they would file suit if the NFL tried to move into any area in which the WFL has a franchise," an indignant Hight noted. "Yet they have turned around and done this exact same thing to us." But the Southwestern League, which paid its players $95 a game, hardly had the money to go toe-to-toe with the brash new bullies on pro football's big-money block, and was soon out of business.

In any case, the WFL had much bigger problems. In its rush to be ready for an inaugural season less than a year after it announced its formation, the league ran into some practical hurdles that raised questions about its viability even before the opening kickoff. One of the most important assets the new league wanted to cultivate was an image of stability, yet had some owners had trouble finding suitable playing fields, and some franchises fled to new cities or changed ownership in the months after the league announced its formation.

Cleveland Indians owner Nick Mileti, the original owner of the Chicago franchise, lost no time in selling it to a local developer. The Hawaii team changed hands, landing with another developer named Chris Hemmeter and restaurateur Sam Battistone, the "Sam" in the Sambo's diner chain. Davidson held the rights to Philadelphia but didn't want to run the team himself; instead, it nearly ended up in the hands (successively) of a deeply indebted Philly businessman and an unemployed lifeguard who promised to recruit other investors before the league decided it wasn't quite that desperate.

Washington, D.C., was supposed to have a team, but was rebuffed in its attempts to secure leases at Robert F. Kennedy Stadium — which the NFL team that played there had no intention of sharing — and Memorial Stadium in Baltimore, home of the similarly possessive Colts. Even the Naval Academy refused to allow the team to use its stadium, even though it had no lights and offered seating for fewer than 30,000 fans. So, team owner E. Joseph Wheeler Jr. announced plans to move down the road to Norfolk's Foreman Field — former home of the Norfolk Neptunes — and rename his team the Virginia Ambassadors. Considering the Neptunes' drawing power in the Continental League, it seemed like a smart move, even if the field did seat a mere 26,000 fans.

But less than a month later, Wheeler was complaining he needed new investors and finally, fed up with the entire situation, sold the team altogether. The buyers, a group of Florida investors, promptly moved it to another former Continental League haunt — Orlando — and renamed it the Suns. Even that name didn't last long, though, as it created all sorts of confusion with another league member, the Anaheim-based Southern California Sun, so at last, the new ownership settled on the name "Blazers" (perhaps referring to blazing suns, although the team logo more closely resembled a comet).

The Boston team was announced as the Bulldogs, then shortened its name to Bulls, then ceased to exist altogether as the ownership group merged its interests with those of the New York franchise. Rights to Boston's draft choices ultimately wound up in Portland with a new franchise (the final original member of the league) that was christened the Storm, while the New York team ended up playing its games in Downing Stadium, the same Randall's Island death trap that had claimed the Continental League's Brooklyn Dodgers eight years earlier.

Detroit's stadium situation was scarcely any better. Rynearson Stadium was at least new, having opened in 1969, but it seated just 22,000 fans and didn't even have lights until they were installed for the benefit of the Wheels. The stadium, used by Eastern Michigan University, wasn't in Detroit or even particularly close: It was 35 miles away in Ypsilanti. The Wheels would come off in Detroit pretty quickly when the franchise folded 14 games into the season, having lost 13 of them.

Even the league's most stable franchise, Toronto, ran into trouble. Bassett had done his best to ingratiate himself to local officials and build a fan base, hiring Leo Cahill, former coach of both the Argos and the Continental League's Rifles, to be his general manager. But even with Cahill on board and the three soon-to-be-former Dolphins under contract, many in Canada's Parliament weren't enamored with the Northmen. A number of legislators, in fact, were strongly opposed — so much so that Health Minister Marc Lalonde introduced the Canadian Football Act to prohibit any team affiliated with a foreign-based league from setting up shop north of the border. The legislation also set a limit on the number of U.S. players allowed on Canadian League rosters.

"The future of Canadian football," he declared, "is too large and too important a question to be left to a few entrepreneurs out for a fast buck."

Lalonde — and many others in Parliament — didn't want Bassett's new team competing with his father's old team, the Argos, and potentially driving them out of business. The bill passed a second reading in the House of Commons and was sent to committee for further consideration, but rather than continue a game of chicken with the Canadian government, the younger Bassett blinked and agreed to move his team.

In scouting around for a new home, Cahill took a trip to Louisville to scope out the possibility of playing at the 40,000-seat Fairgrounds Stadium. When that didn't pan out, the Northmen wound up even farther south in the Memphis market abandoned by the franchise that had moved to Houston (and would, before the first season was over, move again to Shreveport, La.). There, the Northmen became the Southmen or, alternatively, the Grizzlies in reference to their logo: a fierce-looking bear on the prowl, superimposed over an image of the sun. These Grizzlies should in nowise be confused with the far-in-the-future NBA team of the same name, which would owe its name not to Bassett's franchise at all, but rather to its own beginnings in Vancouver, B.C.

Confused yet?

Downing Stadium, where the New York Stars played their games, seen here c. 1990. *Robert S. Anthony, Stadium Circle Features.*

Dickering with the rules

Even if you somehow managed to follow the shell game the league was playing with its franchises, some of the league's various innovations might have left you scratching your head. The ball was a lighter-colored football that was somewhere between tan and gold, adorned at the end with red-orange stripes.

Even stranger, perhaps, was the comically named Dicker Rod. Instead of using chains to measure for first downs, the league employed a device patented by George Dicker, a retired aerospace engineer from Orange County. The nearly 9-foot-tall stick could be used by a single individual, eliminating the need for a two-person "chain crew." The rod was set in the ground at the spot where the ball was placed, then a moveable marker — about a foot long and sticking out perpendicular to the rod — was positioned at the nearest 5-yard stripe. A single sideline official simply had to reposition the rod 10 yards up the field (with the marker remaining at the same distance up the pole), and could use it to measure for first downs if called upon.

Its inventor touted another advantage of the Dicker Rod: safety.

"The person manning the instrument stands with it at the point where the next first down would be achieved," Dicker explained. "But if the play comes right at him, he merely picks it up and runs away. Chain gangs have to drop their stakes and markers at that spot, creating safety hazards for tumbling players."

The WFL ditched the Dicker Rod after its first season. The devices broke twice during games, though neither incident led to a botched measurement, and the league's head of officiating lamented it was more trouble that it was worth. "It was supposed to speed everything up," John McKenna said. "What it did was slow everything down. It took more people to use it."

While the Dicker Rod lasted just one year, another bizarre innovation never made it to the regular season: A fellow named Bill Finneran pitched the idea that team members playing different positions wear different-color pants. Receivers were to wear orange, offensive lineman purple, defensive linemen blue, linebackers red and defensive backs yellow, with quarterbacks and kickers adorned in white. Talk about a kaleidoscopic gridiron: The proposal made the American Basketball Association's red, white and blue ball look positively retro.

Finneran "explained" it as follows: "It's the concept of implementing means whereby one's visual appreciation of dynamic movement is significantly increased."

Huh?

The idea was never tried in an actual game, but another of Finneran's innovations was:

the "action point." Before its maiden season, the league decided — on Finneran's recommendation — to eliminate the kicked extra point and replace it with the action point. Touchdowns were automatically worth seven points, and the team had the chance for an eighth, bonus point by crossing the goal line on a conversion attempt from 2½ yards out.

The rule would prove decisive in the league's first (and only) championship game, when the Birmingham Americans defeated Florida 22-21 after the Blazers failed to convert all three of their action point attempts.

Other changes were more basic, and several made so much sense that they were later adopted by the NFL — a few of them the very same year. ("It looks like they went right down the line and copied our rule book," cracked Tom Origer, owner of the WFL's Chicago Fire).

For starters, the WFL reduced the penalty for offensive holding from 15 yards to 10, and the goal posts were moved from the goal line to the back of the end zone. Another change made it illegal for defensive backs to touch a receiver more than three yards past the line of scrimmage, and still another allowed an offensive back to go in motion toward the line of scrimmage before the ball was snapped.

More new wrinkles:

- Each team would play 20 games, in contrast to the NFL's 14-game season. At the time, NFL teams played six exhibition games during an extended preseason that wasn't particularly popular with fans. The WFL eliminated all preseason games and made every contest count.
- In the event of a tie, teams would play two 7½-minute overtime periods (not relying on sudden death).
- Fair catches on punts were outlawed.
- Hash marks were moved closer to the center of the field.
- Kickoffs were moved back to the 30-yard-line from the 40 (where they were in the NFL at the time) to encourage more runbacks.
- A catch was ruled legal if a receiver gained possession of the ball with one foot inbounds, rather than two.

Many of the changes were designed to encourage a more wide-open style of offensive play and higher scores. The league founders had taken note of how the AFL had won fans with its high-octane offenses a decade earlier and sought to do the same. The results were visible on the field, where the league's winningest team, Memphis, scored 629 points for the season, including a 60-8 rout of the Hawaiians on Aug. 21 at the Liberty Bowl.

At the other end of the spectrum, the hapless Chicago Fire *gave up* 60 points to the same

Hawaiians later in the season. The Fire, who actually started the season with a shutout win, went into a tailspin around midseason as injuries took a toll on the defense. Even though the team folded with three games left on its schedule, it had already allowed a staggering 600 points — an average of 37.5 points — in 16 games (another scheduled game, against Detroit, was canceled when *that* franchise folded). The Fire actually boasted a 7-2 record when it roared into Birmingham for a Sept. 7 showdown with the Americans, who won a 41-40 shootout before nearly 55,000 fans at Legion Field. This was exactly the kind of excitement the league had hoped to generate; unfortunately, it was the beginning of the end for Chicago, which never won another game in its final 10 starts.

The Fire was one of several teams that exemplified another WFL innovation: the singular team name. Until the advent of the WFL, sports teams had chosen to identify themselves using plural nouns with an "s" at the end. There had been a few exceptions, such as the Providence Steam Roller in the early NFL, the Alabama Crimson Tide at the college level and the Wheeling Ironmen in the Continental League, but not until the WFL debuted did the practice come into widespread use. In addition to the Fire and the Southmen/Northmen, the new league had the Southern California Sun in Anaheim, the Bell in Philadelphia and the Storm in Portland.

Some observers chuckled at the practice initially (how can a bell play football?), but it caught on to some extent and long outlived the league itself — though no NFL team has, to date, adopted such a nickname. Modern examples include pro basketball's Utah Jazz, Miami Heat and Oklahoma City Thunder and pro hockey's Colorado Avalanche, Tampa Bay Lightning and Minnesota Wild. The practice was more the rule than the exception for years in Major League Soccer, which even granted a franchise to Chicago called (guess what?) the Fire.

The King and his court

The league had succeeded in luring several big-name players away from the NFL, but many of them wouldn't be free to join the league for its inaugural season and even those who could were scarcely enough to fill out 12 rosters. To do so, some teams cast their nets close to home. More than 45 percent of the Southern California Sun's roster, for instance, had collegiate ties to California. Among them: running backs Kermit Johnson and James McAllister, a pair of rookies from UCLA who had been considered potential first-round draft picks in the NFL.

The Philadelphia Bell took a different approach. The advent of the WFL had brought an end to an expansion of minor-league and semipro football that had begun in the early 1960s and barely managed to stagger into the '70s. The NFL-AFL merger, completed as the new decade began, had solidified the establishment's hold on the American dollar, insofar as it was being spent on professional football.

The Continental League folded in 1970, with four of its teams being absorbed by the Atlantic Coast Football League — which itself folded for good three years later. Bell head coach and general manager Ron Waller had been an assistant for the Pottstown Firebirds, which in three short seasons had dominated that league, and he had a hunch some former Firebirds would make excellent additions to his new team. Among them were Claude Watts, who led the ACFL with 1,062 yards rushing on 7.1 yards per carry in 1970, and dual-threat back John Land, who ran for 548 yards and caught 33 passes for 461 yards more that year. Receiver Ron Holliday and offensive lineman Walt Hughes, two other former Firebirds, also signed on, and the Bell picked up another key Atlantic Coast League import in Don Shanklin, a receiver for the Jersey Jays who had once hauled in nine passes for 314 yards in a single game.

The ACFL imports made a huge impact for the Bell. Land was the league's fourth-best rusher and Watts ranked eighth, combining for more than 2,000 yards between them. The passing game was formidable, as well, with Land, Shanklin and Watts all finishing among the top league's top 15 receivers. But the Bell's most visible offensive weapon was another former Firebird, a quarterback who had signed the richest minor-league football contrast in history to that point.

The New York Jets had Broadway Joe, but the Pottstown Firebirds had The King: not Elvis, but the gridiron equivalent: Jim "King" Corcoran.

Decades before tennis star Andre Agassi declared "image is everything" in a series of Canon camera commercials, Corcoran personified the slogan. He was a larger-than-life character in a small-time world, but saying he was a big fish in a small pond doesn't quite describe his impact. He would have been a big fish in any pond ... or at least his legend would have been.

Typical of that legend is the story that Corcoran led the University of Maryland to a 27-22 victory over Roger Staubach's Navy team in the 1964 version of the Crab Bowl rivalry game. That would have been difficult, however, considering, he wasn't even on the field. The *New York Times* account of that game indicates that, in fact, Corcoran didn't play a single down against the Midshipmen. The myth of his supposed exploits that day grew out of a game three years earlier, when Corcoran threw for two touchdowns and ran for a third in a 29-27 victory over Staubach's Navy team in a *freshman* game. (This was during an era before freshmen were eligible to participate in NCAA varsity sports.)

During most of his college career, Corcoran warmed the bench behind Dick Shiner, who would go on to play 11 seasons in the NFL. When Shiner moved on to the pros after the 1963 season, the starting nod went to not to Corcoran, but to converted halfback Ken Ambrusko. And when Ambrusko went down with a dislocated elbow in the season opener, the King was passed over again, in favor of Phil Petry — the man who was, in fact, at the controls for the '64 triumph over Navy.

Although he'd been a third-stringer for the Terrapins, Corcoran had a strong arm and took his act to the pros in 1966, the beginning of a storied career in which he always seemed to be on the verge of breaking into the big time. Ultimately, James Sean Patrick Corcoran never played in the NFL, and the sum total of his AFL experience was a single game with the Boston Patriots in 1968, during which he threw seven passes and had two of them intercepted. But it wasn't as though he didn't have his chances; he just had a tendency to implode when he was on the verge of a breakthrough.

Corcoran's first stop was with the Denver Broncos, who sent him to the Wilmington Clippers of the ACFL for seasoning. He ranked third on the league's passing list in '66 but failed again to catch on with the Broncos the following year (according to one account, he was kicked out of camp when coach Lou Saban caught him with six girls in his room after curfew) and found himself relegated to the taxi squad. The New York Jets picked him up from there and assigned him to their ACFL affiliate in Waterbury, Connecticut, the Orbits. The Orbits finished last in their division, but the King led the league in virtually every passing category and earned a spot in training camp with Jets in the summer of 1968. There, the man who would earn a reputation as the "poor man's Joe Namath" ran into the real McCoy. The pair actually roomed together during camp. Namath was the better quarterback, but Corcoran had a reputation as a ladies' man that surpassed even Namath's.

Bill Murphy, who roomed with Corcoran the following year when the two played together on the ACFL's Lowell Giants, recalled that the King "had a bullhorn on his Lincoln Town Car. When he saw a girl he liked walking down the street, he would talk to her from his bullhorn. Before you knew it, the girl was falling all over him. He did this almost every day."

Corcoran refused to ride the team bus and drove to games on his own in that Lincoln, which was equipped with a phone, copier and bar, not to mention a Coke machine in the trunk. He wore green shoes for good luck.

Corcoran soon wound up back in the ACFL with the Jets' affiliate but relegated to a backup role even there. A couple of games into the season, the Jets sold his contract to the

Boston Patriots, who kept him in the Atlantic Coast League with their own affiliate in Lowell. But it was with his next team, which he joined in 1969, that he made a name for himself, partly for what he did on the field but also for what happened before he even got there.

Catching fire in Pottstown

The Pottstown Firebirds paid a king's ransom for Corcoran.

The Firebirds were the Green Bay Packers of the ACFL. Playing in a town whose population hovered around 25,000, they were among the league's smallest markets, but their ambitions were definitely king-sized. Ed Gruber, a multimillionaire who had made his fortune in the underwear business, provided the primary backing for the team and made it clear he was interested in signing Corcoran — whatever the cost.

The King had a connection in Pottstown, whose offensive coordinator had been an assistant on the Wilmington Clippers team that Corcoran had led three years earlier. Ron Waller, like Corcoran, was a Maryland grad who would go on to coach the San Diego Chargers for a six-game stint in '73 before taking over the Philadelphia Bell the following year. It was there that Waller would give the King his first — and, as it turned out, last — taste of top-level professional football.

Gruber, whose team had gone 6-5-1 in its inaugural season, thought the King could help him crown the Firebirds as champions. He had assembled a team that included more than a dozen members of the old Philadelphia Bulldogs, who had won the Continental League title in 1966 before going belly-up, but the Firebirds' offense — and their passing game in particular — had been anemic. So, when the Philadelphia Eagles (Pottstown's parent club) put Corcoran on waivers late in the summer of '69, Gruber jumped at the opportunity to sign him.

Money was apparently no object.

The charismatic QB made headlines by dropping this bombshell. "You won't believe it, but my three-year contract with the Firebirds will be worth around $100,000," he boasted, "not all of it in salary, of course, but a lot in benefits including two food franchises in Maryland."

Corcoran's contract immediately paid dividends for the Firebirds, who raced out to a 5-1 start before the King suffered a season-ending shoulder separation in the third quarter of a 33-6 rout of Harrisburg. Backup Benjamin Franklin "Benjy" Dial stepped in and took Pottstown the rest of the way, not only that evening but all the way to the league title with an 11-2 record that included a 20-0 demolition of Hartford in the championship game.

Corcoran was back at the controls for the rechristened Pennsylvania Firebirds when 1970 rolled around. This time, he guided the team through the entire season, leading the league in passing touchdowns (24), yardage (2,129), completions (164) and attempts (297). Eight of those touchdowns came in consecutive drubbings of the Roanoke Buckskins and Richmond Saints to begin the season. In the season opener, the spotlight found Corcoran — as it was wont to do. NFL Films was in town, filming a special about minor-league football that focused on the Firebirds. The cameras loved the King, who responded by throwing for three touchdowns and running for another in a 41-0 rout of Roanoke.

"I was really prepared for this game," he said. "I worked all week preparing. ... I wanted to show them what the King can do, and I want to prove I'm an NFL quarterback — that I belong up there."

Corcoran never got to the Super Bowl, but at least in one sense, he got close. The one-hour NFL Films special on the Firebirds titled *The Making of a Championship Season in a Small Pennsylvania Town* was shown right before Super Bowl VI in January of 1972, a month after the Firebirds wrapped up their second straight championship by shutting out the Hartford Knights for the second straight season.

It was the last ACFL game played in Pottstown. After the season, the team merged with the Norfolk Neptunes and moved to Virginia, taking Corcoran and their championship tradition with them. The new phantom Firebirds, now called the Neptunes, won the league title yet again with a third consecutive victory over Hartford as Corcoran led the league in TD passes again.

His efforts landed him a two-year contract with Montreal of the Canadian Football League at the start of 1972.

"I've already promised Sam Etcheverry a Grey Cup," he boasted, referring to the Alouettes' coach and the trophy awarded to the league champion. "They'll appreciate my talent up there."

But *Ottawa Citizen* columnist Bob Mellor called him simply "the best off-season publicity gimmick the Montreal Alouettes ever hired." He was just one of three quarterbacks, including the previous year's starter, who were vying for the job. And when Etcheverry penciled Corcoran in at No. 2 on the depth chart, he walked out. The Alouettes then suspended him, but refused to let him go.

Corcoran threatened to sue.

"I don't play backup quarterback anywhere," he declared, threatening to buy the Alouettes himself. "I have real estate partners who are millionaires. There would be no problems getting the money. And I would add a touch of class to the team."

Instead, he wound up playing with the Chambersburg Cardinals, another semipro outfit in Pennsylvania who played their games about two hours east of Pottstown.

1974 World Football League	W	L	T	PF	PA	Pct.
Eastern Division						
Florida Blazers	14	6	0	416	280	.700
New York Stars / Charlotte Hornets	10	10	0	467	350	.500
Philadelphia Bell	9	11	0	493	413	.450
Jacksonville Sharks	4	10	0	258	357	.286
Central Division						
Memphis Southmen (Grizzlies)	17	3	0	629	365	.850
Birmingham Americans	15	5	0	500	394	.750
Chicago Fire	7	13	0	446	599	.350
Detroit Wheels	1	13	0	209	358	.071
Western Division						
Southern California Sun	13	7	0	485	441	.650
The Hawaiians	9	11	0	411	422	.450
Portland Storm	7	12	1	264	424	.375
Houston Texans / Shreveport Steamer	7	12	1	240	415	.375

Championship game: Birmingham 22, Florida 21

Get your (free) tickets!

That was his last stop before Waller brought him to the Bell, a team that made a king-sized splash of its own when it took the field for the first time on July 10, 1974 at home against the Portland Storm. Corcoran completed 21 of 38 passes with a 25-yard scoring pass and no interceptions as the Bell opened with a 33-8 victory before an announced crowd of 55,534 at JFK Stadium.

The next week, Corcoran threw a pick-six for the game's only touchdown in a dull 11-0 loss at Houston, where the Texans barely managed to draw 26,000 fans for their home opener despite a "nickel beer night" promotion. Houston had such an anemic offense that the team (which had been shut out the previous week in Chicago) never managed to score more than 17 points in any of its first 14 games.

By the time the Texans' offense hit its stride with 30- and 31-point games in weeks 16 and 17, they weren't the Texans anymore. The team, which had been picked by some to win its division, lost fans and money hand over fist as it struggled to a 3-8-1 start and was moved to Shreveport, a town of fewer than 200,000 people that had more in common with the minor-league outposts of the old Continental League than it did with the "worldly" ambitions of the WFL. Coach James Garrett scoffed at the move, calling the team's new home "rinky-dink" — and was promptly relieved of his duties for remarks detrimental to the league. Shreveport, meanwhile, welcomed the team, renamed the Steamer ("Texans" would hardly do for a team in Louisiana), with a downtown parade, but the team averaged only slightly better attendance for its five remaining home games than it had for its first five, in Houston.

A week later, the New York Stars pulled up stakes and moved to Charlotte, where they began calling themselves the Hornets — a name used by that city's minor-league baseball team from 1901 until it folded in 1973 and, later, by two different NBA teams. The Stars had drawn a total of just 14,000 fans to their final three home games at Downing Stadium before owner Upton Bell moved them to Charlotte, where they averaged a much healthier 22,000 a game for their final four home dates.

Speaking of attendance, the Bell seemed to be doing far better than the Texans, the Stars — or any of the league's other teams, for that matter. The team returned home for the third week of play and, despite the previous week's shutout loss, drew an even bigger announced crowd than had shown up for the opener: 64,719.

The key word being "announced."

The Bell later acknowledged that attendance figures for both of its first two home games had been exaggerated to the point of absurdity. The actual paid figures were just 13,800 and 6,200, respectively; the rest of the tickets had been given away. (The few fans who did pay for seats in Week 3 didn't even get to see the home team chalk up a win: Philadelphia took an early 8-0 lead on an 18-yard Corcoran scoring strike, but lost when two different kickers missed field goal tries of 36 and 26 yards in the waning moments.)

The Bell had to disclose the actual paid attendance figures for tax purposes, and management was forced to come clean: "I did lie, no question," said Barry Leib, the team's executive vice president, adding that the team "papered the house" because "we felt it was the only way to sell the thing."

That didn't say much about the league's appeal.

"I don't see where it hurt anyone," Leib added. "It's not like it was malicious. We estimated that the more people who saw the game, the more fans we could make."

The same problem surfaced in Jacksonville, where more than 4 in 10 tickets at the

Sharks' first two home games were freebies. The announced crowds of 59,111 and 46,780 weren't anywhere near that large.

In reality, the announced crowds for Philly's first two home games, taken together, added up to more than the actual paid attendance for the Bell's entire 10-game home schedule. Jacksonville actually did draw decent crowds, despite the initial inflated figures, but the team wound up in financial trouble anyway. The owner borrowed $27,000 from his head coach, Bud Asher, to meet payroll ... then proceeded to fire him after the team lost four of its first six games. Things didn't get better after that folded 14 games into the season.

The Sharks shared that fate with the Detroit Wheels, who won just once — a one-point upset of the Florida Blazers — and barely drew 10,000 fans on average to Eastern Michigan University's 22,000-seat stadium in Ypsilanti.

When the Wheels filed for bankruptcy after 14 games, the team listed 122 debts.

The Chicago Fire almost made it to the end of the season, but forfeited their final game to the Bell, which gave Philadelphia a 9-11 record on the season. The Bell shouldn't have made the playoffs. The Charlotte Hornets, formerly the New York Stars, had seemingly clinched a playoff spot early by starting off at 10-6, then fell into a tailspin and lost their last four games. But the league's playoff field was downsized midstream from eight teams to three, reflecting the loss of the Wheels and the Sharks. Some owners whose teams had been left out of the playoffs protested, and the field was then expanded again to six.

Still, Charlotte's 10-10 record put it one game ahead of Philadelphia (9-11) and should have assured the Hornets of a spot in the playoffs.

Except it didn't.

When the final field was announced, the Hornets were out and the Bell, inexplicably, was in. This gave the team one more chance to showcase King Corcoran, whose passing yardage ranked second in the league and whose 31 touchdown passes led all quarterbacks. (On the flip side, his 30 interceptions led the league, as well.) But the Bell promptly lost to division champion Florida 18-3 in the opening round, and Corcoran's season was over.

Another 9-11 team, the Hawaiians, fared better, scoring a 32-14 upset over Southern California to advance. Birmingham knocked the Hawaiians out of the playoffs in the semifinals, where Florida won its second straight by upsetting the team with the league's best record, Memphis (17-3). The Blazers' winning streak ended in the finals, however, when they fell behind 22-0 going into the fourth quarter and a furious rally fell short a furious rally fell short: Florida scored three touchdowns but missed all three action points to drop a 22-21 decision.

After the game, sheriff's deputies arrived in the Americans' locker room to confiscate their uniforms. Although the team had led the league in attendance with an average of more than 37,000 a game, ownership had overextended itself with extravagant deals such as the Stabler contract.

The Raiders quarterback eventually got out of that pact and never played a down in the WFL. Instead, he led Oakland to a Super Bowl title in 1977.

Plan B

Amid all the chaos, the league tried to reset for its second season, when several NFL stars were set to join the league. Buyers representing San Antonio, Louisville, Tulsa, Montreal and Toronto were in the pipeline, with groups in line to put the league back in New York, Chicago and Jacksonville (along with new groups in Portland and Charlotte).

Bassett considered, but eventually decided against, selling the Southmen and taking on a new team in New York, so signees Csonka, Kiick and Warfield could be given the marquee treatment in the Big Apple. There was also talk of merging the Southmen with the defunct Chicago Fire and having the team operate in Chicago, but that didn't happen, either. Ultimately, the following changes took place:

- Four first-year cities still had teams, but new nicknames: In Portland it was the Thunder, in Birmingham the Vulcans, in Chicago the Winds, and in Jacksonville the Express.
- The Blazers had been moved from Orlando to San Antonio and rechristened the Wings.
- The league contracted to two divisions with 11 teams total, one fewer than the year before, declining to give the Detroit area another try.

Most importantly, the league had a new commissioner: Chris Hemmeter, the owner of the Hawaiians. Among the owners from the first season, only Bassett and John Bosacco in Philadelphia remained. Hemmeter's partner in the Hawaii franchise, Sam Battistone, moved his operations to the mainland and took over the Southern California Sun.

Bassett had summed up the league's future near the end of its first season by quipping, "If you want to look at the WFL optimistically, you can make a hell of a story. If you want to look at the situation pessimistically, you can make a hell of a story. If you want to look at things realistically, you've got a problem."

Hemmeter looked at it the third way, which meant he had a problem ... but one he believed he could overcome. He had a plan (called "the Hemmeter Plan," naturally), to control costs by designating 42 percent of a team's gate receipts and income from TV/radio deals to players' and coaches' salaries. Ten percent would go to stadium rentals, 10.5 percent to merchandising and related costs, and 37.5 percent into a fund that would cover everything from publicity and travel expenses to telephone and mailing costs. Maximum cost: $650,000 per team.

According to Hemmeter, if the league were to only draw half as many fans as attended games the previous year, it would take three seasons before them money ran out.

"The plan," he declared, "is mathematically infallible."

The second season began with a few new big names in the bag. Daryle Lamonica joined a Southern California team that found itself without

Joe Namath, seen here in 1978, turned down a contract with the Chicago Winds, who promptly folded after five games.

Tony Adams, the league's leading passer from the previous year. But Lamonica would see less time than Pat Haden, the former USC quarterback who formed a potent local combo with ex-Trojan running back Anthony Davis in the Sun's backfield. Haden ranked third in the league in passing, and Davis was far and away the leading rusher with 1,200 yards and 16 touchdowns through a dozen games as the Sun took the lead in the Western Division.

Dallas Cowboys running back Calvin Hill joined the Hawaiians. The Chicago Winds signed John Gilliam, a Pro Bowl receiver, away from the Minnesota Vikings.

The Winds also signed Babe Parilli, Joe Namath's backup for the Super Bowl-winning Jets, to his second WFL coaching job following a stint with the New York Stars in '74. When Parilli's signing was announced, he confidently predicted that the Winds would sign Namath himself to a contract within the week. The team offered Broadway Joe a $4 million deal over four years and even designed its uniforms and color scheme to mimic the Jets' green-and-white attire. None of it was enough to sway Namath, however, and he ultimately remained in the NFL.

That led to a big problem, because TVS, the syndicator that had broadcast the league's games the previous season, got wind (pun intended) of the negotiations and said it would only continue to do so with Namath in the fold. The network wasn't interested in televising games from markets like Shreveport and Charlotte — which had yet to see its boom years and had a population, at the time, of fewer than 300,000 — unless it had a bona fide star like Namath to bring in viewers.

Under Hemmeter, the league was more responsible, but also less exciting.

The Bell was no longer inflating its attendance figures, but there wasn't much attendance to inflate. The team had left cavernous JFK Stadium, with its seating capacity of 102,000, for the cozier confines of 60,000-seat Franklin Field, but it scarcely mattered. The Bell averaged a meagre 3,613 fans for its first four home games and found itself abandoned even by Ron Waller, who resigned as head coach after a single exhibition game. Corcoran, meanwhile, found himself demoted to second string behind Bob Davis, who had played with the Florida Blazers the previous season and had seven AFL/NFL years of experience with the Oilers, Jets and Saints.

The Bell staggered to a 4-7 start. At one point, the team fired its cheerleaders because it couldn't afford to pay them.

They were only making $10 a game, as it was. Corcoran recalled "clunking along" in a yellow school bus and arriving to play a road game against the Southern California Sun. But the guard wouldn't let them through the gate.

"He thought we were migrant workers — honest," Corcoran told Sports Illustrated. A teammate finally convinced the guard of their identity by showing him a Bell T-shirt. "Then, when we started to get out of the bus, the back door broke open and two or three players fell out like cartoon characters."

Another bus broke down in Philadelphia, he said, and the team had to hitchhike.

Attendance was bad in most other cities, as well. Six teams had averaged 20,000 fans or more in 1974, but just one franchise managed that feat in '75. And even there, in Birmingham, attendance was less than two-thirds what it had been the previous year. The Chicago Winds drew just 3,470 fans to their only home game (and only win) of the season, a 25-18 victory over Portland, and two of the team's investors pulled out $175,000 they had deposited with the league, sealing the Winds' fate. The franchise folded after six games on Sept. 2.

Wide receiver Gilliam saw his season end just in time to return to the Vikings, where he played all of the team's games that fall. Parilli, who had been hired with the expectation that he could lure Namath to the team, had been fired before the season even began.

Even with Hemmeter's austerity plan in place, the league wasn't making enough to stay afloat.

"We found that paying the bills was not enough to save the WFL," he said. "We failed at marketing. Possibly I was the wrong person to head up the league. Maybe pro sports are a little too swinging for me. I'm conservative and I don't have the public appeal or flamboyance. We had excitement on the field, but the league (itself) lacked excitement. Most of us are bankers, and we lacked charisma, mystique."

The league went out of business before it could conclude its second season, with the last games being played Oct. 19. The Birmingham Vulcans won their second straight game against archrival Memphis that day to finish the abbreviated season with the league's best record, 9-3.

Those two teams weren't quite dead yet. Both expressed the hope that they might be admitted to the NFL as expansion teams, and Bassett even kept 30 of his WFL players under contract in the hope that he might be able to swing a deal. In the end, however, the NFL decided to wait on further expansion, and as of this writing, both those cities remain without an NFL team.

As to King Corcoran, he retired from football for good after his stint with the Bell and focused on real estate. His future included performances in Las Vegas as a singer with Engelbert Humperdinck and six months in federal prison for tax evasion. He died of cardiac arrest in June of 2009.

Bassett, however, would be back.

Spring Hopes Eternal

Most people don't realize it, but the idea for the United States Football League was nearly two decades old by the time it got off the ground.

The league, which debuted in 1983, almost happened 17 years earlier. It was the brainchild of David Dixon, a French Quarter antiques dealer who in the early 1960s began lobbying to win a pro football team for New Orleans. That team had nearly been the Oakland Raiders: After an abysmal 1961 season in which the Raiders won just one of their 14 games, Dixon led a syndicate that pursued moving the team to the Gulf Coast. The effort, however, eventually fell apart, and the New Orleans Raiders never happened.

Undaunted, Dixon charted a new course. In 1965, he announced plans to start a new pro football league — with a team in New Orleans, of course — that would play in the spring, with kickoff slated for January 1966. Other cities announced for the league were New York, Houston, Miami and Anaheim, with a championship game set for Memorial Day and games limited to two hours (with no halftime and rules that would speed up play) for maximum TV appeal.

Dixon dropped the idea like a hot potato when he landed a spot among the ownership of an NFL franchise awarded to New Orleans in 1966. Dixon's threat to form the rival league may well have given the NFL a nudge toward the Gulf Coast. He already had the name for the team (Saints) picked out; he'd even run it past Archbishop Philip Hannan and obtained his blessing. Another key piece in the puzzle was Dixon's proposal for a domed stadium, based on an idea championed by architect/futurist Buckminster Fuller for domed centers in metropolitan areas. Plans for the stadium were drawn up in 1967, and it was completed in 1975.

Dixon ultimately left the Saints, but he wasn't done with football. He still believed the idea of playing football in the spring would work, having received encouragement from none other than coaching legend Paul Brown. Back in the early '60s, Brown had assured Dixon that spring football was an idea whose time had come: It would work, Brown was sure, and he urged Dixon not to let anyone talk him out of it.

The NFL had talked him out of it by giving him a piece of the big pie in the Big Easy, but suddenly, in 1979, another factor came into focus. On television.

Plugging in

Cable TV had been around for a while, flying under the radar. It had started out as a way for frustrated viewers to bypass the obstacle course of rabbit ears and fuzzy screens to get a clear, dedicated signal — especially in remote areas. In 1962, the nation had nearly 800 cable systems with 850,000 subscribers run by people such as Jack Kent Cooke, future owner of teams in the NFL, NBA and NHL — including the Los Angeles Lakers. But federal regulators wouldn't allow cable systems to develop their own programming. They were carriers, not creators ... at least until 1972.

Four years earlier, the Federal Communications Commission had argued that a ban on original programming protected broadcast stations from competition that could "cripple" them. The following year, though, it changed its tune, not only allowing but *ordering* cable TV providers with more than 3,500 subscribers to start creating their own programs. The FCC's rationale was that original programming was needed to fill in the gaps where local stations didn't provide adequate options.

Now it was cable operators' turn to cry foul. Midwest Video, which owned cable systems in three states, argued that the cost of creating its own programs would be prohibitive: Just converting from carrier-only status would cost $95,000 for color broadcasts, with annual operating costs of $33,000 on top of that. The FCC, as a regulatory body, didn't have the authority to order cable systems to "engage in the entirely new and different business of originating programming," Midwest argued in court.

The Supreme Court, disagreed, though, and in doing so paved the way for the modern era of cable TV.

Where cable operators like Midwest saw problems, others saw opportunity. Charles Dolan and Gerald Levin of Sterling Manhattan Cable lost no time in seizing that opportunity, launching the nation's first pay cable network, Home Box Office, in 1975. Ted Turner followed by converting his Atlanta-based broadcast station into a satellite-powered "superstation," which he sold to cable operators across the country. Little-known fact: Turner originally dubbed his station WTCG, for "Watch This Channel Grow." In 1978, he changed the call letters to WTBS, reflecting what he dubbed the Turner Broadcasting System.

Turner used this national platform to bring reruns of shows like *Gilligan's Island* and *The Beverly Hillbillies* into homes across the country — and something more, as well: sports. Turner had bought the rights to televise Atlanta Braves baseball games in 1973 and, three years later, he bought the team itself, along with the NBA's Atlanta Hawks. That helped set the stage for the next phase of the cable revolution: specialization.

Before the end of the decade, Turner would launch his 24-hour all-news cable station, CNN, and another pair of entrepreneurs would create a 24-hour cable network to focused on sports. Initially dubbed ESP for Entertainment and Sports Programming, it was the brainchild of Bill Rasmussen, a sports executive who suddenly found himself with time on his hands. It was 1978, and Rasmussen had just been fired from not one but two jobs. He'd served as communications manager for the Hartford Whalers and executive vice president for Gordie Howe's Howe Enterprises.

During his time with the Whalers, Rasmussen and his son Scott had produced a monthly sports program called *Sports Only* for a religious station in Hartford. They hit upon the idea of using a show very much like that (which would be called *SportsCenter*) as the launching pad for a 24-hour cable sports network. In partnership with Ed Eagan, an insurance agent interested in the television business, they incorporated their new network for a fee of $91.

But ESP — soon rebranded as ESPN — couldn't run *SportsCenter* 24 hours a day. It needed actual events to cover. In a coup, they persuaded veteran Chet Simmons, president of NBC Sports, to leave the network after 15 years and lead their new venture. This was important because Simmons had been involved in securing the rights to televise such major sporting events as the American Football League, Major League Baseball and the 1972 Olympics.

ESPN debuted Sept. 7, 1979, with an episode of *SportsCenter* hosted by George Grande and Lee Leonard that featured scores accompanied by video highlights from the broadcast networks. Leonard served up the following introduction: "If you're a fan, *if* you're a fan, what you'll see in the next minutes, hours and days to follow may convince you you've gone to sports heaven." Other programming that night consisted of wrestling, college soccer and a game in the American Professional Slo-Pitch Softball League's championship series matching the Kentucky Bourbons against the Milwaukee Schlitz, named for the beer company. (Unfortunately, ESPN had obtained a big sponsorship deal with *another* beer company, Budweiser.)

If the network were to survive, however, it would need something with a little more drawing power than college soccer and men's slow-pitch softball. Spring football would be just the ticket, Dixon realized, and the birth of ESPN helped reignite his vision of creating a second major pro football league. The World Football League had foundered in part because it only managed to secure a minor TV contract with syndicator TVS. By contrast, the AFL had succeeded thanks in large measure to its contract with a major network, NBC.

Simmons, who'd had a hand in the AFL deal with that network was, fortuitously, now heading up the new cable kid on the block that was looking for more sports programming.

What if Dixon could get ESPN on board with the new league? Better yet, what if he could get Simmons on *his* side of the table?

By 1983, Simmons' relationship with ESPN had soured, and he was open to new opportunities. Dixon had one for him: Become president of the USFL. Simmons had no experience running a sports league, but he had experience in the thing Dixon felt would be most crucial to his league's success. Television. Actually, Dixon had tried (and failed) to sign NFL commissioner Pete Rozelle away from the big boys before he turned to Simmons. By this time, the league had already landed a $9 million TV deal with ABC to televise a Sunday game of the week and a $4 million contract with ESPN to serve up offerings on Saturdays and Mondays.

Dixon had some other credible names involved, as well. He'd hired former Denver Broncos coach John Ralston as the league's first chairman, and Ralston would coach the new league's Oakland Invaders. George Allen, a former NFL head coach with the Rams who had led Washington to the 1972 Super Bowl, had been so excited about the USFL concept that he'd signed on to coach the Chicago Blitz.

When word reached the press about the league, it was planning 12 teams, with franchises set in Boston, Chicago, Detroit, Houston, Los Angeles, New York, Orlando, Philadelphia, San Jose and Washington. Eight cities were in the running for the final two spots: Atlanta, Birmingham, Memphis, Minneapolis, New Orleans, Phoenix and San Diego.

The lineup wound up changing a little, as lineups often do when new leagues are in the planning stages. Birmingham and San Diego both ended up making the cut, while Houston and Orlando didn't (although both would be represented in future seasons). The San Diego owners, however, couldn't secure a lease to play in Jack Murphy Stadium and wound up in L.A. instead. The Bay Area owners moved to Phoenix, and a new team was placed in Oakland. That team, called the Invaders, filled a void left when the NFL's similarly named Raiders had departed to play in Los Angeles.

Competition?

What isn't often remembered is that another spring league was in the works at the same time. In March of 1981, a Los Angeles real estate developer named Alex Belle announced he was planning to launch the International Football League, with an eye toward placing franchises in Tokyo, Osaka and Mexico City. The travel costs, he recognized, would be considerable, but he was confident that local television revenue would pay the bill for flights across the Pacific.

Belle's consultants included several people who had been involved in the WFL, including its legal counsel, and Dennis Murphy, founder of the American Basketball and World Hockey Associations. The league was supposed to hold a draft the following January and start play after that, but 1982 came and went with nary a peep from Belle and company. By the time the IFL re-emerged, it was two years later, and Belle was shooting for a 1984 kickoff. He had dropped any immediate plans for teams overseas and had added former L.A. Rams coach Ray Malavasi to his team of organizers. Jerry Saperstein, son of Globetrotters founder Abe Saperstein, was enlisted as chairman of the IFL's executive committee. Former Rams quarterback Roman Gabriel was named coach of the Charlotte-based Carolina Storm.

Malavasi said the league was considering making longer field goals worth four points and, in a move that prefigured a later rule change in the NFL, "having an extra point from an area that isn't a sure thing."

Now, Belle was talking about placing teams in L.A. (with Malavasi as general manager), Shea Stadium in New York, San Francisco and Chicago. Other teams were slated for Charlotte, Fort Lauderdale/Miami, Honolulu, Houston, Indianapolis, Nebraska, Ohio and Tennessee, with El Paso in the running for a possible team at the Sun Bowl. An international division with four teams in Australia and Japan would have to wait until the league's second season in 1985.

The Ohio team, supposedly based in Canton and named the Bulldogs after the NFL's original powerhouse, nonetheless was tabbed to play its home games in Akron's Rubber Bowl. News broke in mid-July that the team was pursuing Art Schlichter, Ohio State's former star quarterback, who had been suspended by the NFL for gambling. (Schlichter ultimately went back to the NFL instead and, in 1990, was named MVP of the Arena Bowl with the Detroit Drive. Things went downhill for him after that, though: He was arrested in 2011 and sentenced to 10 years in federal prison for stealing thousands of dollars to fund his gambling addiction.

He wouldn't have had anywhere to play in the IFL.

Paul Zarynoff, co-owner of the proposed Tennessee franchise, which was to play its games either in Memphis or Nashville, appears to have been well aware of the on-again, off-again nature of the league. He vowed, however, that "there will be a kickoff next spring, even if I have to kick it myself."

No word on whether Zarynoff kicked a football in the spring of 1984, but the IFL didn't. The league postponed the start of its first season yet again, until '85 — and it didn't happen then, either: The IFL never got off the ground.

Heisman heist

By that time, the USFL was already playing games: 18 of them in a season. That was two more than the NFL had on its schedule, although it wasn't the 20 games Dixon had originally envisioned. Dixon's vision and organizational skills, coupled with Simmons' TV savvy, had gotten the league off to a strong start. George Allen had taken the bull by the horns in Chicago, where the Blitz were installed early on as the team to beat.

Allen lured former NFL quarterback Greg Landry to the USFL to lead the Blitz. The 13-year veteran had led the Detroit Lions to the playoffs during his second NFL season back in 1970 and had been a Pro Bowl quarterback the following year, but he had been waived by the Baltimore Colts and was 36 years old by the time he took his first snap in the new league. That didn't stop him from putting up some impressive numbers, throwing for 2,383 yards in 1983 and racking up 3,534 the following season with the Arizona Wranglers. (In an odd swap, the Wranglers and Blitz swapped franchises between the league's first and second seasons, with Chicago's players moving to Arizona and vice versa.)

One of Landry's favorite targets was Trumaine Johnson, who signed with the Blitz out of Grambling. Johnson would play two seasons in the USFL, leading the league with 81 receptions in his first campaign, and twice rolling up more than 1,200 yards receiving.

It's easy to forget how many top-of-the-line players played in the USFL. The World Football League had made news a decade earlier by signing three big stars (Larry Csonka, Paul Warfield and Jim Kiick) away from the NFL champion Miami Dolphins, but that was nothing compared to what the USFL managed to accomplish. There was talk that the Los Angeles Express might be able to land Pitt quarterback Dan Marino, the league's No. 1 draft pick, but he ultimately passed and signed with the Dolphins.

No matter. The league soon had someone even better: running back Herschel Walker, the best player in college football.

Walker *would* have been the most sought-after football player in the country during his Heisman season at the University of Georgia, when he led the Bulldogs to a No. 1 ranking before a narrow loss to Penn State in the Sugar Bowl. If, that is, he'd been a senior. Under NFL rules at the time, Walker couldn't turn pro after the season because he was just a junior, and underclassmen weren't allowed to play in the established league. But with the USFL now in business, Walker had a potential option. The new league would be hungry for a defining moment to put itself on the map.

Walker could provide that moment.

His motivation was personal. His family relied on the $30 his father earned each week as a tenant father to keep the family fed and clothed. He'd already had three very successful seasons at Georgia, averaging more than 1,750 yards a season. Before his junior season, however, he'd suffered a broken thumb that was expected sideline him for as long as six weeks. It didn't turn out to be that long, and Walker actually played in a cast during the season opener against Clemson. He rushed for just 20 yards on 11 carries in that game, but regained his form as the season wore on, surpassing 200 yards less than a month later against Mississippi State and again during a 44-0 rout of No. 20 Florida in early November.

Herschel Walker gave the USFL instant credibility when he signed with the New Jersey Generals.

But even though he recovered, the thumb injury served as a potential warning: A football player can be injured at any time, and if a college player were to suffer a debilitating injury, he could kiss a big pro contract goodbye.

Long story short: Walker signed with the USFL's New Jersey Generals. He would play three seasons with the team, leading the league in rushing during his first and third seasons. His 2,411 yards in '85 set an all-time record for professional football, and he also led the league in scoring that year, but he never led the Generals to a championship. The team didn't make the playoffs in its first year, then lost in the quarterfinals each of the following two seasons.

Walker's signing paved the way for other stars to join the league. Players like running back Joe Cribbs, who jumped to the Birmingham Stallions in 1984 after rushing for 1,000 yards or more three times in his first four seasons with the Buffalo Bills. Cribbs was the USFL's leading rusher in 1984, the only season Walker didn't set the pace. Then there was University of Michigan receiver Anthony Carter, who stayed close to home and joined the Michigan Panthers for their inaugural season. Unlike Walker, Carter won a championship. Although he ranked outside the USFL's top 10 in catches, it was his big-play ability that stood out: His average of 18 yards per reception was better than anyone else in the league. When the Panthers reached the finals, Carter caught a 48-yard touchdown pass from Bobby Hebert with 3 minutes left that turned out to be the difference in a 24-22 win over Philadelphia.

The USFL also gave Reggie White, a defensive end from the University of Tennessee, the chance to stay near his college roots. The NFL didn't have a team in Tennessee at the time, and the upstart league's Memphis Showboats chose White in the 1984 territorial draft, a process that allowed teams to select players from their own geographic region. White would record 23.5 sacks in two seasons with the Showboats before moving to the NFL, where he would play 13 All-Pro Seasons with the Eagles, Packers and Panthers.

1984 United States Football League	W	L	T	PF	PA	Pct.
Eastern Conference						
Atlantic Division						
Philadelphia Stars	16	2	0	479	225	.889
New Jersey Generals	14	4	0	430	312	.778
Pittsburgh Maulers	3	15	0	259	379	.167
Washington Federals	3	15	0	270	492	.167
Southern Division						
Birmingham Stallions	14	4	0	539	316	.778
Tampa Bay Bandits	14	4	0	492	347	.778
New Orleans Breakers	8	10	0	349	395	.444
Memphis Showboats	7	11	0	320	455	.389
Jacksonville Bulls	6	12	0	327	455	.333
Western Conference						
Central Division						
Houston Gamblers	13	5	0	618	400	.722
Michigan Panthers	10	8	0	400	382	.556
San Antonio Gunslingers	7	11	0	309	325	.389
Oklahoma Outlaws	6	12	0	351	459	.333
Chicago Blitz	5	13	0	340	466	.278
Pacific Division						
Los Angeles Express	10	8	0	338	373	.556
Arizona Wranglers	10	8	0	502	284	.556
Denver Gold	9	9	0	356	413	.500
Oakland Invaders	7	11	0	242	348	.389

Championship game: Philadelphia 23, Arizona 3

John Walton, again

While the league was signing big names fresh out of college, it also gave players like Landry in the twilight of their careers a way to hang on a few more years. Or, in the case of John Walton, one last chance to make it big.

Walton, the hero of the Continental Football League's 1969 title game, had left the Indianapolis Capitols after the season for another shot with the L.A. Rams. During the 1971 preseason, however, Raiders defensive end Ben Davidson blindsided Walton, leaving him with a separated shoulder. He was in a body cast for eight weeks and ultimately released, eventually hooking up with the Columbus Barons of the Midwest Football League.

Walton's next shot at the pros had come in 1974, when he tried out for the Chicago Fire of the World Football League … only to be released after Virgil Carter, who had defected from the NFL's Cincinnati Bengals, won the job. As luck would have it, however, Walton got at second chance with the WFL the following year, after his coach at Columbus, Perry Moss, was named to coach the Florida Blazers. (Ironically, the Blazers had just moved to San Antonio, the city represented by the Toros in Walton's historic championship victory more than five years earlier). Moss named Walton his starting quarterback, and the journeyman responded by leading the league in passing with 19 touchdowns and 2,405 yards through 13 games.

It might have been a storybook comeback had the team not folded at that point — along with the rest of the league.

Still, Walton's story wasn't over. His WFL experience landed him a spot on the Philadelphia Eagles roster, where he served as a backup for the next three seasons. He played sporadically and hung up his cleats for good (or so it seemed) after the 1979 season, moving to the sidelines as head coach of his alma mater, Elizabeth City State. As fate would have it, though, he wasn't through on the field just yet. Once again, a connection from his past gave Walton an opportunity to prove himself, and once again, he made good.

This time, that connection was Dick Coury. The receivers coach for the Eagles during Walton's time in Philadelphia, Coury had been named head coach of the USFL's Boston Breakers.

Coury knew who he wanted as his quarterback from the outset — even though Walton hadn't played pro football in four years. As he had in San Antonio, Walton responded with a banner year, throwing for 3,772 yards and 20 touchdowns as he led the Breakers to an 11-7 record. He ranked third overall among the league's quarterbacks and set a record, at age 35, for the most passing attempts in a season. The next year, his numbers were nearly as impressive: 3,554 yards with 17 touchdowns, but the team finished the season by losing 10 of its last 13 games, and Walton retired once again — this time for good.

Thus concluded a career in which he played quarterback in four major professional football leagues and became the first black quarterback to win a pro championship.

No one else can say that.

Enter Trump

As important as the players were, it was the owners who set the tone for the league. Among them were John Bassett of the Tampa Bay Bandits, who'd owned the Memphis Southmen in the WFL, as well as the Toronto Argonauts of the Canadian Football League from 1957 until 1974, and a franchise in the World Hockey Association. Bassett was joined in the Bandits' ownership by "the Bandit" himself: Burt Reynolds, who played a popular character by that name on the big screen in *Smokey and the Bandit*. Reynolds, who also starred in the football-themed film *The Longest Yard*, had hoped to pursue a football career in college but had switched course after suffering a series of injuries as a sophomore halfback at Florida State. Now, he had the next best thing: an ownership stake in a professional team.

Bassett, meanwhile, was among the most level-headed owners in the league. He'd seen the WFL collapse during a bidding war with the NFL and had no desire to repeat that mistake. He didn't have a Herschel Walker or a Reggie White, but he did have a popular coach in former pro quarterback Steve Spurrier, whose three-year stint with the Bandits was his first head coaching job.

Spurrier's quarterback was John Reaves, a journeyman from the University of Florida who'd never thrown for more than 790 yards in eight NFL seasons. In the USFL, however, he was a different player, rolling up 4,000 yards through the air in 1984 — second in the league behind Jim Kelly — and duplicating that feat the following year. Reaves' top receiver, Eric Truvillion from Florida A&M, had a pair of 1,000-yard seasons with the Bandits, but his time in the NFL was limited to a stint with the Detroit Lions' replacement team during the 1987 strike.

The Bandits weren't the best team in the league, but they were among the biggest draws, ranking second at the turnstiles during each of their three seasons and averaging more than 43,000 fans for their home games. They also posted three straight winning records and made the playoffs two out of the three years they were in business, just as often as the Generals made the postseason with Walker.

Speaking of the Generals, they wound up being the Bandits' nemesis — but not on the field. The rivalry, or rather the feud, wasn't between the players but between Bassett and the Generals' second owner, a 35-year-old New York real estate developer who would one day wind up being president of the United States.

Donald Trump had been on board to be the Generals' owner back in 1981, but they hadn't been his first choice. He and five partners had enlisted George Allen as the front man for a proposal to buy the Baltimore Colts from Robert Irsay in the late spring of that year. According to Irsay, Allen spent several weeks trying to talk him into selling the team for $50

million, only to be rebuffed. Said Irsay: "I've just bought a big condominium in Baltimore. ... If I was going to sell the Colts, I doubt if I would spend a couple hundred thousand dollars on a condominium." (That condominium must not have meant so much three years later, when Irsay packed up the Colts and moved them to Indianapolis.)

Trump admitted talking to Irsay but denied at the time making any offer. Still, Trump's interest in owning an NFL team would resurface over the years. In 2014, he would try to buy another NFL team, the Buffalo Bills, only to be outbid by Terry Pegula, owner of hockey's Buffalo Sabres. And then, there were his dealings with the USFL.

With the Irsay deal having fallen through, Allen had hooked up with the new league, and so did Trump — at least temporarily. But before an October organizational meeting, Trump

Donald Trump in 1987

apparently got cold feet. In his book *Football for a Buck*, Jeff Pearlman relates that Trump simply failed to show up. After the meeting started, however, he called the hotel where it was being held, and Dixon put him on speaker phone. Where was he?

Trump said he was backing out of his commitment so he could focus on his casino project. Then, he hung up.

Suddenly, the league was left scrambling to find an owner for the New Jersey team, its entry in the nation's largest media market. *Not* having a team in the New York area was not an option. Without it, the league would take a huge hit in terms of both credibility and potential revenue. Fortunately for Dixon and the other owners, an Oklahoma oil man named

J. Walter Duncan agreed to take the reins. (Few remember today that it was Duncan, not Trump, who signed Herschel Walker.)

But the league hadn't seen the last of Trump. In September of 1983, the developer was back in as owner of the Generals, having purchased the team he'd walked out on a couple of years earlier. Duncan, the team's owner, had been eager to sell: He'd lost a significant amount of money on the team during its first season and wanted to stay closer to home in Oklahoma. The commissioner and the other owners were apparently willing to forgive and forget Trump's earlier flakiness, not wishing to look past the dollar signs he was waving at them. They didn't realize he intended to undermine the league's entire *raison d'être*.

Expanding horizons

Meanwhile, the league was raising the stakes by adding not one, not two, but six expansion franchises. The number was originally supposed to be eight, and perhaps as many as 10. In April, the league announced it was scrapping its original play to add just four teams for its second season, going with a more aggressive plan instead.

Why?

The franchise fee for each new team was $6 million, which got split among the existing owners. Expansion was, in short, a source of revenue. And with teams like Boston, Washington and Chicago having pulled in paltry crowds, a shot in the arm was sorely needed. The league listed "priority" cities as Atlanta, Houston, Jacksonville (or Miami), New Orleans, Pittsburgh, San Antonio, San Diego and Tulsa (or Oklahoma City).

Other cities under consideration were Anaheim, Charlotte, Cincinnati, Cleveland, Dallas, Des Moines, Kansas City, Memphis, Milwaukee, St. Louis and Seattle. Bassett was put in charge of scoping out the target cities and narrowing down the field.

New Orleans dropped out of the mix when the Boston Breakers moved there. Seattle was viewed as the strongest contender, according to one report, and San Diego was targeted for the second time in as many years. But the same problem reared its head again when the team couldn't get a lease at Jack Murphy Stadium, and the franchise was shifted to Tulsa, where it became the Oklahoma Outlaws.

Outlaws owner Bill Tatham hired former Chargers head coach Sid Gillman as the team's director of player development, and Gillman signed quarterback Doug Williams away from the NFL's Tampa Bay Buccaneers. (Williams, who would win Super Bowl MVP honors for Washington's 42-10 rout of Denver four years later, was far less effective in Tulsa, where he threw for 15 touchdowns and 21 interceptions as the Outlaws limped to a 6-12 season.)

The first expansion franchise to be approved was the Pittsburgh Maulers, owned by Edward DeBartolo Sr., father of the San Francisco 49ers owner. The Maulers would sign Mike Rozier, the University of Nebraska running back who had won the Heisman Trophy the previous year, but Rozier failed to crack the league's top 10 in rushing for his rookie season, and the Maulers would finish a disappointing 3-15 while drawing an average of just 22,000 fans.

In addition to the Outlaws and Maulers, the league settled on four other new teams: the Houston Gamblers, Jacksonville Bulls, Memphis Showboats and San Antonio Gunslingers. Honolulu was approved for the 19th team, contingent upon a 20th team being approved for Seattle, but neither of those franchises ever got off the drawing board.

The Gamblers signed quarterback Jim Kelly from the University of Miami and hired Darrell "Mouse" Davis from Portland State as their offensive coordinator. Over the next two seasons, Kelly would use Davis' innovative run-and-shoot offense — which employed four receivers — to pile up an astounding total of nearly 10,000 yards passing and 83 touchdown passes. He led the league by a large margin in both categories both seasons, winning the league's MVP *and* Rookie of the Year awards in 1984.

The Gamblers would make the playoffs both years but would fall in the first round of the playoffs each time. Of course, Kelly would go on to lead the Buffalo Bills to four consecutive Super Bowls, though they came up empty in each one.

Express and regrets

Still, Kelly wasn't the biggest-name quarterback to sign with the USFL that year. Steve Young, runner-up for the Heisman to Rozier, inked a contract worth an astonishing $40 million with the L.A. Express, who were under new ownership in the person of J. William Oldenburg. He called himself "Mr. Dynamite." If there was anyone Trumpier than Donald Trump in the USFL, it was Oldenburg, a developer and financier who had made a ton of money on the previous year's real estate boom. At one social event, he was introduced as "the gentleman who invented life in the fast line."

"I'm used to winning, to nothing less than becoming the best," he said in an interview with *Sports Illustrated*. "Donald Trump can get all the press he wants, but when it comes to business, he can't carry my socks."

But Oldenburg was long on style and short on substance. He threw temper tantrums when he didn't get his way, as when Young took too long — in his estimation — to sign on the dotted line. He was giving Young the biggest contract ever offered a football player. Why was he wasting time reading the fine print? In the end, Young did sign, but not before some tense moments in Oldenburg's office when it looked as if the entire deal might fall through, thanks to the (inebriated) owner's impatience.

With Young on board, Oldenburg promised the Express would fill the L.A. Coliseum and bring home a championship, but when they fell behind by surrendering a pair of early touchdowns in their season opener against the Denver Gold, Oldenburg blew a gasket. According to *The Denver Post*, "he began beating on the walls of his private box, and his fury spilled outside as the quarter ended."

Attendance for that game was just 32,000 in the 92,000-seat Coliseum, and the Express wound up losing 27-10.

But that turned out to be the least of Oldenburg's problems. It soon came to light that his exaggerated "guarantees" about the Express' success weren't the only hyperbole he had spewed. He lived in a mansion in an exclusive Bay Area suburb, shopped on Rodeo Drive in Beverly Hills, and rented an opulent San Francisco office space — complete with wet bar and jacuzzi — for $2 million a month. He celebrated its grand opening by hiring Las Vegas icon Wayne Newton and a 34-piece orchestra to perform *The Impossible Dream* as mist rose from dry ice onstage.

For all that, Oldenburg was "not a billionaire" after all, "despite his Rolls Royces, chartered jets and ostentations parties." That was the assessment of *The New York Times* in a piece that ran less than four months after the Denver game.

Oldenburg soon found himself under investigation for an alleged improper real estate deal: He'd purchased 363 acres of property in a San Francisco suburb for $800,000, then sold it for $55 million to State Savings and Loan of Salt Lake City — which Oldenburg also happened to own. The deal ran afoul of Utah state regulations that limited the value of real estate an S&L could own at 10 percent of its assets. According to Utah financial commissioner Elain Weis, the $55 million was well above that limit. "He tried to bail himself out with the land sale," she said.

Mortgage banker John French of Grubb & Ellis in San Francisco was even more blunt: "There have always been people with ambition and dreams who thought they could make 2 plus 2 equal 5," he said. "Mr. Oldenburg is trying to make 2 plus 2 equal 50."

Mr. Dynamite's deal had blown up in his face and left him strapped for cash. As a result, he was forced to sell the Express. The buyer, another real estate man named Jay Roulier who was a minority owner of the Houston Gamblers, made it his top priority to settle Young's contract and ensure he'd be around for a second season.

"There's no question Steve thought Oldenburg was a fruitcake," Roulier said. "If an owner hadn't come in and the defaults weren't remedied, he was gone."

Soon, however, Roulier was gone, as well. He had used his equity in the Gamblers to buy the Express, but when Houston couldn't find anyone to take up the slack, *that* franchise was suddenly in jeopardy. So, about three after he was announced as the savior of the Express, Roulier was on his way back to Houston. No one else, however, wanted to pick up the tab for the expensive team Oldenburg had assembled, so the league was forced to operate the franchise in its final season, with each of the remaining owners kicking in somewhere between $500,000 and $800,000 to cover the tab.

Allowing the Express to fold was not an option: The league's TV contract with ABC required that it field teams in each of the nation's top three markets, and L.A. ranked No. 2.

Trump vs. Bassett

No. 1, of course, was New York, where Trump — who had "won" his rivalry with Mr. Dynamite by default — found himself king of the USFL.

Trump went after New York Giants linebacker Lawrence Taylor, giving him $1 million to join the Generals after his contract was up in 1987. Taylor took the money, then returned it after signing a more lucrative contract with the Giants and paying an additional $750,000 (which he was able to afford courtesy of the big NFL contract) to get out of the deal. Trump didn't have Taylor, but at least he was $750,000 richer. And the Generals wouldn't survive long enough to play when Taylor would have been free to join them, anyway.

Trump also tried to lure Miami Dolphins head coach Don Shula away from the NFL, but he came up empty there, too. The first big name he signed was Cleveland Browns quarterback Brian Sipe, who had been the NFL's Most Valuable Player in 1980. But Sipe failed to match his numbers from that season, throwing for 17 touchdowns with 15 interceptions and 2,540 yards with the Generals. More importantly, at 35 years of age, he wasn't the kind of matinee idol Trump wanted as his leading man. As it so happened, a quarterback who fit that bill was available: Boston College's diminutive "miracle man," Doug Flutie.

Flutie, who had thrown perhaps the most famous Hail Mary pass in college football history to give BC a victory over the University of Miami, had all-American looks to go with his Heisman Trophy. (Yes, the USFL did land three consecutive Heisman winners.) So, Trump signed him for $1 million-plus a year, dealing Sipe and his $700,000 contract to the Jacksonville Bulls.

Chet Simmons saw Trump as injecting new energy into the league. "Donald Trump is what this league needs," he said. "You have to promise the fans something. You have to show the fans you're trying. You have to be enthusiastic about trying to get the best product you can."

Trump's theatrics, however, were greasing the wheels for his campaign to move the USFL's schedule to the fall. He'd had his eye on autumn almost from the beginning, and had owned the Generals for less than three months when he tipped his hand at a forum of in New York City. Ticket sales, he said, were "going through the roof," and with a good season, the Generals could look forward to filling the stadium. It wasn't quite the audacious optimism of Bill Oldenburg, but it was close.

"I believe that over the next two or three years the USFL — after it becomes competitive and we're taking a lot of NFL players — will switch seasons. I see this league going from the spring and summer into the fall and competing directly against the NFL. I'll be able to challenge the Giants and the Jets and everyone else."

Trump proposed the idea directly to his fellow owners in January, but no vote was taken. Still, someone leaked the story to *The New York Times*, which ran it on April 15, 1984 under the headline, "U.S.F.L. envisions fall schedule beginning in 1987." The paper credited two anonymous sources as stating that an "executive decision" had been made by "the people who control the league" to switch to the fall.

The sources named six "people who control the league," including Trump, who acknowledged he was the "primary instigator" of the proposal. Also on the list: Simmons and John Bassett, owner of the Tampa Bay Bandits. But while Trump had been pushing the idea from the beginning, the other two men were outraged.

Bassett fired off this missive — on Bandits letterhead — to Trump the next day, copying Michigan Panthers owner (and league chairman) Al Taubman, along with Simmons:

> *"On a number of occasions over the past meetings, I have listened with astonishment at your personal abuse of the commissioner and your various partners if they did not happen to espouse one of your causes or agree with one of your arguments.*
>
> *"It is obvious from the record that you are a talented and successful young man. It is also a fact that I regard you as a friend and an owner who has made a contribution to the league in general and been a savior to New York/Jersey in particular.*
>
> *"While others may be able to let your insensitive and denigrating comments pass, I no longer will.*

"You are bigger, younger and stronger than I, which means I'll have no regrets whatsoever punching you in the mouth the next time an instance occurs where you personally scorn me, or anyone else, who does not happen to salute and dance to your tune.

"I really hope you don't know that you are doing it, but you are not only damaging yourself with your associates, but alienating them as well.

"I think before you shoot and when you do fire, stick to the message without killing the messenger."

Bassett had been a steadfast opponent of moving to the fall. His team was doing just fine in the spring, thank you. He also didn't appreciate Trump's free-spending ways. The league had started out with a mandate to contain costs. Dixon's original framework called for each team to have a salary budget of $1.845 million, with an additional $500,000 for a couple of high-profile players. It wasn't a mandate; it was a handshake deal among the owners.

It quickly went out the window.

A revolving door of owners, especially those like Trump and Oldenburg, hadn't been around at the beginning and couldn't have cared less what had been agreed to back then. In fact, but the time the league folded after just three seasons, the Bandits were the only team representing the same city they'd started out in, with the same owner and the same coach.

Bassett, whose team had also drawn more fans in those three seasons than any other in the league, was obviously doing something right.

But it didn't matter outside of Tampa.

The other owners had unrealistic expectations of the kind of crowds they could draw and the kind of money they could spend. They were used to being winners and wouldn't settle for anything less, the bottom line be damned.

"Guys would lose three games, and they'd go out and buy the Pittsburgh Steelers' offensive line," Bassett told *Sports Illustrated*. "They'd win the championship, but they'd lose $10 million!" Which would leave Bassett and the others holding the bag when those teams went under. A prime example: the $500,000 he and the surviving owners paid in 1985 to keep the Los Angeles Express afloat.

"They spent too much on every conceivable budget item," Bassett said. "People didn't act in a professional, businesslike manner, except our team. The original concept worked; it was the people who screwed it up. Now, instead of making money, we're losing our asses. Our payroll is 2½ times what it's supposed to be. We never budgeted $800,000 this year to help save the L.A. franchise."

Simmons, meanwhile, had been inclined to stay in the spring. The league hired a consultant to study both options, and the company recommended staying in the spring for the '86 season, starting its season four weeks earlier, shortening it by two weeks and expanding regional TV coverage. But Simmons found the moves impractical and ultimately went along with Trump's pro-spring bloc.

Even so, Simmons, who had been trying to mediate between Bassett and Trump, didn't seem much happier than the Bandits owner when news of the fall concept was leaked. This was supposed to have remained in-house. The same day Bassett sent his letter to Trump, Simmons fired off a memo of his own to all the owners, denouncing the leak as "unconscionable" and a "malicious" distortion of the truth. He confronted Trump directly, but the Generals owner wouldn't confirm or deny being the source of the story. Instead, he took the dispute public: A piece in the *Los Angeles Herald Examiner* a week later quoted him as calling Simmons "useless" and maintaining "you just sit there."

Trump told Simmons he hadn't said that, but nine months later, Simmons was out as commissioner, having been replaced by Harry Usher, an attorney who had helped organize the 1984 Olympics. In the meantime, owners did, in fact, vote to shift the USFL season to the fall, beginning with the league's fourth season. The owners were losing money, and they panicked.

Fall fallout

The Philadelphia Stars, who had just won the league title, abandoned the City of Brotherly Love to avoid going up against the Eagles and landed in Baltimore, which had recently been forsaken by Irsay's Colts.

And that was just the tip of the iceberg.

Instead of expanding, teams were folding or relocating in a desperate attempt to stay afloat. Pittsburgh went out of business after just one year rather than take on the Steelers. After pondering a move to Dallas — a move that wouldn't have made much sense — Chicago ultimately just suspended operations rather than go up against the Bears. The pitiful Washington Federals announced they were moving to Miami, then switched gears and chose Orlando instead to avoid competing with the NFL Dolphins in the fall. The New Orleans Breakers moved for the second time in as many seasons, fleeing the Saints' city for Portland in the Pacific Northwest.

The 1983 champion Michigan Panthers, meanwhile, merged with — and moved to —

Oakland, while the Oklahoma Outlaws moved west to merge with the Arizona Wranglers, although the new hybrid team was still the Outlaws. (Oklahoma was originally supposed to merge with Oakland, with the Panthers simply disappearing, but that deal fell through).

All this chaos merely highlighted the fact that the league was no longer the shiny new plaything it had been three years earlier, and ABC decided not to continue televising its games once it moved to the fall. Commissioner Usher admitted it was unlikely the league would be able to replace ABC's coverage with another broadcast network contract.

"When we couldn't negotiate a TV contract within 60 or 90 days," Bassett told Sports Illustrated, "we should have either gone out of business or voted to go back to the spring."

Owners, however, did neither. Instead, they reaffirmed their intention to play in the fall with another vote in the spring of '85, with only the Denver Gold and Bassett's Tampa Bay Bandits dissenting.

The Gold which had led the league in attendance during its inaugural season, was drawing fewer fans after starting 7-1 in 1984, then collapsing to finish at 9-9 and miss the playoffs altogether. Owner Doug Spedding knew his team couldn't compete with the NFL Broncos, either. Bassett, meanwhile, still believed in the spring concept and knew it would be suicide to go head-to-head in a battle for fans with the NFL's Buccaneers. So, he took his ball and went home. Well, not exactly home: Bassett announced that he was pulling the Bandits out of the league and starting a new spring league of his own.

"I'm not going to sit back and take orders from a lot of guys who don't know how to run a business," Bassett said. "I think the chances of the USFL succeeding in the fall are very slim."

Bassett had big plans for his proposed league, which he said would be a multi-sport entity encompassing football, golf and indoor soccer in addition to football. Meanwhile, Usher fell out of favor with Trump, and the league settled on a new strategy: a $1.32 billion antitrust suit against the NFL that could provide enough money to keep the league alive, or enough leverage to force a merger for the remaining teams.

A merger would, of course, give Trump what he'd failed to achieve when he tried to buy the Colts back in '81: membership in the NFL.

In a letter dated Jan. 17, 1984, Trump told the league's other owners that spring TV revenues couldn't sustain the league. "The NFL knows this and are just waiting," he wrote. "Their only fear is a switch of our league to the winter, an event which will either lead to a merger, or, in the alternative, a common draft with a first-class, traditional league."

In the fall of 1985, after the USFL played what would be its final season, sources close to Trump were reporting he had met with NFL commissioner Pete Rozelle to talk about just such a merger. According to this version of events, the discussions revolved around the possibility of the NFL adding six USFL teams: Oakland, Baltimore, Memphis, Jacksonville, Arizona and, of course, Trump's Generals, the only one of the six to share a market with any NFL teams. The NFL reportedly dropped the talks when they became public, but Rozelle claimed they never took place at all.

The merger idea became a liability for the upstart league when the NFL used it as a defense in the lawsuit. It obtained documents, most of them in-house memos between USFL owners, that referred to a "merger strategy" as early as 1983 — and the fact that Trump was the driving force behind it. In the end, the jury sided with the USFL in ruling that the NFL was, indeed, a monopoly and awarded the younger league treble damages ... of a $1 award.

The USFL was effectively out of business.

What became of Bassett's plans to form an alternate league? Unfortunately, they were not to be. Bassett died of cancer on May 14, 1986, and spring football was dead — at least for the time being.

Epilogue

David Dixon, however, wasn't ready to give up just yet. In July of 1987, a year after the USFL played its last game, he announced he was forming a new spring football league called the American Football Federation. The league, he said, was open to signing players right out of high school and would avoid the kind of free spending that had helped doom the USFL.

Teams were planned in New York, Philadelphia, Chicago, Detroit, Dallas, Houston, Tampa, Los Angeles and either Miami or Orlando.

"We have the owners and we have the cities," said Dixon, who was supposedly negotiating with Fox Broadcasting to televise the league's games.

A few more news items appeared on Dixon's proposal through the spring of 1988. After that, there was nothing.

As for Bassett's proposed spring league, it never happened, either. He died in May of 1986 at the age of 47 after undergoing treatment for brain tumors for two years.

Another outfit, dubbed the Professional Spring Football League, seemed poised to kick off in 1992, announcing plans for a 16-game schedule and teams in 10 cities: Albuquerque, Boston, Columbia, Las Vegas, Little Rock, Miami, Portland, Tampa and Salt Lake City. The league held a draft, formed rosters, set a season schedule and made preparations to begin play. A championship game called the "Red, White and Blue Bowl" was even scheduled for Fourth of July weekend.

But organizers pulled the plug less than three weeks before the season was scheduled to start. More than 600 players on 10 rosters were told they wouldn't be playing football, after all. Apparently, league organizers had thought it wouldn't have to pay insurance premiums on players for workers' comp until the players became full-time employees. They thought wrong and found themselves in a $1 million hole before the season even started. Despite earlier claims of solid financial backing, it turned out they didn't even have enough cash on hand to meet their first payroll. After scrambling frantically to find new investors over the next couple of weeks, they finally threw in the towel.

Other proposals for leagues came and went, all of them failing at various stages. The United Football League, an obscure four-team outfit, toiled in relative obscurity from 2009 to 2012 before calling it quits. Teams during the first season were the California Redwoods, Florida Tuskers, Las Vegas Locomotives and New York Sentinels. The Tuskers won all six regular-season games before falling to Las Vegas 20-17 in the finals, but none of the teams averaged as many as 15,000 fans a game.

New York moved to Hartford as the Colonials the next season, and the Redwoods moved from the Bay Area to Sacramento. The league boosted its schedule to eight games and looked at adding two expansion teams among San Antonio, Los Angeles, Omaha and Salt Lake City, but the Omaha Nighthawks were ultimately the only new franchise for the second season. They were also the only team to draw more than 20,000 fans a game, but they didn't make the finals, where Las Vegas beat Florida, 23-20, for the second time in as many years.

The Tuskers folded during the offseason, and Hartford's owner was in charge of a new team called the Virginia Destroyers — who won the title by defeating two-time champ Las Vegas. The regular season, however, was reduced from six games to four games when the final two games were abruptly canceled, and none of the games that actually were played drew as many as 20,000 fans, the end was in sight.

The league did, however, return for one more season — or at least part of one. It planned to play eight games again, but suspended operations midway through the campaign and, this time, there would be no coming back. The top attendance figure was just 8,023 for a game in Sacramento, and one in Las Vegas pulled in just 601 fans. The Locomotives were unbeaten and atop the standings at 4-0 when the whole league went out of business.

Other planned leagues, including a supposed USFL revival and something called the A11FL, which would have made all offensive players eligible receivers depending on how they lined up, never got off the ground.

The A11FL set up teams in a number of old USFL markets and adopted the nicknames that league had once used: the Tampa Bay Bandits, L.A. Express, Philadelphia Stars, New

Jersey Generals, Denver Gold and Michigan Panthers were all on board, with updated logos and helmets designs. There was also a Wranglers team, but in Dallas instead of Arizona. Oakland's team would be called the Bay Area Sea Lions, and Chicago's the Staggs (with two "Gs" in honor of Amos Alonzo Stagg). But trouble emerged when Oakland and Los Angeles had to drop out because California's workers' compensation laws made the cost of operating those teams prohibitive.

The A11FL arranged with ESPN to televise two "showcase games," in Tampa and Dallas, during the spring of 2014, but those games were mysteriously called off a few weeks beforehand, and the league announced it was regrouping without the "all-11" gimmick.

It then faded into oblivion — although its Facebook page still existed, more than three years after its last post.

The Canadian Football League even tried to get into the act, expanding into the United States in 1993 by placing a team in Sacramento called the Gold Miners. Three others — the Las Vegas Posse, Baltimore Colts (later renamed the Stallions when the NFL Colts objected) and Shreveport Pirates — followed the next season. But attendance in Las Vegas was anemic, and the league approved a move to Jackson, Mississippi, then to Miami as the Manatees before giving up and folding the franchise.

Before the 1995 season, the league added to U.S. expansion teams, the Birmingham Barracudas and Memphis Mad Dogs. Sacramento, meanwhile, was moved to San Antonio.

The most successful franchise, both on the field and the gate, throughout the three-year experiment was Baltimore, which averaged more than 30,000 fans and even won the Grey Cup in 1995 with a 37-20 victory over Calgary. It was, however, the last game they — or any of the other American teams — would play. With the Stallions on the brink of the CFL title, the NFL's Cleveland Browns announced they were moving to Baltimore, effectively undercutting the Canadians' only real U.S. success story.

All five U.S. franchises were dropped at a league meeting on Feb. 2.

Fans attend a Kansas City Brigade game in 2006. *Kansas City Royalty.*

Arena Football League, 1987-2009

Inside Job

Believe it or not, indoor football got its start in the NFL.

Sort of.

And it was the league's first true championship game. Not exactly the perfect time to be experimenting with the game.

But the 1932 contest between the Chicago Bears and Portsmouth Spartans wasn't intended as an experiment. It was a case of improvisation. At the time, the NFL champion was the team with the best regular-season record. There were no playoffs, as such. But the 1932 season featured an unusually close race involving three of the league's eight teams. The Green Bay Packers had a chance to clinch their fourth straight title with a victory in their final game of the season, against the Spartans of Portsmouth, Ohio.

But the Spartans were on the rise behind former halfback Glenn Presnell, the old Ironton

Tanks standout, who had once led Nebraska to a 14-0 victory over Red Grange's Illinois team. Presnell had joined the Spartans a year earlier, and they'd finished second to the Packers, just a game out of first place. Now, playing at home before a capacity crowd of 15,000, the Spartans were ready to take the next step. Presnell completed a 26-yard scoring pass for the only touchdown Portsmouth would need, then connected on another 26-yard strike that set up his own TD run from a couple of yards out. The final score was 19-0, and with the victory, the Spartans knocked the Packers out of contention. They hadn't clinched the title for themselves, though: They had to sit and wait as the Bears and Packers squared off in the final game of the season the following Sunday.

A Green Bay victory would give Portsmouth the title, but a loss would leave the Spartans in a tie with the Bears with identical 6-1 records, and the two teams had played to a draw in their two previous meetings. (In fact, Chicago had played six tie games and Portsmouth four, but those didn't count in the standings one way or the other). Surely, the mighty Packers, who had lost just once all season before succumbing to the Spartans, wouldn't lose two games in a row … or would they? With no way to win the title, the Packers had nothing to play for except pride, and now they had to face a strong Chicago team on the Bears home field.

The Bears, who had suffered their only loss of the year against the Packers in October, weren't just playing for a shot at the title, they wanted revenge.

On top of that, winter was setting in, with a storm moving into the Great Lakes region and blanketing the field with snow. The weather was so bad Portsmouth had to cancel a nonleague exhibition against a semipro team from Columbus that day, but the Bears and Packers, with more at stake, forged ahead. Amid these less-than-ideal conditions, the two teams battled to a scoreless tie through three quarters before Bronco Nagurski took over. The future Hall of Famer ran to the Packers' 5-yard-line, setting up a field goal — the only points Chicago would need. Then, with time running down, he sealed the victory with a 56-yard scoring run.

The Bears thus forced the Spartans into a playoff the following week at Wrigley Field, the Bears' home stadium.

The weather, however, wasn't getting any better. Wind and snow continued to buffet the region, so organizers decided to take a drastic step: They would move the game indoors. Chicago Stadium was available. The floor was concrete, but dirt was being brought in for a circus the following week, and a six-inch layer of bark could be added in the hope of breaking the players' fall … not their bones. Portsmouth coach Potsy Clark suggested the move, and the Bears' George Halas agreed.

It wasn't the first time the stadium had been used for football: The Bears had played their crosstown rivals, the Cardinals, in a charity game there two years earlier. But some adjustments would definitely have to be made.

The game would be played on a condensed field just 80 yards long and 45 wide — 20 yards shorter and 10 yards narrower than usual. There was so little room on each sideline that the field was directly adjacent to the stands. To compensate for the shorter field, the ball would automatically be moved back 20 yards whenever a team crossed the opponent's 10-yard line. Goal posts were moved up to the goal lines, but teams wouldn't be allowed to take advantage of the shorter distance by trying field goals, which were ruled illegal for this game only.

Despite these restrictions, the Associated Press predicted that "the shorter distance between the goal lines … probably will result in more scoring and thrills."

It didn't turn out that way.

A partisan crowd of 11,198 turned out in hopes of seeing Chicago's dream backfield of Nagurski and Red Grange attempt to claim the title. But the matchup wasn't the epic battle it might have been because, on the other side of the field, the Spartans were without their leading offensive weapon. Dutch Clark had led the team in rushing, passing and receiving yards, if you can imagine that, and led the league in scoring. But he hadn't counted on playing an extra game and had made arrangements to start his offseason job, as basketball coach at Colorado College, before the scheduled playoff.

The game was, in some ways, a replay of the previous week's contest against the Packers. Once again, the Bears found themselves in a scoreless deadlock through three quarters, but once again, they found a way to win it in the fourth by an identical 9-0 score. As he had against Green Bay, Nagurski came through when it counted, throwing a short pass to Grange in the end zone for the only touchdown of the game.

The remaining points came the Portsmouth punter fumbled the ball out of the end zone for a safety in the closing moments.

1932 NFL Championship Game

Portsmouth Spartans	0	0	0	0	– 0
Chicago Bears	0	0	0	0	– 9

Chicago Stadium, Dec. 18, 1932
Attendance: 11,198

Fans fill Chicago Stadium for a 1930 hockey game, two years before the NFL played its championship game there.

Shrinking everything

The NFL must have liked having a championship game, because the following season, it actually planned for one, splitting into two divisions and arranging for the winners to play for the title. Chicago won again in '33, clinching the division by beating the Spartans in Portsmouth's last two games. They also turned out to be the team's final two games representing southern Ohio: The following season, they moved to Detroit and became the Lions.

Indoor football, meanwhile, probably would have become a footnote in the history of the sport if it hadn't been for Jim Foster.

A former NFL promotions director, Foster must have been aware of the 1932 title game, but that isn't where he got the idea for Arena Football. The inspiration came from indoor soccer, and the motivation came from a future president of the United States. According to Foster, he formulated the concept for the game while attending an indoor soccer game at

Madison Square Garden in 1981. He'd come straight from work, so he still had his briefcase with him. Following his muse, he reached inside, pulled out an envelope and sketched a field that looked like a hockey rink and some ideas for how indoor football might work. Then he called NBC, suggesting that the network could show games during the spring and summer months, when football fans were hungry for something other than baseball.

NBC thought it was a good idea. But it was so good that David Dixon beat him to the punch with the outdoor United States Football League. Suddenly, the spring and summer months were spoken for, as was most of the talent not already playing in the NFL. Foster therefore left his idea on the drawing board and, in a case of "if you can't beat 'em ...," joined the USFL. He eventually became executive vice president of the Chicago Blitz, but he never forgot about the Arena Football concept.

When the USFL ran into trouble, he saw his chance. New Jersey Generals owner Donald Trump had persuaded his fellow owners to abandon their springtime business model and go head-to-head with the NFL during prime time: the fall. It never happened. The USFL tried to stay afloat by filing an antitrust suit against the established league, and when that didn't pan out, it collapsed.

But Trump's folly turned out to be Foster's big break. Foster didn't mince words when describing how it went down, telling *The Cleveland Plain Dealer* that "the reason Arena Football happened was because of Donald Trump. He ruined the USFL."

Foster was in business. In one sense, he picked up where indoor football had left off more than a half-century earlier: in Illinois, with a team representing Chicago. The first game, played in April of 1986, matched a team called the Chicago Politicians against the Rockford Metros in a test game at Rockford's Metro Center. Neither of the teams played any more games after that, having served as the initial guinea pigs for Foster's new enterprise.

He patented the idea the following year.

In most ways, it didn't bear much resemblance to its distant ancestor, that 1932 title game. Foster wasn't trying to squeeze 11-man teams on a regulation field into an undersized container. He was shrinking everything. Teams had eight men on the field at a time, and the field itself was just 50 yards long and slightly more than 25 yards wide, with end zones eight yards deep. The rosters consisted of just 21 players, most of whom played both offense and defense. The speed of the game favored smaller players, too. The only thing that wasn't smaller was the scoring. In fact, fewer points were scored in that game between the Bears and Spartans than were ever scored in an Arena Football League game. (The low-water mark was a 16-12 victory by the Albany Firebirds over the Washington Commandos in 1990, and the record for most points was set 11 years later when the New York Dragons blasted the

Carolina Cobras 99-68.)

Doug Buffone, a Hall of Fame linebacker for the Bears who signed on as Foster's director of development, compared the arena game to Rollerball, a futuristic and fictional blood sport based on roller derby, featuring motorcycles and a steel ball. Arena Football wasn't quite as crazy as the 1975 James Caan movie, but it did bear a certain resemblance to human pinball. The sidelines were lined with walls, like a hockey rink, and missed field goal attempts bounced at odd angles off tightly strung netting on either side of the narrow goalposts. Players on the opposing team could field the ball and run it back.

Following the test game of 1986, Foster patented the sport and launched a six-week demonstration season featuring four teams: the Chicago Bruisers, Denver Dynamite, Pittsburgh Gladiators and Washington Commandos. Denver won the title game, avenging an earlier loss to Pittsburgh with a 45-16 rout. More importantly, the games were gold at the gate: Only two of the 13 games played drew crowds of fewer than 10,000.

A bona fide star

Attendance dropped a bit over the next three seasons, but by the 1990s, the league had found its footing and had begun to expand. Eight teams played a 10-game season in 1991, with two games added in 1993 and two more three years later. The league got perhaps its biggest boost in 2000, when Kurt Warner became the first quarterback to throw for more than 400 yards in a Super Bowl as he led the St. Louis Rams to a 23-16 victory over Tennessee. It marked the pinnacle of an unlikely Cinderella story for Warner, who had failed to catch on with the Green Bay Packers after graduating from Northern Iowa in 1993. He'd been an all-conference selection for the Panthers, throwing for more than 300 yards four times. But the Packers were already well stocked at quarterback with Brett Favre, Mark Brunell and Ty Detmer ahead of him on the depth chart. As a result, he soon found himself stocking shelves at a local supermarket for close to minimum wage.

The next thing anyone heard about Warner, his name appeared in the small-print "Transactions" section of the sports page on March 23, 1995, where it was reported that the new Iowa Barnstormers — an arena team owned by Jim Foster himself — had signed him and a lineman named Brian Krulikowski. That was the extent of the news. Nothing about the size or duration of his contract. No background. No scouting report. Nothing. Warner was, at that point, just a football footnote.

Iowa played to the hometown crowd by stocking its roster with local products: Nearly one-third of the team had played college ball at one of three universities in the state. Was

Warner just a gimmick? Not according to Art Haege, the team's director of player personnel. A few days after Warner signed with the club, his picture appeared in the *Des Moines Register* with the caption "Starter?" and the following from Haege: "He'll have as much a chance to start as anyone else we have. He throws the ball well and has good judgment. He came from a passing-type offense and was well-coached in college. That will really help him here."

It wasn't long before that question under Warner's photo was answered in the affirmative. Not only was Warner in the starting lineup for Iowa's season opener against Milwaukee, he threw for 285 yards and five touchdowns as the two teams matched the then-league record for most points in a game. Iowa won, 69-61.

Warner followed that up with four more touchdowns and 241 yards passing in another Iowa victory the following week. The team finished at 7-5 on the season, but it was a sign of bigger things to come.

In 1996, Warner led Iowa to a 12-2 record in the regular season and a berth in the championship game. The quarterback on the opposite sideline? Jay Gruden. Before he became head coach of Washington in the NFL, Gruden was the Arena Football League's marquee quarterback, winning four Arena Bowls with the Tampa Bay Storm (and, later, two more as coach of the Orlando Predators).

Warner finished the game with an Arena Bowl record 316 yards passing and four touchdowns, while Gruden racked up yards and five TDs. Warner set another record with 19 passing first downs, but he also threw three interceptions, including a pick-six in the second quarter that gave Tampa Bay a 28-21 lead. Iowa tied it at halftime but was never able to take the lead. Still, the Barnstormers had a chance to win it in the final minutes when, trailing by four points, Warner scrambled away from pressure and found Lamart Cooper on the right sideline near the 16-yard line. Cooper pivoted and ran toward the center of the field, turning upfield and slamming into the wall right at the pylon. The officials called him out of bounds a half-yard short.

Cooper felt otherwise. "I was in," he said after the game. "I hit on the other side of the end zone line. I'm in. It's that simple."

On the next play, Warner handed the ball to fullback Ron Moran, who ploughed up the middle and thought he was in the end zone as well. But he dropped the ball after his forward progress appeared to have been stopped, and Warner fell on the ball at the 3. It was ruled a fumble, and the Barnstormers were left with three more chances. A slant pass went through the receiver's hand, and Warner's next two passes were knocked away.

Tampa Bay held on to win, 42-38.

Warner would find redemption of sorts in the 2000 Super Bowl, when he helped the Rams build a 23-16 lead and then watched as Tennessee receiver Kevin Dyson's lunge for the goal line fell a single yard short in the closing seconds.

First, however, Warner would lead the Barnstormers to the Arena Bowl again in '97, where they lost to Arizona in what turned out to be his final arena game. He might have been named MVP in either of his two Arena Bowl seasons, but the league didn't present that award between 1996 and 2010. Still, he earned all-league honors at quarterback before moving to the NFL's European league, which he led in touchdowns, and passing yards while playing for the Amsterdam Admirals.

Warner would go on to lead the NFL in completion percentage during each of his first three seasons in the league, leading the Rams to the Super Bowl as a rookie and then again two years later. He reached the Super Bowl one last time, with the Arizona Cardinals at age 37, when he fell just short of engineering a huge upset of the Pittsburgh Steelers. He played one more season and retired, later becoming the only player ever inducted into both the Arena Football and Pro Football halls of fame.

Arena Football, meanwhile, continued to grow after Warner's departure. By 2001, the league had expanded to 19 teams, and a couple of years later, teams were playing as many games in a season as their NFL counterparts (16). In 2000, the circuit even added its own minor league, af2, featuring 15 teams, most of them in smaller markets. Rock star Jon Bon Jovi became a high-profile owner of the Philadelphia Soul, which won the league championship in 2008. But that turned out to be the league's last season — at least in its original incarnation. By then, the league had overextended itself and, even though average attendance was the highest in league history, it declared bankruptcy and suspended operations at the end of the year.

Oddly enough, af2 remained in business for one more year, and some of its teams joining some revived Arena Football League teams to form a new league (which was originally called AF1 before assuming the familiar Arena Football League name) in 2010. That league had contracted by 2018 to become a regional league of four teams, all in the Northeast, while some teams folding and others such as Arizona and Iowa departing to join the Indoor Football League.

That league, formed in 2008, was centered on the Midwest and upper plains states, but still had a bigger geographic footprint as of 2018 than the league that started it all. In addition to the Rattlers and Barnstormers, it featured the San Diego Strike Force, Green Bay Blizzard, Bismarck Bucks, Sioux Falls Storm, Quad Cities Steamwheelers, Tucson Sugar Skulls, Nebraska Danger (Grand Island) and Cedar Rapids RiverKings.

ArenaBowl results 1987-2008

1987	Denver Dynamite 45, Pittsburgh Gladiators 16
1988	Detroit Drive 24, Chicago Bruisers 13
1989	Detroit Drive 39, Pittsburgh Gladiators 26
1990	Detroit Drive 51, Dallas Texans 27
1991	Tampa Bay Storm 48, Detroit Drive 42
1992	Detroit Drive 56, Orlando Predators 38
1993	Tampa Bay Storm 51, Detroit Drive 31
1994	Arizona Rattlers 51, Orlando Predators 38
1995	Tampa Bay Storm 48, Orlando Predators 35
1996	Tampa Bay Storm 42, Iowa Barnstormers 38
1997	Arizona Rattlers 55, Iowa Barnstormers 33
1998	Orlando Predators 62, Tampa Bay Storm 31
1999	Albany Firebirds 59, Orlando Predators 48
2000	Orlando Predators 41, Nashville Kats 38
2001	Grand Rapids Rampage 64, Nashville Kats 42
2002	San Jose SaberCats 52, Arizona Rattlers 14
2003	Tampa Bay Storm 43, Arizona Rattlers 29
2004	San Jose SaberCats 69, Arizona Rattlers 62
2005	Colorado Crush 51, Georgia Force 48
2006	Chicago Rush 69, Orlando Predators 61
2007	San Jose SaberCats 55, Columbus Destroyers 33
2008	Philadelphia Soul 59, San Jose SaberCats 56

X Marks the Spot

When I worked as a prep sports intern at my local newspaper, two things surprised me. One: The newspaper carried occasional bits of wrestling news. Not Olympic Greco-Roman wrestling or arm wrestling or thumb wrestling or steer wrestling. This was the kind of wrestling I grew up watching as a kid on my still-black-and-white TV when there was nothing else to watch on Saturday afternoon.

Even back then, my prepubescent self knew one thing about wrestling: It was fake. The outcome was predetermined; this was entertainment, *not* sports.

The other thing that surprised me was that many of the people who worked in the sports department seemed just as interested in wrestling "news" as they did in the pennant race or the NCAA Tournament.

These two facts say something the popularity of pro wrestling, which had long ago evolved from a legitimate sport into a scripted show that owed as much to afternoon soap operas as it did to athleticism. As with soap operas, there were heroes and villains — "faces" and "heels" — who occasionally switched roles to keep things interesting. Trademark moves, colorful names and even more colorful costumes became pro wrestling's stock-in-trade as it morphed from sport to entertainment. Something similar happened to roller derby about the same time: It, too, had begun as a real competition before promoters started picking the winners and writing complex storylines for skaters to follow.

But in the mid-1970s, banked-track roller derby began a period of decline. It might have disappeared altogether had it not been for renewed interest in it as a recreational sport. Gradually, it began to catch on again as a real competition (mostly for women's teams) in local flat-track races at the start of the 21st-century.

More on roller derby in a later chapter.

Wrestling, meanwhile, went in the opposite direction. Participants became more flamboyant and storylines more elaborate. In the early 1980s, it entered a period of ascendancy when Vince McMahon bought his father's promotion and raised its profile with the help of 6-foot-7 strongman Terry "Hulk Hogan" Bollea. Within a few short years, the World Wrestling Federation went from a regional operation to a national phenomenon that made McMahon a billionaire. McMahon surrounded Hogan with charismatic wrestlers like

Jesse "the Body" Ventura, Ric Flair, Rowdy Roddy Piper and The Undertaker. Later superstars like Stone Cold Steve Austin and The Rock only added to the success. Ventura went on to become governor of Minnesota, and The Rock (Dwayne Johnson) parlayed his wrestling image into a career as one of Hollywood's leading men. John Cena hit the big screen, as well.

But even the money Johnson made at the box office pales in comparison to McMahon's portfolio. Wrestling might be fake, but McMahon's bank account sure isn't.

Neither was the football league he ran in 2001.

XFL founder Vince McMahon in 2006

McMahon had never been shy about admitting that his wrestling matches were pure entertainment. He even drove that point home by renaming his promotion World Wrestling Entertainment about the time he started his football venture. But the XFL, as he called it, would be something different. The games would count, the scores would be earned and the results would be 100 percent real. McMahon planned to take all the in-your-face attitude of pro wrestling and infuse it into real, honest-to-goodness American football.

It would be a balancing act, to be sure. In describing his vision for the new league, he immediately sought to draw a distinction between it and his wrestling promotion: "The WWF is 100 percent entertainment, but the XFL is 100 percent sports."

Would the outcomes be scripted?

"Nooo."

Wrestlers wouldn't be suiting up for XFL teams (although McMahon was open to players climbing through the ropes). He reinforced the new league's legitimacy by bringing in former Dallas Cowboys receiver Drew Pearson to serve on the league's advisory committee and joining forces with Dick Ebersol, head of NBC Sports, which would televise its games. Like its two immediate predecessors, the WFL and USFL, McMahon's league would play its games during the spring to avoid a direct conflict with the National Football League.

On top of that, he sought to draw a distinction between the two products in more fundamental ways. Labeling the NFL the "No Fun League," McMahon promised an alternative that would not feature "an overregulated, antiseptic brand of football."

There would be a moving "Skycam" suspended over the playing field to follow the action; live microphones on some players; and jerseys bearing the kind of colorful nicknames wrestlers might have used: "Dirty Durden" and "Death Blow" (Reggie Durden and Jamal Duff, both of Los Angeles), "Mantis" (Darryl Hobbs of Memphis), and of course Rod Smart's "He Hate Me" in New York.

2001 XFL	W	L	T	PF	PA	Pct.
Eastern Division						
Orlando Rage	8	2	0	213	185	.800
Chicago Enforcers	5	5	0	186	184	.500
New York / New Jersey Hitmen	4	6	0	132	145	.400
Birmingham Thunderbolts	2	8	0	131	239	.200
Western Division						
Los Angeles Xtreme	7	3	0	235	166	.700
San Francisco Demons	5	5	0	156	161	.500
Memphis Maniax	5	5	0	164	166	.500
Las Vegas Outlaws	4	6	0	169	143	.400

Championship: Los Angeles 38, San Francisco 6

Lost in translation

McMahon wanted to translate wrestling's aggressive, high-energy atmosphere to the gridiron. His league would feature confrontational, smash-mouth football, with no holds barred. No fair catches on punts. No kicked extra points. Defensive backs could slam into receivers in the open field. And there would be an opening scramble for the ball, like a rugby scrum with momentum, to replace the coin toss.

Even the team names were designed to sound like something out of a Clint Eastwood movie. Hitmen. Rage. Enforcers. Demons. The XFL seemed to be stocked almost entirely with dropouts from an anger management class. The Memphis Maniax and Los Angeles Xtreme incorporated the signature X from the league title in their names, even though that letter didn't really stand for anything.

"The XFL will take you places where the NFL is afraid to go because, quite frankly, we are not afraid of anything," McMahon said confidently. "This will not be a league for pantywaists and sissies."

What he should have been afraid of was that his approach might not work. Reason number one: It was one thing to present an in-your-face mentality when everything was scripted, and quite another to let that kind of attitude play out live without a net. Reason number two: Smash-mouth football isn't always the most exciting — or telegenic — form of the game. People don't tune in to watch "3 yards and a cloud of dust," and they're not interested in seeing a bunch of passes fall incomplete because defensive backs have leveled receivers running their route. On the contrary, the AFL and, to a lesser degree, the USFL had succeeded by offering a wide-open, high-scoring version of football. A fast-paced shootout, not a barroom brawl. The game's most successful innovations over the previous 30 years had been things like the shotgun formation in Dallas, the run-and-shoot with the USFL's Houston Gamblers and Bill Walsh's West Coast offense in San Francisco.

Without much excitement on the field, the league had to rely solely on its gimmicks to keep viewers interested, which created another problem. Even with a wrestling promoter at the helm, no one suspected the league was fake: The games were just too bad. But it quickly became apparent that the league was trying too hard for style points in an attempt to distract from what it lacked in substance.

Too often, McMahon resorted to wrestling tie-ins in an attempt to keep people interested. The pregame hype featured a recorded message by The Rock (who said he was "geeked" and "pumped," among other adjectives, about watching the XFL). Jesse Ventura was one of the announcers, and Stone Cold Steve Austin warned NFL Commissioner Paul Tagliabue that the new league "might bite you on your ass." The regional broadcast team consisted of two other WWF veterans, Jim Ross and former wrestler Jerry "King" Lawler, who admitted he neither knew nor cared much about football and quit midway through the season because McMahon had fired his wife from his wrestling organization.

McMahon even resorted to putting scantily clad cheerleaders front and center, inviting viewers into *their* locker room during one game. Family entertainment this was not. It was smoke and mirrors and bad taste, all wrapped into a package that made football look like a bad imitation of pro wrestling, even if the games *were* real. Bob Costas, who worked for NBC — the same network that was televising the league's games — pontificated: "It has to be at least a decade since I mused out loud, 'Why doesn't someone combine mediocre high school football with a tawdry strip club.' Finally, somebody takes my idea and runs with it."

Eventually, the league had to get around to playing football. But the games left a lot to be desired. The *New York Times* headline after the opening game, a dull 19-0 victory by Las Vegas over New York/New Jersey, said it all: "Novelty Upstages Game On the XFL's First

Night." No one scored in the second half, so the network cut away to the league's other game that night, a much more entertaining 33-29 victory by Orlando over Chicago.

The XFL opened the season with an encouraging 9.5 rating on NBC, but the audience was less than half that in the second week, and it continued to fall over the course of the season. By the time it was over, McMahon was probably grateful he'd opted for a less ambitious 10-game season rather than 18 or 20, as the USFL and WFL, respectively, had slated. Playoff berths were on the line in the ninth and 10th weeks, but those games nonetheless drew the season's worst ratings — with only modest increases for the playoffs and championship "Million Dollar Game." TV Guide ultimately named the league's broadcasts the third-worst television show of all time.

Seeking to somehow stop the bleeding, the XFL made a series of changes on the fly as the season progressed. It eliminated the rule allowing defensive backs to hit receivers running their patterns, and, for the playoffs, added 2- and 3-point conversion attempts from the 5- and 10-yard lines, respectively. (Previously, the only option was to attempt a 1-point run or pass from the 1-yard line.)

Stadium attendance was more encouraging than the TV ratings, with San Francisco pulling in more than 35,000 fans a game for its five home dates and the league's eight teams drawing an average of 23,410. Still, the Los Angeles Xtreme seemed to be playing in a near-empty stadium even when it hosted the championship game, because the Coliseum held more than 90,000 people and only 24,000 showed up. The home team won, but the game was far from exciting, with the Xtreme racing to a 21-0 halftime lead and winning 38-6. The opposing San Francisco Demons failed to score at all until the final 25 seconds, when they managed a meaningless touchdown run in front of virtually no one who cared.

Despite all the downsides, there were a few highlights. L.A. quarterback Tommy Maddox, the league MVP, went on to lead the Pittsburgh Steelers to the playoffs in 2002 but said the most fun he ever had was playing in the XFL. The Xtreme's first home game produced plenty of excitement, with Maddox throwing for 412 yards and four touchdowns in a 39-32 come-from-behind double-overtime win over Chicago. But even that game was punctuated with oddities: One fan waved a sign that read, "I'm here for nothing but the cheerleaders." Another, a Chicago partisan, got pelted by food, beer and wads of paper by L.A. fans, many of whom arrived in Raiders gear. The game was supposed to be televised, but viewers missed most of the first quarter because a generator ran out of gas.

Even before the season started, there was trouble. Franchises announced for Washington and Miami were shifted to Memphis and Birmingham, but that wasn't unusual for a new league getting its footing. More bizarre, in a portent of things to come, was the blimp incident. It happened in early January, a month before the scheduled start of the season: The pilot of an airship carrying the XFL logo lost control of the craft and attempted an emergency landing at Oakland Airport, but he and his copilot had to bail when a landing crew couldn't tie it down. The blimp floated away, meandered through the air for several miles before its gondola snagged a sailboat mast and crashed into a seafood restaurant.

The XFL ultimately crashed, as well, but a lot less spectacularly. Even with cost controls in place to keep player salaries manageable, the league still lost $50 million. The partnership between McMahon and Ebersol lasted just one season, after which NBC pulled the plug and the league dissolved. McMahon thought long and hard about going it alone, without a TV contract, for a second season, but he ultimately decided against it. Still, he never quite got the football bug out of his system. So, in 2018, he announced plans to try again, with a rebooted XFL aiming for a 2020 debut.

No sooner had McMahon thrown his helmet back into the ring, however, then another spring league announced plans to begin play a year earlier. The person behind it? A fellow named Chris Ebersol: you guessed it — Dick Ebersol's son.

Part IV
Other Sports

In a Jam

Roller Derby is an odd pastime that doesn't fit neatly into any particular box. The object of the game isn't to deposit a ball into the opponent's goal; indeed, there *isn't* a ball at all. It might be best described as a combination of ice hockey and stock-car racing, with human bodies taking the place of cars, donning wheels and crashing into one another at high speed. The object of roller derby, however, isn't to reach the finish line (there isn't one) but to pass your opponents. The more skaters of the opposite team you pass in the space of 60 seconds, the more points you pile up.

Unlike most sports, men and women both took to the oval track — although not at the same time — and the points they scored counted equally in the final tally.

It's a highly original idea, and its history is as unusual as the sport itself. It started out as a leisure craze, evolved into a competitive sport, morphed into "sports entertainment" and then, finally, hit its stride as a recreational sport in the 21st century.

At the height of its popularity in the mid-20th century, the emphasis was on entertainment. Like the Harlem Globetrotters, who always seemed to beat their potential foils, the Washington Generals, teams like the L.A. T-Birds and Bay Bombers managed to come back "in the nick of time" to defeat visiting teams like the Texas Outlaws, Chicago Hawks and Reilly's Renegades.

Teams barnstormed across the country, too, taking their show on the road much as the Globetrotters did. The sport would be immortalized in such films as *The Fireball* (1950) with Mickey Rooney and Marilyn Monroe; *Kansas City Bomber* (1972) with Raquel Welch and *Rollerball* (1975) starring James Caan in a fictional and futuristic variant of the sport that featured a metal ball and motorcycles.

Evolution

The term "roller derby" originally meant something different. It was used to describe races on skates, which gained popularity in the early 20th century. By that time, activities on wheels ranged from speed skating and "polo skating" to a hybrid that combined skating with ballroom dancing. Seven thousand people attended opening night at a public roller rink at the Coliseum in Chicago in 1902.

Ten years later, in 1912, *The Corpus Christi Caller-Times* contained a passing reference to "a Southwest service roller derby tournament." And three years later in the nation's capital, a story in *The Washington Herald* announced that the National Skating Association had granted a sanction to a Mrs. B.W. Hawkesworth "to hold a professional championship roller meet race" that would be known as "the Great American Roller Derby."

A dance marathon in 1923; the kind of event that paved the way for walkathons and, ultimately, Roller Derby.

It wasn't the first race of its kind: Not long before the Washington event was held, a 24-hour race had been held at Madison Square Garden, which had added roller skating to its calendar in 1908.

The 100-mile race would include at least 20 sprints that would be key in determining the winner. Scoring would be done based on something called the Berlin Point System, with the winner of each sprint getting five points, and the top three overall finishers receiving 15, 10 and 5 points, respectively. Players would compete in two-man teams, with the race starting in front of the White House and ending at the Convention Hall. The pre-race favorites, world champions Roland Cioni and Arthur Eglington, lived up to their billing and won the event, which marked the culmination of a four-day carnival.

But it wasn't until 1935, when former cinema salesman Leo "Bromo" Seltzer got involved with skating, that roller derby began to move toward its modern form.

Seltzer began promoting events at a time when endurance contests were all the rage. Four years earlier, he'd staged the first "walkathon," in Denver. A walkathon was what a dance marathon turned into when the dancers got so tired they could barely move their feet. But Seltzer insisted his events were different — even though they, too, involved couples. The distinction was an important one, though: In Indiana, a Seltzer walkathon nearly didn't happen when police threatened to arrest everyone involved for violating a ban on dance marathons. A judge sided with Seltzer, and the event went on after an hour's delay.

In all, Seltzer would gross about $2 million staging 23 walkathons across the country, before the fad cooled off, forcing him to look for the "next big thing." He found it in the pages of *Literary Digest*, which informed him that 93 percent of American fathers bought skates for their kids. He thought to himself: "Anything you're good at as a kid, you'll stick with it if there's an outlet." Seltzer aimed to provide that outlet with a takeoff on the old walkathons called roller derby. *The New York Times* would later describe it as "an endurance scramble with less drama than dance marathons and less speed than six-day bicycle races."

Seltzer dubbed it the Trans-Continental Roller Derby, and in 1936 massive crowds were turning out to see it: as many as 225,000 in Chicago for one competition. It even brought the stars out: In Los Angeles, the likes of Jack Benny, Milton Berle, George Burns, Eddie Cantor, W.C. Fields and Cary Grant turned out for events at the Pan Pacific Auditorium in 1937. Actress Eleanor Powell was even linked romantically to star skater Wes Aronson.

Under the Derby's original format, skaters would cover about 4,000 miles over the course of a competition, with top prize money running as high as $1,000, but most of them coming away with "nothing more than a pair of worn-out roller skates," syndicated columnist Lyle Spencer wrote. As with his walkathons, roller derby became a traveling road show, with the best skaters going along for the ride, gypsy style, in a caravan that crisscrossed the country.

The events themselves, however, weren't cross-country affairs — although they were designed to give that impression. An event staged in Miami took place entirely on an oval track under a tent downtown, but lights on a huge board followed the skaters' progress as though they were coming from San Francisco. Each light indicated when the skaters had "reached" a city or town between San Francisco and Miami. Fifteen teams (of one man and one woman each) from Seltzer's traveling group were joined by several local teams in an event that was very much a race: Prizes were awarded for lap winners and the total distance covered each day.

But that format soon began to change.

Full contact

Seltzer was continually tweaking the concept, trying out new ideas and making them permanent parts of the derby if they proved popular. By the time his troupe pulled into Louisville in November 1935, he was already running one-on-one match races, which would remain a fixture of the derby for decades to come. The Louisville stop also gave him a chance to try out something new: an "Australian Pursuit" race in which four skaters were placed a quarter of a lap apart. Each one was then charged with passing the competitor in front of him and eliminating him from the race. The event, which was borrowed from cycling, served as a basis for the scoring system used in later versions of the derby.

A story in the *Muncie Evening Press* of Indiana from May of 1937 showed another stage in the sport's transformation from distance race to modern roller derby in progress. The derby still pitted a number of two-person teams against one another, all trying to cover the distance from Los Angeles to Miami, New York or wherever the race was being held. It was still a race, with the fastest time winning. Although the races lasted for 21 days or more, they weren't endurance tests: The teams would race from 7:30 p.m. to midnight, prime time for the crowds of paying customers who came to watch. The racers slept on cots in the "infield" overnight; then, when the event started up again, they competed in a series of 15-minute sprints called "jams," with women and men taking turns on the track.

But the two-person teams would soon be a thing of the past. *The Evening Press* reported that the skaters had begun to form cliques, with several competitors joining forces to block a particular skater from scoring. All of a sudden, the event was much more of a contact sport. As the newspaper reported: "This causes numerous spills, fist-fights (hair-pullings in the case of the girls) and, now and then, painful injuries. Nearly all of the boys and girls are burned and scraped on the legs and arms and shoulders from skidding along the wooden floor."

At the end of it all, the de facto teams would split the prize money.

The increased contact wasn't some skaters' cup of tea. Joseph "Joie" Ray, a distance runner who competed in three Olympics and finished third in the 1928 Boston Marathon, had been one of the Derby's first big-name attractions. He'd even competed in at least one dance marathon, and he'd won a 1935 match race in Louisville. But with the Derby's emphasis shifting from endurance to rugby-style contact, Ray was out of his element. The future belonged to skaters willing to mix it up, like former boxer Billy Lyons and 42-year-old Ma Bogash, who teamed up with her son to became one of the circuit's best-known skaters.

It wasn't long before the cliques became actual teams, wearing different-color jerseys. Some competitors might wear white jerseys and the others red; white-versus-black was also common. In one variation, three teams took the track at once, with black, white and green teams facing off. This innovation didn't last, though, because two of the teams wound up banding together against the third. (In later years, the home team would typically wear white, with the visiting squad attired in red.) In 1940, Seltzer tried another wrinkle: identifying various teams using the names of Native American tribes: the Pawnees, Mohicans, Aztecs, Navajos, Apaches, Seminoles, Comanches and Iroquois. That changed didn't last, either.

While the sport evolved gradually through trial and error, derby lore identifies a clear tipping point between old-style mock transcontinental races to modern jam-based scoring. That tipping point, according to Seltzer, took place in Miami early in 1938, in an encounter with sportswriter Damon Runyon. Seltzer invited Runyon to check out a practice session, and some players got tangled together in close quarters during a jam. He liked what he saw and suggested to Seltzer that the game would be more exciting if such contact became an integral part of the game. Seltzer took the suggestion to heart, and voila, modern banked-track roller derby was born.

It probably wasn't quite that cut-and-dried. Jostling and blocking on the oval were already taking place in the spring of '37, as the Muncie press report made clear. But the sport was beginning to coalesce around the new format, with Seltzer dropping "Transcontinental" from his organization's name and referring to it simply as Roller Derby, a name he trademarked and would later defend in court. (This is why the group's primary competitor during the 1960s and early '70s never used the term: It referred to itself as "Roller Games.")

Sport or spectacle?

Almost from the beginning, there were questions about whether Roller Derby was a legitimate sport, or merely a staged spectacle. As early as the summer of 1938, *San Francisco Examiner* columnist Harry Borba was writing that Roller Derby was "not a sports event but an amusement." Borba pointed out that Seltzer's publicity man made no effort to announce how the racers stood from one day to the next, and there wasn't any comprehensive record book or list of champions. The skaters, he asserted, were actors, plain and simple.

Roller Derby, he wrote, "is the poor man's delight. For 30 cents and three passes ... he can take the family and get four hours of thrilling amusement. He can boo the 'villain' who gives the poor honest skater a push on his puss. He can cheer the unfortunate when he gets up and gives the villain the earnest elbow. In short, he can have a whale of a time, and perhaps a bottle of pop, for 10 cents apiece and not strain the family roll more than 50 cents."

It was a good deal, especially during the Depression, when tickets to a baseball game or a boxing match were a good deal more expensive.

Skaters countered that the sport was real because the injuries they sustained were real. In 1962, another columnist, Frank Gianelli of the *Arizona Republic*, asked Shirley Hardman of the Texas Outlaws whether "this roller derby stuff" was "on the level or sort of like wrestling on wheels?" If looks could kill ... she fixed him with the kind of expression that made him think she was going to pop him in the nose.

She didn't, but she offered the following rebuttal: "I've been skating seven years and had a broken jaw, a busted leg, two dislocated shoulders (and) four concussions. Does that sound 'fixed'? ... If I don't stay a winner, I don't make money. It's as simple as that."

Some critics viewed the Derby as fake *because* of the injuries — or at least the rough-and-tumble skating that caused them. They argued, with some justification, that more fans

Skaters leap over two fallen competitors.

showed up at the oval to view the fisticuffs and see bodies fly over the railing than to watch the match itself, so it was natural that the Derby emphasized fighting over fair play.

On the other hand, this is exactly the kind of appeal Runyan had suggested a full-contact sport could have. And while Rodney Dangerfield would come up with the classic line, "I went to a fight the other night, and a hockey game broke out," even critics of the on-ice fisticuffs weren't suggesting hockey games were staged. There was certainly a high degree of showmanship involved in the Derby, but the same could be said for barnstorming teams in general during the 1930s. The all-black Ethiopian Clowns earned a reputation as the Harlem Globetrotters of baseball during a period when the Globetrotters were hamming it up on court and still beating the likes of the Minneapolis Lakers in legitimate games.

What raised suspicions, ultimately, had little to do with violence or showmanship. It had much more to do with the results. As with staged wrestling matches (and the Globetrotters' later staged exhibitions), the white-clad home team was typically cast in the role of hero, while the red-clad visitors were portrayed as villains. Wrestling matches had their "faces" and "heels" engaged in soap-operaesque storylines, and the Derby followed a similar format that made it seem like a live-theater melodrama or a *Dudley Do-Right* cartoon on skates.

By the 1960s, the two major skating organizations were centered in San Francisco (Roller Derby) and Los Angeles (Roller Games). Not coincidentally, the home teams for those two cities almost always came away with league championships. From 1960 through 1971, the San Francisco Bombers appeared in all 12 championship rounds, winning 10 of them. Likewise, the L.A. Thunderbirds — almost perpetually marketed as "the World Champion L.A. T-Birds," appeared in all 20 Roller Games championship series, and lost just three.

Contests almost always came down to the final jam, with the home team staging a near-miraculous comeback to snatch victory from the jaws of defeat as time expired.

(And the crowd goes wild!)

It's also worth pointing out that the teams in Roller Games and Roller Derby weren't owned by different people, the way George Steinbrenner owned the Yankees or George Halas owned the Chicago Bears. All the teams were run by a single individual: Leo Seltzer's son Jerry in San Francisco and Bill Griffiths in Los Angeles. Players weren't drafted or traded; they were allocated to one team or another based on the league owner's preferences. Standings never appeared in the newspaper, as they did for Major League Baseball or the NFL; indeed, some sports editors refused to run any news about the Derby, deeming it entertainment rather than sport.

Despite all this, it wasn't always perfectly clear that the results were staged. With most games coming down to the final jam, it was always possible that a skater could "go rogue" and flip the script, as apparently happened when the Detroit Devils stunned the T-Birds in 1968. More significantly, though, is the fact that Leo Seltzer always envisioned Roller Derby as a legitimate sport. There was a constant tension, however, between that vision and the need to make money if he wanted to stay in business. Setting ticket prices so low made the Derby accessible, but it also kept profit margins low. Translated: The Derby had to draw a boatload of fans just to break even.

In the early days, Runyan took a $20,000 portable track from one city to the next on his barnstorming tour, charging just a dime or a quarter for admission. Derby operated on a shoestring until the postwar years, with few skaters getting much more compensation than room and "board" (that cot in the infield) on the road.

Then came television.

TV boom and bust

In the late 1940s, when fledgling networks were hungry for programming, they turned to Roller Derby to fill timeslots. Exposure during a 13-week run on CBS elevated the Derby's profile, and the trickle of fans that had been coming to see events at armories along the East Coast turned into a flood — so much so that Seltzer was able to book an event at Madison Square Garden in June of 1949 that drew 55,000 fans over five days. That same year, Seltzer created a six-team National Roller Derby League, with teams based in various cities, mostly on the East Coast.

The league consisted of the Brooklyn Red Devils, Jersey Jolters, New York Chiefs, Philadelphia Panthers, Washington-Baltimore Jets and the only Midwest entry, the Chicago Westerners.

An ad touts a late-night Roller Derby telecast in the late 1940s, when the sport was a TV staple.

The league took a hybrid approach to scheduling, which combined barnstorming with the traditional "league" format in which each team plays its home games at a single venue, such as Boston Garden or Wrigley Field. The Jolters, for examples, used armories in Jersey City, Paterson and Teaneck, while the Westerners moved around from Chicago to Columbus, Ohio, and even made appearances in Miami, one of the Derby's longstanding hotbeds.

Among the league's participants that first year were Ann Calvello of the Westerners, who would skate for 33 teams in a 45-year career that spanned seven decades, and Midge "Toughie" Brasuhn of the Brooklyn Red Devils, a holdover from the barnstorming era who skated for the Brooklyn Red Devils. Brasuhn would continue her career through the late 1960s, when she jumped to Roller Games.

After the Derby's run on CBS ended, Seltzer signed a three-year deal with ABC, which often televised matches three times a week. During the league's five-year run of championship contests, the Chiefs dominated but weren't a shoo-in. They won three times, but the Jolters also won twice, and the Chiefs didn't even make the finals in 1951. Seltzer would insist those matches were legitimate competitions, not staged shows. But the wind went out of the Derby's sales in the early '50s, when the military took over many of the armories where the teams had been playing for the Korean War, and when fans grew tired of the constant barrage of TV coverage.

TV, on the other hand, didn't need the Derby anymore. It was filling its timeslots with more original programming, and Derby couldn't match the appeal of *I Love Lucy*.

In 1954, the league added a West Coast team, the San Francisco Bay Bombers, and Seltzer moved the Chicago Westerners to Los Angeles as the Braves the following season, creating a natural rivalry. (The Panthers, meanwhile, were shifted form Philadelphia to Chicago and took over the Westerners name.) For four seasons starting in 1955, there was no Roller Derby World Series, with the New York Chiefs claiming the title each year.

Seltzer, meanwhile, moved his base of operations to Los Angeles, and inked deals with independent TV stations in L.A. and San Francisco to televise the Braves and the Bombers. But the idea that so many people thought the Derby was fake still galled him. According to author Ed Koch in *Roller Derby Requiem*, he became even more determined to prove otherwise after a news conference where the Duke of Windsor asked a reporter whether Roller Derby was real.

In response, he arranged for a series in New York between the Chiefs and the Bay Bombers, giving the teams clear instructions to play all-out. No scripts. No melodrama. No predetermined outcome.

The games were most definitely *not* fake. It was easy to tell because the underdog Bombers not only defeated the champion Chiefs, but humiliated them. In 18 meetings, the Bombers won 18 times, with every game a rout. The lopsided results, which understandably turned off the hometown crowd in the nation's largest market, demonstrated one thing: Fans liked the scripted game better — especially when the home team came out on top.

Leo Seltzer canceled the TV contract for the Braves and dropped out of the Derby after that, handing the baton to son Jerry, who moved the base of operations to San Francisco. There, he built a 1960s dynasty around the Bay Bombers, featuring Joanie Weston and player/coach Charlie O'Connell. Filling the void in Los Angeles was Bill Griffiths, who established a team called the Thunderbirds as the centerpiece for his Roller Games operation. The stars of his show included Ronnie "Psycho" Rains, Big John Hall, Sally Vega and Ralphie Valladares. Regarded as one of the best jammers ever, Valladares provided a key link to the Los Angeles Braves, with whom he spent five seasons starting in 1954, and became, more than any other skater, the face of the T-Birds. In all, he spent 40 seasons with 13 different teams.

Syndicated show

During the '60s, games were no longer live, but videotaped and shipped out across the country, so the Bay Bombers and T-Birds became "America's Teams" before Ted Turner used the label for his Atlanta Braves when he put them on cable TV from coast to coast. Turner, incidentally, was among the local TV station owners to air those skating videotapes, which were edited to fit neatly into a one-hour timeslot: Only the second half of games made it to the small screen, and the eight periods had been shortened from 12 minutes to 10 minutes each for the benefit of viewers at home.

In this new age of syndicated TV, most of the visiting teams never set foot anywhere near the cities they supposedly represented: The New York Chiefs and Brooklyn Red Devils no longer had home arenas by the late 1950s; neither did Roller Games' Western Renegades, Texas Outlaws, Detroit Devils and Chicago Hawks.

This was actually a return to the Derby's roots: During its early barnstorming era, contests were staged between a white-clad "home" team, representing the current stop on the tour, and a red-clad "visiting" team identified with a big, bad metropolis: Chicago in the Midwest and New York everywhere else. The difference was that, in the 1960s, most contests took place in a single city. In the Derby, it was San Francisco or Oakland. For Roller Games, it was the dingy old Olympic Auditorium in downtown Los Angeles, where Dick Lane called the play-by-play while skaters, coaches and referees played out scripted scenes of comedic bravado between the jams. (Playing off fans' natural distrust of officials, Roller Games often created scripts that depicted the refs as conspiring with the evil visitors against the virtuous T-Birds.) Former T-Birds coach Danny Reilly became a bad guy as the coach of the rival Reilly's Renegades, only to become a hero again when he rejoined the home team. The comparisons to staged wrestling were too obvious to ignore. But even so, the spectacle drew rabid followers, just as wrestling did — and would continue to do.

A rare cross-league showdown between the T-Birds and the Derby's Midwest Pioneers, featuring the legendary Joanie Weston, pulled in more than 50,000 fans at Chicago's Comiskey Park. The Pioneers, as the home team, naturally won, but the event marked the beginning of the end for skating's second boom period. Within a year, Roller Derby was out of business, having been hurt by the Arab oil embargo and resulting gas shortage. Part of the appeal of skating was its low cost, but if it was more expensive to get to the arena than it was to buy a ticket, that put a big damper on the deal.

Roller Games absorbed many of the skaters from Roller Derby and stuck around, in one form or another, until 1986, but was never the kind of draw it had been during the late '60s and early '70s. A few attempts were made to revive the banked-track derby. One featured inline skates. Another, created by Griffith, had skaters using a figure-8 track with one heavily banked curve that made it look like an amusement park ride ... and a pit full of alligators(!). Even a new version of the T-Birds couldn't save that one. Indeed, none of these latter-day efforts met with such success. In 2001, however, a grassroots movement spawned a number of local all-female leagues, this time on a flat track and without the scripted outcomes.

Skaters kept a bit of the old flair by adopting colorful nicknames, but the results were, refreshingly, not in doubt. Leo Seltzer has passed away in 1978. But he would undoubtedly have been happy to see the sport he created finally be recognized as legitimate.

Bowled Over

Don Carter was the Michael Jordan of the 1960s. He dominated his sport, signed huge endorsement contracts, and had one of the most recognizable names in athletics — right up there with Mickey Mantle and Arnold Palmer.

Carter didn't shoot hoops or swing for the fences. Neither did Fred Flintstone, his animated prehistoric wannabe counterpart. Instead, they both hurled a heavy ball with three little holes in it toward 10 white pins at the end of a shiny, slick stretch of hardwood. Carter, at least, had an uncanny ability to knock them all down with a single crash-bang flourish.

In the 1960s, Carter did what much of Middle America did — he just did it better. The advent of the automatic pinsetter, pioneered by American Machine and Foundry (AMF) in 1951, had streamlined the process of bowling and opened up the game. No more waiting several minutes after each ball while a "pin boy" hurried to restore the scattered targets to their full and upright position. Suddenly, it was all done for you. And, seemingly just as suddenly, bowling grew from a fringe activity with a few participants to a mainstream sport that captivated the nation.

By 1955, there were 6,600 bowling alleys (or centers) scattered across the country; eight years later, the number had almost doubled to 12,000 — and the number of people taking part local leagues rose from 3 million to 7 million. Anyone with a few bucks available to rent some shoes and a lane for the hour could try his or her hand at the game, and Friday nights for many became regular bowling nights, when TGIF meant heading down to the local lanes for a beer or three and some friendly team competition. Monogramed shirts in matching colors spread across America, sponsored by companies eager for a little publicity — many of them brewers that made the same beer the bowlers indulged in.

TV shows like *Bowling for Dollars* allowed ordinary Joes and Josephines to compete for a jackpot, awarded to any contestant who could bowl two consecutive strikes. The jackpot started at a couple of hundred dollars and went up in $20 increments each time a bowler failed to claim it, settling for smaller amounts of a dollar a pin and $20 for a single strike or a spare. But the big money was on the Professional Bowlers Association (PBA) tour, where pros competed regularly in high-stakes tournaments. Each Saturday afternoon for more than three decades, announcer Chris Schenkel (also a regular on the network's college football telecasts) would present a PBA event from one of more than 30 locations across the country

— places as diverse as Louisville, Tucson, Mobile, Fresno and Boston. The telecasts, which started in 1962, drew consistently strong ratings while offering the drama of 7-10 splits, 10th-frame turkeys and even a few 300 games.

A year earlier, however, a group of entrepreneurs had tried a different approach, one that directly challenged the PBA. Instead of organizing the sport in a series of tournaments, similar to golf, they thought it made more sense to start with the immensely popular Friday night league concept and take it national. Bowling would be more like baseball than golf: a team sport that would draw fans based not only on personalities, but regional allegiances.

This was not some fly-by-night proposition. There was big money to be made in bowling, and companies tied to the sport were already making a killing. Between 1957 and 1961, for example, stock in the Brunswick Corp — which manufactured bowling equipment and had pioneered the transition from wooden to plastic bowling balls — soared an astonishing 1,590 percent between 1957 and 1961.

It was therefore no real surprise that billionaire Texas oilman Lamar Hunt, the mastermind behind the American Football League, put his outsized personality and bankbook behind the new venture. The year was 1960, and Hunt set about building the cornerstone of the league: a $3 million project known as the Bronco Bowl that would feature more than 70 lanes, seating for thousands of spectators and a whole lot more. The project would be a recreational amusement park, featuring billiards, pinball, miniature golf, slot cars and archery. Food concessions and even a barbershop were incorporated into the design, along with a concert hall.

Other large-scale bowling "arenas" were planned in the other cities that applied for membership. One of the league's showcase teams was, naturally, planned for New York City, where columnist Red Smith wrote that plans called for $3 million bowling stadium to be "suspended in midair in the Grand Central Terminal."

Irving Fagenson, an investor in the New York team, proclaimed that "bowling can be a very big spectator sport. It just never before has catered to spectators. You have to give them the accommodation — plush seating and good service in the refreshment line, as well as close-up seats and good competition. We're going to do all this."

Other teams were expected to build arenas, as well. There would be no back-alley alleys for the National Bowling League: It planned a first-class presentation all the way. Plush seats were arranged in a horseshoe pattern around four- or six-lane spotlight bowling areas for maximum viewing comfort, with a press box at each arena installed to facilitate media coverage. The arenas weren't huge, seating between 1,500 and 3,500 fans, so many spectators had what amounted to a ringside (or alleyside) seat.

In the beginning, this was part of the attraction, but it had a downside as well. Joe Joseph, a marquee name who bowled for the Kansas City Stars, later recalled that some team owners brought in friends to heckle their opponents from the front row. These hecklers might yell, "What step are you in?" during a bowler's approach or "Throw it in the gutter!" as he was just about to release the ball. Joseph said the competitors' averages began to suffer, and fans began to stay home, reasoning they could see mediocre scores for free at their local bowling alley.

Early gutter balls

Even before the season started, not everything went as planned. The Miami and Birmingham franchises were unable to complete their arenas in time for the season and had to drop out. The San Antonio Cavaliers couldn't find a home, either, but stayed in the league as a road team, while the Kansas City Stars wound up playing in a converted movie theater that dated from 1927. And that fancy Grand Central arena planned for the Big Apple? It never came off. A zoning permit for the project was denied, and the New York Gladiators wound up in Totowa, N.J., a town of barely 10,000 residents 21 miles northwest of NYC. The Gladiators, like the Stars, had to settle for playing in a refurbished movie theater.

Early plans for teams in Indianapolis, Sacramento, Raleigh and Houston failed to pan out, and the league found itself without a major market when the Chicago franchise dropped out — replaced by a team called the Bombers in Fresno. They would be that city's only major league team in any sport, but this much could be said for them: Even though they entered the league late in the fall of 1960, they managed to build their own arena (NBL Lanes) northeast of town in Clovis, and get it ready for the start of the season.

Rounding out the league membership were teams in Detroit, Fort Worth, Los Angeles (which played in Culver City), Minneapolis and Omaha.

Even with the turmoil heading into its inaugural season, hopes for the league weren't just high — they were off the charts. An Associated Press story published Feb. 5, 1961, proclaimed that "no new professional sports venture ever faced the future with as much confidence as the NBL."

"The reason is that the NBL finds its success virtually assured before it starts," the story continued. "There is a television contract paying each club more than $100,000 a year. It is estimated that a club won't have to average more than 1,000 attendance a night in order to bring in a nice profit." That was not to mention profits from concessions, advertising in a magazine the league planned to publish and various other sources.

When the NBL held its inaugural draft, teams made headlines with some of their selections. The Dallas Broncos picked Yankees slugger Mickey Mantle in the 16th round, while the New York squad made his teammate, catcher Yogi Berra, their final selection. The Omaha Packers used one of their picks to go after Johnny Chapman Jr., a local phenom with an impressive average of 185. His best game to date at the time of the draft was 260, with a top three-game series of 682. Even more impressive was the fact that Chapman had just graduated … from the eighth grade: He was only 13 years old and weighed in at a scant 87 pounds.

"I think it's swell. I'm very happy about it," Chapman told a reporter who asked him what he thought of being drafted. Still, he as pragmatic about the fact that he'd have to schedule league appearances around his high school schedule. "I'll be willing to bowl when the team's in town," he said.

Apart from such blatant headline grabs, NBL teams did select a number of big-name bowlers — many of whom expressed interest in competing for the league. Fred Riccilli was the first to sign on the dotted line, agreeing to a $10,000 contract with the Los Angeles Toros, and more than 80 others followed suit. The league set a minimum salary of $6,000 — the equivalent of more than $50,000 in 2018 — and some bowlers signed up to earn more. Second-round pick Carl Richard, for instance, signed with the Kansas City Stars for $15,000 a year (well into six figures in 2018 dollars) on top of a $5,000 signing bonus.

Among the top players who signed with the NBL was a Hungarian cabinetmaker from Cleveland named Steve Nagy who had bowled a memorable 300 game in a televised match on "Championship Bowling" in 1955 — the same year he was named Bowler of the Year for the second time. He signed with the Toros, as well.

Veteran Buzz Fazio had wowed audiences that same year by becoming the first bowler to roll an 800 series on live television. Fazio, who had converted not one but two 7-10 splits en route to winning the Masters Championship in '55, was still a force to be reckoned with even though he was past 50 when Detroit picked him seventh overall in the NBL draft. It was his son Joe, however, who wound up playing for the Thunderbirds, while Buzz signed on with the Omaha Packers.

Joe Joseph, who would later win one of the PBA's four majors — the Tournament of Champions — signed a $20,000 contract to bowl for Kansas City.

Ed Lubanski, a two-finger bowler who had started out as a pitcher in the St. Louis Browns organization, signed on with Detroit, as well. Lubanski would go on to earn a spot in the Guinness Book of World Records for having the highest lifetime average (204) over a period of 25 years. He was coming off an impressive feat just a year earlier, in which he appeared in a televised event from Miami's Bowling Palace played under a Scotch mixed-doubles format. Under the rules of the competition, Lubanski would bowl the first ball of each frame, and his partner Lois Davis would go after the spare … except there were no spares for Davis to attempt.

Instead, Lubanski reeled off 24 consecutive strikes in unprecedented back-to-back 300 games.

Ed Lubanski, who once rolled consecutive 300 games, was one of the biggest names to join the NBL.

Some of the big names, however, stuck with the PBA. In addition to the coveted Don Carter, No. 1 draft pick Billy Welu and Dick Weber were among those who stayed on the sidelines. (Carter and Weber, incidentally, would rank 1-2 on the Bowlers Journal International list of the top 100 bowlers of the 20th century.) Carter, the No. 2 overall draft pick, reportedly turned down a $50,000 contract to play for Fort Worth. It seems to have been an easy decision, since he was already earning twice that much.

"Our first year, we naturally couldn't afford to pay the $100,000 some stars like Don Carter are earning," league commissioner Dick Charles said. "But we have signed some stars to $20,000 contracts and have a minimum contract of $6,000 for the 26 weeks of our season."

Other incentives for signing with the circuit included plans for a match-play tournament over 13 weeks at the end of the season, a cross-country odyssey that was to begin in Los Angeles and wind up in New York, with the winner taking home a $100,000 prize. This was in addition to a 26-week season, to be followed by a championship series.

That was a lot of bowling. In fact, the grueling schedule called for each team to bowl 135 matches in competition that spanned five nights a week throughout the season. It wasn't quite as long as a baseball season, but it was close.

The league sought to attract fans by instituting a novel scoring system, awarding one point for each victory and bonus points based on scoring: one for a game over 210, two for a game over 220 and so forth up to 10 points for a perfect game. If two teams were deadlocked at the end of a match, total pinfall would serve as the tiebreaker.

Matches were split into halves, with the first featuring a team rotation contest involving five bowlers from each side and the second involving five head-to-head matches. The league took cues from baseball and basketball in an attempt to liven things up. Each player was assigned a "position" in the lineup: leadoff, pressure, pivot, cleanup and anchor. Teams could even use a wild-card substitution, calling a player off the bench to complete a tricky shot.

Bowlers were often introduced using colorful nicknames, such as Johnny "the Brooklyn Bomber" Meyer and J.B. "Mr. Stoneface" Solomon. Actress Jayne Mansfield did the honors at a ribbon-cutting ceremony to dedicate the Bronco Bowl in Dallas, and the NFL debuted with a marquee matchup there between the home team and the visiting New York Gladiators in the fall of 1961. Some 2,000 fans showed up to watch the spectacle, enjoying the sounds of a Dixieland jazz band and marveling at the gigantic scoreboard.

The league had its share of excitement. In December, Ed Lubanski rolled a 300 game to rack up 11 points for the Detroit Thunderbirds, who eked out a 29-28 victory over the Fresno Bombers.

1961–62 National Bowling League

	City	Arena
Eastern Division		
Detroit Thunderbirds	Allen Park, Mich.	Thunder Bowl
Kansas City Stars	Kansas City	Midland Theatre
New York Gladiators	Totowa, N.J.	Gladiator Arena
Omaha Packers	Omaha	Packer Stadium
Twin Cities Skippers	Bloomington, Minn.	Convention Ctr. Arena
Western Division		
Dallas Broncos	Dallas	Bronco Bowl
Fort Worth Panthers	Fort Worth	Panther Hall
Fresno Bombers	Clovis, Calif.	NBL Lanes
Los Angeles Toros	Culver City, Calif.	Jefferson Arena
San Antonio Cavaliers	None	Road team

Championship: Detroit d. Twin Cities 3 games to 0
Kansas City, Los Angeles, Omaha and San Antonio folded

Pulling the plug

But problems began when the television contract failed to pan out. This put the onus on fans to turn out for the live matches, but weeknights weren't necessarily the ideal time for working Americans to spend their evenings watching a spectator sport (unless, of course, that sport was baseball), and many started to lose interest as the long season wound on.

By mid-December, the Omaha and San Antonio teams had both ceased operations. Kansas City pulled out of the league a week later, and Los Angeles followed 15 days into the new year, leaving just two teams — Fort Worth and Fresno — in the Western Division. All the teams that folded were near the bottom of the standings and struggling at the gate when they called it quits. The league staggered forward with just six teams, scrapping its two-division format and decreeing that the first-half champion would meet the second-half winner for the title.

First-half winner Detroit faced the Twin Cities Skippers for the title in a best-of-five championship series, swept by the Thunderbirds in three games. Only 1,000 fans bothered to turn out for the clinching contest, which wound up being the final match in the league's short history. NBL executives set a meeting for May 3 to take stock of where they stood — and tally up their losses — but organizer Curtis Sanford was confident the league would be back for a second season.

"We're over the biggest hump now," he said, announcing that the league would likely scale back to weekend-only play in its second season. "We're established. We have six stadiums built. Things should be better next year."

Soon, the league unveiled plans to add two teams, bringing its contingent up to eight, while a bowling equipment manufacturer provided a needed boost with an infusion of $100,000. There was talk of changing the league's pay structure, replacing guaranteed salaries with prize money for the winners.

But the players had other ideas. They weren't thrilled with the concept of competing for prize money rather than earning guaranteed paychecks, especially over such a long season. Lubanski, who had captained Detroit to the championship, said he had polled the league's players and found that the majority were inclined to give up on the league and try their luck with the PBA.

"We kept going on promises the past season," Lubanski said. "The league is going to have an awfully rough time getting most of the bowlers to come back. They'll be able to fill the teams, of course, but I'm talking about the 'name' performers.

"We heard all about fabulous prize money this year, but we didn't get it," he added.

"They'll have to put the money in front of us before we'll believe it."

That was more than the struggling league was able to do, and two months later, it announced it was suspending operations. The mammoth bowling center built as the home arena for the Fresno team was demolished just a few years after it was built. The Midland Theatre in Kansas City went back to being a theater. (It went through a series of ownership and name changes, becoming the Arvest Bank Theatre at The Midland in 2013).

As for the Bronco Bowl in Dallas, it gave way to a teen nightclub in 1963 and subsequently became a 2,550-seat concert venue, hosting the likes of Bruce Springsteen, David Bowie, Metallica, U2 and Adam Ant, along with a stripped-down bowling center — 22 lanes instead of 78 — arcade and sports bar. For a couple of years in the mid-'60s, owner Lamar Hunt staged an event there called the "Broncothon," a sort of indoor pentathlon in which participants paid $1 to bowl a game, take a swing at nine baseballs, hit 10 golf balls, shoot 10 arrows and take eight shots at a rack of billiard balls.

Hunt, who conceived and built the Bronco Bowl, later admitted he had probably gone overboard with the lavish project.

"We were originally just interested in the bowling, but it was overbuilt, and we've been trying to make the best use of the space ever since," he told *The New York Times* in 1984, adding that he probably wouldn't have built it if given a chance to do it all over again. "It wasn't all that well thought out."

Home Depot had different thoughts about the site. The home improvement retailer purchased it in 2003, and the destruction of the Bronco Bowl followed that same year.

Kicking and Dreaming

If you came of age during the 1970s, chances are you remember being "encouraged" to accept a couple of European imports. One was the metric system. The other was soccer. These things were supposed to be good for you. The rest of the world embraced them, so America should, too.

The best way to get Americans to reject an idea is to tell them the rest of the world knows what's good for them. So, even though the metric system is firmly entrenched everywhere else, the big push in the '70s for your average American to measure things in meters, weigh things in grams and buy gasoline in liters, never panned out on this side of the pond.

It's the same story for soccer. It remains, by far the most popular sport in the world, but statesiders seem to be waiting for their country to win a World Cup, or for the sport to morph into some high-scoring approximation of NBA basketball. It's likely to be a long wait in either case. These days, soccer seems to be making some inroads, courtesy of its popularity among the younger set, better exposure and more interest in European soccer. Still, it's a long way from becoming America's Game.

In fact, one of the first major pro soccer leagues in the United States simply imported a dozen teams from overseas, slapped American-sounding names on them, and let them loose to play one another on U.S. soil. There were three teams from England, three from Scotland and one each from Uruguay, Brazil, the Netherlands, Ireland, Northern Ireland and Sardinia. Yes, Sardinia. Some of the team names betrayed their point of origin: Stoke City became the Cleveland Stokers, and the Wolverhampton Wanderers played as the Los Angeles Wolves, who beat the Washington Whips (aka Aberdeen FC of Scotland) 6-5 for the United Soccer Association championship.

The year was 1967 — the same year, as fate would have it, that another pro soccer league got its start. The National Professional Soccer League had a TV contract with CBS and the backing of owners from other pro sports. Dan Reeves of the Los Angeles Rams was behind the L.A. Toros, and John Rooney of the Pittsburgh Steelers owned the Philadelphia Spartans. The Oakland Clippers defeated the Baltimore Bays for the title.

But the league didn't last long enough to enjoy its two-year television deal, merging with its rival league after a single season to form the North American Soccer League.

1979 North American Soccer League

	W	L	GF	GA	Pts.
American Conference					
Eastern Division					
Tampa Bay Rowdies	19	11	67	46	169
Fort Lauderdale Strikers	17	13	64	63	165
Philadelphia Fury	10	20	60	51	111
New England Tea Men	12	18	56	41	110
Central Division					
Houston Hurricane	22	8	61	46	187
Chicago Sting	16	14	61	63	159
Detroit Express	14	16	56	49	132
Memphis Rogues	6	24	38	74	73
Western Division					
San Diego Sockers	15	15	59	55	140
California Surf	15	15	56	50	140
Edmonton Drillers	8	22	43	78	88
San Jose Earthquakes	8	22	41	74	86
National Conference					
Eastern Division					
New York Cosmos	24	6	84	52	216
Washington Diplomats	19	11	68	50	172
Toronto Blizzard	14	16	65	49	133
Rochester Lancers	15	15	57	42	132
Central Division					
Minnesota Kicks	21	9	67	48	184
Dallas Tornado	17	13	53	51	152
Tulsa Roughnecks	14	16	61	56	139
Atlanta Chiefs	12	18	59	61	121
Pacific Division					
Vancouver Whitecaps	20	10	54	34	172
Los Angeles Aztecs	18	12	62	47	162
Seattle Sounders	13	17	58	52	125
Portland Timbers	11	19	50	75	112

Soccer Bowl: Vancouver 2, Tampa Bay 1

Scoring: 6 points for a win; 1 point for each regulation goal scored up to three per game

Pele's league

The NASL was memorable primarily for one name: Pele.

The Brazilian superstar retired after 19 seasons in 1974 and signed a contract to play with the league's New York Cosmos. The $2.8 million deal made him the highest-paid athlete in the world, and he turned out to be worth it. Bringing the sport's biggest star to the nation's biggest city created just the sort of buzz the league needed, with 10 million people switching on their sets to watch his televised debut with the Cosmos.

Fans packed Giants Stadium in New Jersey to see him, as well. The Cosmos drew more than 62,000 fans to see Pele score a hat trick at the age of 37 against the Tampa Bay Rowdies in 1977, and nearly 78,000 turned out that same year for a playoff game against Fort Lauderdale. The next week, in the semifinals, more than 73,000 showed up in the rain to see Pele score what would be the final goal of his career.

The Cosmos went on to win the title, capping Pele's three seasons in the league, which would never again reach such heights.

Building a league around one player is always problematic. The first American Football League tried to do it with Red Grange and failed after one season. George Mikan was the centerpiece of a 16-team league called the Professional Basketball League of America in 1947, which collapsed just three weeks into its inaugural season. The NASL lasted a bit longer, but despite some successes, it will always be known as the league that brought Pele to the United States.

Aside from the huge crowds that came to watch the Brazilian superstar, seats at stadiums across the league were mostly empty. Average attendance was always less than 8,000 until Pele arrived, and even afterward, it never topped 15,000: the kind of crowd that would fit comfortably into a large basketball arena. I remember attending a Los Angeles Aztecs game at the Rose Bowl one sunny afternoon during the mid-'70s and marveling at how most of the 90,000 seats were empty.

The Aztecs won the league title in 1974 but, although they signed Irish superstar George Best two years later, he couldn't propel them back to the winner's circle. Best played with the Aztecs for two seasons and led the league in assists during the 1977 season. Teammate Steve David scored a league-leading 26 goals that year, but their combined efforts were only good for a third-place divisional finish.

The team picked up another European star in 1979 in the person of Johan Cruyff, who had been named the World Cup's top player after leading the Netherlands to a runner-up finish in the 1974 tournament. Cruyff retired in 1977 but reportedly lost most of his money in bad investments (including a pig farm!) recommended by a scam artist who, according to Vice Sports, had "possibly seduced his wife." Cruyff was named the league's MVP for the Aztecs in 1979, even though the team failed to win its division and lost in the second round of the playoffs.

Cruyff would only play one more season in the league, earning first-team all-league honors for the Washington Diplomats in 1980 but failing to lead that team beyond the first round of the playoffs.

The Aztecs, meanwhile, averaged more than 10,000 fans a game just twice in eight years, suffering their worst attendance, ironically, during their championship season: It was just over 5,000 a game. To put that in perspective, team owner (and devoted soccer fan) Elton John would welcome as many fans for a single concert up the road at Dodger Stadium the following year as the Aztecs had drawn for their entire home schedule in '74.

Johan Cruyff in Barcelona in 1975

While few fans bothered to turn out for live games, TV audiences were apathetic, too … when the league could find them. Pele's star power convinced CBS to televise his debut with the Cosmos, an exhibition game against the Dallas Tornado in the summer of 1975. Pele assisted on one goal and scored the second in a 2-2 tie at aging Downing Stadium on Randall's Island, previously home to the Brooklyn Dodgers of the Continental Football League and New York Stars of the WFL. It was hardly the kind of stage befitting the greatest star in the game, and the field was reportedly spray-painted ahead of time to make it look better on television.

CBS also carried the championship game (known as the Soccer Bowl) in 1975 and again '76, although the Cosmos failed to make the finals either time. They won each of the following two years, with a handful of regular season games being shown on TVS, the same syndicated sports network that had broadcast the WFL, and ABC picked up coverage on a semi-regular basis for the next two years. But with Pele retired and the U.S. audience still unenthusiastic, ratings were anemic, averaging a "dismal" 2.6 for six games in 1980 according to *Sports Illustrated.*

Not the NFL

As with any struggling league, teams moved around frequently, and membership rose and fell from season to season. San Diego had three different teams over the years (the Toros in 1968, the Jaws in 1976 and the Sockers in from 1978 to '84). Well, that's not exactly true: The Jaws moved to Las Vegas and became the Quicksilvers for one season before moving back to San Diego as the Sockers.

The league made three attempts in Washington, too, while smaller markets like Tulsa and Fort Lauderdale also had teams.

League membership was five in 1969 and grew to 24 in six divisions by 1978 before it started contracting again in 1981. By the time the NASL's played its final season three years later, just nine teams remained. One reason for the decline was the advent of the Major Indoor Soccer League, which began play in 1978 on a smaller field designed for indoor arenas that produced faster play and more scoring. Some American fans, lulled to sleep by 1-0 and 2-0 games outdoors, took to the new version more easily, and although attendance wasn't huge, 8,000 fans in a 12,000-seat arena *looked* a lot better than the same number in a 60,000-seat stadium.

With two leagues and 30 franchises in 1978, the sport was an unwieldy mess. The talent pool was so badly diluted that the quality of play — never remotely comparable to European or South American soccer — suffered even more. It was as though U.S. soccer wanted to dress a double-A product up in major league uniforms and hope fans wouldn't know the difference.

They did.

"We tried to compare ourselves to the National Football League of the 1970s," Chicago Sting president Lee Stern explained to *The New York Times* in 1983, "when we're really more like the NFL of the 1940s or '50s, when it was struggling before TV made an impact on that sport."

To make matters worse, the NASL tried to bolster its quality of play by paying enormous sums to lure marquee European and South American players to play in the States. In addition to Pele, the Cosmos brought in Italian standout Giorgio Chinaglia, who wound up setting the league record for most goals in a career, and Franz Beckenbauer, captain of West Germany's

1974 World Cup championship team. Chinaglia came relatively cheap: His initial contract paid him about $80,000 a year over three years. But Beckenbauer cost the team $2.8 million over four years.

With the formation of the MISL, a bidding war ensued, putting both leagues even deeper in a financial hole, and a one-game players' strike in 1979 further hindered the NASL's credibility.

Games were played during the weekend of the walkout, with some players striking and others suiting up, but filling the gaps in the rosters proved problematic: Eddie McCreadie, coach of the Memphis Rogues, had been a world-class defender before retiring in 1974; now, he was forced to play goalie against the Detroit Express, which teed off on the 37-year-old for six goals in a shutout victory. Four of those goals were scored by Bob Rohrbach, normally a second-string player who didn't score a single goal the rest of the season.

Ron Newman, 44-year-old coach of the Fort Lauderdale Strikers, hadn't played in nearly a decade but was forced into action during the second half of a 4-0 loss to Washington. It wasn't the first time Newman had taken drastic action. A year earlier, after the Strikers had dropped their first three games, Newman knew he had to do something to keep fans' hopes alive. So, he rode onto the field in a hearse before their next home match, emerged from a coffin and ran up to a microphone, proclaiming, "We're not dead yet!"

After that, the team used a different mode of transportation to arrive at every match, ranging from horses to motorcycles, from fire engines to a double-decker bus. The team wound up making the playoffs that season.

The NASL responded to the MISL by forming its own indoor spring league, but it suspended play in 1982 and allowed three of its teams to play that season in the MISL. One of those, the Sockers, wound up winning the league championship. After the NASL folded in 1984, the Sockers moved over to the indoor league full time and proceeded to win seven championships during their eight seasons in the league. They also played four seasons in the Continental Indoor Soccer League before finally folding in 1996, the last remaining NASL team still in business.

That year was also the first for Major League Soccer, the top-tier league that would succeed where the NASL had failed. Ron Newman turned out to be a bridge between the two leagues. After his years with the Strikers, he guided the San Diego Sockers through their glory years from 1980 until 1993. Then, in '96, he was the first manager chosen to lead an MLS team, the Kansas City Wiz (later known as the Wizards and Sporting Kansas City). He coached the team for just over three seasons.

A footnote: A second soccer organization took the name North American Soccer League in 2009 and played through 2017. Teams like the New York Cosmos, Tampa Bay Rowdies and Fort Lauderale Strikers took their names from clubs in the original NASL, and the two finalists played in a game called the Soccer Bowl, just as finalists from the first league had. But the league was only recognized as a second-tier league, and a planned 2018 season was canceled after the U.S. Soccer Federation declined to renew that status.

All the Puck in the World

It's no coincidence that the World Hockey Association looked a lot like the ABA on ice. It was the brainchild of Dennis Murphy, the same guy who thought up the ABA, and the two leagues had plenty in common.

There were big-name signings. There were unstable franchises. And there was, after less than a decade, a merger that brought four teams into the established league.

When it came to signing top players, the WHA was even more successful than the ABA had been. George Mikan had quit as commissioner of that league after it failed in a $1 million bid to sign a young UCLA graduate named Lew Alcindor (later Kareem Abdul-Jabbar), but the WHA managed to grab not one but both of the biggest names on ice: Bobby Hull and Gordie Howe.

The birth of the WHA continued a period of sudden, almost out-of-control growth for professional hockey. The established National Hockey League had held steady at just six teams — the so-called Original Six — for a quarter of a century, ever since the 1942-43 season. The "National" in the name had been a misnomer in more ways than one: The circuit included two Canadian teams and four others based in the U.S., but all were clustered in the Northeast and Upper Midwest.

Then, suddenly, in 1967, the league doubled in size, adding six new teams, including two on the West Coast.

Why the sudden expansion?

For the same reason Major League Baseball allowed the Dodgers and Giants to move west, then approved the expansion New York Mets to replace them: West Coast fans were tired of being treated like second-class citizens; they wanted big-league teams of their own to support.

Much like baseball's Pacific Coast League, the second-tier Western Hockey League had been making noise about stepping up in class and challenging the NHL as far back to 1959. It was then that president Al Leader said his league, which was then concentrated in the Pacific Northwest and western Canada, was looking at putting teams in the Bay Area and Los Angeles.

"With larger arenas and larger crowds, the owners would be in a position to pay the salaries needed to attract the top stars of ice hockey and keep them," Leader said. "Within five to seven years we could be a major hockey league, and if that comes the National Hockey League would welcome a playoff and world series of hockey."

That was speculative and optimistic at best, but the WHL wasn't bluffing when it talked about moving into the West Coast's two biggest markets. Dan Reeves, owner of the Los Angeles Rams, led an ownership group that bought the Victoria Cougars and moved them to L.A. for the 1961-62 season. The league also granted an expansion franchise to San Francisco, replacing the Winnipeg Warriors team that had suspended operations after the previous season. (Winnipeg was the easternmost franchise in the league, and travel costs contributed to the Warriors' decision to call it quits.)

The new Los Angeles team was christened the Blades, and the San Francisco entry was named the Seals. The Seals would win the league title in just their second season, and would repeat as champions the following year by besting the Blades. By the time the 1966-67 season faced off, the WHL and American Hockey League were playing an interlocking schedule in preparation for a full-fledged merger and rebirth as a single 15-team major league. In addition to San Francisco and Los Angeles, the alliance would include Vancouver, Victoria, Portland, San Diego and Seattle from the WHL, along with Providence, Baltimore, Buffalo, Cleveland, Pittsburgh, Rochester, Quebec and Hershey (Pennsylvania) from the AHL.

The NHL wasn't about to let that happen. Not only did it disrupt the ambitious plan by placing expansion teams in two of those markets — Pittsburgh and Los Angeles — it stole the San Francisco Seals from the WHL. The merger plans collapsed then and there, with the Los Angeles Blades folding and the Western League reduced to a five-team circuit that never again challenged the big boys.

Blindsiding the big boys

But if the NHL thought it had insulated itself from future competition, it was wrong. It added two more expansion teams, in Buffalo and Vancouver, for good measure in 1970, and it didn't pay much attention when rumors of a rival league began to swirl. It didn't know much about the upstarts, but what it did know didn't seem a cause for concern. For one thing, the people behind this venture weren't hockey people; they were people who went around starting new leagues, then jumping ship for the next "big thing."

Both Murphy and Gary L. Davidson had been involved in the ABA, and hockey was a lot different than basketball. Davidson was a Southern California lawyer who looked more like a surfer dude than a hockey player. In fact, he'd never even seen a hockey game in person. His ideas included eliminating the center line to speed up play and using a fluorescent red puck (this was before A's owner Charles O. Finley proposed using an orange baseball).

There *were* a few real hockey people on board with the project, most notably "Wild Bill" Hunter, who had served as general manager of a junior hockey team called the Edmonton Oil Kings and had sought to buy the NHL's Pittsburgh Penguins. He'd been rebuffed, and the new league offered him a chance to get into pro hockey while sticking it to the NHL at the same time. Ben Hatskin, a former football player for the Canadian League's Winnipeg Blue Bombers, also had an ax to grind: He'd applied for an NHL expansion franchise back in 1967 and had been turned down.

But people like Hunter and Hatskin hadn't been credible enough (at least to the NHL) to give them the time of day before. Why worry about them now? Besides, they were largely working behind the scenes. Hockey neophyte Davidson was the first president and served as the face of the league ... at least for a year and a half, after which he quit to kick-start yet another longshot endeavor: the World Football League.

That kind of instability would plague the league throughout its existence. Even before it played its first game, there were signs that things would often fail to go as planned. The Dayton Arrows couldn't find a place to play and moved to Houston, where they became the Aeros. The San Francisco Sharks franchise couldn't meet its financial obligations, so a group of Canadians stepped in and moved the club to Quebec City as Les Nordiques.

The Calgary Broncos never played a game, either, and the franchise was transferred to Cleveland. So, the Edmonton Oil Kings broadened their marketing plan and renamed themselves the Alberta Oilers — if only for one season. It was like the Keystone Cops meets musical chairs. The NHL didn't seem to be vulnerable to such a rag-tag, disorganized lot ... except where it mattered most: when it came to the players.

Like baseball, the NHL used its monopoly power to keep salaries down by inserting a reserve clause in player contracts. This effectively bound players to their teams as long as the teams had use for them. It was a one-sided arrangement that kept salaries down and players in a bind: They had to accept the reserve clause in order to play in the NHL, which also controlled minor-league teams and, by extension, the pay they offered.

The WHA announced that its contracts wouldn't include a reserve clause. Players unable to come to terms on new contracts with their current teams could appeal to a three-person arbitration board — with one member each appointed by the player, the club and the first two members. If the arbitration hearing failed to produce a satisfactory result, the player could become a free agent.

That sounded good to a lot of players. Perhaps foremost among them was Bobby Hull, the league's best player during the sixties.

Hull was, in many ways, the face of the NHL. He'd led the league in goals seven times, his Chicago Black Hawks had won the Stanley Cup in 1961, and five years later, he had become the first player in league history to score more than 50 goals in a season. Hull would match that feat four more times. But his career with the Black Hawks hadn't produced the kind of numbers he wanted in his bank account.

Bobby Hull with the Winnipeg Jets on the cover of the team's program in 1973.

Specifically, he argued that the team had reneged on a subsidiary contract that promised certain fringe benefits, including deferred payments meant to reduce Hull's tax liability.

Hull sat out 14 games in late 1969 before returning to the Black Hawks, saying, "I was wrong" and that he had received "poor advice" encouraging him to walk out. But despite the apparent contrition, Hull knew the team had put him over a barrel, and the episode left him with a bad taste in his mouth.

Three years later, when Hatskin came calling on behalf of the Winnipeg Jets, he was willing to listen — even if he, like the rest of the hockey establishment, didn't take the new league too seriously. Hull's name first appeared in connection with the Jets in a February report that the WHA had reversed its earlier intention not to pursue big-name players and had placed him on a pre-draft "negotiation list."

Hull, whose nickname was The Golden Jet, certainly would fit right in with a team called the Jets, but despite his problems with the Black Hawks, he still expected them to come through with a good offer when his contract expired at the end of the year: "My contract with

Chicago runs out at this season. If they're good to me, I expect to stay. I think they will be." In fact, Hull had sought to take the Jets out of the running by demanding a $1 million contract. It was an absurd figure, something he figured no established team would pay him, and no fledgling club *could afford* to pay him.

But he wasn't about to disparage the new league, getting in a dig at the NHL's salary structure in the same interview from the locker room at the Black Hawks' game against the Detroit Red Wings: "You know there are fellows in this (locker) room and fellows in that (locker) room over there who would go" to the new league if they were offered a contract. "They won't have any problem getting players. Far from it. There are a lot of $15,000 players in the NHL who will go for a raise. There will be some surprises, you watch."

The Golden Jet turned out to be one of them. When Hatskin said he'd meet Hull's $1 million demand, Hull agreed to join the new Winnipeg team ... as soon as the money was in place. Hatskin himself didn't have that kind of cash, so he had to go begging to other league owners to pay a share, arguing that Hull's presence would benefit them all by giving the WHA instant credibility. Not all of them opened their wallets, though, and it came down to the final few hours before Hull was scheduled to sign.

But somehow, Hatskin got the money in place, and Hull was officially a Jet.

The playboy and the toupee

Other players followed — 67 of them in all — although that wasn't always a good thing. According to one report, the top four names on the WHA's wish list, after Hull, were Ken Dryden, Stan Mikita, Brad Park and Derek Sanderson, in that order. The league whiffed on the first three but nabbed Sanderson along with goalie Gerry Cheevers, both of whom had helped the Boston Bruins win Stanley Cups in 1970 and '72.

Cheevers wound up playing three-plus seasons for the Cleveland Crusaders before returning to the Bruins for the rest of his career. Sanderson didn't work out so well. He had been the NHL's rookie of the year in 1968 and had assisted on the game-winning goal in overtime of Game 7 in the 1970 Stanley Cup Finals, giving the Bruins their first title in 29 years. Unfortunately, he had a drinking problem and a playboy image to go with his success on the ice. He spent money like it was going out of style and drove a Rolls Royce; *Cosmopolitan* named him one of the sexiest men alive.

Sanderson was fresh off the Bruins' second Stanley Cup championship in three years when the WHA's Philadelphia Blazers — who already had NHL refugee Bernie Parent on their roster — offered him a staggering $2.6 million multi-year contract on Aug. 4, 1972, that was the richest in pro sports at the time. He'd be making more money Wilt Chamberlain, Joe Namath or Pele. Not only that, his contract stipulated that he didn't have to play in road games that required an airplane ride, because of his fear of flying.

"Like the Godfather," he said. "They made me an offer I couldn't refuse."

In hindsight, the Blazers probably wished he would have. One reporter labeled a "playboy worth his weight in bourbon and water," and that description didn't turn out to be far wrong. He injured his back and had to sit out for more than a month. According to Jim Barniak of *The Philadelphia Bulletin*, a disagreement among the team's two owners over whether to sign Sanderson in the first place broke up their partnership ... with the anti-Sanderson guy, Bernard Brown, sticking it out. The few fans who bothered to show up at Blazers games didn't seem to like Sanderson much, either, greeting him with boos. As Barniak put it, "Derek has captured Philadelphia with all the pizazz of a cup of yesterday's ice water."

The Blazers couldn't even sell out their home opener and promptly lost their first seven games. Their home opener, against the New England Whalers, had to be rescheduled after the ice cracked beneath the weight of a Zamboni machine that was supposed to smooth out the surface, not break it. When fans found out the game had been canceled, they started bombarding the ice with souvenir orange pucks they'd been given at the gate, throwing them toward Sanderson, who had been given the task of announcing the game was off. "Maybe this is what we get for trying to open on Friday the 13th, said team president Jim Cooper.

He was the guy who wanted to sign Sanderson and who left the ownership team in the next few weeks. His partner Brown, lasted until the end of the season before he sold the team to a new owner, who moved the franchise to Vancouver.

It played two seasons there and two more in Calgary before disbanding.

As for Sanderson, he played in just eight games for Philadelphia, notching a paltry three goals and three assists, before his WHA playing career ended. The Blazers had to pay the Bruins between $500,000 and $1 million just to take him back. Sanderson was out of hockey altogether six years later, penniless and sleeping on a park bench in New York City. He eventually turned things around, overcoming alcoholism and embarking on a successful second career as a money manager.

While Sanderson was a dud, Hull turned out to be a smash. Not only did he play every season of the WHA's seven-year existence, he earned MVP honors twice and scored more than 50 goals during each of his first four years in the league. In 1974-75, he found the net 77 times in 78 games, by far the most of his career and the most in a single season for any WHA player. He finished his run with the Jets as the league's No. 2 all-time scorer and helped Winnipeg win three championships.

The biggest glitch? A game against the Birmingham Bulls (a team that had retained its alliterative name *and* its bovine connection after moving from Toronto, where it had been the Toros.) It happened during the 1977-78 season, courtesy of Dave Hanson, a journeyman best known for playing a role in the '77 Paul Newman vehicle *Slap Shot*. Hanson actually inspired one of the characters in the film, a guy named "Killer" Carlson, but wound up playing a different role instead: one of three bespectacled brothers (named Hanson!) who help Newman's team reverse its sagging fortunes by starting fights all over the ice.

Hanson played parts of three seasons in the WHA and a couple of more in the NHL. His career highlight was probably the only point he scored — an assist — in one of five playoff games he appeared in with the Bulls in 1978. But his most memorable moment came in a regular-season game against Hull and the Winnipeg Jets. During a scuffle, Hanson came up from behind Hull and ripped off the Golden Jet's ... toupee.

Frank Mahovlich, playing for the Bulls in the final season of a Hall of Fame career, witnessed the hairy scene. "In those days, the wigs were sewn in, they were stitched to your head," he recalled in a 2007 interview on the NHL's website. "And Bobby started to bleed from the top down, and blood was coming down all over, and he had to walk off the ice. It was an embarrassment in a lot of ways."

The Rocket and the legend

It was that kind of hit-and-miss luck that made the WHA so exciting — and so confounding. For instance, the Quebec Nordiques managed to hire legendary player Maurice "Rocket" Richard (pronounced "ri-SHARD") as their first head coach. But he only lasted two games, and one press report said he was "nervous, shaking occasionally like a leaf" during the team's home opener, even tough it ended in a resounding 6-0 victory over Alberta.

General manager Marius Fortier said, "We can't ask Maurice Richard to die behind the bench. We aren't tyrants. And it's obvious that this has become a superhuman task beyond his powers. He has visibly lost weight since he's been with us. His morale is very low."

A few days later, the Nordiques released Richard from his contract, and he returned to private business.

But while the WHA ended Richard's career in hockey, it did the exact opposite for Gordie Howe.

The hockey legend was already in the Hall of Fame and when the WHA got ready to begin its second season in 1973. He had begun his career way back in 1945 with the Omaha

Knights of the old U.S. Hockey League, and had played the next quarter-century with the Detroit Red Wings, finally retiring in 1971 to take a front-office position he described as his "mushroom job." In other words, management kept him in the dark most of the time, and opened the door just long enough to shovel some shit on him.

Howe preferred to be on the ice, but he was 46 years old and focused on his sons, Mark and Marty, both of whom were up-and-coming junior league players for the Maple Leafs' farm team, the Toronto Marlboros. The Marlboros won their league title, thanks in large part to the two teenagers, but the Howe kids were making just $60 a game. They could make a lot more than that in the WHA, and the NHL wasn't an option because that league didn't allow anyone younger than 20 to sign a contract.

Houston Aeros head coach Bill Dineen knew all this, plus he had a connection to the family: He'd played five seasons with Gordie Howe for the Red Wings back in the '50s. Dineen thought Howe would be receptive to the idea to his two sons playing for the Aeros, and he had a hunch the family patriarch might want to lace on the skates again himself. Playing alongside his two sons would be a dream come true, and even if the old man couldn't play much, his name would put fans in the seats and his sons' talent would put pucks in the net.

Given the elder Howe's frustration with his front-office job, his passion for his sons' career and his friendship with Dineen, it shouldn't have come as a big surprise when all three Howes agreed to contracts with the Aeros. Gordie signed for $1 million, with his two sons each making $600,000 over four years. What was a surprise was how well Gordie could still play. During his first three campaigns with the Aeros, he averaged over 100 points (goals plus assists) a season — a figure he had reached just once in the NHL. He was named the league's MVP in his first season and led the Aeros to the first of back-to-back championships.

All three Howes moved to the New England Whalers for their final two seasons in the WHA, and all played long enough to get back into the NHL when it absorbed four WHA teams in a 1979 merger. Mark Howe played the longest, lasting 16 seasons with Hartford, Philadelphia and Detroit. Marty Howe played six seasons with Hartford and Boston. Gordie Howe played one more season with Hartford, becoming the only player to compete in five different decades, before retiring for good at the age of 52. (He would add a sixth decade in 1997 when he played one shift on the ice for the Detroit Vipers of the International Hockey League.)

1975–76 World Hockey Association	W	L	T	Pts.
Eastern Division				
Indianapolis Racers	35	39	6	76
Cleveland Crusaders	35	40	5	75
New England Whalers	33	40	7	73
Cincinnati Stingers	35	44	1	71
Canadian Division				
Winnipeg Jets	52	27	2	106
Quebec Nordiques	50	27	4	104
Calgary Cowboys	41	35	4	86
Edmonton Oilers	27	49	5	59
Toronto Toros	24	52	5	53
Western Division				
Houston Aeros	53	27	0	106
Phoenix Roadrunners	39	35	6	84
San Diego Mariners	36	38	6	78
Minnesota Fighting Saints	30	25	4	64
Denver Spurs / Ottawa Civics	14	26	1	29

Championship: Winnipeg d. Houston, 4 games to 0
Points: 2 for each win, 1 for each tie
Minnesota disbanded during season
Denver moved to Ottawa, then disbanded

Chicken wire and stolen cars

Teams came and went over the years as the WHA expanded from an original 12 teams to as many as 14, adding expansion teams in Phoenix, Indianapolis, Denver and Cincinnati — with only the last surviving to the end. Teams in major media markets fared poorly, with the Los Angeles Sharks and the New York franchise (which went by three different names) each leaving after two seasons.

Some teams played in rundown arenas in bad neighborhoods where chicken wire was used instead of plexiglass along the boards, and the ice wasn't always entirely even. The

Cleveland Crusaders spent two years in Cleveland Arena, built in 1937. The neighborhood was so dangerous that two team members had Thunderbirds stolen from the parking lot on the same night, and team trainer Steve Thomas got mugged three times in a single winter. When one mugger demanded his watch, Thomas replied: "They got that one last week." The Crusaders went to the other extreme after two seasons by moving to the brand-new Richfield Arena, easily the best facility in the league ... but so far outside of town that fans had to drive an hour to get there.

The Chicago Amphitheatre, home to the Chicago Cougars franchise that lasted three seasons, was even older than Cleveland Arena. Built in 1934, it was right next to the old stockyards. Elvis and the Beatles had both performed there, but that didn't make it a great place for hockey. It was intended to be a temporary home for the Cougars until the Rosemont Arena could be built, but that venue didn't open until 1980 — five years after the Cougars folded.

The only time the Cougars made the playoffs, in 1974, they did so as the fourth and final seed in the Eastern Division in a year when they allowed more goals than they scored. But they surprised everyone by beating the first-place New England Whalers in the opening round, meaning they had more games to play. That's where they ran into a problem: The Amphitheatre, assuming they wouldn't get that far, had already scheduled a traveling production of *Peter Pan*, featuring onetime Olympic gymnast Cathy Rigby, at the same time.

The Cougars had a backup plan: They'd signed an agreement to use Chicago Stadium, home of the Black Hawks, if the Amphitheatre wasn't available. But the Black Hawks were in the playoffs, too, so *that* option was off the table. They considered playing at the Cleveland Arena, site of those muggings and car thefts, but finally settled on the Randhurst Twin Ice Arena, a skating rink in a shopping mall with room for 2,000 spectators. (Don't think about going to visit the rink: It's no longer there. All you'll find is a Home Depot.)

Against the odds, the underdog Cougars won again, eliminating Toronto in the second round. Fortunately, *Peter Pan* had finished its run. But the arena staff had been so sure the Cougars would lose that they had melted the ice surface and started to dismantle the pipes that were used to cool the ice. So ... back to Randhurst they went for the finals. Their Cinderella run ended there, where they were swept by Gordie Howe and the Houston Aeros.

Amazingly, neither Cleveland nor Chicago had the worst arena in the league. The New York Golden Blades drew pitifully small crowds at Madison Square Garden in 1973 and couldn't even manage to meet their second payroll. So, the league took over and moved the team to Cherry Hill, New Jersey (a suburb of Philadelphia, not New York), where an arena was available because the Jersey Devils, a team that had played there since 1960, had just gone out of business along with the rest of the Eastern League.

If you could call it an arena.

Cherry Hill Arena seated just over 4,400 people, so at least the few fans who showed up wouldn't look quite as lost. But the players often did. The visiting team's locker room didn't even have showers, so teams were forced to keep their uniforms on until they could get back to their hotel. There wasn't enough room for the coach on the bench, so he had to sit behind the team in the stands. Then there was the ice: It was so uneven that the visitors actually had to skate uphill for two periods, and it caused the puck to fly at crazy angles. One player was on the receiving end of a pass that caromed up off the ice and hit him right between the eyes.

The league started each of its first two seasons with a team in New York and ended up running the team itself both times when the owners bailed. It assured its fans that it would return to the Big Apple area, but it never did. The Jersey Knights, for their part, went on a new crusade — to the West Coast, where they became the San Diego Mariners. Los Angeles never got another team after the Sharks left, either, relocating to Michigan as the Stags and failing to last a full season there before moving to Baltimore and limping into oblivion as the Blades at the end of 1975.

The league had a charter member called the Minnesota Fighting Saints that played until 1976 before folding. Then the Cleveland Crusaders moved to Minnesota for a season and started calling themselves the Fighting Saints, too. They went out of business at the end of 1977.

As franchises fell by the wayside, the league filled out its membership in curious fashion by allowing teams from the Soviet Union, Czechoslovakia and (for one game) Finland to play games against its "regular" teams that counted in the standings. The Soviets finished 7-5-2 in two seasons, playing each WHA team once, awhile the Czechs were less successful at 2-10-2.

WHA Avco Cup series		
1973	New England Whalers d. Winnipeg Jets	4-1
1974	Houston Aeros d. Chicago Cougars	4-0
1975	Houston Aeros d. Quebec Nordiques	4-0
1976	Winnipeg Jets d. Houston Aeros	4-0
1977	Quebec Nordiques d. Winnipeg Jets	4-3
1978	Winnipeg Jets d. New England Whalers	4-0
1979	Winnipeg Jets d. Edmonton Oilers	4-2

The end is the beginning

The Indianapolis Racers held the distinction of having two of the sport's best players at the beginning of their careers, just when the WHA was closing in on the end of the line. Mark Messier played five games without scoring a goal for the Racers in 1978, and Wayne Gretzky signed lasted only slightly longer.

Wayne Gretzky in 2006. *Kris Krug.*

Gretzky was coming off a monster season with the Sault Ste. Marie Greyhounds junior team of the Ontario Hockey League, where he had hoped to wear No. 9 in homage to his idol, Gordie Howe, but had to settle for 99 because the single-digit number was already taken. Gretzky, just 17 at the time, scored 70 goals and assisted on 112 others for a team-record 182 points that year and instantly became the most coveted junior skater in North America. Ineligible for the NHL because minimum age requirement, he found himself courted by both the Racers and the Birmingham Bulls in the WHA, ultimately signing a seven-year personal services contract with the Racers' owner worth $1.75 million.

He didn't last seven years with the Racers. He barely lasted seven games After scoring three goals and assisting on three others in eight outings, he was informed that the team couldn't afford his contract. Even with him in the lineup, the Racers lost five of their first six games, including four at home, and were bleeding money. They needed an infusion of cash just to stay afloat, so the owner sold Gretzky and two other players were sold to the Edmonton Oilers for $850,000 in early November.

The Racers folded scarcely a month later, anyway, and Gretzky went on to a storied career with the Oilers, who joined the NHL in a merger the following year. From 1984 through 1988, Gretzky led the Oilers to four Stanley Cups in five years, helping the team become easily the most successful former WHA team to join the NHL. Gretzky retired holding the record for most points in a career with 2,857, more than 1,000 more than his idol, Gordie Howe, who ranks fourth on the list. (Messier, incidentally, ranks third).

Merger talks between the WHA and NHL fell apart more than once over the years. A 1977 proposal would have likely resulted in six teams from the junior circuit surviving in a combined league: Cincinnati, Edmonton, Houston, New England, Quebec and Winnipeg.

But that deal fell apart, and when the merger actually did occur two years later, Houston had gone out of business and the older league didn't want any part of Cincinnati. Instead, it paid the Stingers and the Birmingham Bulls $1.5 million each to shut up and go home.

The remaining four teams did join the NHL, with New England being rebranded as the Hartford Whalers, but only Edmonton remained in its original city. The Quebec Nordiques moved to Denver in 1995 to become the Colorado Avalanche, and the Hartford Whalers moved to North Carolina, playing in Raleigh's PNC Arena. The Winnipeg Jets, meanwhile, moved to Phoenix in 1996, but Winnipeg got another team (also named the Jets), when the Atlanta Thrashers moved there in 2011.

A few final notes:

The Western Hockey League, whose major league dreams stimulated the NHL's initial expansion, faded away in the early 1970s, but not entirely without a trace.

The NHL effectively put the league out of business when it announced in the summer of '74 that it was granting two Western League teams — the Denver Spurs and Seattle Totems — NHL franchises for the 1976 season. The move was intended to keep the WHA from expanding into those cities. But the Seattle group couldn't put together the necessary financing, so the team never played in the NHL.

The Denver expansion squad never happened, either. When Spurs ownership found out about a plan to instead move the California Golden Seals (another former Western League team) to Colorado instead, they abandoned their NHL plans and applied to join the WHA instead. The Phoenix Roadrunners, left out in the cold when the Western League folded, also joined the upstart league.

As it turned out, the Seals never moved to Denver, winding up in Cleveland instead; the Kansas City Scouts, an expansion team created to keep the WHA out of *that* market, moved to Denver after just two seasons and became the Rockies. (The franchise survives as the New Jersey Devils). The Spurs, meanwhile, lasted less than one season in the WHA before moving to Ottawa for a few games and then folding; Phoenix held on for a second season before doing the same.

Meanwhile, Dennis Murphy, who had started the WHA, wasn't quite through with hockey. He would revisit the concept of a rival hockey league in 1990, when he was involved in an effort to start what would have been known as the Global Hockey League. Teams were awarded to Albany, Providence, Saskatoon and Hamilton, while others were expected in California and the southeastern United States, as well as the Czech Republic.

In May, a franchise was placed in Birmingham, and plans for an entire "European division" consisting of Prague, London, Lyon, Berlin, Milan and Rotterdam were announced. The league was supposed to begin play Nov. 1, 1990, but it never got off the ground. First, plans were pushed back a year, then Murphy dropped out and the league was rebranded the Continental Hockey League. After that, it simply disappeared.

Strings Attached

Quick quiz: World Team Tennis in the 1970s … a) was Billie Jean King's idea; b) cost Jimmy Connors a chance to complete a grand slam; c) inspired a No. 1 song on the pop charts; d) featured cheerleaders, multicolored courts and trash talking; e) all of the above.

If you picked "all of the above," you just aced this quiz. Or at least avoided an unforced error. World Team Tennis rode in on the coattails on King's straight-sets victory over Bobby Riggs in the "Battle of the Sexes" tennis showdown of 1973. The court clash proved two things: that women could compete with men and that tennis American style — with attitude — could get fans' attention.

But even before that historic match, King and her then-husband Larry had set the wheels in motion on another project: an arena league for

Billie Jean King defeated Bobby Riggs in their 1973 Battle of the Sexes match.

tennis players. To create World Team Tennis, the Kings joined forces with Leonard Bloom, owner of the ABA's San Diego Conquistadors, and the ubiquitous Dennis Murphy, who seemed to have a hand in just about every new league that popped up in the late 1960s and early '70s. The concept was modeled after other American team sports, and it would be everything traditional tennis wasn't: loud, colorful and audacious.

"I think the team concept and the league are Americana," said George MacCall, the league's first commissioner. "Every major spectator sport is built around those concepts."

Born at the dawn of the disco era, WTT had everything except mirror balls. Wimbledon might require players to wear all white and only white, but WTT went to the opposite extreme: the courts themselves were multicolored, with blue and green service areas near the net, brown near the baselines and bright orange in the doubles alleys — and no white lines separating any of them. Teams had cheerleaders, and trash talking was encouraged, and confrontational "bad boys" like Jimmy Connors and Ilie Nastase were celebrated.

During a match in 1975, Connors responded to heckling from the crowd by mooning them, flipping the bird and pretending to masturbate the handle of his racket. But one of those hecklers went over the line when he started to make obscene references to Chris Evert, who at the time was Connors' fiancée. Connors rushed into the stands and had to be restrained by a guard; he later admitted he "wanted to kill the guy."

Other were less demonstrative.

Tennis journalist Bud Collins once wrote that Ken Rosewall, playing for the Pittsburgh Triangles, "looked like he was confessing to an ax murder" when he admitted clapping for an opponent's double faults.

Jimmy Connors brought his fiery game to World Team Tennis, and it may have cost him the Grand Slam.

To traditionalists, it was all very un-tennis-like … and that was the point. King and her fellow organizers were thumbing their noses at the entrenched culture of strawberries and cream, curtsies and accepted etiquette in general.

It wasn't just the trappings that were different, but the game itself. WTT matches consisted of five sets: one each of men's and women's singles, men's and women's doubles and mixed doubles. If a player wasn't on his or her game, substitutions were allowed. Gone were interminable deuces and advantages, replaced by no-ad scoring. The first player who reached four points won a game, period (you didn't have to win by two), and the traditional Love-15-30-40 scoring progression gave way to 0-1-2-3-4.

On top of all that, the new league challenged the traditional business model of tournament play and prize money based on performance. Instead, players would receive guaranteed contracts, as in other team sports.

The International Lawn Tennis Federation initially balked at allowing players to participate and had threatened to bar King, John Newcombe and Linda Tuero — who had all signed to play in the nascent league — before relenting. Key factors in its reversal: The league agreed to pay $48,000 a year and schedule its matches around Wimbledon, the U.S. Open and Davis Cup. That deal, however, didn't include the French and Italian Opens.

When it came down to it, the French Open held its ground, barring Connors and fellow WTT players Evonne Goolagong and John Newcome from playing in 1974. It was the best year of Connors' career: He won 15 of the 21 tournaments he entered, including the other three major events; his ban from the French Open deprived him of his only opportunity to complete the Grand Slam in a calendar year (he's still one of only six men to have won three or more). Connors tried to get a court injunction against the ban but was denied.

World Team Tennis began to take shape in the summer of 1973, with an announcement that the league planned to begin play the following year with a dozen teams. That list eventually grew to 16 and included franchises owned by Gary L. Davidson of ABA, WHA and WFL fame in Phoenix, as well as Jerry Saperstein, the 32-year-old son of Globetrotters founder Abe, in New York with a team called the Sets.

In announcing his involvement, Saperstein set World Team Tennis apart from anything that had come before it, including Murphy's other enterprises. "The ABA, AFL and WHA were all imitations of something that already existed," he said, adding that the circuit would be "the only major league experience with men and women competing on the same floor, the same night for the same points."

Other teams included the Los Angeles Strings, Boston Lobsters, San Diego Swingers and Golden Gate Otters. Rounding out the list were teams in Chicago, Cincinnati, Cleveland, Denver, Detroit, Houston, Philadelphia and Toronto.

As with any other startup league, several franchises shifted before the start of play. The Swingers never played a game in San Diego, moving to Hawaii as the Leis (they would relocate again after three seasons to the Pacific Northwest as the Cascades). The Otters wound up being known as simply the Golden Gaters.)

Davidson's involvement turned out to be short-lived: He sold the Phoenix team to new owners, who moved it to Baltimore and renamed it the Banners. Cleveland dropped off the list, and the Cincinnati entry moved in to take its place. St. Louis was added, then moved to Miami and became the Florida Flamingos. Minnesota, which would be known as the Buckskins, was also added to the mix.

John Bassett of Toronto owned teams in the WHA and WFL, but tennis was particularly close to his heart: He'd won the Canadian Open Junior Doubles Championship at age 15 and later competed in the U.S. National Championships in singles. Bassett signed on to own the Toronto-Buffalo Royals.

Houston's team was named the E-Z Riders after owner E.Z. Jones, but easily the most famous team name belonged to the Philadelphia Freedoms, who were built around Billie Jean King and made it to the championship round in the league's inaugural season before moving to Boston the following year after the original Lobsters folded.

Freedom and struggle

Elton John in 1975, when his song "Philadelphia Freedom," inspired by Billie Jean King's WTT team, hit the top of the charts.

But even though the Freedoms lasted just one year, their name became immortalized in song by Elton John. The English rock star was hitting the height of his popularity in 1973, when he met King at a party in Los Angeles. The two hit it off, and when King went to London for Wimbledon, John popped in to visit her — driving up in a Rolls Royce with 28 speakers. The two just sat in the car and talked until the wee hours of the morning, listening to music the entire time.

The next summer, John hit on an idea: He told the tennis star he wanted to write a song in her honor. She asked what he wanted to call it, and he came up with the idea of "Philadelphia Freedom," after her team. He thought the "iambic" rhythm to the city's name would work well, but it would be up to lyricist Bernie Taupin to come up with the words. Taupin said he couldn't write a tennis song, so the words don't have anything to do with tennis, but what he came up with worked — both for King and the record-buying public. John recorded a demo in Colorado and delivered the tape to King during the Freedoms' championship match against the Denver Racquets in August of 1974. He played it for her and the entire team right there in the locker room.

Everyone loved it. Unfortunately, it wasn't quite enough motivation for the Freedoms to beat the Racquets, but King did win the league's MVP award and the song itself reached

No. 1 on the Billboard charts in April of 1975. The timing was ironic, because just three weeks earlier, the Freedoms were sold to a group led by future New England Patriots owner Robert Kraft, who moved the team north to Boston.

John's song had a lot more staying power than the team that inspired it. "Philadelphia Freedom" stayed on the charts for 21 weeks, including a two-week stint at No. 1, and by the time the Bicentennial rolled around, it had established itself as the third-most-popular song of the year. ("Philadelphia Freedom" didn't appear on any album and was actually the first song John and Taupin had written specifically as a single. The label on the single read "with Love to B.J.K. and the sound of Philadelphia.")

The Freedoms weren't the only casualty of that first season. In all, seven teams folded and another, the Detroit Loves, moved to Indiana. One new team, the San Diego Friars, was added for the 1975 season, bringing league membership to an even 10 teams, where it remained for its final four years.

Tennis columnist and broadcaster Bud Collins called the first season "a disaster" involving "too many teams, too many games, wrong time of year." King and her husband, looking to stop the bleeding, came up with an idea they called "spectaculars": weekend extravaganzas involving six to eight teams, playing three or four matches a day. It's exhausting just thinking about it, which is probably one reason only 352 fans turned out to watch one such event in Boston, pitting the Lobsters against Cleveland, Indiana and Phoenix.

As Phoenix's Jeff Austin pointed out, "Who in Boston wants to come inside to watch Phoenix and Indiana? It's like scheduling a baseball game between the Giants and Dodgers at Fenway Park."

King had her doubts that the league would last: "We just hope we can hang on this year, get some TV (coverage) and get reorganized next year."

The season wasn't all bad, though. The Pittsburgh Triangles rose to the top of the league behind the play of Goolagong and Vitas Gerulaitis, defeating the Golden Gaters for the title. Pittsburgh had another strong season in '76, advancing to the semifinals, but the team folded the following year and was replaced in the WTT lineup a team called The Soviets, a traveling team made up of players from the Soviet Union. (The team finished last in the Eastern Division but did manage to knock off the defending champions from New York in one match, 27-24.)

Despite that setback, 1976 and '77 were good seasons for King. With the Freedoms having flown the coop to Boston, she went on to play for the New York Sets, taking them to the playoffs after a last-place finish the previous year. The league would, in fact, survive, and she would lead New York to championships each of the next two seasons.

Also in 1977, Renee Richards signed a contract to play with the Cleveland Nets. Richards, a transgender ophthalmologist from Southern California, had undergone sex reassignment surgery two years earlier and had recently been barred from playing in the French and Italian Opens after failing chromosome tests. The WTT, by contrast, accepted her.

"I signed her because she is a good player and it will add depth to our team," Cleveland owner Joe Zingale said simply, though he also admitted, "This also will be a tremendous drawing card for us."

Richards, 42, eventually was teamed in mixed doubles with John Lucas, better known for his 14-year career as an NBA point guard. Lucas had been an All-American in both tennis and basketball at the University of Maryland. He joined the New Orleans Sun Nets in 1978 after his Houston Rockets (whose season would otherwise have overlapped with WTT) missed the NBA playoffs.

Richards would compete in five U.S. Opens, advancing as far as the women's doubles final in 1977, the same year she joined WTT. Lucas would go on to coach teams in both the NBA — with three teams in six seasons ending in 2003 — and in World Team Tennis' successor league, where he coached a Houston Wranglers team that featured Steffi Graf for one match in 2005.

In addition to King, Connors and Goolagong, most of the sport's best players participated in World Team Tennis at one time or another. Female MVP awards for the regular season went to Goolagong in '75, Chris Evert of Phoenix each of the next two seasons and Martina Navratilova of Boston in the league's final year. All won Grand Slam tournaments multiple times. On the men's side, Gerulaitis was the playoff MVP for Pittsburgh in 1975, and a parade of other top men swung their rackets in the league. Among them were six-time Wimbledon winner Bjorn Borg; Rod Laver, who had dominated the sport in the 1960s; two-time Wimbledon and U.S. Open singles champ Ken Rosewall; three-time Wimbledon winner John Newcombe; and Ilie Nastase, who was as well known for his fiery temper and outrageous antics as he was victories at the French and U.S. Opens.

Given his demeanor, Nastase might have been the last person you'd expect to serve as coach. But he did just that for the L.A. Strings, leading them to the championship in the league's final season. Evert, who played on that team, said "Nasty" did a good job in the role, and that there wasn't any friction on the team. As for Nastase's attitude toward Evert, then the world's No. 1 player, he didn't provide much actual coaching: He knew when to leave well enough alone.

1974 World Team Tennis	W	L	Pct.
Eastern Division			
Atlantic Section			
Philadelphia Freedoms	39	5	.886
Boston Lobsters	19	25	.432
Baltimore Banners	16	28	.364
New York Sets	15	29	.341
Central Section			
Detroit Loves	30	14	.682
Pittsburgh Triangles	30	14	.682
Cleveland Nets	21	23	.477
Toronto-Buffalo Royals	13	31	.295
Western Division			
Gulf Plains Section			
Minnesota Buckskins	27	17	.614
Houston E-Z Riders	25	19	.568
Florida Flamingos	19	25	.432
Chicago Aces	15	29	.341
Pacific Section			
Denver Racquets	30	14	.682
San Francisco Golden Gaters	23	21	.532
Los Angeles Strings	16	28	.364
Hawaii Leis	14	30	.318

Championship: Denver d. Philadelphia, 55-44

Buss bows out

World Team Tennis struggled through five seasons of disappointing attendance without a television contract, and when all was said and done, it went out, not with a bang, but with a series of whimpers. First, the Boston Lobsters and New York Apples — the top two teams in the Eastern Division — called it quits, trimming the number of teams from 10 to eight.

The biggest blow, however, came when Jerry Buss announced he was folding the league champion Los Angeles Strings. The team was coming off a banner year, having set a WTT attendance record with average crowds of 7,219. To top it all off, the finals against Boston had been a thrilling affair, with Nastase defeating Tony Roche 7-6 in men's singles and Chris Evert edging Martina Navratilova by the same score in women's singles.

The encore was shaping up to be even better: The team had already sold 1,500 season tickets, easily ahead of the previous year's pace.

But Buss, a chemist who made his fortune in real estate, had bigger fish to fry: The next year, he would purchase the NBA's Los Angeles Lakers, hockey's L.A. Kings and the building where they both played (The Forum in Inglewood, for 67.5 million).

The rest of the league, meanwhile, was suffering. San Francisco was drawing well, but other teams were having trouble attracting spectators. Many league members had begun to search farther afield for fans, playing matches at satellite venues in the hinterlands. The New Orleans Nets, who had moved from Cleveland after the '77 season, were sometimes called the Sunbelt Nets because they played matches all over the South — from Baton Rouge to Houston; from Biloxi, Miss. to Lakeland, Fla. The Lobsters, meanwhile, played some matches 90 miles from Boston, in Yarmouth, Mass.

There might have been some hope if the league had still been attracting top players, but the stream of big names that once played team tennis had slowed to a trickle, most having focused their energy once again on tournament tennis. Even in 1978, WTT was having a hard time gaining commitments from stars. Connors and Borg hadn't played that season, and some marquee players who did take the court skipped matches to play in tournaments whenever they felt like it. Gerulaitis and Nastase, who was fined $15,000 for missing three matches to play in a New York tournament after Wimbledon, were among them. Nastase laughed it off, but the league was suffering.

Evert was by far the biggest draw, accounting for 40 percent of the league's total attendance, according to one estimate. She was making $175,000 in cash, and more than double that when other financial incentives such as annuities were taken into account. But, she said, "I've got more money than I need." Why should she subject herself to the rigors of a 44-game season on top of regular tournament play?

After the season ended, teams were having even more trouble lining up major stars for the '79 season. Gerulaitis had made $137,500 playing for the New York Apples, but he wanted $300,000 to return for another season.

Apples owner Sol Berg saw the writing on the wall and folded his team in the fall of 1978, in part because the WTT had yet to sign a single major star. When Boston owner Robert Kraft pulled out, he cited "new pressures being put on several top players by major tournaments" in explaining his decision. "We were not confident that the necessary quality level of player will be in the league next season," he said.

Buss echoed that rationale: "The critical element in this decision is my concern that we will not be able to deliver a quality product in 1979," he said in a statement. "Anything less than last year would not be fair to the great number of fans who have been loyal to us, and would have an economic as well as credibility impact on the following year."

Domino effect

The Strings, Lobsters and Apples not only played in three of the league's biggest markets, they also represented three of the most successful franchises.

But Buss' decision to fold was even more devastating because he owned all or part of three other teams in the league — the Indiana Loves, Anaheim Oranges and San Diego Friars. Each of them promptly folded, as well, as did Seattle and New Orleans. That left just two clubs, in San Francisco and Phoenix, still operating.

The Golden Gaters' general manager announced plans in January for a shorter season and said teams in San Diego, Tampa, Atlanta and Houston were possibilities. But none of them ever materialized, and neither did the 1979 season, shortened or otherwise. In March of 1979, the Phoenix Racquets finally suspended operations, leaving the Golden Gaters as the last team standing.

The golden age of World Team Tennis was over, but what appeared to be the end was just a brief interruption.

King resurrected the concept in a scaled-back version for a new season in 1981. The schedule was shorter (just three weeks), the venues were smaller (no NBA arenas), and the pay was far more modest — most of it based on performance rather than wrapped up in guaranteed salaries, and only four teams were involved. Since all four were in California, it really didn't make sense to call it "World" Team Tennis anymore, so King dropped that global pretense and simply called it Team Tennis.

Notably, Jerry Buss was involved again, as owner of the revived Los Angeles Strings. Buss won the first pick in the draft and immediately chose the most recognizable player who had committed to the new league: Martina Navratilova. The Strings won the first title in the rebooted Team Tennis season, and the league doubled in size for 1982, expanding into the heartland with new teams in Phoenix, Chicago, Dallas and Houston.

With more realistic aspirations, this new version of the sport survived — and continues to survive as of this writing — once again attracting some of the sport's top names. Navratilova won three straight women's MVP awards while playing for the Atlanta Thunder from 1992 to '94, and Connors returned for a time, as well, winning a share of the men's MVP award in '92. Other top stars such as John and Patrick McEnroe, Venus Williams, Andy Roddick and Lindsay Davenport also took the court, and the organization expanded to once again include teams from coast to coast. Familiar team names like the Strings and San Diego Friars were joined by new franchises such as the Washington Kastles and Newport Beach Breakers. By 1992, organizers had gained enough confidence to restore the dropped "World" to the league's name.

Then, in 2001, another new team with a familiar name joined the circuit. After more than a quarter-century King's first team had returned:

The Philadelphia Freedoms were back.

WTT Finals	
1974	Denver Racquets 55, Philadelphia Freedoms 44
1975	Pittsburgh Triangles 74, San Francisco Golden Gaters 65
1976	New York Sets 91, San Francisco Golden Gaters 57
1977	New York Apples 55, Phoenix Racquets 39
1978	Los Angeles Strings 108, Boston Lobster 93

Sources

"4 and 5-Pt. Field Goals In Con. Loop," El Paso Herald Post, p. 22, March 16, 1970.

"13-Year-Old Proves Age Little Factor In Bowling," Bristol Daily Courier (Pa.), p. 18, July 22, 1960.

"35 Gridders Survive Apaches' Screening," San Francisco Chronicle, p. 46, July 31, 1967.

"120 girls start softball drill," Chicago Tribune, pt. 2, p. 1, May 16, 1944.

"1969 Mexico Golden Aztecs," Fun While it Lasted, funwhileitlasted.net, May 16, 2013.

"1972-73 Chicago Cougars Ron Anderson Jersey," thirdstringgoalie.blogspot.com, July 18. 2011.

"1978-1980 New York Stars," Fun While It Lasted, funwhileitlasted.net, Jan. 8, 2013.

"1978-1981 New Jersey Gems," Fun While It Lasted, funwhileitlasted.net, May 22, 2013.

"1979 Philadelphia Fox," Fun While It Lasted, funwhileitlasted.net, May 11, 2011.

"1979-80 California Dreams," Fun While It Lasted, funwhileitlasted.net, Dec. 18, 2011.

"1984 Columbus Minks," Fun While It Lasted, funwhileitlasted.net, May 20, 2011.

"1996-1998 Atlanta Glory," Fun While It Lasted, funwhileitlasted.net, Nov. 22, 2014.

"1997-1998 Long Beach Stingrays," Fun While It Lasted, funwhileitlasted.net, March 16, 2012.

"1996-1998 New England Blizzard," Fun While It Lasted, funwhileitlasted.net, Sept. 23, 2013.

"1998 Chicago Condors," Fun While It Lasted, funwhileitlasted.net, Nov. 7, 2012.

"69-61! Iowa wins opener," Des Moines Register, p. S1, May 13, 1995.

"Aggies' 'Spring' Tilt Due," Hobbs Daily News-Sun (N.M.), p. 7, April 30, 1976.

"Akron Falcons (sic) Lose CFL Finance Support," Bridgeport Post (Conn.), p. 33, Sept. 20, 1967.

"Akron Vulcans Axe Tobin Rote, Doak Walker," Bridgeport Telegram, p. 15, Aug. 22, 1967.

"Akron Will Remain in Continental Loop," Bridgeport Post, Aug. 24, 1967.

"Alberta Oilers WHA name," Edmonton Journal, p. 57, June 8, 1972.

Alcock, J.J. "History of Federal League One Battle After Another," Chicago Tribune, chicagology.com, Dec. 23, 1915.

"All-Stars Show Snap in Driving Workout," Los Angeles Times, pt. 2, p. 14, Jan. 26, 1934.

Amador, Abe. "The Girls of Summer," Indianapolis News, p. B1, May 8, 1990.

"American League Can't Agree On New Brown Home," New Philadelphia Daily Times, p. 6, Sept. 29, 1953.

"American Women in World War II," history.com, March 5, 2010.

"Anaheim Club Signs Bunce," San Bernardino County Sun, p. C-4, June 30, 1967.

Anderson, Cerisse. "The NFL introduced documents showing former USFL Commissioner ..." UPI Archives, upi.com, June 30, 1986.

"Anderson Packers Quit Pro Cage Loop," Marshfield News-Herald (Wis.), p. 10, April 11, 1950.

Andrews, Evan. "10 Things You May Not Know About Satchel Paige," history.com, Sept. 22, 2015.

"Another New Grid Loop Set," San Rafael Daily Independent Journal, p. 41, Oct. 5, 1973.

"Another (yawn) pro football league is born, Salina (Kan.) Journal, p. 11, July 1, 1983.

Applebome, Peter. "Wide-open spaces of Texas – Indoors," New York Times, nytimes.com, Feb. 22, 1984.

Arenafan.com.

"Argos deal Wilkinson in one of two trades," Brandon Sun (Manitoba), p. 7, April 24, 1971.

Ariail, Cat. "Steph Curry ... The 'Male Machine Gun Molly?' " ussportshistory.com, May 12, 2016.

Asato, Bart. "USFL sees Hawaii on its horizon," Honolulu Advertiser, p. 8, July 20, 1983.

Ashwill, Gary. "The Negro League You've Never Heard of: The National Association of 1907-1909," Agate Type, agatetype.typepad.com, Feb. 5, 2014.

Ashwill, Gary. "Negro Leagues DB Update: 1932 East-West League," seamheads.com, Aug. 13, 2015.

"Attendance Project: USFL," kenn.com.

"Attendance Project: WFL," kenn.com.

"Azar seeks finances for IFL franchise," El Paso Times, p. 8, Sept. 7, 1983.

"Aztecs Are Homeless," Brownsville Herald, p. 15, Sept. 21, 1969.

"Bakersfield Eleven Opens Against Oaks," Bakersfield Californian, p. 15, Sept. 16, 1940.

"Baltimore Colts Quit Pro League," Los Angeles Times, pt. 4, p. 2, Jan. 19, 1951.

Barber, Red. "Not all the drama was on the field in famous 1950 pennant battle," christiansciencemonitor.com, July 29, 1988,

"Barnstormers' update," Des Moines Register, p. 17, March 31, 1995.

Basketball-reference.com.

"Bears, Bulldogs End League Season Sunday," Los Angeles Times, p. 24, Dec. 16, 1941.

"Bears vs. Spartans," Milwaukee Journal, pt. 2, p. 1, Dec. 18, 1932.

Becker, Josie. "Pro Football in Los Angeles – A History," josiebeckerfc.blogspot.com, Oct. 23, 2011.

Begley, Kathy. "Mod Derek 'Turns On' Fans At Mid-City Signing," Philadelphia Inquirer, p. 21, Aug. 4, 1972.

"Bell Fails To Ring True," Pittsburgh Press, p. 22, Aug. 6, 1974.

"Belles to Play Sox Tonight; Name All Star Team Lineup," Racine Journal-Times, p. 10, June 30, 1943.

Bellis, Mary. "The History of Roller Skates," ThoughtCo., thoughtco.com, April 24, 2017.

Benny Kauff, sabr.org.

"Bill Bridges Stopped – But Only for Half," El Paso Herald, p. 24, Dec. 12, 1962.

Birks, Tom. "Perfect Games Wind Up News' Bowling Clinic," Miami News, p. 7B, Aug. 6, 1959.

Blackistone, Kevin B. "It's time for baseball to acknowledge Cap Anson's role in erecting its color barrier," Washington Post, washingtonpost.com, Dec. 2, 2015.

Blackistone, Kevin B. "When Will time come for women's pro hoops?" McAllen (Texas) Monitor, p. 11, April 20, 1993.

"Blazers Idled By Unsafe Ice," Pittsburgh Post-Gazette, p. 10, Oct. 14, 1972.

Blickenstaff, Brian. "Baseball's Forgotten Brotherhood, The First Athlete Union in American Pro Sports," Vice Sports, sports.vice.com, Oct. 20, 2016.

"Blimp crashes into boat, restaurant in Oakland," Harrisburg American (Pa.), p. 8A, Jan. 10, 2001.

Blitz, Matt. "The Black Babe Ruth," Today I Found Out, todayifoundout.com, April 9, 2015.

"Bobby Hull, the Golden Jet, Is Back," Boston Globe, p. 29, Dec. 5, 1969.

"Bolin too much for Wranglers," Lincoln Journal Star, p. 14, March 24, 1981.

Bona, Marc. "How Arena Football was created, why it endures," cleveland.com, Aug. 18, 2014.

Borba, Harry. "Roller Derby Isn't Sport," San Francisco Examiner, p. 21, July 16, 1938.

"Borg, Nastase To Miss First Round in France," Austin American-Statesman, p. 35, June 5, 1974.

Bradley, Hugh. "Four Major Baseball Leagues By 1960 Predicted," Arizona Republic, p. 23, Oct. 31, 1951.

Brehm, Keith. "All American Girls League Reveals Plan for Operation," Racine (Wis.) Journal Times, p. 10, April 27, 1943.

"Brisker of the A.B.A. arrested in fight," New York Times, nytimes.com, Oct. 13, 1971.

"Bronco Bowl," Texas State Historical Association, tshaonline.org.

Brown, Bruce. "Cuban Baseball," theatlantic.com, June 1984.

"Browns will quit if two leagues merge," Tampa Tribune, p. 22, Nov. 17, 1949.

Bruns, John. "New York will have team in new World Tennis League," Central New Jersey Home News, p. 7, June 23, 1973.

"Buffalo Bid For Franchise Favored by Packer Officials," Green Bay Press-Gazette, p. 19, Jan. 19, 1950.

"Bulldogs in 17-14 Win," Los Angeles Times, pt. 2, p. 9, Dec. 6, 1937.

"Bulldogs Lucky to Nip Bullies," Los Angeles Times, p. 21, Dec. 11, 1939.

"Bulldogs Slate Charity Game," San Bernardino Sun, p. 23, Nov. 26, 1966.

Burley, Craig. "Free Benny Kauff," The Hardball Times, fangraphs.com, April 12, 2004.

Byers, Walter. "Brown Signs To Coach In New Loop," Ogden Standard-Examiner, p. 8, Feb. 9, 1945.

Byers, Walter. "Coast Bid As Major Is Nixed," Dayton Herald, p. 24, Dec. 12, 1945.

Canning, Whit. "Texas Longhorns: Where Have You Gone?" p. 60, 2005, Spring Publishing, Champaign, Ill.

"Capitols Withdraw from CFL," Tipton Tribune (Ind.), p. 4, Feb. 17, 1970.

"Cardte Hicks," thelegends.org.

Carson, Dick. "The 25 best nicknames from the NFL, ranked," foxsports.com, Nov. 11, 2016.

"Carter Signs With WFL In Chicago," Piqua Daily Call (Ohio), p. 12, Feb. 8, 1974.

"CFL Boss Resigns Post," Lubbock Avalanche-Journal, p. 6-D, March 11, 1970.

"CFL May Add An Extra Team," Beckley Post-Herald, p. 2, July 3, 1965.

"CFL Owners Award 2 New Franchises," Raleigh Register, p. 6, Jan. 9, 1967.

"CFL Owners Judge Vulcans' Fate Today," Medina County Gazette (Ohio), p. 15, Aug. 23, 1967.

Chait Geils, Donna. "Making a dream come true, and watching it fade away," New York Times, nytimes.com, Nov. 15, 1981.

Chamberlain, Charles. "Continental League Paves Way for Majors to Expand," Hagerstown (Md.) Morning Herald, p. 10, Aug. 3, 1960.

Chamberlain, Charles. "Girls' Loop Costs $100,000," Des Moines Register, p. 10, May 1, 1943.

Chapman, Scooter. "Slogan happy Green Bay has a new one," Port Angeles Daily News (Wash.), p. 14, July 16, 1975.

"Cheryl Miller named," Carlisle (Pa.) Sentinel," p. B2, June 6, 1986.

"Chicago Bears Win Again, 23-0," Stevens Point Journal (Wis.), p. 5, Jan. 29, 1934.

"Chicago club loses in second overtime," Mattoon Journal Gazette (Ill.), p. 15, Feb. 12, 2001.

Chick, Bob. "Dicker Rod: Last Snicker," St. Petersburg Independent, p. 1-C, July 18, 1975.

Christoph, Ella and Lutz, Eric. "Tale of the Whales," Newcity, newcity.com, Aug. 2-5, 2018.

"Cioni and Eglington Win 100-Mile Derby," Washington Times, p. 21, March 28, 1915.

Clark, Dick and Holway, John B. "1930 Negro National League," SABR Research Journals Archive, research.sabr.org.

"Cleveland Is Out Of Federal League," Elmira Star-Gazette, p. 8, Dec. 18, 1913.

"Coach Was a Genius, Not Prophet," Los Angeles Times, articles.latimes.com, Feb. 3, 1985.

"Coast League Men Still in Dreaming Stage Over Majors," Oregon Daily Journal, p. 17, Jan. 16, 1919.

"Coast League Moguls Hear Plan For Pro Football Loop," Santa Cruz Sentinel, p. 6, Feb. 16, 1940.

"Coast Pro Football League Organized," Oakland Tribune, p. 13, Aug. 24, 1940.

"Colonels Court Disaster Unless Muskies Bite Hook," Louisville Courier-Journal, p. B6, March 26, 1968.

"Comets Folding!" Racine (Wis.) Journal Times, p. 21, July 11, 1951.

"Connie Kunzmann," Wayne State Wildcats, wswildcats.com.

"Conscription Fear Wrecks Grid Loop," Bakersfield California, p. 13, Aug. 29, 1940.

"Continental Can 'Fight Or Quit,'" Salem Statesman Journal, Ore., p. 38, May 13, 1960.

"Continental Football League Established," Daily Times (Salisbury, Md.), p. 2, Feb. 8, 1965.

"Continental Football League Makes Debut," Anderson Daily Bulletin (Ind.), p. 11, Aug. 14, 1965.

"Continental Grid League, New TV Network Sign Contract," Troy Record, p. 90, Nov. 23, 1966.

"Continental League Meets With Others," Kalispell Daily Inter Lake (Mont.), p. 4, Aug. 2, 1960.

"Continental League Ready (Well, Practically) to Roll," Binghampton Press, p. 12, Jan. 30, 1960.

"Continental League To Support Class D Circuit," Danville Bee (Va.), p. 13, March 16, 1960.

"Continental League Wants Unrestricted Player Draft," Eau Claire Leader, p. 17, May 25, 1960.

" 'Cornets' Trumpet Women's Pro Basketball," Quad-City Times, p. 17, March 22, 1978.

Crawford, Denis M. "Hugh Culverhouse and the Tampa Bay Buccaneers," McFarland & Co., Jefferson, N.C., 2011.

"Crockett, Zachary. "The Rise and Fall of Professional Bowling," priceonomics.com, March 21, 2014.

Crowe, Jerry. "How basketball became three-dimensional," Los Angeles Times, articles.latimes.com, May 6, 2008.

"Crucial Meeting Held," Rocky Mount (N.C.) Telegram, p. 10, Nov. 18, 1974.

"Csonka, Kiick, Warfield Jump To WFL," Playground Daily News (Fort Walton Beach, Fla.), p. 11, April 1, 1974.

"Cumnock Plans New Athletic Field and Gym," Los Angeles Times, pt. 2, p. 10, Feb. 1, 1934.

Curran, Pat. "Who'll have the last laugh in Bobby Hull saga?" Montreal Gazette, p. 15, Oct. 22, 1969.

Curtis, Charles. "Official Says Hockey Would Go Big Here," Los Angeles Times, pt. 4, p. 1, March 27, 1959.

Cutler, Teddy. "Does Donald Trump Hate the NFL Because of the Buffalo Bills," Newsweek, newsweek.com, Sept. 25, 2017.

Dahlem, John S. "Cumnock School," cifss.org.

Daly, Dan. "The Battle of Ohio," Sports on Earth, sportsonearth.com, Nov. 27, 2013.

"The Day the Money Ran Out," Sports Illustrated, si.com/vault, Dec. 1, 1975.

Davis, Reyn. "A Nowhere Ride," sportsillustrated.com, May 28, 1979.

DeFord, Frank. "Five Strides on the Banked Track," Open Road Media, 2014.

"Dennis Kuno on the History of the Continental Football League," Pittsburgh Sports Daily Bulletin, Jan.13, 2012.

Doran, Nick. "Did You Know the Reds Had a Black Player Before Jackie Robinson?" Redleg Nation, redlegnation.com, Aug. 5, 2015.

"Dorothy Schroeder," aagpbl.org.

Dougan, Steve. "Arkansas Lassies Have Distinct Michigan Look," Lansing (Mich.) State Journal, p. 13, Dec. 31, 1974.

Down, Fred. "Third Loop Expects Organized Baseball to Cooperate," Provo Daily Herald, p. 8, July 28, 1959.

"Doxie Moore Sizes Up NPBL as Nov. 1 Opening Game Approaches," Waterloo Courier, p. 15, Oct. 25, 1950.

Doxsie, Don. "Women's pro league tires to stay alive, awaken fan support," Quad-City (Iowa) Times, p. 1S, April 26, 1994.

Doyle, Pat. "Branch Rickey's Farm, baseball-almanac.com/minor-league/minor2005a.shtml.

Dufresne, Chris. "New Owner for Express Sought," Los Angeles Times, pt. III, p. 13, Feb. 1, 1985.

Dulo, Ken. "In the Sporting Nook," The Saint Joseph (Mich.) Herald-Press, p. 10, Oct. 13, 1953.

Dunmore, George J. "McClendon Is Turning In Top Job With Pipers," Pittsburgh Courier, p. 26, Jan. 23, 1960.

Elderkin, Phil. "Team Tennis, staging a return, looks much fitter," Christian Science Monitor, csmonitor.com, July 20, 1981.

Eskenazi, Gerald. "How W.T.T. Became World Team-less Tennis," New York Times, nytimes.com, Nov. 20, 1978.

"ESPN, Inc. History" fundinguniverse.com.

"Evansville Quintet Is Joining Pro League," Muncie Star Press (Ind.), p. 14, Feb. 8, 1951.

"Ex-Continental Players Supplying Als and Argos," Ottawa Journal, p. 17, Aug. 25, 1967.

"Ex-Nittany Lion Stars in Minors," Lock Haven Express (Pa.), p. 12, Dec. 2, 1968.

"Falkenberg Sold To Newark Feds," Brooklyn Daily Eagle, p. 33, March 28, 1915.

"FCC Wins Authority to Order Original Cable TV Programming," Asbury Park Evening Press, p. 8, Jan. 11, 1972.

"Federal League To Play In Brooklyn," New York Times, p. 9, Feb. 14, 1914.

Fidler, Merrie A. "The Origins and History of the All-American Girls Professional Baseball League," McFarland & Co., Jefferson, N.C., 2006.

Finch, Frank. "Bulldogs Beat Packers," Los Angeles Times, pt. 2, p. 9, Dec. 20, 1937.

Finch, Frank. "Bulldogs Rout Salinas by Score of 34-0," Los Angeles Times, pt. 2, p. 9, Sept. 15, 1938.

Finch, Frank. "North Defeats South, 17-12, in Drab Football Game," Los Angeles Times, pt. 2, p. 10, Jan. 31, 1938.

Finch, Frank. "PCL Accepts $900,000 in Indemnities," Los Angeles Times, pt. 4, p. 2, Dec. 3, 1957.

Finch, Frank. "Scouting the Pros," Los Angeles Times, p. 27, Sept. 12, 1948.

"Five Founding Cities Named By 3rd Major," Atlanta Constitution, p. 29, July 28, 1959.

"Fleet Walker," Baseball Reference, baseball-reference.com.

Fleming, David. "Report: Rendell fired off angry letter to Tagliabue," pottsvillemaroons.com, Nov. 20, 2007.

"Forbes Releases 16th Annual NBA Team Valuations," forbes.com, Jan. 22, 2014.

"Forest Hills lures top players," Lowell Sun, Jan. 2, 1973.

"Former Hawks dot Barnstormers' roster," Iowa City Press Citizen, p. B1, April 26, 1995.

Fraley, Oscar. "Plans underway for 12-city National Bowling League," Bend Bulletin (Ore.), p. 2, Nov. 17, 1960.

"Frick Would Not Permit Player Pool," Sedalia Democrat (Mo.), p. 10, March 24, 1960.

"From the SABR archives: Judge Landis dismisses 1915 Federal League lawsuit," sabr.org.

"Gabriel Named Coach of Storm," Asheville Citizen-Times, p. 12, Aug. 6, 1983.

"Gangway! Women's Softball League Prepares for Season," Wisconsin State Journal, p. 13, May 17, 1943.

"Gems Clinch Spot," Morristown (N.J.) Daily Record, p. 22, March 10, 1981.

Gems, Gerald. "Nancy Lieberman-Cline," Jewish Women's Archive Encyclopedia, jwa.org.

"Generals Give Job to Flutie; Sipe Is Traded," articles.latimes.com, Feb. 7, 1985.

"Gigantic Baseball War Is Threatened," Springfield News-Leader, p. 6, Jan. 7, 1912.

"Gilbert Is Asking For Top Money," Beckley Post-Herald (W.Va.), p. 3, June 28, 1969.

Gill Bob. "Outsiders I: Minor League and Independent Football, 1923-1950," St. Johann Press, Haworth, N.J., 2010.

Gill Bob. "Outsiders II: Minor League and Independent Football, 1951-1985," St. Johann Press, Haworth, N.J., 2010.

Gill, Bob. "The Bulldogs: L.A. Hits the Big Time," 1984 PFRA Annual No. 5, Gill, Bob. "Thorpe's Farewell Season," The Coffin Corner, Vol. 15, No. 3, 1993.

"Girls' Baseball," Life, p. 63, June 4, 1945.

"Global Hockey League Plans Czech Franchise," Los Angeles Times, p. P11, March 19, 1990.

Gloster, Rob. "American Basketball League folds," apnews.com, Dec. 22, 1998.

Goldberg, Dave. "If it's good for fall football, it's good for spring football," Port Clinton (Ohio) News Herald, p. 8, Dec. 20, 1983.

"Golden Jet could buy one," Brandon (Manitoba) Sun, p. 6, Feb. 15, 1972.

"Good-bye For Denver Quint; Record Broken," Quad-City Times, p. 9, Jan, 22, 1951.

Gordon, Greg. "WTT Still Part Of Tampa Bay Area's Future?" Tampa Tribune, p. 10-C, Jan. 25, 1979.

Gossett, Gary. "Toros Won't Play Again This Year," San Antonio Express, p. 33, Dec. 2, 1970.

Gottehrer, Barry. "The Giants of New York," Longmans Canada Limited, Toronto, 1963.

"Government mum on Drapeau pass at NFL," Ottawa Journal, p. 17, Jan. 24, 1978.

"G.R. Chicks Fold For '54 Season," Benton Harbor (Mich.) News-Palladium, p. 17, Sept. 30, 1953.

Graham, Tony. " 'Fox trot' is over for Dave Wohl," Asbury Park (N.J.) Press, p. D8, July 13, 1980.

"Grant Jets 6 Home Dates at Sports Arena," Long Beach Independent, p. D-2, Sept. 14, 1961.

Grasso, John and Hartman, Eric R. "Historical Dictionary of Bowling," p. 120, Rowman & Littlefield, Lanham, Md., 2014.

Gregory, Sean. "The NFL Fought Donald Trump's Bullying 30 Years Ago and Won. Should It Do It Again?" time.com, Sept. 12, 2018.

Greene, Nick. "Good, Honest Football: Re-Watching the XFL," Mental Floss, mentalfloss.com, Sept. 8, 2014.

Grett, Wayne. "Bolin scores big in new cage loop: $30,000," Des Moines Register, p. 21, Sept. 25, 1980.

Grett, Wayne. "Cornets tab Bolin their most valued," Des Moines Register, p. 3S, April 14, 1980.

Grett, Wayne. "Women's basketball league folds before first game," Des Moines Register, p. 3S, Feb. 2, 1987.

"Grid Debut Won by Los Angeles," Harrisburg Evening News, p. 17, Nov. 8, 1937.

"Grid League Adds Tulsa," Lake Charles American-Press (La.), p. 8, July 17, 1965.

Griffin, John. "Sports Parade," San Mateo Times, p. 25, Nov. 15, 1951.

Grimes, H. Coleman. "Spartan Victory Sunday Will Give Them Claim To State Title," Portsmouth Times, p. 16, Nov. 16, 1929.

Groller, Keith. "After Caravan crown, Pate A's hope to avoid Blues," Allentown Morning Call, p. C3, Aug. 4, 1997.

Gustkey, Earl. "Inventor Makes Chain Gang Obsolete," Los Angeles Times, p. C10, Oct. 29, 1970.

Gustkey, Earl. "Women's League Is Calling It Quits," Los Angeles Times, p. B1, Dec. 23, 1998.

Hackleman, Jim. "A.B. 'Happy' Chandler Quits Commissioner Job With CFL Over Changes," Danville Register (Va.), p. 11, Jan. 15, 1966.

Hageman, William. "Before there was Wrigley, there was a seminary," Chicago Tribune, March 30, 2014.

Halvonik, Steve. "Brisker ruled dead, but disappearance still a mystery," Pittsburgh Press, p. D3, June 23, 1985.

Hanlon, Steve. "Wilt the stilt," nwitimes.com, Oct. 13, 1999.

Hannigan, Dave. "America at Large: Soccer evangelist Ron Newman's dream became a reality," irishtimes.com, Sept. 5, 2018.

"Happy Bows Out as Boss Of Grid Loop," Syracuse Post-Standard, p. 10, Jan. 15, 1966.

" 'Happy' Opens Football Office," Beckley Post-Herald (W.Va.), p. 2, April 1, 1965.

"Harvey Hester Dies; Sportsman Was 70," Atlanta Constitution, p. 3, March 29, 1967.

Harvey, Steve. "Orange County Rhinos beat the NFL to local TV," Los Angeles Times, March 6, 2011.

Haupert, Michael. "Ed Bolden," Society for American Baseball Research," sabr.org.

Hecken, Phil. "Too Good for the Ticker," uni-watch.com, Nov. 15, 2014.

Hembree, Barbara. "Hoosier Gals Lose Pro Loop Opener," Indianapolis News, p. 26, Jan. 6, 1975.

"Hershey To Get Pro Grid Games," Lebanon Daily News (Pa.), p 26, Feb. 25, 1970.

Hessler, Warner. "USFL in command of NFL at the half," Newport News (Va.) Daily Press, p. B2, June 29, 1986.

Hicks, Dave. "Offers roll in for Karen," Arizona Republic, p. D-3, Feb. 9, 1975.

Hill, Shandy. "Pottsville May Lose Pro Grid Title," Reading Times, p. 12, Dec. 14, 1925.

"History of the American Basketball League," Association for Professional Basketball Research, apbr.org.

"History of Women's Professional Basketball," Association for Professional Basketball Research, apbr.org.

"Hockey," Lowell (Mass.) Sun, p. 5, Feb. 12, 1972.

"Hockey loop to open next October," Minneapolis Star, p. 3D, Nov. 2, 1971.

Holmes, George R. "O.B. Has An Eye On The Federals," Winfield Daily Free Press, p. 3, Aug. 25, 1915.

Holmes, Tommy. "Pepper Martin and The Grid Dodgers," Brooklyn Daily Eagle, p. 11, Aug. 13, 1948.

Hooper, Milton. "Friday Flashback: American Professional Slow Pitch League (APSPL)," The Knight Writer, March 31, 2017.

"Hopes Fading for Kern Pro Eleven," Bakersfield Californian, p. 16, Sept. 26, 1940.

"Horace Fogel: The Strangest Owner in Phillies History," Philly Sports History, phillysportshistory.com, July 6, 2011.

"Hot 100 chart run Elton John Philadelphia Freedom," Jimmy's Charts, racpro.com.

Hruby, Dan. "Hang On, You Football Widows; New League, Season in the Wind," Hartford Courant, p. D1, Jan. 29, 1981.

Hughes, Jill Elaine. "These girls of summer played in skirts," Chicago Tribune, p. 19, June 22, 2014.

Husman, John R. "Fleet Walker," Society for American Baseball Research, sabr.org.

"IFL's Bulldogs chase Schlichter," Dayton Daily News, p. 21, July 15, 1983.

"International Football League A Reality in'74?" Lakeland Ledger, p. 4B, Oct. 6, 1973.

Jacobs, Proverb G. "Autobiography of an Unknown Football Player," p. 676, 684, AuthorHouse, 2014.

Janofsky, Michael. "U.S.F.L. Owners' Strategy in '84 Revealed," New York Times, nytimes.com, June 8, 1986.

Janofsky, Michael. "U.S.F.L. envisions fall schedule beginning in 1987," New York Times, nytimes.com, April 15, 1984.

"Jean Faut" biography, aagpbl.org.

Jenks, Jayson. "Is John really dead?" Seattle Times, seattletimes.com, May 11, 2017.

"Joe Tinker Signs With Federal League" Decatur Daily Review, Page 5, Dec. 28, 2013.

"Joie Ray Wins Roller Derby Match Race; Nygra-Thomas lead," Louisville Courier-Journal, p. 16, Nov. 7, 1935.

Johnson, Dan. "The Cornet Legacy," Des Moines Register, p. S-1, July 28, 1997.

"Johnson Joins Federals," Salem Daily Capital Journal, p. 1, Dec. 3, 1914.

Johnson, Michael Simon and Rosario, Daisy. "Latino Players Blurred MLB's Color Line Before Robinson's Debut," Only A Game, wbur.org/onlyagame, July 11, 2015.

Johnson, Roy S. "The Lady Is A Hot Shot," Sports Illustrated, si.com, April 6, 1981.

Kahler, Kalyn. "Tommy Maddox on XFL, Elway and Big Ben," si.com, Feb. 17, 2017.

Kale, Gary. "CFL Gives Chandler Full Powers as Commissioner That Baseball Wouldn't," Daily Courier (Connellsville, Pa.), p. 7, April 8, 1965.

Kaufman, Michelle. "Women's league's success not skintight," Baltimore Evening Sun, baltimoresun.com, Feb. 20, 1991.

"KC's Bill Bridges New ABL Scoring Record Holder," Sayre Evening Times (Pa.), p. 10, Dec. 10, 1962.

Kearney, Jim. Column, Vancouver Sun, p. 18, Feb. 12, 1972.

Kee, Lorraine. "Women's Pro Hoops Gets Another Shot," St. Louis Post-Dispatch, p. 2B, Oct. 12, 1996.

Keener, Sid C. "Barnes Reveals Transfer Plan," St. Louis Star-Times, p. 14, Dec. 9, 1941.

Keeney, Stephen R. "Blurring the Color Line: How Cuban Baseball Players Led to the Racial Integration of Major League Baseball," Society for American Baseball Research, sabr.org.

Keese, Parton. "N.H.L. Gives Franchises To Denver, Seattle For '76," nytimes.com, June 13, 1974.

Kelly, Cathal. "American football, eh? Who cares?" The Star, thestar.com, Nov. 22, 2008.

King, Susan. "National Film Registry selects 25 films for preservation," Los Angeles Times, articles.latimes.com, Dec. 19, 2012.

Knecht, G. Bruce. "The Unraveling of a 'Billionaire'," New York Times, gbruceknecht.com, June 3, 1984.

Koch, Ed. "Roller Derby Requiem," 2015.

Kranish, Michael and Fisher, Marc. "Trump Revealed," Scribner, New York, 2016.

"L.A. Loses Out in Bid for Browns," Los Angeles Times, p. 1, Sept. 30, 1953.

"Lakers Rip Sheboygan," Minneapolis Star Tribune, p. 23, Feb. 29, 1952.

"Lance Tibke," The Dark Side of Nebraska, thedarksideofamerica.com.

Lardner, Rex. "Bowling's Big League — A $14 Million Gamble," Sports Illustrated, si.com/vault, Oct. 30, 1961.

"Larry Kelley Enters Boston Shamrocks," Helena Independent Record, p. 9, Oct. 21, 1937.

"Larry Miller: The ABA's All-Time Single-Game Scoring Leader and an ACC Legend," 20 Second Timeout, 20secondtimeout.blogspot.com, March 8, 2008.

"Las Vegas Team Heads for Memphis," Des Moines Register, p. 21, Dec. 15, 1969.

"Last Season For Purple Spartans In Portsmouth?" Portsmouth Daily times, p. 8, Dec. 3, 1933.

Laughman, Casey. "Oldest NFL veteran going strong at 97," Indiana Gazette (Pa.), p. 15, Aug. 10, 2002.

"Lawsuits threaten to kill WPBL," Arizona Daily Star (Tucson), p. F-3, Dec. 28, 1979.

"Leaders," usflsite.com.

"League Knocks Out Ramblers; S.B. Apparently Without Team," San Bernardino Sun, p. B-7, May 20, 1969.

Levitt, Daniel. "State of pay: tennis has huge gender gap in earning power," theguardian.com, July 14, 2018.

Levitt, Daniel R. "The Battle that Forged Modern Baseball," Rowan & Littlefield Publishing, Lanham, Md., 2012.

Lewis, J.D. "Pink Panthers' Show Tour Hits Seymour," Columbus (Ind.) Republic, p. 18, Nov. 1, 1974.

Lewis, Michael. "The forgotten story of ... the 1979 NASL players' strike," theguardian.com., March 8, 2015.

Lieber, Jill. "Rebels With a Good Cause," Sports Illustrated, si.com, June 3, 1985.

Lilley, Bill. "Professional team Akron Vulcans amassed debt, losses at Rubber Bowl in 1960s," Beacon Journal, Nov. 4, 2008.

Livingston, Bill. "Signing Jerry Lucas made George Steinbrenner a star," Cleveland Plain Dealer, cleveland.com, Nov. 27, 2015.

"Long Beach Continental grid team dissolved," Redlands Daily Facts, p. 16, Aug. 30, 1967.

Longley, Neil. "An Absence of Competition," Springer, New York, 2013.

Lorge, Barry. "World Team Tennis Is Something Else," Washington Post, washingtonpost.com, Aug. 13, 1978.

"Los Angeles Bulldogs End Undefeated Season," Wilmington Morning News, p. 11, Jan. 3, 1938.

Lowery, Steve. "After only one year ... Adios, Amigos," Los Angeles Times, articles.latimes.com, July 14, 1988.

Lowitt, Bruce. "Padded WFL Attendance Disclosed," Pensacola News Journal, p. 2C, Aug. 7, 1978.

"Lubanski bowls perfect game in competition," Redlands Daily Facts, p. 11, Dec. 14, 1961.

Luhm, Steve. "NBA draft: Jazz draft woman in '77" Salt Lake Tribune, elpasotimes.com, June 20, 2009.

Luttermoser, John. "Only the owners are in the know in the secretive USFL," Tampa Bay Times, p. 3C, Oct. 22, 1984.

"Majors Rebuff Minor Moves," Arizona Republic, p. 22, Dec. 10, 1951.

"Majors Reject Demand To Double Draft Price," Rochester Democrat and Chronicle, p. 14, July 14, 1945.

Mann, William C. "Denver obtains WHA franchise," Greeley (Colo.) Daily Tribune, p. 19, May 20, 1975.

"Manton's Field Goals Nip Collegians, 15-14," Los Angeles Times, p. 9, Jan. 22, 1940.

"Mary Jo Peppler Superstars' champ," Arizona Republic, p. G-2, Jan. 30, 1975.

Mayor, Larry. "Bears played NFL's first indoor game," chicagobears.com, March 1, 2014.

Malbert, Gus. "Lease For Ballpark Signed By Landgraf," Richmond Times-Dispatch, p. 6, Jan. 9, 1912.

Marshall, Joe. "The Once and Future League," Sports Illustrated, si.com/vault, April 21, 1975.

Matthews, C. Starr. "Gilmore For 10c. Ball," Baltimore Sun, p. 5, Aug. 10, 1915.

Matthews, Matty. "A-A Debut Here Tonight as Hawks Oppose 49ers," Miami News, p.2-B, Oct. 8, 1946.

Matthews, Matty. "Hawks' Dismal Debut Shakes Pro Grid Foundations Here," Miami News, p. 8-B, Oct. 9, 1946.

Mayer, Scott Patrick. "The First Fifty Years of Professional Baseball in Richmond, Virginia," scholarship.richmond.edu, May 2001.

McCann, Richard. "Roller Derby roughness and spills are providing real thrills for spectators," Muncie Evening Press, p. 18, May 6, 1937.

McDermott, Barry. "The WTT reigns in Plains," Sports Illustrated, si.com., May 9, 1977.

McDonough, Will. "They're split on merger," Boston Globe, p. 64, Sept. 22, 1985.

McDuling, John. "The great 1960s bowling bubble was so awesome," qz.com/192783, March 28, 2014.

McGregor, Robert Kuhn. "A Calculus of Color: The Integration of Baseball's American League," McFarland & Co., Jefferson, N.C., 2015.

McKenna, Brian. "Bud Fowler," Society for American Baseball Research, sabr.org.

McNeil, William F. "Black Baseball Out of Seasons: Pay for Play Outside of the Negro Leagues," McFarland & Co., Jefferson, N.C., 2007.

McShane, Larry. "WWF formulator pledges legitimate football with XFL," Palm Springs Desert Sun, p. 25, Feb. 4, 2000.

Mellor, Bob. "It's Question Period," Ottawa Citizen, p. 23, March 9, 1972.

Mellor, Bob. "NHL-WHA merger ends five-year war," Ottawa Citizen, p. 1, June 25, 1977.

Merlino, Doug. "Harlem Globetrotters: Godfathers to the NBA's Best and Flashiest Stars," Bleacher Report, bleacherreport.com, April 1, 2011.

Mifflin, Lawrie. "Why N.A.S.L. is in trouble," New York Times, Nov. 13, 1983.

Mikan, George. "Mikan Explains 12-Foot Lane Rule," Minneapolis Star, p. 52, Dec, 14, 1951.

"Mikan, George," American National Biography, anb.org, March 2011.

Miller, Ed. "The WHA – A Look Back at the Upstart League," thehockeywriters.com, July 6, 2018.

Miller, Geoffrey. "World Team Tennis Gets Boost From ILTF Group," Jackson Clarion-Ledger, p C5, Feb. 15, 1973.

Miller, James Andrew and Shales, Tom. "Those Guys Have All the Fun: Inside the World of ESPN," Back Bay Books, New York, 2011.

Miller, Jeremy. "Iowa Star Signs Pact With Rens," Pittsburgh Post-Gazette, p. 21, Sept. 10, 1961.

Miller, Jim. "$50 million offer rejected by Irsay: Colts staying here," Baltimore Evening Sun, p. 1, July 13, 1981.

Miller, Lou. "Pepper Martin Makes Major League Grid Debut at 44," Franklin News-Herald, p. 14, Sept. 2, 1948.

"Minor League Football Owner to Meet With CFL," Paris News (Texas), p. 12, Sept. 17, 1972.

Moackler, Jim. "Iowa gets franchise in women's pro cage loop," Des Moines Register, p. 1S, Feb. 23, 1978.

Monson, Sam. "The Pottsville Maroons: A Forgotten Icon," Split Coverage, splitcoverage.com, Jan. 9, 2013.

Monteith, Mark. "Jerry Harkness plays game-changing role in basketball history," nba.com/pacers, Sept. 17, 2013.

Moore, Jack. "Cold Mountain," The Classical, theclassical.org, Jan. 23, 2013.

"Moses Fleetwood Walker," jockbio.com.

"Ms. Richards signs with World Team Tennis," Wilmington Morning Star, p. 1-C, June 3, 1977.

Mueller, Bobby. "Cleveland Indians 1948 Champs Helped by Negro League Players," Fansided, calltothepen.com, 2016.

Mule, Marty. "Dave Dixon, driving force behind Superdome, dies," Times-Picayune, Aug. 8, 2010.

Murphy, Bill. "Why The Gold Cartel Messed With The Wrong Irishman," kitco.com, Jan. 10, 2006.

"NAFL To Stay At 13 Members," Frederick News (Md.), p. 10, Jan. 21, 1950.

"NASL TV: A Short History," kenn.com.

"National 'Pro' Gridiron Laurels at Stake Today," Los Angeles Times, p. 64, Dec. 18, 1932.

Nelson, Murray R. "Abe Saperstein and the American Basketball League," McFarland & Co., Jefferson, N.C., 2013.

"New Baseball League," Binghamton Press and Sun-Bulletin, p. 9, Jan. 7, 1913.

"New Cage Loop Expands, But Delays Start for year," Titusville Herald, p. 8, May 11, 1960.

"New Cleveland Pro 11 Changes Name," New Philadelphia Daily Times (Ohio), p. 9, Aug. 14, 1945.

"New football league has designs on Shea," New York Daily News, p. 43, July 1, 1983.

"New football league may sign prep stars," The Tennessean, p. 7, July 7, 1987.

"New football league with international aspirations plans to kick off in spring," Orlando Sentinel, p. B-3, July 1, 1983.

"New Major Grid League," Dayton Daily News, p. S-3, Sept. 3, 1944.

"New Major League Agreement" (1921), roadsidephotos.sabr.org.

"New Outbreak in Chicago Race War," Rock Island Argus, p. 1, July 28, 1919.

"New Outlaw League Announces Its Plans," Decatur Herald, p. 1, Dec. 22, 1911.

"New Women's League Will Alter the Game," New York Times, nytimes.com, Dec. 18, 1990.

"New York Giants Beat All-Stars in Los Angeles Game," Belvidere Republican-Northwestern (Ill.), p. 6, Jan. 17, 1939.

"New York rallies to eliminate Iowa," Sioux City Journal, p. A17, April 11, 1980.

"NFL Owners Make Rule Changes To Enliven Game," Brownsville Herald, p. 13, April 26, 1974.

"NFL sets draft date, rejects Memphis bid," Dayton Daily News, p. 16, March 17, 1976.

"Oakland's Tart Hits 49 But Amigos Win By Three," Indianapolis Star, p. 26, Nov. 1, 1967.

"Oaks Trade ABA's Number One Scorer," Eureka Times Standard, p. 12, Jan. 19, 1968.

"O.J. Has Pineapple Land Bid," El Paso Herald-Post, p. 24, July 31, 1969.

"O'Connor Hopes for 'New' PCL With Triple-A Status," Long Beach Independent-Press-Telegram, p. C-4, Sept. 15, 1957.

O'Connor, W.J. "Beaten For Title By .00086, Terriers Appear Satisfied," St. Louis Post-Dispatch, p. 14, Oct. 4, 1915.

O'Connor, W.J. "Stifel's Support Puts Columbian League 'In Good'" St. Louis Post-Dispatch, p. 14, Feb. 13, 1912.

O'Donnell, John P. "Pottsville stages late rally to beat Four Horsemen," Philadelphia Record, Dec. 13, 1925.

O'Keefe, Michael. "Document from 1945 – two years before Jackie Robinson broke MLB color barrier – saying black players couldn't make it in baseball is up for sale," New York Daily News, nydailynews.com, Jan. 14, 2015.

"On This Day In Kansas City Sports History," allstarsports.com, Feb. 18, 2012.

"One More Club Needed To Complete U.S. League," Philadelphia Inquirer, p. 10, Jan. 4, 1912.

O'Neal, Bill. "The Pacific Coast League, 1903-1988," Eakin Press, Austin, Texas, 1990.

"O'Neal extends gesture to predecessor's family," Associated Press, espn.com, June 2, 2005.

O'Neil, Buck and Wulf, Steve. "I Was Right On Time," p. 41, Fireside, 1997.

"Opening Up Weeghman Park (Wrigley Field) in 1914," miscbaseball.wordpress.com, 2009

Oren, Paul. "Crusaders Following in the footsteps of 'World's Tallest Team,' nwi.com, Jan. 28, 2015.

"Outlaws Make Bid For "OTD: Maurice Richard signs with WHA's Quebec Nordiques," canadiancoinnews.com, July 20, 2018.

Outlar, Jesse. "The Miracle of Miami," Atlanta Constitution, p. 1-D, Dec. 27, 1972.

"Outlaws Make Bid For Toronto Player," Bridgeport Times and Evening Farmer, p. 7, Jan. 17, 1912.

Overpeck, Keith F. "Colonel Crowds down 1,400 a game; pro basketball up overall," Louisville Courier -Journal, p. B5, Jan. 9, 1976

"PCL Next Major Loop, Says Frick," Santa Rosa Press Democrat, p. 10, March 25, 1952.

"Packer Stock On Sale Today," Rhinelander Daily News (Wis.), p. 1, April 6, 1950.

"Panthers? Now they're the Cleveland Browns," Akron Beacon Journal, p. 16, Aug. 14, 1945.

"Paul Fagan: The Owner Who Banned Peanuts From the Ball Park," baseballpastandpresent.com.

Pearlman, Jeff. "One man's letter to Donald Trump," jeffpearlman.com.

"Philly Wins CFL In Overtime," Lincoln Star (Neb.), p. 14, Dec. 5, 1966.

Pierson, Don. "Football's Back, And It's Indoors," Chicago Tribune, Feb. 22, 1987. articles.chicagotribune.com.

"Plan Companion League To NBA, Says Podoloff," Akron Beacon Journal, p. 5C, April 16, 1950.

"Plans Announced for Pro Football League," Los Angeles Times, pt. 2, p. 10, March 20, 1934.

Plaschke, Bill. "No Spark and Little Fanfare," Los Angeles Times, articles.latimes.com, Oct. 21, 1997.

"Pleased With Opening Of The U.S. League," Reading Times, p. 5, May 3, 1912.

Pluto, Terry. "Loose Balls: The Short, Wild Life of the American Basketball Association," Simon & Schuster, New York, 2007.

"Politicians are blamed for riots," Decatur (Ill.) Daily Review, p. 1, July 29, 1919.

"Portsmouth is New Leader of 'Pro' Circuit," Salt Lake Telegram, p. 9, Dec. 5, 1932.

Posanski, Joe. "Satchel Paige's MLB debut was pitching magic," mlb.com, July 12, 2018.

"Potent, Pediculous Or Putrid They're Paul's Pro Panthers," Akron Beacon Journal, p. 26, June 8, 1945.

"Pottsville, Pa., Barters Trophies For Recognition," Anderson Herald (Ind.), p. 18, Dec. 23, 1962.

"Pro Debut Tough Chore For Mrs. Pat Palinkas," Palm Beach Post, p. B5, Aug. 17, 1970.

Pro Football Archives, profootballarchives.com.

Probasketballencyclopedia.com.

"Problem Of Coast League Is Survival," Mt. Vernon Register-News (Ill.), p. 6, June 3, 1957.

"Proposed Grid Loop Wants Owens," Lawton Constitution (Okla.), p. 26, March 12, 1970.

Pruett, Brad. "The Unraveling of a Billionaire," grryo.com, April 11, 2013.

"Raiders May Be Without A Hometown," San Rafael Daily Independent Journal, p. 23, Nov. 28, 1962.

"Ramblers Gird For San Jose," San Bernardino Sun, p. 37, Oct. 6, 1967.

Rasmussen, Cecilia. "The Man Who Got Roller Derby Rolling Along," Los Angeles Times, p. B3, Feb. 21, 1999.

"Reading Without Baseball Team," Altoona Tribune, p. 11, June 3, 1912.

"Reading's Men Sign With Other Teams," Richmond Times Dispatch, p. 7, June 1, 1912.

Reddit, reddit.com/r/nba/comments/39nhd6/no_player_in_the_nba_has_ever_worn_number_58_59/

"Redskins refuse to share stadium with Ambassadors," Anniston Star (Ala.), p. 19, March 31, 1974.

Reinsdorf, Jonathan M. "The Powers of the Commissioner in Baseball," Marquette Sports Law Review, Article 6, scholarship.law.marquette.edu, Vol. 7, Issue 1 (Fall).

"Reisling Wants Job," Altoona Tribune, p. 10, Feb. 17, 1912.

"Resigns As Continental Loop Boss," News-Palladium (Benton Harbor, Mich.), p. 16, Jan. 15, 1966.

"Richard bowled during NBL's only season," Joplin Globe, joplinglobe.com, Nov. 14, 2009.

Roberts, M.B. "Paige never looked back," espn.com.

Roberts, Rich. "Attn: NFL ... Get Ready for the IFL and the USFL," Los Angeles Times, pt. III, p. 10, March 5, 1981.

"Rocket's bag not coaching," Ottawa Citizen, p. 30, Oct. 17, 1972.

"Rockets Picked For Playoff By About 28-14," Charleston Daily Mail, p. 5, Nov. 27, 1965.

"Rockets Streak By Rifles, 24-7, Capture CFL Crown," Raleigh Register (W.Va.), p. 8, Nov. 29, 1965.

"Roller Skaters Go Rolling Downtown Here Tomorrow," Miami News, p. 17, March 11, 1936.

"Rote Signed," Ames Daily Tribune (Iowa), Jan. 3, 1967.

Rothe, Emil H. "Was the Federal League a Major League?" Research Journals Archive, research.sabr.org.

Rothenberg, Matt. "AAGPBL shined a light at Wrigley Field in 1943," baseballhall.org.

Rowley, Storer. "'Philadelphia Freedom,' a musical tribute to Billie Jean King," Northwestern Now, news.northwestern.edu, June 15, 2017.

Rumore, Danielle. "ABL, WNBA are in leagues of their own; ABL has the better talent, but WNBA has a following," The Baltimore Sun, baltimoresun.com, Aug. 12, 1997.

Russell, Lars. "The greatest Seahawks team of the ... 1940s?" fieldgulls.com.

Ruzzo, Bob. "Fate of the Federal League: Were the Federals Incompetent, Outmaneuvered, or Just Unlucky?" Fall 2013 Baseball Research Journal, sabr.org.

"Sacramento Pro Grid Team Folds," San Rafael Independent-Journal, p. 13, July 3, 1970.

Salter, Stephanie. "Pioneers give Diamonds a lesson in teamwork," San Francisco Examiner, p. 51, Dec. 3, 1979.

"Sammy Baugh Hired at Tulsa As Pro Coach," Amarillo Globe-Times, p. 13, June 17, 1965.

"Sanction Granted for Roller Skating Races," Washington Herald, p. 10, March 15, 1915.

"Sanderson: 'Too Good to Refuse,'" Spokane Spokesman-Review, p. 25, Aug. 4, 1972.

"Saperstein Cries: Cut Big Scores and Big Men," Minneapolis Star, p. 11, Jan. 4, 1958.

Sargent, Jim. "Doris Sams Biography," aagpbl.org.

Schaerlaeckens, Leander. "Johan Cruyff's Complicated Legacy," sports.vice.com, March 25, 2016.

Schmidt, J.R. "100 Top Bowlers of the 20th Century," Jr. Jake's Bowling History Blog, bowlinghistory.wordpress.com.

Schmidt, J.R. "Steve Nagy's 300 Game on Championship Bowling," Bowl-A-Roll Lanes, Nov. 2, 2011. bowl-a-roll.blogspot.com.

Schudel, Matt. "King Corcoran," Post Mortem, voices.washingtonpost.com.

Schwartz, Larry. "Galloping Ghost scared opponents." espn.go.com/sportscentury.

Schwartz, Nick. "The first game in XFL history was a disaster," Jan. 25, 2018. ftw.usatoday.com.

Schwartz, Seth. "The Johnnie Walton story," National Football Post, nationalfootballpost.com.

Segell, Michael. "Jimmy Connors: The Games He Plays," Rolling Stone, rollingstone.com, Sept. 4, 1980.

"Senate Kills Controversial Baseball Draft Bill, 73-12," Jefferson City Post-Tribune, p. 10, June 29, 1960.

"Seven Professional Teams Will Meet In American Roller Derby," Washington Herald, p. 10. March 27, 1915.

"Shamrocks, Cubs Clash," Los Angeles Times, p. 25, Oct. 10, 1934.

Shappell, Lee. "Austere budget key to survival of cage league," Arizona Republic, p. F5, Dec. 7, 1980.

"Sheboygan, Denver, Waterloo Quit NBA, Plan Rival Loop; 12 Clubs Remain After Rift," Rochester Democrat and Chronicle, p. 24, April 25, 1950.

Shipley, Amy and Hente, Paul. "Women's Pro Hoops Leagues Battle For Position," St. Louis Post-Dispatch, p. 7F, May 18, 1997.

"Slach, Duvall on girls' all-state team," Iowa Press-Citizen, p. 10, March 21, 1975.

Slusser, Susan. "American Basketball League Folds," San Francisco Chronicle, sfgate.com, Dec. 23, 1998.

Smith, Red. "Abe Saperstein's Boy Jerry," New York Times, nytimes.com.Feb. 3, 1978.

Smith, Red. "Continental Crybabies," Tampa Bay Times, p. 1-C, April 28, 1960.

Smith, Red. "Views of Sport," Warren County Observer (Pa.), p. 16, Nov. 21, 1960.

Smith, Wilfrid. "Bears win, 9-0; Pro Football Champions," Chicago Tribune, p. 19, Dec. 19, 1932.

Smits, Ted. "Pro Grid Post To Jackie Robinson," Hagerstown Morning Herald (Md.), p. 15, May 3, 1966.

Smyser, Bob. "Hollywood in 17-10 Victory," Los Angeles Times, pt. 2, p. 9, Dec. 22, 1941.

Snyder, Brad. "Antitrust ball started rolling in Baltimore," Baltimore Sun, articles.baltimoresun.com, Sept. 1, 1994.

"Softball Stars Sign Contracts," Akron Beacon Journal, p. 20, April, 14, 1943.

"Spartans and Bears to Play Game at Night," Green Bay Press-Gazette, p. 15, Dec. 16, 1932.

"Spartans Must Battle Bears," Akron Beacon Journal, p. 18, Dec. 12, 1932.

"Sports Roundup," Corpus Christi Caller-Times, p. 8-B, Jan. 29, 1912.

Spencer, Lyle. "'Twas This Way," Bayard (Iowa) News, p. 6, Dec. 21, 1936.

Spousta, Tom. "Novelty Upstages Game On the XFL's First Night," New York Times, nyt.com, Feb. 4, 2001.

"Spring Football League Planned," Corpus Christi Caller-Times, p. 30, April 11, 1965.

"Spring league closes doors," Mussouilian, p. 27, Feb. 14, 1992.

"Stags Become Bruins in Pro Basketball," Chicago Tribune, pt. 2, p. 2, Aug. 15, 1950.

Stevens, David. "Baseball's Radical for All Seasons," Scarecrow Press, Lanham, Md., and London, 1998.

Sullivan, Dean A. "Late Innings: A Documentary History of Baseball, 1945-1972," University of Nebraska Press, 2002.

Stellino, Vito. "Irsay says Colts losing Maxwell – too," Baltimore Sun, p. E6, June 29, 1983.

Steve Dimitry's Extinct Sports Leagues, oocities.org.

Stevenson, Jack. "Roman Gabriel Considers Fling With Minor League," Hazelton Standard-Speaker (Pa.), p. 26, April 13, 1973.

Stockton, J. Roy. "Browns Will Stay in St. Louis, American League Decides," St. Louis Post-Dispatch, p. 2B, Dec. 9, 1941.

"Storm follows USFL decision," Vancouver Sun, p. C8, April 30, 1985.

"Strike Coming, Says Simpson," Clearfield Progress (Pa.), p. 21, April 24, 1974.

"Strikes again!" Anniston Star (Ala.), p. 29, April 7, 1974.

"Suspended King Corcoran May Buy Club," Newport News Daily Press, p. D3, Aug. 20, 1972.

Tanier, Mike. "First in War, Third in the AAFC: The Story of Pro Football's Yankees and Dodgers," bleacherreport.com, July 3, 2015.

Terp, Christine. "Women Still Determining A Direction," The Palm Beach Post, p. 55, July 24, 1981.

"Texas Loop Challenges Continental," Abilene Reporter-News, p. 4, March 4, 1968.

" 'That Poodle Could Cover Our Team's Payroll For A Month' – The Story of the WABA's Atlanta Comets," Fun While It Lasted, funwhileitlasted.com, Feb. 4, 2013.

Thornley, Stew and Holgunin, Marc. "Minnesota Hoops," Minnesota Historical Society, milkeespress.com/fillies.

Tiefenbach, Arnie. "Mary Baker: A bonnie girl of autumn," Regina Leader-Post, p. C4, Aug. 1, 1984.

Tignor, Steve. "1974: The World Team Tennis Experiment Begins," tennis.com, April 23, 2015,

"Time Here To Get That Bowling Ball, Son," Redlands Daily Facts, p. 13, Nov. 25, 1960.

"Tinker Gets Offer from the Outlaws," Coshocton (Ohio) Tribune, Page 1, Dec. 25, 1913.

"Toronto girls turn pro," Ottawa Journal, p. 17, April 12, 1943.

"Toronto seeking new home, eyes Louisville," Hamilton Journal News (Ohio), p. 7, April 23, 1974.

"Toros Hold Last Meeting," San Antonio Express, p. 34, June 27, 1971.

"Troubled Akron Loses Another," Medina County Gazette (Ohio), p. 8, Sept. 18, 1967.

"Trump envisions USFL moving to fall schedule," Casper Star-Tribune, p. D2, Dec. 16, 1983.

"Trump buys New Jersey Generals," Danville (Ky.) Advocate Messenger, p. 11, Sept. 22, 1983.

"Tulsa to Have Pro Football in 1966," Des Moines Register, p. 14, May 20, 1965.

"Tulsa's Proposed Entry In CFL Without Stadium," Danville Register (Va.), p. 9, Aug. 4, 1965.

"Two Babes Enter WFL Wilderness," Zaneseville (Ohio) Times Recorder, p. 13, May 16, 1975.

Tye, Larry. "Satchel Paige," Society for Professional Baseball Research, sabr.org.

Tygiel, Jules. "Revisiting Bill Veeck and the 1943 Phillies," Baseball Research Journal, p. 109, Cleveland, 2007.

"UFL Champs May Play in Philly," Daily Reporter (Dover, Ohio), p. 16, Feb. 17, 1965.

"Union Oil Backs Move To Los Angeles," The Missoulian (Mont.), p. 8, Aug. 20, 1953.

"United States League Flirting With Ty Cobb," Baltimore Evening Sun, p. 8, April 10, 1913.

"United States League Plans For This City," Baltimore Evening Sun, p. 8, Jan. 8, 1913.

"United States League Proves Failure In All Cities In Its Circuit," Binghamton Press and Sun-Bulletin, p. 9, June 6, 1912.

Urban, Robert. "Corcoran Given 'King' Size $125,000 Package By Firebirds," p. 1, Pottstown Mercury, Aug. 26, 1969.

Urban, Robert. "Firebirds Deny Offering Corcoran $100,000 Package," p. 22, Pottstown Mercury, Aug. 22, 1969.

"Urge Coast League Back Pro Football," Santa Ana Register, p. 10, Jan. 17, 1940.

"Usher in line to replace Simmons as USFL head," Chippewa (Wis.) Herald-Telegram, p. 11, Jan. 15, 1985.

"USFL may add up to 10 teams," Helena (Mont.) Independent-Record, p. 9, April 9,1983.

"Veeck Glum About Move to Los Angeles," Chillicothe Gazette (Ohio), p. 11, July 21, 1953.

Vetel, Phil. "The Cubs get lights at Wrigley Field," Chicago Tribune, chicagotribune.com, Jan. 3, 2008.

Vitez, Michael. "Remembering days when women wore spikes to work," Tallahassee Democrat, p. D1, July 6, 1992.

"Walkathon hoofers hurdle ordinance," Indianapolis Star, p. 1, Sept. 20, 1933.

"Walker Breaks Thumb," Ocala Star-Banner, p. C1, Aug. 22, 1982.

"Walker injects life into Georgia," Wilmington Morning Star, p. 2D, Sept. 8, 1982.

"Walter Johnson Jumps Back," Atlanta Constitution, p. 5, Dec. 20, 1914.

Ward, John Montgomery, "Is the Base-Ball Player a Chattel?" Lippincott's Magazine, xroads.virginia.edu, August 1887.

"Washington Park," covehurst.net.

"WBL," Sports Illustrated, Oct. 15, 1979.

Weiner, Evan. " 'Slap Shot' had nothing on the Birmingham Bulls," nhl.com, Nov. 16, 2007.

"WFL drafts 'big names'," Las Vegas Optic (N.M.), p. 4, March 19, 1974.

"WFL signs another star; Stabler to leave Oakland," Pocolo Record (Stroudsburg, Pa.), p. 12, April 3, 1974.

"WFL Week II: Opening Night Crowds Absent," Pittsburgh Press, p. 29, July 18, 1974.

"White Plains Diamond On Top Of Station," Evening Review (Liverpool, Ohio), p. 5, Jan, 30, 1912.

Witosky, Tom. "Stormers a half-yard short," Des Moines Register, p. 21, Aug. 27, 1966.

"WHA Blazers Trying to Unload Sanderson," Detroit Free Press, p. 4-B, Dec. 16, 1972.

"Wheeling Football Franchise Revoked," Cumberland News (Md.), p. 15, Dec. 16, 1969.

"Who's saying what," Louisville Courier-Journal, p. C2, Feb. 18, 2001.

Wiggins, Robert Peyton. "The Federal League of Base Ball Clubs," McFarland & Co., Jefferson, N.C., 2009.

Williams, Lena. "Former Team Official Recounts the A.B.L.'s Dizzying Descent," New York Times, nytimes.com, April 2, 1999.

Wilson, Austin. "Rugged Opening For Shreveport," Alexandria (La.) Town Talk, p. 12, Sept. 25, 1974.

"Witman Fixes Up At Baltimore," Reading Times, p. 2, April 18, 1913.

"Women to take field again as players reunite at County Stadium," Fond Du Lac (Wis.) Commonwealth Reporter, p. 18, Aug. 25, 2000.

"Women's cage – a pro sport," Santa Rosa Press Democrat, p. 17, March 22, 1978.

"Women's History Month: The WBL (1978-81)," Las Vegas Aces, aces.wnba.com, March 9, 2018.

"Women's pro basketball league will include a team from Iowa," Iowa City Press-Citizen, p. 14, March 23, 1978.

Wood, Hal. " 'Pants' Wants Coast Part in Major League," San Mateo Times, p. 9, May 14, 1945.

"Work Begins On Arenas For Bowling," Ogden Standard Examiner, p. 18, Feb. 5, 1961.

"World Football League Rule Changes," wflfootball.tripod.com

"Wrigley Says No Dice To Giving Veeck Los Angeles," New Philadelphia Daily Times, p. 8, Aug. 19, 1953.

Wrinkle, Jim. "61 hear Joe Joseph," Bryan Times, p. 9, March 24, 1972.

Yannis, Alex. "Chinaglia, Unpredictable Star of Cosmos, Happy About Trading Italy for America," nytimes.com, March 27, 1977.

Yannis, Alex. "Cosmos Will Sign Beckenbauer for 4 Years, $2.8 Million Today," nytimes.com, May 25, 1977.

Yannis, Alex. "Miss Meyers Agrees To Sign With Gems," New York Times, nytimes.com, Nov. 15, 1979.

"Year In Review: 1884 American Association," Baseball Almanac, baseball-almanac.com.

Yorgey, Ken. "Montreal Signs 'King' To Two-Year Contract," Pottstown Mercury, p. 25, Jan. 14, 1972.

Young, Linda. "Time Right, Cornet Coach Believes," Quad-City Times, p. 2S, Nov. 11, 1978.

Zimmerman, Paul. "Bears Do Missionary Work on West Coast; Beat All-Stars, 26-7," Davenport Democrat and Leader (Iowa), p. 11, Jan. 15, 1934.

About the author

Stephen H. Provost is a lifelong sports fan who served as sports editor of two daily newspapers in California. *A Whole Different League* is his 18th book. During more than three decades in journalism, he has worked as a managing editor, copy desk chief, columnist and reporter at five newspapers. Now a full-time author, he has written on such diverse topics as American highways, dragons, mutant superheroes, mythic archetypes, language, department stores and his hometown. He currently lives in Virginia. And he loves cats. Read his blogs and keep up with his latest activities at stephenhprovost.com.

Made in the USA
Middletown, DE
24 July 2023

35682838R00190